AF565084

Designing Enterprise Client/Server Systems

Beth Gold-Bernstein
David Marca

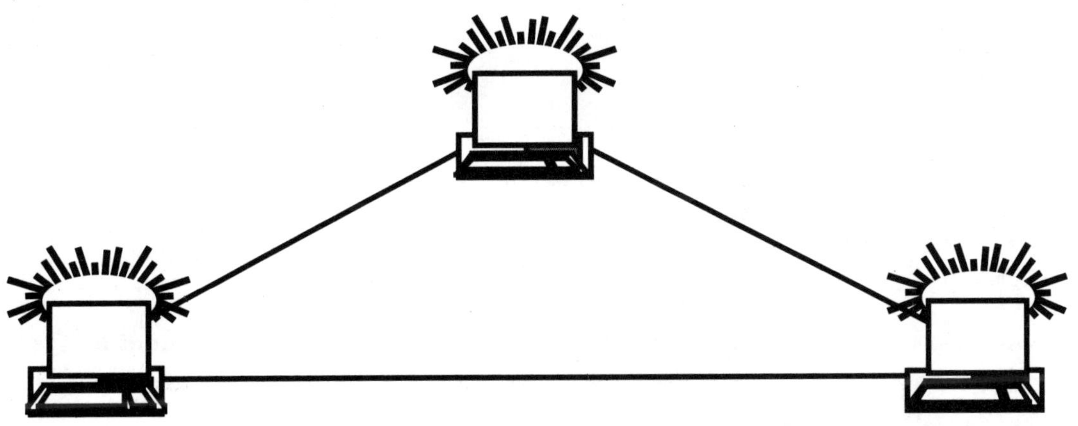

Foreword by
Shaku Atre

To join a Prentice Hall PTR Internet mailing list, point to:
http://www.prenhall.com/mail_lists/

Prentice Hall PTR
Upper Saddle River, New Jersey 07458
http://www.prenhall.com

Library of Congress Cataloging-in-Publication Data

Gold-Bernstein, Beth.
Designing Enterprise client/server systems / Beth Gold-Bernstein, David A. Marca : foreword by Shaku Atre.
p. cm.
Includes bibliographical references and index.
ISBN 0–13–890195–3
1. Client/server computing. 2. Distributed databases 3. Business—Data processing. I. Marca, David. II. Title.
QA76.9.C55G65 1998
004'.3681—dc21 97–14595
CIP

Acquisitions editor: Mark L. Taub
Cover designer: Bruce Kenselaar
Cover design director: Jerry Votta
Manufacturing manager: Alexis R. Heydt
Marketing manager: Dan Rush
Compositor/Production services: Pine Tree Composition, Inc.

Prentice-Hall, Inc.
A Simon & Schuster Company
Upper Saddle River, New Jersey 07458

Prentice Hall books are widely used by corporations and government agencies for training, marketing, and resale.

The publisher offers discounts on this book when ordered in bulk quantities. For more information contact:

Corporate Sales Department
Phone: 800-382-3419
Fax: 201-236-7141
E-mail: corpsales@prenhall.com

Or write:

Prentice Hall PTR
Corp. Sales Dept.
One Lake Street
Upper Saddle River, New Jersey 07458

Printed in the United States of America
10 9 8 7 6 5 4 3 2 1

ISBN: 0-13-890195-3

Prentice-Hall International (UK) Limited, *London*
Prentice-Hall of Australia Pty. Limited, *Sydney*
Prentice-Hall Canada Inc., *Toronto*
Prentice-Hall Hispanoamericana, S.A., *Mexico*
Prentice-Hall of India Private Limited, *New Delhi*
Prentice Hall of Japan, Inc., *Tokyo*
Simon & Schuster Asia Pte. Ltd., *Singapore*

Beth's Dedication:

To my father-in-law, Harvey Bernstein, with love and gratitude, for his support and encouragement.

David's Dedication:

To the four extraordinary teens in my life:

Michael Kellogg, for his strength of character.
Kyle Kellogg, for his spirit of invention.

Katherine Shuemaker, for her love of family.
Susan Shuemaker, for her spirit of adventure.

Every life you have touched has been the better for it.
Thank you for sharing your lives with me, and with the world!

Contents

Foreword

Organizations are now using distributed client/server technology to build large and complex mission critical systems. Many organizations are solving their Year 2000 problems by replacing their legacy systems with client/server applications. The new enterprise systems will reach across geographic and organizational boundaries, integrate with existing and new systems, and even directly connect to customers and suppliers via the Internet. The ability of organizations to deploy and maintain these systems and utilize technology for competitive advantage requires a business centric approach to ensure a return on investment. It also requires a predictable, repeatable process that enables the successful collaboration of business and I/S professionals in defining the requirements, design, and implementation of the system.

Up till now, the overall success rate of client/server projects has been only "fair to poor." Client/server is far more complex to implement than previous technologies because it involves many more decisions about which components to choose, how to integrate components from different vendors, and how to distribute and integrate data and processing across different hardware platforms and locations. The challenge is to create robust, secure, and manageable systems, architected to meet the evolving needs of a fast paced and highly competitive business climate. These challenges require a comprehensive multi-dimensional solution that includes people, process, and technology.

Technology alone is not sufficient to solve the complex issues involved in developing and deploying large scale mission critical applications. In other words, choosing the right products is not in itself enough to ensure success: The risk of failure is too great and too costly. It is essential to find and apply correct techniques for defining and negotiating requirements for multiple business units, for partitioning data and processing across clients, servers, hosts, and geographic locations, and for performing traffic analysis. In order to minimize risk, designers and developers need to understand the design alternatives and tradeoffs. Designs must be evaluated against both best design practices and metrics tied to business performance. The process for designing these systems must therefore provide the necessary information for making the right decisions. The right decisions will enable organizations to adapt easily to changes in business process, competitive climate, and technology.

Critical design issues for large scale distributed systems include: how to define and provide access to shared data across the organization; how to manage distributed data; how to determine the optimal allocation of data and processing across different computing platforms; how to perform capacity planning and performance analysis on a site-by-site basis; how to design for maximum reusability; and how to manage and maintain distributed systems. The focus must be on building flexible systems that provide maximum reuse and responsiveness as business needs change.

The IllumiSys™ Design Method is a comprehensive framework for developing enterprise client/server systems. It defines a process to enable business and systems professionals to collaborate in developing the requirements, design, and implementation of systems in a way that ensures that both the current and future needs of an organization are met. The method includes techniques for creating granular software components that can be modified and reused. It also covers the organizational issues that so often derail the development and deployment of large scale systems. Techniques and best practices are defined for choosing technology components that integrate with existing and new technology, and minimize maintenance costs.

While smaller client/server projects may succeed with prototyping alone, large scale distributed solutions are far more complex, expensive and risky. The IllumiSys™ Design Method can help minimize the risks and maximize the adaptability, manageability, and reusability of the system, while ensuring that it meets the business goals.

Shaku Atre
President
Atre Associates, Inc.
Port Chester, NY
email: shaku@atre.com

Preface

Our purpose in writing this book was to provide executives, project managers, and implementers, with the knowledge necessary for building enterprise distributed systems. Today's systems must meet the current needs of the business, and easily adapt as the business grows, evolves, and changes to seek competitive advantage in a global economy.

This book has been designed to adapt to the different needs of our readers. It can be read cover to cover as an in-depth tutorial on how to design enterprise distributed systems. Busy executives can gain an understanding of distributed systems, and the tasks required to build them, simply by reading the overview sections in each chapter. The book is also designed to be used over and over again as a reference. It provides templates and a full case study containing complete distributed design specifications.

The design elements throughout this book are provided as a guide to the reader. A basic understanding of the structure of this book can help the reader use it in a flexible manner to maximize its value.

The book has five parts. "Part I: Context for Understanding Distributed Systems" describes the business need for distributed systems, modeling, and the IllumiSys™ Design Method. "Part II: Business Components—The Essential Model" describes how to create a requirements specification. "Part III: Software Components—The Implementation Model" describes how to create a distributed design specification, including multi-tier design and traffic analysis. "Part IV: Organizational Enablers" describes organizational factors critical to the success of distributed systems. "Part V: Case Study" contains a case study that covers the entire process. The examples are used throughout the book. Parts II and III define how to create the specifications. The case study is a beginning to end example of how the process is used on a project. It explains all the examples in context of the project. There is extensive cross-referencing between the case study and the examples in the book.

Each Part of the book (except the case study) has its own roadmap. Each roadmap is a graphic, depicting each chapter in that part of the book. The roadmaps are given in Figure P–1.

Each section of the roadmap represents a chapter in that part of the book. The appropriate roadmap appears at the beginning of each chapter, with the appropriate section shaded. These roadmaps are intended to guide readers through the steps in the design process and subsequently to help them quickly find particular information.

Each section within each chapter contains a heading and one sentence which describes the purpose or contents of that section. The section titles and sentences are included in the Table of Contents to help readers quickly find the information they seek. The Table of Contents also provides a high level overview of the design process.

In addition, we have included specific information for different types of readers to optimize the value that each can obtain from this book.

For **executives**, we have a section on objectives in the beginning of each chapter. It includes a high level overview of the information presented in greater detail within each section. Busy executives may want to start with the Table of Contents, then scan and/or read

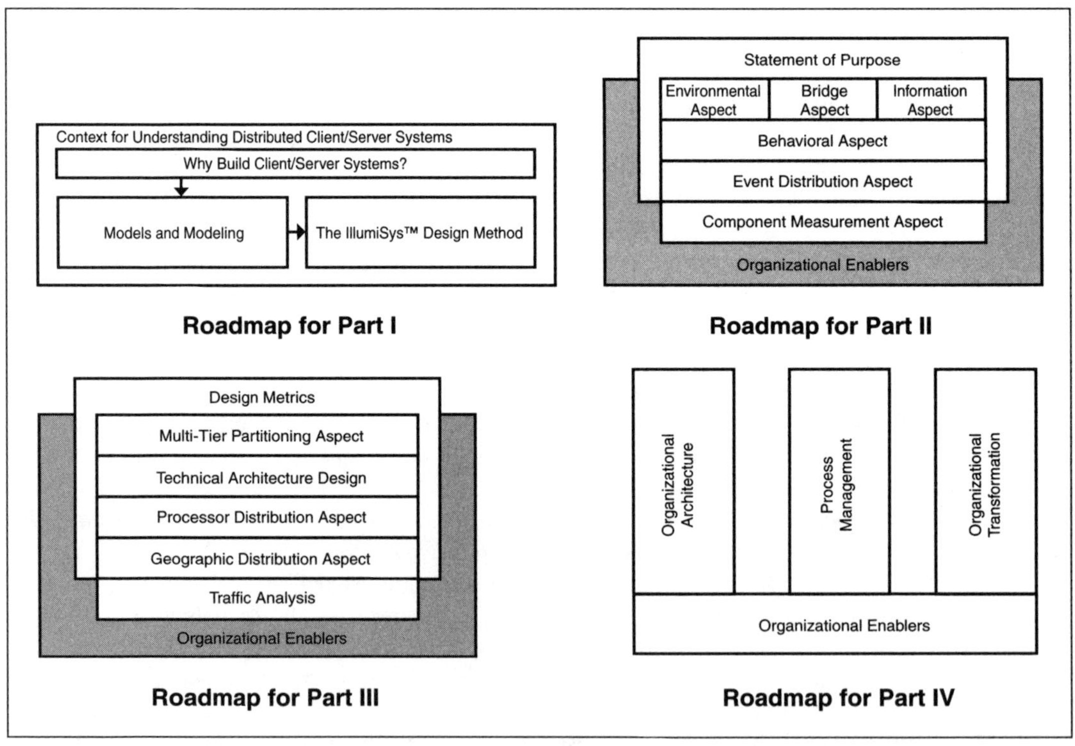

Figure P–1 The Roadmaps for This Book

particular sections of interest. Part I of the book defines the business drivers mandating a change in the way we develop systems. New types of systems are required to support the dynamic needs of today's successful organizations. Repeatable processes based on best practices can lead to more predictable success in building scaleable, reusable, adaptive systems. Parts II and III describe the design process in detail. Chapter 14 serves as a tutorial on client/server technology and the decision points for choosing technology. Part IV of the book describes the organizational factors including roles and responsibilities, business processes, and other non-technical factors that determine the success or failure of a system.

For **project managers** we have provided examples of design deliverables and scenarios for building the models. There is a table at the beginning of each chapter in Parts II and III that lists the design activity, and artifacts produced. Appendix F is a list of all the design artifacts, designating which are mandatory, recommended, and optional. Project managers will also be interested in the section on objectives for each design phase. Thereafter we describe the deliverables of each aspect of the distributed systems design and how to create the deliverables. These deliverables are models, tables, and specifications describing all the aspects of designing large-scale distributed systems. We believe they can be used with almost any SDLC (System Development Life Cycle) present in a company.

For **project implementers**, we have provided a case study and used the models in the case study as examples throughout the book. The purpose of the study is to lead the reader through all the steps for fully designing a multi-tier enterprise application that will span geographic locations. The examples serve as templates for project deliverables. The deliverables are artifacts of the system design, providing views of different system dimensions that can be reviewed and validated by all necessary parties. After implementation, the artifacts serve as documentation for the system. We have also included metrics, goals, guidelines and recommendations for making design and implementation decisions and tradeoffs.

We recommend all readers start with Part I of the book, then go to Part V, "The Fleury Market Case Study." Chapter 21 gives the background describing Fleury Market (a busy French commodities market with colorful characters). This will provide the reader the context for understanding the examples used throughout the book. Chapters 22, "The Fleury Market Essential Model," and Chapter 23, "The Fleury Market Implementation Model," give an overview of the entire design process. Part V acts as a reference to the examples used in other parts of the book.

We recognize that there may be minor inconsistencies or inaccuracies in the case study, but we felt these errors did not warrant delaying publication of the book. If you find inconsistencies and inaccuracies, or have an alternative design, please let us know. We will give a T-shirt or mug for all valid submissions. Please include your name, company, and return address with your submission to:

IllumiSys Corp.
53 Carville Avenue
Lexington, MA 02173
617-863-8589
FAX: 617-861-0261
bgb@illumisys.com

Remember, finding mistakes in your design is not bad, it's good. Mistakes are much easier, faster and less expensive to fix before they're implemented. This is the benefit and purpose of having design models to review.

We sincerely hope this book illuminates your task of utilizing technology to provide strategic benefit to your organization.

Beth Gold-Bernstein
David Marca

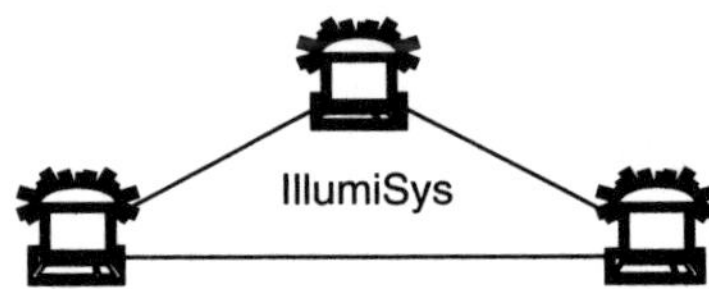

Acknowledgments

We wish to acknowledge Corrine Brandi for her contribution of intellectual content to this book and the development of the design process. She also contributed to the design and structure of the book, including the innovative design for the Table of Contents.

We wish to acknowledge Larry DeBoever for his conceptual view of Adaptive Systems. We believe it is the right message for enterprise computing today.

We wish to thank CGI Systems (a wholly owned subsidiary of IBM) for their permission to use the Fleury Market case study and other material for the Essential Model.

We wish to thank Phil Sully for his work on the Fleury Market case study.

We would like to acknowledge Ken Schoman for his early work on the design method and his ideas on managing distributed data.

We would like to thank our wonderful reviewers, Corrine Gregory and Dick Angus, for their thoughtful and excellent suggestions. They both greatly contributed to the clarity of this book.

Finally, we would like to thank our editor, Mark Taub, for his continued patience with this project.

On a personal note, Beth would like to thank her family for their patience and forbearance while this book tagged along on many weekends and vacations. David would like to thank his close friends Mike Albert, Beth Perdue, Sandi Claudell, and Adam Kline for their support during this project.

PART I

CONTEXT FOR UNDERSTANDING DISTRIBUTED CLIENT/ SERVER SYSTEMS

Part I of this book will give you a framework for thinking through the implications of developing enterprise client/server systems. It explains why client/server technology and distributed systems are required to meet the dynamic needs of business today, and how a modeling method can contribute to business success. Figure I–1 depicts the Road Map for Part I of the book.

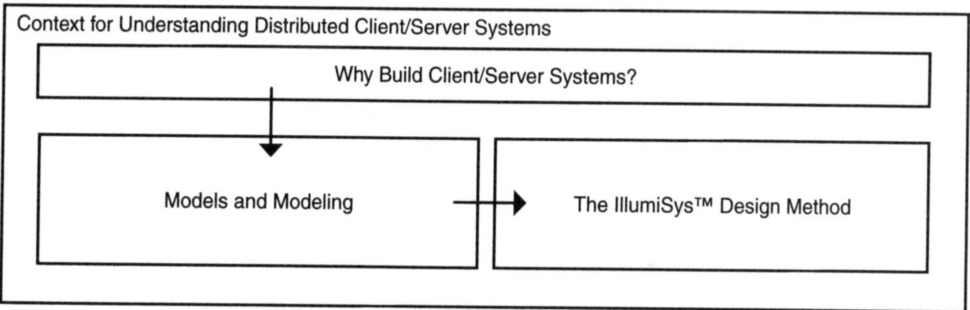

Figure I–1 Road Map for Part I—Context for Understanding Distributed Client/Server Systems

Chapter 1, "Why Build Client/Server Systems?", discusses how modern business, in an attempt to dramatically reduce its cycle times, is demanding that technology enable it to adapt to a rapidly changing marketplace. We will discuss how traditional computing technology has stifled business mobility and how business is viewing client/server as a potential for enabling adaptability.

With client/server technology comes increased technical complexity due to the need to partition system functionality across a changing technical infrastructure. This requires computer professionals to create a design *before* writing the software. In other words, "design" is a fundamental skill for successful client/server projects. For client/server solutions, "design" means using an iterative approach that creates multiple, interrelated models. Chapter 2, "Models and Modeling," explains how models can help reduce risk and manage complexity.

Chapter 3 is an overview of the IllumiSys™ Design Method. It provides the background and overall view of the language and a process for designing large-scale distributed systems. Its language uses standard graphic symbology to illuminate the particulars of client/server. The design process, however, is new. The presentation of the method is organized by vital design questions we feel you will have to answer to achieve client/server success. In addition, the presentation is interspersed with design heuristics—each one intended to help you make technical or project trade-offs.

1

Why Build Client/Server Systems?

The Primary Design Goal for Information Systems Must be to Facilitate Change in Business Processes and the Applications which Enable Them

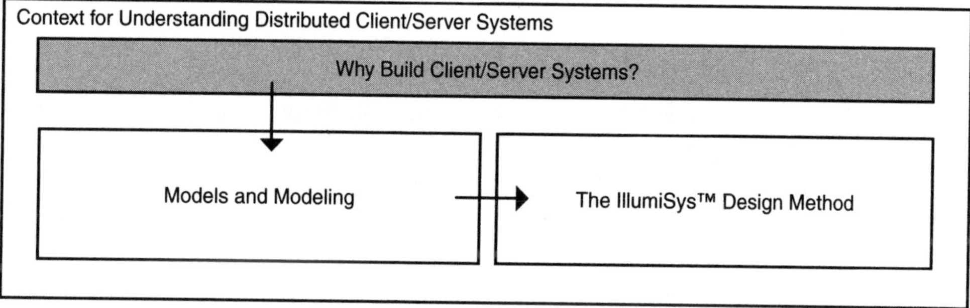

Figure 1–1 Road Map for Part I—Context for Understanding Distributed Client/Server Systems: Why Build Client/Server Systems?

Currently, client/server computer architectures are a focus of information system (I/S) organizations around the world. Massive migration from host-centric to network-centric systems is underway in every major public and private business. The cost of this migration is enormous. Organizations report that the cultural shifts needed to be successful are difficult at best. During our changing times, we must ask ourselves what is wrong with our existing I/S architectures? There are many advantages to "traditional" systems, including less complexity and previously trained staff. Before debating the technical merits of message oriented middleware (MOM) against object request brokers (ORBs) we must first answer this question.

What is wrong with our existing I/S architectures? To put it simply our existing I/S architectures are failing. They are failing to meet the changing demands of business. Previously successful I/S practices and technologies for meeting business requirements and providing solutions are suddenly no longer effective. The very architectures that were effective in the 1970s and 1980s are now inhibiting our ability to service business in the 1990s. One of the reasons for this is because the design point of legacy systems was to optimize expensive mainframe processing and storage resources. However, systems designed to optimize computing resources can not easily adapt to changing business needs because *they were not designed* for that purpose.

We assert that competitive *advantage* was a goal for the 1980s. Organizations which had not achieved competitive advantage are out of business. And new businesses must achieve it just to start. The real game in the 1990s is *sustainable* competitive advantage. By sustainable competitive advantage we are referring to a company's ability to deliver the right goods and services today and also be able to sustain that ability over time. The only constant is rapid change.

Companies that are effectively deploying client/server technology to achieve sustainable competitive advantage are all doing the same thing. They are not organizing themselves around traditional measures of usability or availability as their primary design point. They are organizing themselves around the principle of adaptability because they realize adaptability enables them to sustain their competitive advantage.

Companies which have come to this conclusion are realizing that it is their traditional technical architectures that are inhibiting their ability to adapt. In fact, technology is holding business back rather than enabling it to move forward. Newer client/server technology promises flexibility and adaptability in the technology and therefore in the very business that it enables. This, then, is the primary justification for the massive technical migration to network-centric systems—the ability to adapt the systems to the changing needs of the business.

This book deals with both the strategic and practical issues that impact our ability to design, build, and deploy client/server systems that enable sustainable competitive advantage.

1.1 BUSINESS UNDER PRESSURE TO CHANGE

Shrinking Business Cycles are Forcing a Major Shift in I/S

The way businesses operate has changed drastically in the past ten years. Today, companies are shedding their long-held beliefs and values of how business should be conducted because today's competitive climate has shifted from "company-driven and product-oriented" to "customer-driven and service-oriented." Those companies which continue to survive are adapting quickly to their changing markets. More and more executives are concluding that business adaptability is the key to survival.

Two key factors are driving organizations to continuously change their business and administrative processes and to "reinvent" themselves on an ongoing basis: globalization and profit margin erosion. If an organization reinvents itself successfully, it then becomes a new competitor in the global arena, and the cycle repeats itself. Let's examine these factors more closely.

Today, companies compete in a global market where the best set the standard for the rest. In a global economy, global communication and global transportation have altered and intensified the competitive environment. Trade barriers are falling, excellent suppliers are driving out inferior ones, and technology is now playing a key role in delivering products and services to customers. For example, today it is extremely difficult to enter the overnight shipping business. A large fleet of planes and trucks, a high speed package sorting facility, and a highly automated package tracking system are all required just to enter the industry!

As competition increases, profit margins erode. If a competitor company is able to cut costs and to return the savings to the customer, while simultaneously delivering a good quality product, there is a serious threat to existing companies in that market sector. A threatening competitor is able to offer goods or services cheaper and faster than the existing companies. This forces the laggards to find a way to achieve at least competitive parity, if not competitive advantage in order to keep their customers. Less margin means less budget dollars, and that means that the existing company must find ways to cut costs. Cutting costs almost always means changing the business and administrative processes of the company to be of higher value and less expense.

Lower profit margins force companies to innovate new ways to bring in profit. The search often begins in core processes. Today's airline industry is a good example, because it has experienced serious erosion of profit margins. If you were to ask United Airlines what business they are in today they would say airline reservations. They plan to earn more on entertaining you in the air than on ticket prices. Since June of 1996 United Airlines has been flying a Boeing 777 with electronic gambling networked into every seat on the airplane. The company's objective—to supplement shrinking profit with new services. Not only must companies cut costs and reinvent existing processes, but they must innovate and invent completely new ones.

The pressures of globalization and profit margin erosion are exacerbated by other factors as well. Rapid changes in technology, economics, policy, and leadership are all forcing administrative and business processes to change. The result is that the internal cycle times of business—pricing cycles, time-to-market cycles, delivery cycles, service cycles, innovation cycles—are getting shorter and shorter. Business cycles have gone from years to months. This rate of shrinkage is accelerating.

Let's use Ford Motor Company as an example. In days gone by, the "shelf-life" of the Model-T car lasted for an entire generation! In the 1980s it took Ford seven years, from design to showroom delivery, to produce a new car model. Today, it takes eighteen months. Another example in the product sector is today's retail business where the average "shelf-life" cycle time is about four months.

Cycle times are under enormous pressure in the service sector as well. An I/S director at a specialty credit card company recently told us that in order to maintain their niche, they must be able to customize product—essentially bring a new product to market—within *one week*. These examples of shrinking business cycles are evidence that companies must be able to adapt to survive.

Competition, margin erosion, and changes in the business and administration processes are technology imperatives for I/S professionals. It is crucial that we understand these forces because our job is to deploy systems that enable our organizations to achieve success in this constantly changing world. In the 1970s and 1980s we utilized technology to report on the business, but today we use technology to literally run the business. In response to shrinking business cycles I/S is forced to drastically reduce its systems delivery cycles to keep up.

One could argue that today's business success depends on technology. Client/server technology has the potential to enable changes in the business to quickly be reflected in the systems that run the business. This is the reason why organizations are adopting this technology en masse. A recent study by Strategic Focus (www.strategicfocus.com) reported that in 1996 non-client/server applications represented 46.9% of all applications. The report predicted that by 1998 non-client/server applications would fall to a total of only 17%. This represents a 200% increase in client/server development. New technology enables companies to deploy business solutions to quickly meet short-term goals *and* build a foundation for a sustainable future.

Companies that have achieved adaptability have done many things well. From a technical perspective they utilize computing technology which is capable of integrating with technology from multiple vendors. This makes it much easier to integrate different kinds of technology and adopt new technology. It also makes it easier to reuse what already exists and add new functionality as needed. These qualities help drastically reduce development cycle times and maximize reuse—keys to achieving business adaptability.

For example, Federal Express customers can now key in a package air bill number over the Internet and see each and every leg of the package's journey, including the name of the person who signed for it and what time it arrived! In every way, shape, and form, modern business is becoming technology-enabled and customer-oriented.

1.2 LEGACY SYSTEMS INHIBIT CHANGE

> *Legacy Code Inhibits Change Because it was Built for Processing Efficiency and not Reuse*

The problem with our legacy systems is that their design and implementation inhibit change. This is not because programmers failed in their original task. Legacy systems were built at a time when business was more stable, and rapid change was not the primary design point. Because memory and storage were very expensive, the primary design point of many legacy systems was processing efficiency. This was often achieved through programming craftsmanship which lead to a culture of artisan programming.

This code is now proving difficult to change because it wasn't built for reuse. Moreover, changes in one section of code often impact other parts of the code. Over the years, the numerous patches that have been made to the code have made these systems even more difficult to change because of the unpredictable and unintended effects changes might have on other modules. This is part of the reason the year 2000 problem is so complex, making it difficult and expensive to correct these systems. Changing the date is a structural change which could ripple through an undetermined number of modules which could then fail, with potentially catastrophic effects on the business. Moreover, legacy systems were built with older technology which is proprietary and does not support the addition of new technology from other vendors. Therefore, it is more difficult to extend the functionality of these legacy systems with new features and capabilities of today's newer technology.

Further, because the deployment cycles of legacy systems was typically three to five years, the methodologies, languages and development processes were built around a long development cycle. Since today's business cycles are typically four to eighteen months, a system delivered in three to five years would have little or no value. To be of value, the I/S systems deployment cycles must be equal to or shorter than the business cycles they enable. The old I/S methods and tools just can't deliver in this environment. Most importantly, the culture of the artisan programmer can't survive, because reuse and component software building is a requisite for the shorter development cycles.

Indeed, it's not just the older systems that inhibit change. Some new client/server systems deployed as little as two or three years ago could be called "client/server legacy systems." They are beautiful, expensive technology solutions that are out of date weeks or months after delivery. The systems fit the definition of legacy in that they can neither be easily scaled nor extended. A sexy graphical user interface (GUI) is of little value to the business if it fails to adapt to business changes. Without understanding the primary design point of adaptive systems, organizations are destined to build yet another generation of legacy systems, regardless of the technology they use. Building systems which can adapt to business changes requires designing for change, not just using client/server technology.

The traditional relationship between the business, systems, and supporting technical infrastructure inhibits change. For example, a business colleague who works for a major telecommunications company recently told us that his company had a new telephone service to offer its customers. People in the marketing department were very excited about the new offer. The only problem, he told us, was that it was six months overdue to be released because I/S had been unable to make the necessary systems changes that would allow them to bill their customers for the new service. This is a classic example of technology-driven architectures and their impact on business.

Executives are concluding that business value must directly drive technology decisions, and not vice versa. To cause this to happen some organizations are demanding a return on I/S investment within twenty-four months. This is what we call a process-driven architecture.

1.3 ADAPTIVE CLIENT/SERVER SYSTEMS ENABLE CHANGE

Process-Driven Architectures Enable Change

Client/server technology is capable of quickly delivering new and better product, service, and value to customers and to the business. Client/server technology is built on open systems standards and enables integration of different systems components. Ultimately, open systems standards make systems more extensible. Standards make it easier to add new technology and new functionality, while still using the old.

Client/server technology is far more user friendly. It makes it easier to put the controls in the hands of the end user and lets them do their analysis and reporting without the intervention of I/S. In turn, this enables rapid decision making. This is essential if companies are going to sustain competitive advantage even while their business is changing more and more rapidly.

Client/server development tools enable rapid application development (RAD). The benefits of RAD are more pronounced when applications are carefully architected for adaptiveness to change and reuse. Because processing power and storage are now cheap, we can afford to opt for less efficient code in favor of more reusable code. It is important to note here, that if the primary design point is adaptiveness to change, design decisions are most often made to accommodate change. That means adding more processing power when necessary to solve performance problems, rather than relying on creative artisan programming.

Artisan programming will always inhibit change in the business, because it does not lend itself to reuse. This in turn, increases the cost and time spent in quality assurance (QA), which in business terms, is a cost: It does not add *business* value. The primary benefits of component architectures and object oriented programming (OOP) is the ability to create reusable components which have already been through QA and testing, thereby significantly reducing development costs. When new business requirements arise, new functionality can be added to existing components.

In fact, today's technology is so adaptable, it gives us the ability to create flexible, business process-driven architectures. This is a relationship where changes in the business drive changes in the application architecture, which in turn drive changes in the technical architecture. Most importantly, process changes can be realized in the applications that enable them inside the shorter cycle times of the business. This is the relationship that executives and line management in organizations have been looking for a long, long time.

Companies that have successfully migrated to client/server technology and created adaptive systems have some common characteristics. They realize that although the technology available today is astonishingly powerful, there are no "silver bullets." No perfect or single tool or technology will ever be "the answer." Most importantly, successful companies realize that success depends on far more than just a new programming tool, it depends on creating process-driven architectures.

1.4 THE EVOLUTION OF COMPUTING

From Host-Centric to Network-Centric Systems

Back in the 1960s, mainframes were the first commercial use of computing technology. They were limited in their capability and extremely large and expensive. Only the most technical people could work on them, and the mainframe's limited capabilities enabled automating only "back room" manual functions such as accounting. Their highly cryptic user interfaces (for example, Job Control Language) and the rigid ways information could be accessed (only via a programming language) made data entry slow and error prone. Business users were dependent on I/S to program and deliver reports. New information needs could not be quickly and easily met. Typically, I/S backlogs of business requests could be measured in years! This was the infancy of computing technology, where business users were totally dependent on I/S.

During the 1970s, the minicomputer made its debut, and proliferated because they filled departmental computing needs. Departments took control and were able to manage their computing resources. Systems were created to fill the needs of a single department; they were not designed to integrate with other systems in the organization. As these so-called "stove pipe" systems increased in vast numbers, work and information duplication were the norm. This was the preadolescent stage in the evolution of computing. While departments had the freedom to create their own applications, business users were still dependent on I/S professionals to deliver their information.

During the 1980s, the computer industry was perfecting miniaturization and thereby constantly improving performance while reducing cost. Inevitably, the personal computer emerged. This marked the beginning of what is now called "end user" computing: The final recipient of business information gained the ability to directly manipulate data. Hundreds of useful applications, and a few key software tools (for example, the spreadsheet), became widely available. But the cost of gaining independence from the mainframe was a highly uncoordinated and almost chaotic way of working. This was the adolescent phase of computing, where end users "did their own thing." Now each PC became its own "stove pipe" system. Inconsistent and unmanaged data proliferated.

In the early 1990s, network computing, the proliferation of servers on those networks, and mature graphic user interfaces emerged. Through the ability of robust networks to link the PCs, servers, and mainframes together, I/S departments can now develop distributed solutions which enable end users to be more productive through technology, while providing a robust and manageable distributed computing infrastructure. Today, the technology is available to create distributed systems that are reliable and powerful enough to support just about any business activity. This is the maturation of computing, where interdependence is key to success. Today, the mainframe is just another processor in the distributed computing environment.

There is, however, a catch to this new era of interdependent computing technology. As powerful as our new network-centric systems are, they must be effectively used to be of value, and this requires collaboration and cooperation among people. (Case in point: just because someone owns a telephone does not mean they will pick it up and call their mother!) Client after client reports to us that the "cultural shifts" and "organizational challenges" are the most difficult in this world of collaboration and cooperation. For this reason we stress that the evolution of client/server occurs in three domains at the same time: people, process, and technology. We refer to this as the Client/Server paradigm. Let's take a brief look at this new paradigm.

The people dimension of the client/server paradigm is actively changing the roles and activities of people in the workplace. Executives are shedding their typical roles as scorekeepers and are being asked to demonstrate true leadership. The role of the worker is also shifting, from one where tasks are done under strict control of management to one where active thinking and decision making are part of every task.

The work itself is also being impacted. There is a growing trend to take work away from "stove pipe" functional departments and give it to designated process teams which are cross-functional in nature. This means the systems must change to support this cross-functional teaming.

Fannie Mae and General Electric are two good examples of the people dimension of client/sever. Fannie Mae reassigned the work of making a loan from its slow-moving centralized departments to highly focused work teams comprised of financial, marketing, and computer experts. General Electric gave its workers flexibility and unprecedented authority to decide how to do their work. This change enabled its Power Systems division to reduce its inventory carrying charges by almost $100 million. Clearly, changing the way people work, and shifting the work accordingly, can result in substantial productivity gains.

The process dimension of the client/server paradigm addresses how work is actually done. More and more, large enterprises are finding ways to reduce duplication of effort and consolidate several similar jobs into one. Centralized work locations are giving way to distributing work to where it makes the most sense to have it done. Client/server technology enables systems to be deployed to support work where and how it occurs in the business.

Timberland and Cleveland's Society National Bank have taken advantage of client/server technology in this way. At Timberland, taking orders and verifying credit, jobs which used to be done in two different departments, were merged into one job. The new computer system supported the new organization and also enabled electronic transmission of the order to manufacturing, which sped up the process even more. Cleveland's Society National Bank took a similar approach. Now, their loan officers have laptops to free them from the confines of their desks and enable them to create refinancing deals at the convenience of their customers.

Clearly, distributed technologies can enable a different way of working. In fact, if an employee can be across town, then why not across the world? Virtual employees and virtual teams are becoming more and more common, requiring more and more coordination and computer systems support between them.

When people, process, and technology evolve together we witness the power of client/server computing. When one facet of the paradigm forges ahead without the others, we see predictable failure. More than ever before, business and I/S professionals need to partner together to be successful. There is no recipe to achieve this partnership. It requires thinking and creativity, on a day by day basis. It can be done, and it *is* being done. When client/server is successful it enables people to do their jobs better which is a goal we believe is worth working toward.

1.5 WHAT IS NEW IN CLIENT/SERVER?

New Thinking for People, New Behavior for Systems

Many people argue that there is *nothing* new about client/server, really. The concepts and capabilities of client/server have really been around for a long time. We agree and we disagree. Although many of the capabilities of client/server have indeed been possible with more traditional technologies it has never been this easy—not across multiple vendor technologies and not this fast. Client/server enables I/S to deploy long-sought practices with relative ease. The tools and technology have finally caught up to the theory:

1. **New Technology.** Client/server is new technology. Operating systems, hardware platforms, application development tools and languages, networks and middleware, and their implications, must all be considered.
2. **New System Complexity.** One major benefit of client/server is its ability to integrate new technology, allowing you to pick and choose components from different vendors. But this also creates complexity in both building and maintaining systems. Increased heterogeneity creates increased maintenance costs and the need to create and manage many more vendor relationships. Integration of heterogeneous components becomes the problem. Because there are so many permutations and combinations possible, predicting system performance is extremely difficult. It also increases the complexity of testing and scaling systems across the enterprise. Design and architecture are key to managing this complexity.
3. **Shorter, Iterative, and Incremental I/S Delivery Cycles.** Just as business is facing shorter delivery cycles, I/S groups are facing shorter development cycles. As discussed previously, the only way to be of value to business in the 1990s is to deliver within or below the shrinking business cycles. Nothing else makes sense. Whereas traditional mainframe development cycles were typically three to five years, the June 1995 issue of *Computerworld Client/Server Journal* cites typical client/server development cycles of nine to ten months (Figure 1–2).

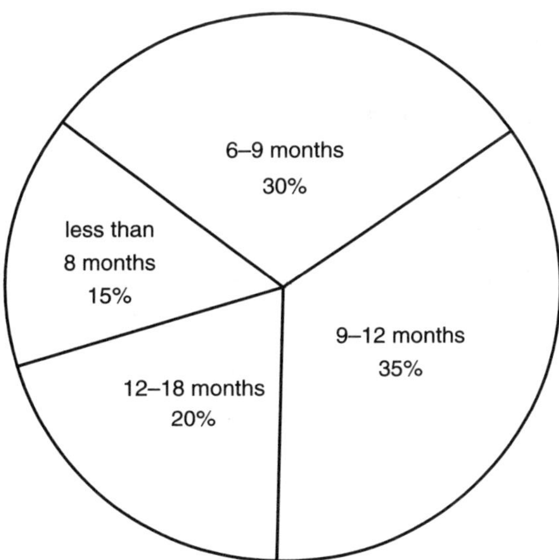

Figure 1–2 Average Development Cycles (*Computerworld,* June 1995)

Shorter development cycles force companies to deliver smaller solutions and incrementally build the "big picture." Incremental deployment of systems allows business to release the most important segments of major initiatives first, and then grow the system to meet the long-term objectives over time. Also, because smaller pieces of the system are studied for each release, project teams often iterate or "go back" to previously released segments of the systems as more is discovered about the overall goals. This iterative and incremental approach is key to success.

4. **New Distributed Computing.** Client/server computing is distributed computing. Producers and users of business information are distributed across the departmental and geographical boundaries of the enterprise. This distribution increases the risk of project failure due to the difficulties in obtaining interdepartmental agreement and coordination. Therefore, and we cannot stress this enough, the success of enterprise-wide client/server systems requires cross-organizational teamwork and infrastructure. Creating these elements requires the cooperation and collaboration of many people across a company. Architecture and design help foster this critical interdependent way of working.

   Client/server applications are also distributed across multiple computers. I/S must be able to look at the component pieces of an application and determine the best place for each component to reside. This is commonly referred to as data and process partitioning. There are three distinct views of partitioning: one business driven and two technology driven. The first is to partition the business rules and information among the responsible organizational work units, and in effect determine the boundaries of responsibility between the work units. The second is a multi-tier partitioning which looks at how the presentation, business rules, and data will be distributed across multiple processors. The third is a geographic partitioning which allocates the multi-tier design geographic locations. All aspects of distributed computing are new to client/server and we are just beginning to reach a level of mastery.
5. **New Roles for Business Users.** Rapid change in the business processes demands full participation of business users in the design and testing of on-line transaction processing systems. For decision support systems, the plethora of end user tools is putting report writing and data access decisions into the hands of end users. In fact, companies *must* have end users be responsible for their own reporting and analysis. In order to stay competitive, decision making must also be accelerated. This is accomplished by giving users direct access to the information they need. Creating competitive advantage depends on business professionals learning to work with these new tools to access their own information thereby accelerating their decision making capabilities. The bottom line is that business users are assuming *equal* responsibility for the success of a systems effort. This is very different from "being involved."
6. **New Roles for I/S.** Although writing code is not "bad," the more code that is written, the more that has to be maintained. The objective of today's I/S professional is *not* to write a new application to solve the next business problem. Instead, the goal is to look at the organization holistically and utilize existing data and software to meet new business needs. Any new code written should be unique to a specific set

of users and/or contain functions that have never previously been coded. Thus, the job of I/S is shifting from application development to building and supporting an infrastructure for information.

7. **New System Behavior.** Inherently, there is little new about client/server. But the power, flexibility, and usability of this technology enables radically new system behavior. Postulate for a moment that there is little new business data. (Oh yes, the data that is now in relational databases may have been in paper files a few years ago, but there is very little that is actually new.) What *is* new is what is done with that data and how a system behaves when business events occur to change that data. New technology can "push" information about key events to the people that need to know, when they need to know it. This accelerates decision making even more than having knowledge workers "pull" disparate pieces of data to see what is happening in their business. For example, with database trigger technology, a junior programmer can learn to build systems which instantaneously notify key business users when critical events are happening. In a world of shrinking business cycles this real-time knowledge is invaluable.

The implications of the client/server paradigm are far-reaching. It requires everyone including the CEO, line managers, business users, and programmers to think about their systems in radically different ways. And so, a successful client/server effort has to do many different things right. It has to correctly analyze the impact the technology will have on business operations and ultimately customer service. It must coordinate multiple organizational units during requirements specification, design, implementation, and deployment. It must work within a shortened development cycle. It must enable itself with tools for all phases of the development cycle. In short, successful client/server efforts have to be well-managed, and the solution they create has to be well-designed.

1.6 WHAT IS NOT NEW IN CLIENT/SERVER?

Rigor and Discipline of a Formal Process of Working Together

Although many mainframe programmers may see their careers passing before them when they see client/server technology come through the door, there is much that is not new about client/server. Many of the concepts have been around for years in the mainframe world and much of the discipline developed for mainframe systems is sorely needed in the client/server arena, especially as more and more client/server systems integrate with mainframe legacy systems.

For example, remote procedure calls (RPCs), are similar to compiled subroutine calls in structured programming. The only difference is that the application modules reside on separate processors. Similarly, data administration is as sorely needed in the distributed world as it was in the centralized world, maybe more. The underlying principles of object oriented analysis, design and programming—high cohesion and low coupling—

have been around since the late 1960s. Of course, nothing ever replaces the need for good requirements analysis or the need to really understand the business itself.

Contrary to popular trade press articles, our experience is that mainframe I/S professionals can be successful in the world of client/server if they are willing to open their minds and to let go of some of the notions of the past that no longer work. Most importantly, seasoned I/S professionals know what it takes to deploy a system. They understand that the process of working together must be well-defined and followed to be successful. For example, GUI prototyping is only one part of the overall effort. Behind the scenes is data modeling, network design, configuration management, security and support issues, quality control and testing, and creating robust reliable systems capable of supporting the business seven days a week, twenty-four hours a day, 365 days a year. Traditional I/S staff have been there and they know what it takes to build mission-critical enterprise systems. Seasoned professionals with a commitment to learn can contribute immense value to companies transitioning to client/server.

1.7 THE NEED FOR DESIGN

Successful Systems Don't Just Happen; They are Engineered

Well-managed projects and well-designed solutions do not happen accidentally. In fact, the current success rate for client/server efforts is low. The January 1995 issue of *Application Development Trends* reported that 16% percent of client/server projects were successful, 53% were so severely challenged that they experienced serious trouble or were put on hold, and 31% were canceled entirely. Several reasons contribute to this low success rate:

1. **Focus on the GUI.** Too much attention is currently being placed on the "drag-and-drop" user interface. Typically, as a percentage of the amount of project resources being used, too many people are developing the user interface (UI) and too much UI prototyping is being done. Although usability is an important requirement, the most difficult technical problems occur: 1) in partitioning system behavior across a distributed processor architecture and 2) in assuring that the various components "fit" together across the enterprise. Careful, continuous, and thorough design, backed by iterative prototyping and design refinement, are needed to solve these problems.
2. **Lack of Methods.** There is a failure to utilize data engineering methods to fully understand business processes and the impact of change in these processes. This results in poor or no database models or data architecture. There is no formal method for defining business rules for maintaining or organizing data for optimal access by each business unit. In turn, this inhibits the ability to optimize enterprise-wide information sharing, and the response to new needs for business information. In addition, unsuccessful projects sometimes fail to separate the data for on-line transaction processing (OLTP) from the decision support system (DSS).

3. **Few Management Tools.** Unsuccessful client/server projects have a dearth of management tools. They often lack widely available code management tools, even though their primary software result is a set of highly interconnected, yet very small, software components. In addition, they sometimes do not employ system management tools for monitoring the network, even though having a "virtual console" of network performance is crucial. They rarely use groupware technology, such as Lotus Notes, or Intranet enabled documents to coordinate the many hundreds of tasks which must be done by many people throughout the enterprise. In addition, while they may use project management tools, those tools are usually built to support a mainframe development style, and hence provide inadequate support for the highly parallel, highly iterative kind of development process a client/server project needs to undertake. In short, client/server projects themselves are poorly designed.
4. **Scope Creep.** Another common reason for client/server project fatalities is the way they are run. Often the exact scope of the system is not clearly defined, thereby causing the infamous "scope creep." In addition, without clear scope definition iterative release cycles are not possible. Quite often a shared understanding of the business implications of the system and the project is also often overlooked in favor of "getting the system out the door." When programming keeps taking center stage, the organizational aspects of both the problem and the solution are postponed until near system delivery, or they are not addressed at all.
5. **Little Infrastructure.** The driving tendency to forsake building a technical infrastructure for code development and testing is also common. For example, we often observe development teams ignoring the "network people" until the very end of the project. This practice may work in the mainframe environment, but it is risky in client/server. All these traditional ways of working, which can be compensated for during mainframe-based projects, eventually become "show stoppers" during client/server projects.
6. **Focus on the Incorrect Design Point.** Finally, unless an organization understands the primary design point of enabling change in the business and administrative processes, client/server systems are not designed to adapt to the continuous changing needs of the business. They may be too focused on the capabilities of the technology, rather than the needs of the business. We are finding many legacy client/server systems being built today.

1.8 THE NEED FOR MODELING

Modeling Produces an Explicit Design Which Can Be Reviewed And Validated

All of the above factors point to the difficulty of managing and coordinating complexity; complexity in the technology, the process, the business, and the development team itself. The solution is simple. Every aspect of the project and the solution must be *explicitly* designed. The design process creates a clear, shared understanding of the system focused on the business needs. The very act of collaborating on a design brings hidden assumptions to the surface and provides a foundation for a group of people to reach a common understanding and to develop agreement about what is to be built.

The act of explicit design is known as "modeling." To convey a shared understanding of the system, the design must be represented in design models; pictures with associated text. Text alone is not enough. Text is highly ambiguous. It can neither be verified nor validated. It requires no thinking to ramble on and on about what a system will do or how it will accomplish its tasks. A wise philosopher put it this way, "I didn't have time to write you a short letter so I wrote you a long one." The difficulty in modeling is not in learning how to draw circles and squares or little clouds with arrows. The difficulty comes when a cross-organizational team of people attempt to align on a specific and measurable design to agree on something. A common misconception regarding models is that they are simply "documentation." Current development cycles leave little time for documentation. Models are a collaborative tool for designing complex client/server systems. The process of design helps minimize the risk by preventing defects before they are code. The result of using models is that documentation is provided as a natural by-product of the effort. This is especially important for delivering system functionality incrementally, building upon what has already been done before.

Modeling is practiced by every major engineering discipline on the planet: civil engineers, electrical engineers, architects, mathematicians, and even musicians. Modeling requires fluency in language (or notation) that can correctly and sufficiently describe the problem space. For software engineers this includes the business, the specific problem, the proposed design, and the implications of the design. For example, a client/server design must communicate such things as the distributed processor architecture, how the system's behavior is allocated across that architecture, and system performance considerations. In addition, the design must be explicitly tied back to a complete statement of system requirements.

We want to emphasize here that the nature of designing client/server is not the "analysis paralysis" activity commonly associated with lethargic development cycles. Designing carefully and thoroughly does not call for long schedules. It calls for thinking "design" during every step of the project. By that we mean continually keeping in mind the design of the system as well as the implications each technical decision has on that design.

None of the winners of the "Client/Server Top Five" at the 1995 Database World in Boston cited the secret of their success as the particular database or application development tool they chose. Instead, they all talked about using technology to deliver business functionality and creating a shared understanding between I/S and the business. Richard L. Hudson, Vice President of Global Marine, Incorporated, sumed it up this way, "Be more insistent on system design."

The design method presented in this book is a blending of the old and the new. It represents a modern object-based method to be used to express client/server solutions. We did not throw out all the tools and techniques developed over the last quarter of a century that work. Instead, we built upon common techniques and added new ones required for

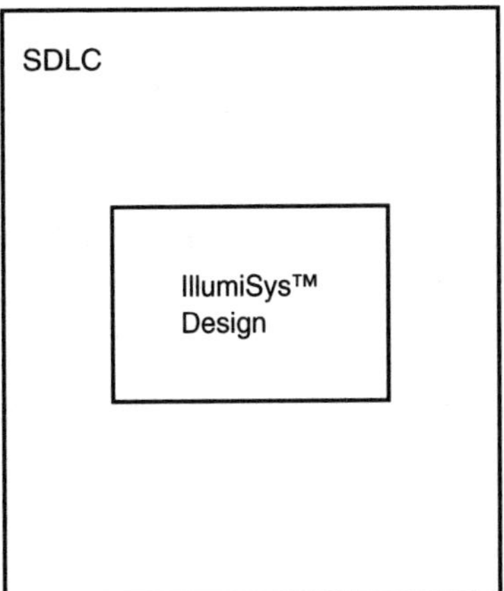

Figure 1–3 The IllumiSys Design Method Fits Within Existing System Development Life Cycles (SDLC)

the specific needs of distributed systems, including partitioning data and processing across processors. This book presents a design method created specifically for such distributed client/server systems. It focuses on "design" as an activity that meets business requirements, maximizes reuse, and allows systems to be easily modified.

The design method focuses on what is necessary to succeed with distributed systems. It is not a complete Systems Development Life Cycle (SDLC). In our experience, every large organization we work with has their own SDLC. What they lacked was the explanation and deliverables of the specific steps necessary for deciding how to distribute data and processing across the distributed environment so the resulting system is flexible, manageable, can be quickly deployed to meet current business needs, and easily changed to meet new needs. This is the purpose of the IllumiSys™ Design Method. It has been designed to fit within or augment existing SDLCs (see Figure 1–3).

2

Models and Modeling

Models Provide the Rigor and Discipline for Engineering Adaptive Systems

As organizations adopt client/server for more and more of their business systems, and as these systems become distributed across the enterprise, design becomes increasingly essential. This book presents a design method created specifically for such distributed client/server systems. It focuses on "design" as an activity that meets business requirements, maximizes reuse, and allows systems to be easily modified.

In the last chapter, we discussed how businesses, in an attempt to dramatically reduce cycle times, are migrating to client/server as a way to adapt to rapidly changing business conditions. Client/server technology is more complex than centralized systems. Client/server systems are comprised of multiple components and must be designed to run over networks. Furthermore, although the systems themselves are more complex, the development cycles are far shorter. This requires iterative development efforts and a design approach that can support it. As Figure 2–1 suggests, modeling is crucial.

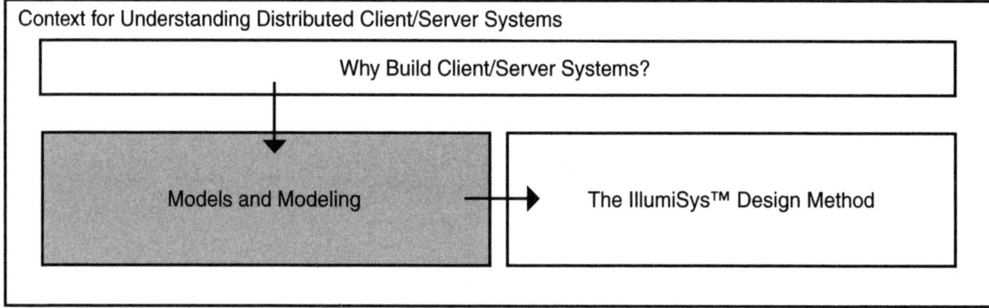

Figure 2–1 Road Map for Part I—Context for Understanding Distributed Client/Server Systems: Models and Modeling

But modeling, like any skill, can be misapplied. For example, during the two decades we have participated on projects to design computer-based solutions, we have seen people model the wrong subjects, spend too much time detailing one particular portion of a system while ignoring other equally important areas, and develop models that do not integrate well. We feel you can avoid these common pitfalls, and achieve greater success in designing client/server solutions, if you can fully answer the following two questions:

1. Why are models of requirements and design beneficial to client/server development?
2. What is the process for specifying and designing client/server solutions using models?

The benefit of answering these two questions can be summarized clearly. During the development of a client/server solution, many decisions have to be made, such as what users need, how these requirements will be met, what computers are needed, and how the actual solution will operate on those computers. Models help illuminate each of these decisions in a way that makes it easier to see the pros and cons of each alternative. They reduce the risk of building complex systems, because they enable better communication among the participants.

To summarize the modeling process, the goal is to, as quickly as possible, develop a concise and coherent story about:

- What the business is
- How the business operates
- How the system will support the business
- The details of what the system will do
- How the system will operate.

Creating distinct, yet well-connected, models for each of these concerns is the desired outcome of the modeling process.

2.1 OBJECTIVES OF MODELING

Models Help Prevent Defects by Making the Design Explicit

The purpose of the model is to describe the proposed system design in sufficient detail so that defects can be found *before* the system is built, when they are much cheaper to fix. The resistance to modeling that many organizations have is due to past experience with "analysis paralysis" when projects studied the problem in depth but never actually built anything useful to the business. Because of the reduced business and development cycle times, we have months instead of years to build systems and cannot afford to engage in lengthy design activities. It is therefore critical to model the system in sufficient enough detail to meet the business need.

The IllumiSys™ Design Method provides guidelines for keeping the modeling process on track and aligned with the business. This is accomplished by answering a set of essential questions that guide and influence the development of the model. It is important to note that models are not created for documentation. Models are intended to be used to prevent system defects. This is accomplished through ensuring the "accuracy" of the design. There are two parts to accuracy. The first is that each and every question in the question set has been answered to the satisfaction of the users. The second is that each response has been answered to a sufficient level of detail for business sponsors, users, and I/S personnel to know what will be built and how, and they must be satisfied that what is planned to be built will meet the needs of the business.

2.2 WHAT IS A MODEL?

A Model is an Accurate, Concise, and Unambiguous Description of a System

A model is an abstract representation of something real. It is a highly organized set of information containing a lot of diverse information about a system. Models provide a description of a system that can be understood and reviewed by all business users and I/S professionals.

A model consists of both graphics and natural language. A model contains aspects which highlight a particular area of the business, such as the business process or the information used by the system. Each aspect pertains to a different kind of information.

The IllumiSys™ models can contain many different perspectives of a client/server system (for example, requirements, design goals, partitioning, technical infrastructure). Historically, the software engineering community has always advocated separating system requirements from the design of the system. We concur with this approach and have practiced it for almost two decades now. We have found that separating requirements from design helps people isolate two important questions: 1) What will the system do? and 2) How will the system be constructed? The IllumiSys™ Design Method actually produces *two* models: one for the business requirements and one for the design.

In this book, the model of requirements is based on the Yourdon Systems Method, an event-driven method (*Yourdon™ Systems Method: Model-Driven Systems Development*, Yourdon Press, Prentice Hall, New Jersey, 1995). We have chosen this method because it uses a modeling language, including data flow diagrams (DFDs), state transition diagrams (STDs), and entity-relationship diagrams (ERDs) that is already familiar to many system designers. We did not wish to start from scratch and force designers to learn a whole new modeling language. Therefore, we do not spend a lot of time in this book describing the requirements model. We cover the requirements model only enough to explain how to develop it so that it becomes a very effective input to developing the design model (Part II is devoted to requirements. Parts III through Part VI address the design model).

2.3 THE MODELING PROCESS

The Modeling Process Focuses on Distinct Subjects Individually, Then the Interaction Between the Different System Components

Each model has a single subject. However, a single subject never functions in isolation, but is always intertwined with its environment. Although it is sometimes very hard to determine where the system ends, setting a narrowly defined scope is critical to successfully delivering systems in the shortened time frames now required. Companies who have successfully implemented client/server systems commonly point to the necessity of having complete alignment between business and I/S on what will be built and when it will be delivered. For these reasons, the first step in the IllumiSys™ Design Method is to precisely define a system's boundary. Many projects have run aground due to scope creep. Defining a project's scope to fit six to twelve month delivery requires large projects to be broken up into phases with a high degree of iteration at all phases in the life cycle. This is very different from traditional development methods.

In more stable times, when business cycles were seven to ten years, we developed design methods that typically produced large-scale systems in three to five years. These long, complex projects were often managed with a "waterfall" life cycle which had distinct phases for analysis, design, coding, testing, implementation, and maintenance. The problem was that requirements were often discovered in the design and coding phase (read: "scope creep"). Most systems went into maintenance mode immediately after being implemented. While the waterfall life cycle was useful for managing the large-scale projects of the past, it is not appropriate for the fast paced development cycles of today.

Client/server demands rapid and concurrent development. It allows for multiple design and development tasks to be occurring on a project at the same time. Also, the results of each can be generated in very short periods of time. Client/server is also incremental and highly iterative. Early versions serve as foundations upon which successive iterations of the system are built. Even if large systems take years to build, they are released in increments which have tightly controlled scopes.

The modeling process in this book starts with defining the overall purpose of the system. Different dimensions of the system are depicted in views that are graphic models, tables, or structured text. The views (also called artifacts) are reviewed by others who have particular understanding of the various dimensions of the system to validate the model. They offer corrections and suggestions and sometimes they even have new insights about the system based on what the model says. This is how the models help prevent defects and reduce risks.

2.4 THE STRUCTURE OF A MODEL

> *Models Have a Hierarchical Structure to Show Interaction Among Components and to Enable Them to be Used for Project and Enterprise Level Efforts*

As we mentioned earlier, the IllumiSys™ Design Method organizes information about the system into two models: requirements and design. The structure for both models is the same, although the actual information in each model, the aspects and views, are different. The structure was created so that the models could be used by system developers to build complex component-based systems.

The first structure is the model itself (see Figure 2–2). A model is an abstraction of something real, or something that will become real; in this case, a system. Models show policy or technology. Each model has a well-defined structure to allow checking for completeness and consistency. Correctness is established by making them understandable to business users so they can be reviewed. In the IllumiSys™ Method the requirements model highlights *what* the system will do, while the design model highlights *how* the system will be built using distributed computers. Thus, a model defines the highest level of importance—the *kind* of information it contains. However, given the nature of the complexity of constructed systems, no one modeling language is adequate to describe a system. This is why models have more detailed structures of aspects and views.

Aspects highlight an area of focus in the model. Weinberg's lump law states that, "in order to understand anything do not attempt to understand everything!" Architectural drawings serve as a useful example. An architect usually creates one set of drawings for the home owner, which needs to look much like the house they are buying. A text description certainly won't do. The buyer wants to *see* where the windows, doors, and walls will

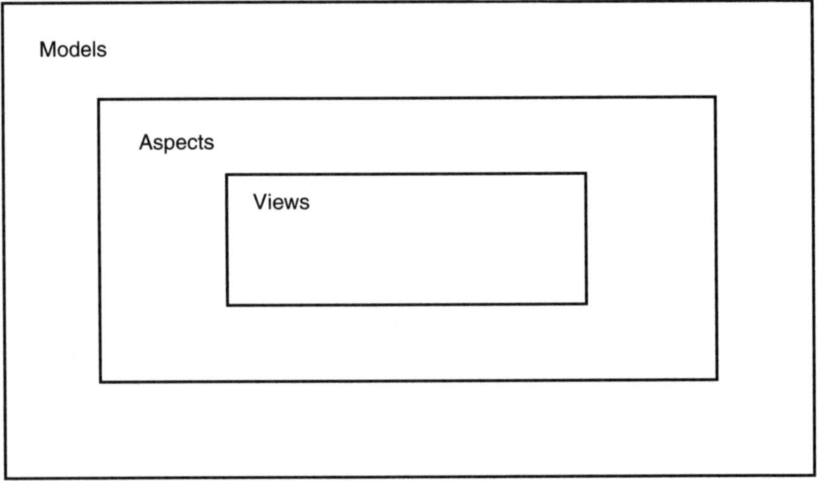

Figure 2–2 The Structure of a Model

be. While they exist only on a drawing, they are much easier to move and change. If the homeowner wishes to move a window once it has been framed, it will be much more difficult, take longer, and cost more money. The drawings that are useful to a homeowner (which may even include shrubbery, walkways and siding) would be of little use for a framer, plumber, or electrician. They each need their own set of drawings that focus on the aspect of the project they are responsible for. If everyone had to work from one drawing, that drawing would be too confusing for anyone to understand. That is the purpose of having different aspects to highlight different areas of the system.

Aspects are comprised of views. A view is a table, diagram, or structured text specification used to highlight a particular area of concern. Each view shows a part of the model and is used by people to discuss one set of issues about the system so they can make informed decisions about the design or the implementation. In other words, a view is a window into the system which does not go beyond people's ability to comprehend what is being communicated. By carefully choosing a set of overlapping views, it is possible to separately describe all parts of the system in a way that forms a complete, consistent, and coherent representation of the system. For example, one view may explain how the system interacts with its environment, while another defines how the system behaves when given a particular stimulus. The views become the actual artifacts of the system. They are the deliverables of the design. As such, they serve as the documentation for the system and specifications for building and implementing the system.

This, in fact, is the general structure of both the requirements model and the design model in the IllumiSys™ Design Method. The method advocates certain views and aspects which we and others have found to be highly effective in communicating what a system should do and how it should operate in a distributed setting. Each model, aspect, and view addresses a critical set of questions about the system.

We recommend you take the method as a starting point for each of your client/server projects, and use the concerns of each project to make your own choices about what views and aspects to keep, which ones to omit, and which, if any, new ones you need to create. If you are tackling your first client/server effort, we suggest you choose a system that is relatively small, or one that has minimal complexity. Use the IllumiSys™ Design Method on it without alteration. In this way, you will gain enough familiarity with the method to allow you to make decisions about how to adapt the method for more complex modeling situations.

2.5 BENEFITS OF MODELING

An Ounce of Prevention is Worth a Pound of Cure

The purpose of models is to prevent defects. Defects found in the design phase are far less expensive to fix than when they are found once they exist in code. In our architecture example, it is far less expensive to move a window or door when the house exists as a drawing than during the construction phase. In fact, it has been estimated that defects found in design cost one tenth to fix than defects found in code reviews. If defects pass through to implementation they cost ten times more to fix than during testing. There is a geometric progression in cost as defects pass through the life cycle.

The benefit of using models to prevent defects is that the models are easier to understand and review than large amounts of text. They are also less ambiguous. They make it easier to find defects and identify areas of risk.

It must be noted that prototyping is a technique to model the user interface. Prototyping alone is not sufficient for modeling the complex behavior of enterprise-wide distributed systems. It can not describe the behavior of the system over wide area networks, or depict how data and processing will be distributed across processors and geographic locations. Large-scale distributed systems represent a higher degree of risk. Therefore, the investment made in modeling can be easily justified if it helps prevent defects that may prevent the successful implementation of the system.

3

The IllumiSys™ Design Method

An Event- and Object-Based Method for Developing Distributed Client/Server Systems

Chapter 2 introduced the fundamental concepts of models for system development. The IllumiSys™ Design Method takes these concepts and applies them to the problem of designing client/server solutions. As its starting point, the method relies on time-tested modeling techniques for specifying system requirements. This chapter is an overview of the IllumiSys™ Design Method (Figure 3–1).

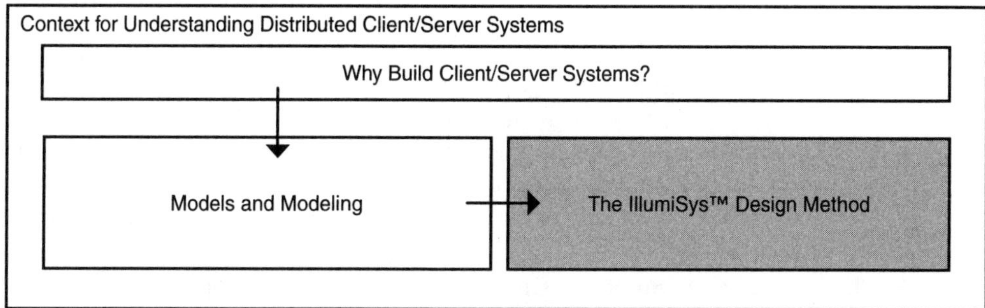

Figure 3–1 Road Map for Part I—Context for Understanding Distributed Client/Server Systems: The IllumiSys™ Design Method

Because we are interested specifically in client/server systems, the method must map well to the "shape" of client/server solutions. In that respect it is both event-based and object-based. The method is event-based because it uses business events to drive the partitioning of the system into a set of event responses. By initiating the requirements effort with a focus on the business events, we never lose track of the business processes which are driving the events. By designing the system as a set of responses to business events, when the business processes change we can more easily change the specific responses to the business event. We call the packaging of the event and its complete response a "business component." This strategy is very powerful for designing client/server systems because each business component represents the complete set of business rules and information needed to respond to each business event. Once defined, these business components can be distributed across the geographic locations of the business, partitioned into software "tiers," and ultimately distributed across technical components of the client/server architecture and even onto intranets and the Internet.

The method is also object-based because it takes into account the practices of encapsulation and inheritance. It partitions the business components into a multi-tier architecture including presentation, business rules, data access rules, and data. The data access rules encapsulate the data because the application does not need to know the location or structure of the data in order to access it. The application just sends a message to the data access tier. The business rules are partitioned into a set of methods which access data through the data access rules. Partitioning business events into a set of granular components is the key to reuse. Finally, even though we use "traditional" entity-relationship diagrams to represent the data, there is a major focus placed on inheriting both attributes and relationships from "supertype" entities. We therefore consider our object-based modeling approach to provide a migration strategy to object oriented development that currently carries much less risk than full object modeling for a number of reasons:

1. **No Standard Notation.** Until the recent (fall 1996) introduction of the Unified Modeling Language (UML) for objects, which represents a common modeling language developed by Grady Booch, Jim Rumbaugh, and Ivar Jacobson, each object method had its own notation and each focused on different dimensions of the object modeling task.
2. **No Theoretical Model to Guide Object Design.** Unlike relational data modeling which is based upon mathematically provable predicate logic, object modeling has no rigorous mathematical basis to prove the correctness of the model. In fact, UML addresses primarily *concepts and notation* because there is as yet little experience using object oriented methods to provide method *content* (engineering experience or rules of thumb).
3. **Immature Technology.** Current client/server technology is far more mature than object technology. The object databases are largely the products of small companies without significant market share. Therefore they are inherently riskier than Oracle, Sybase, DB2, or Informix. Further, the introduction of object/relational databases from the large database vendors may make large organizations reluctant to bet on pure object databases from small unknown companies.
4. **Evolving Middleware.** Technology for object communications, Object Request Brokers (ORBs), is still evolving. There are competing standards, and ORBs cannot

yet handle the on-line transaction volumes and rates required for many mission-critical enterprise systems.

At this point in time, most companies are using object oriented technology to develop the client side of the application. The objects being used are mostly application objects such as menu bars, windows, buttons, and so on. The application objects communicate with relational databases and traditional programming modules on the server. These application objects are different than business objects, such as customers, products, and contracts. By using object-based modeling throughout a system specification and design effort, the IllumiSys™ Design Method maps well to today's technical solutions and leaves the designer in a position to easily move to full object modeling in the future.

Finally, if you are in a shop which has adopted full object oriented analysis, design, coding languages, and databases we *still* believe that it is worth reading this book. The clear and concise description of the partitioning and distribution strategies for client/server, as well as the guidelines for selecting the technical architecture are valuable no matter what notation is being used. We believe UML is a very important piece of work and will enable the object oriented community to move full speed ahead. Stay tuned for further updates to this book as UML and object technology matures. In the meantime, we have found that Use Case Studies can be easily substituted for requirements (see Chapter 9, Section 9.2).

3.1 OBJECTIVES OF THE ILLUMISYS™ DESIGN METHOD

The Method Creates a Blueprint for Building Adaptive Systems

Adaptive systems require a reusable component approach to systems development to enable rapid deployment of business solutions. Traditional design methods do not address how to design and distribute these components across the distributed technical architecture and across the distributed business architecture of regional, national, and global operations. This is the primary focus of the IllumiSys™ Design Method.

The IllumiSys™ Design Method extends proven design techniques to address the difficult task of partitioning components across a distributed client/server architecture in a way that allows them to be managed, shared, and reused. The first part of the method, The Essential Model, creates business components that are comprised of business events and responses to those events, including the dimensions of processing, data, and time. These components are then distributed across geographic locations by considering how events naturally occur within specific locations of the business. The second part of the method focuses on distributing these components across the distributed client/server technical architecture, at specific geographic locations and across the geographic locations, and defining how components interact and communicate.

3.2 CREATING BUSINESS COMPONENTS: THE ESSENTIAL MODEL

The Design of Adaptive Systems Must be Business Driven

When we refer to "Business Driven" systems we mean systems that use technology to solve business problems, as opposed to technology-driven systems which are built to find a use for the latest and greatest technology. Business Driven systems are possible only if the systems are designed with a thorough understanding of the business events that drive them. Of course, well-defined requirements have always been critical for designing systems. Today's shrinking business cycles and complex distributed computing environments make it more important than ever before. Reusability depends upon creating components that accurately reflect the business processes they model.

Part one of the IllumiSys™ Design Method is a technology-free statement of what the system must accomplish. We call this the "Essential Model." It is based on the Yourdon Systems Method (*YSM Yourdon Systems Method: Model-Driven Systems Development by YOURDON Inc*, published by PTR Prentice Hall, 1995), and we have significantly extended it by adding the Event Distribution Aspect and Component Measurement Aspect to address the issues of partitioning for distributed systems. Figure 3–2 is the road map for the essential model. It is so-called because it represents the essential processes, rules, and information of the business.

The Essential Model begins with looking at the business requirements as a set of system responses to real world business events. Once the events are identified, the data and processing required to respond to the event are defined. These "business components"

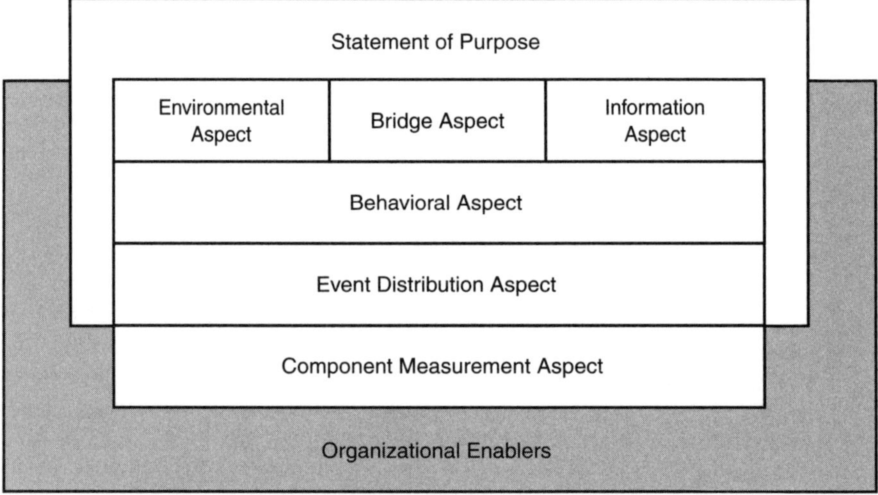

Figure 3–2 Business Components: The Essential Model

package together information and processing. The Behavioral Aspect of the Essential Model then further partitions these event components into highly granular, highly cohesive, loosely coupled response components which are comprised of response processes and data. The method then distributes the event components along the lines of organizational business units to define the logical boundaries of responsibilities for managing the business events. (Note that this is again a business-driven design step.) This creates a distributed design that is manageable because from its very beginning, the design defines the business responsibility for each distributed component. Business units are then mapped to the geographical business locations of regional, national, and global operations. We note here that although typically design methods differentiate between logical and physical design, we differentiate between business and technology. These locations, although physical, relate to business operations, not technology.

There are eight major steps to building the Business Requirements Model (called the Essential Model in YSM). They are: the Statement of Purpose; the Environmental Aspect; the Bridge Aspect; the Information Aspect; the Behavioral Aspect; the Event Distribution Aspect; the Logical Location Distribution Aspect; and the Component Measurement Aspect. Further details and examples on each of these Aspects can be found in Part II of the book.

1. **The Statement of Purpose.** The Statement of Purpose documents the business reason for the system, complete with at least one metric which will be used to measure the success of the system in enabling the business. (For further details see Chapter 4.)
2. **The Environmental Aspect.** The Environmental Aspect states the essential business events which drive the system, and how the system connects to and operates within its business environment. It is the primary aspect which defines the system's scope. (For further details see Chapter 5.)
3. **The Information Aspect.** The Information Aspect defines the business rules and information needed for the correct operation of the system, followed by what changes that information undergoes during each business event. (For further details see Chapter 6.)
4. **The Bridge Aspect.** The Bridge Aspect brings process and data together to make sure that the Environmental and Information Aspect agree, and that the overall Essential Model is complete and consistent. (For further details see Chapter 7.)
5. **The Behavioral Aspect.** The Behavioral Aspect describes in detail how the system behaves in response to each business. This aspect rigorously defines all the business policy inside the system boundary and is organized (partitioned) by the business events. (For further details see Chapter 8.)
6. **The Event Distribution Aspect.** The purpose of the Event Distribution Aspect is to map the system requirements to the real world environment of a distributed business by taking the Event Components and distributing them across business units.

   The purpose of forming logical locations is to determine which areas of the business are responsible for responding to business events. For example, in a manufacturing business, whose responsibility is it to notify the customer of back-order situations? Is the business based on just-in-time-inventory? Is it the responsibility of the Order Entry work unit to assign the warehouse location where the order will be sent to? These are critical decisions. (In object oriented analysis Use Case Studies are often used. These groups of users are identified, then it is determined how they use the system. This can be used for requirements instead of YSM.)

Next we distribute Logical Locations across the geographic locations of the enterprise. Although this seems to be a "physical" design step, it is really defining the business geography, not the technical implementation. It defines the requirements of different geographic business locations and enables a very flexible and reuseable design. For example, business units in Japan and the United States may share many of the same processes, but may have unique business rules as well. It also defines the communication between different business units which is necessary to accomplish the work of the overall enterprise. We have in effect defined our "logical" application boundaries and application interfaces. (For further details see Chapter 9.)

7. **The Component Measurement Aspect.** Measuring the components of the Essential Model provides critical information for defining the technical requirements in Part Two of IllumiSys™ Design Method: The Implementation Model. The Component Measurement Aspect of the Essential Model defines the occurrences of each component, including averages, peaks, and expected growth. This yields an understanding of the natural business cycles and performance requirements for the technical implementation. (For further details see Chapter 10.)
8. **Organizational Enablers.** Organizational Enablers appear on the diagram because they are the organizational factors which "wrap around" the system requirements. They include things such as organizational structure, process management, and operational support. They are the part of the diagram to remind us that the requirements are not complete without a consideration of Organizational Enablers. They are covered in Part IV of the book.

3.3 DISTRIBUTING COMPONENTS ACROSS THE DISTRIBUTED TECHNICAL ARCHITECTURE: THE IMPLEMENTATION MODEL

The Primary Design Point for Client/Server Systems is Adaptability

The Essential Model assumes perfect technology and in that model the business requirements are the complete focus of the effort. In a perfect world, the technical implementation of the system would look just like the Essential Model. However, there is no such thing as perfect technology or perfect operating conditions. All organizations are bound by real world constraints and technical limitations. Therefore, Part Two of the IllumiSys™ Design Method, the Implementation Model, defines how the business components are partitioned into software components and how these software components are distributed across processors and geographic locations. These decisions and design trade-offs are guided by design metrics and heuristics derived from the best client/server design practices which can be found in manufacturing, retail, finance, insurance, higher education, utilities, and state and local government.

The purpose of the Implementation Model is to create the blueprint for building the system. Figure 3–3 is the Road Map for creating the distributed design specifications. The business components defined in the Essential Model are first partitioned across the software tiers of a multi-tier client/server architecture. These include presentation, business rules, data access, and data. This partitioning is independent of the technology with which the system will be implemented. This step creates "multi-tier components" which are then distributed across a Technical Architecture consisting of clients, servers, mainframes, and other technical platforms (for example, the Internet/Intranet). Design Metrics are used throughout to provide guidelines for defining the Technical Architecture and evaluating the distribution of multi-tier components across it. The design is then distributed to the geographic locations of the business units defined in the Essential Model. The network requirements, which often determine the feasibility of the design, can be determined through traffic analysis. The overall success of the system is greatly dependent upon the organizational enablers in place. The organizational dimension is addressed in Part IV.

The Implementation Model consists of seven parts: Design Metrics, Multi-tier Partitioning, Technical Architecture Design, Physical Partitioning, Geographic Partitioning, and Traffic Analysis.

1. **Design Metrics.** Because design alternatives exist, much discussion often arises in order to select one of the alternatives. Design metrics are included to help people make better and faster design decisions. Design metrics include enterprise-wide guidelines as well as metrics specific to the project. They include such things as

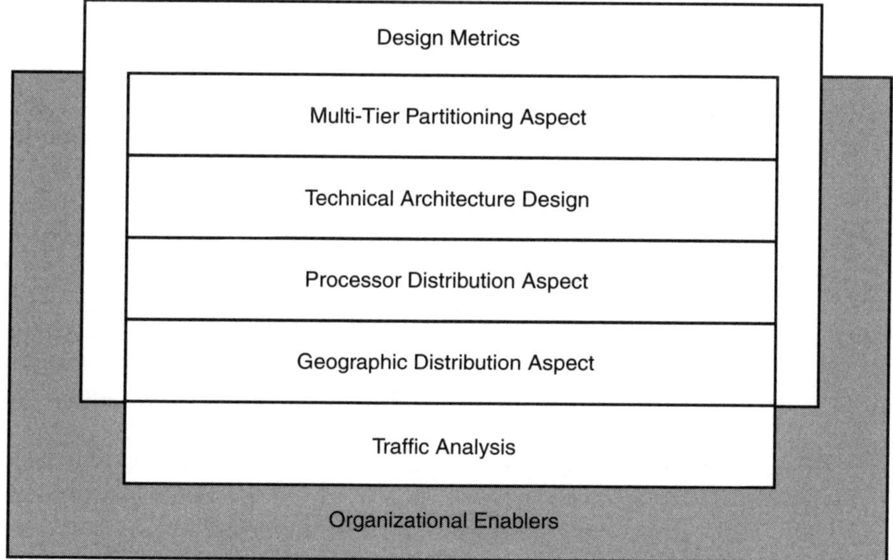

Figure 3–3 Software Components: The Implementation Model

availability, maintainability, scalability, usability, transportability, and reusability. They also include factors such as security, speed, data "freshness", reliability, and recoverability. Project specific design goals, such as minimizing training, rapid application deployment, reduced maintenance costs, will also be defined. (For further details see Chapter 12.)

2. **Multi-Tier Partitioning Aspect.** Multi-tier partitioning, a concept common to scaleable client/server design, involves taking each business event and partitioning it into the following design tiers: presentation, business rules, data access rules, and data. We recommend first doing this partitioning without giving consideration to the technology which will be used to implement the design. This is critical because if it is done well, it is possible to design for scalability, extensibility, and reuse at the beginning of the system's life, even if it will be physically implemented all on one processor. Multi-tier partitioning results in data encapsulation and granular methods representing business rules. This leaves designers with the maximum flexibility to change their systems rapidly when business rules change, when data sources and legacy systems are replatformed, when the business grows and the systems must accommodate more users, when reorganization of the business results in repartitioning of responsibilities, when new technology is introduced, or any other change occurs. (For further details see Chapter 13.)
3. **Technical Architecture Design.** This is the stage of the method where the technical components of the system are defined. This includes vendors for hardware, operating systems, development environments, network components, management tools, Internet/Intranet components, and configuration standards. Technical Architecture decisions are guided by business requirements, and by any enterprise standards that may exist. (For further details see Chapter 14.)
4. **Processor Distribution Aspect.** The next stage of the method defines how the multi-tier components will be implemented in the chosen technology, including clients, servers, mainframes, middleware, development languages and environments, and network components. The goal is to create a set of "software blueprints" for clients, servers, and mainframe integration from which the system will be built. The IllumiSys™ Design Method provides heuristics for guiding the designer through the decision making process of processor distribution.

   An adaptive design will enable you to *re-distribute* the tiers as necessary. As the technical architecture matures, and more and more applications are brought into the fold, there will be an ongoing need to shift and adjust the physical placement of components to sustain or improve system performance. This strategy will create designs that can adapt to being deployed on maturing client/server platforms, and/or Internet and Intranets. The IllumiSys™ Design Method leaves you with a set of tools for doing this with minimal redesign effort. (For further details see Chapter 15.)
5. **Geographic Distribution.** Once the multi-tier components have been mapped to processors the next step is to map the processors to geographic locations. Heuristics for mapping processors to locations are also provided in this step. For example, we recommend that servers be distributed to geographic locations to move data closer to where it will actually be accessed, thereby increasing performance, but *only* if the

company has implemented a virtual data center to support the geographic distribution. (For further details see Chapter 16.)

6. **Traffic Analysis.** Traffic Analysis focuses on the message traffic across the network and the contention on each processor due to that network traffic. The purpose of this step is to determine the feasibility of the design. For example, the design may be restricted due to the inability of the network to handle the expected message sizes and volumes, and to provide input for capacity planning for both the network architecture and the server processors. Traffic analysis is also used to determine if each software component is indeed running on the "correct" processor. We often find that some repartitioning is necessary due to the network constraints identified during a traffic analysis. (For further details see Chapter 17.)
7. **Organizational Enablers.** Organizational Enablers are also part of the Implementation Model because the actual implementation may be dependent upon the organizational factors as well as all the other requirements. For example, the first implementation of the system may need to consider a lack of distributed support capability.

3.4 ORGANIZATIONAL ENABLERS

Creating an Organization to Enable Change

Organizational Enablers allow for the rapid deployment of adaptive systems. They are critical to the success of enterprise client/server systems. Organizational Enablers include an organizational architecture optimized for cross functional teaming and change, process management that propagates best practices across the organization, and organizational transformation to enable the organization itself to adapt to change (see Figure 3–4).

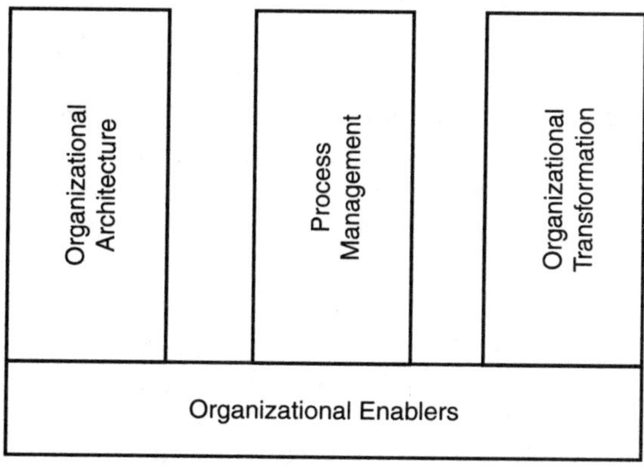

Figure 3–4 Road Map for Part IV—Organizational Enablers

Organizational Enablers enable new applications to be deployed more rapidly. Organizations that do not have this infrastructure struggle with these issues at the project level. This often slows or sometimes stops deployment. It may also result in an overall architecture that is difficult to integrate with new or existing systems.

Note that Organizational Enablers wrap around both the Essential and Implementation Models. That is because they profoundly effect the ability of the organization to succeed with distributed client/server systems. (For further details see Part IV.)

3.5 FLEURY MARKET CASE STUDY

An Example of the IllumiSys™ Design Method

Part V of the book is an example of a design effort using the IllumiSys™ Design Method. All the models and examples in the book come from the Fleury Market Case Study. For background on the case study, see Chapter 21. We recommend you read Chapter 21 before proceeding with the rest of the book because all examples used in the book come from the case study. It will help you to understand the example models and tables if you first understand the background for the Fleury Market System.

3.6 BENEFITS OF THE ILLUMISYS™ DESIGN METHOD

Building Enterprise-Wide Scalable Distributed Systems

We truly believe that client/server technology is now robust and mature enough to build enterprise-wide mission-critical systems. Client/server technology is an evolutionary trend, not a buzz word. These systems will grow and change over time. The design method presented here will enable you to build enterprise systems in today's technology that will adapt to tomorrow's business needs and technology. The modular partitioned design technique is equally suitable for maturing client/server technologies and the emerging Internet/Intranet technologies.

The IllumiSys™ Design Method provides a process based on best practices in the industry for building scalable systems which can easily adapt to changing business needs. It defines a way to build granular, reuseable components based on business events. The modeling techniques are based on standard techniques which have been widely used by many organizations. The benefit provided by the IllumiSys™ Design Method is that it provides a repeatable sustainable process for defining how components are distributed across a multi-tier architecture and across geographic locations.

PART II

BUSINESS COMPONENTS—THE ESSENTIAL MODEL

Part I analyzed the business, technical, and human factors surrounding client/server design efforts. Now, we are in a position to cover the first stage of the IllumiSys™ Design Method—the business requirements for the system under development. A clear and coherent statement of requirements is *the* starting point for client/server design, and it is so for two reasons.

First, the purpose of the system is to meet business objectives. Everything else is secondary in importance. The need for "cross-organizational" systems which share information and processing across logical, geographic, business units, and enterprise boundaries increases the challenge of building the "right system." It is only with *intensive* collaboration and cooperation among people that this is possible. An Essential Model provides an unambiguous description of the business that can be reviewed, verified, and shared across the organization.

Second, client/server technology enables organizations to design and deploy systems that closely resemble the way business processes are actually performed, and are also capable of adapting to new business requirements. The business components defined in the Essential Model must be correctly partitioned across your distributed architecture of clients, servers, and mainframes in a flexible and adaptable manner. The Essential Model provides specifications for Business Components that can easily be mapped to the distributed architecture.

As discussed in Chapter 2 models are an abstract representation of something real. It takes several different aspects of a model to arrive at a complete understanding of the overall area under study. Figure II–1 is a road map of the aspects of system defined by the Essential Model of business requirements.

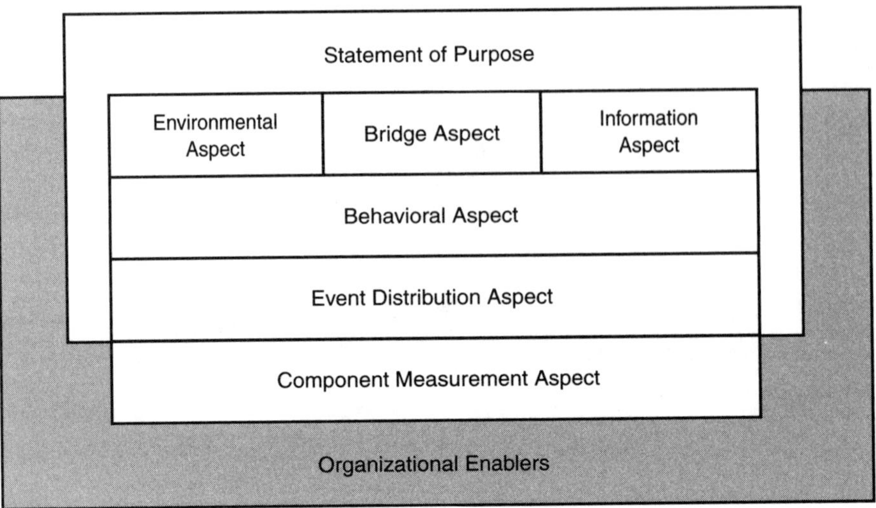

Figure II–1 The Aspects of Essential Model

Following is a brief description of the chapters of Part II, "Business Components—The Essential Model." The models used as examples throughout the book are taken from the Fleury Market Case Study. We suggest you first read Chapter 21, which contains the background for the case study, and look over Chapter 22, which presents all the artifacts of the Essential Model in the context of the business case study. Understanding the case study will help you understand the model views or artifacts. The chapters in Part II explain how to create the artifacts.

Chapter 4, "The Essential Model Overview," provides an overview of the Essential Model, its purpose and its structure, and heuristics for creating the model in practice. It also covers the primary textual specification that states the purpose and scope (inclusions and exclusions) of the system and drives all other aspects of the model.

Chapter 5, "The Environmental Aspect," focuses on declaring the scope of the system and understanding the logical boundaries between systems. It addresses how to negotiate and define these boundaries as areas of responsibility within business units.

Chapter 6, "The Information Aspect," describes the information required to support the system. It helps organize information and define what it means. It organizes the information to reflect business policy and declares the rules of association between the information components.

Chapter 7, "The Bridge Aspect," literally "bridges" together the view of the environment and the view of the information. It assures that the two views "fit" together and that our understanding of the system is consistent and complete. It does this by examining the impact of business events on the information that the events maintain.

Chapter 8, "The Behavioral Aspect," is built to rigorously define the business policy inside the system boundary. This aspect is the major specification for system design. It details the system responses to business events, and how data is used by each response.

The more detailed the Behavioral Aspect specifications, the less needs to be done in design.

Chapter 9, "The Event Distribution Aspect," takes the business events defined in previous aspects and groups them together into logical locations that are based on events serviced together by a particular work unit or type of location. These logical locations bear some resemblance to Use Case Studies often used in object oriented analysis techniques. We then define the geographic locations of the distributed business and where events occur. The Event Distribution Aspect is built to understand the national and global requirements of distributed systems. This aspect is the primary input to determining the need for client and server processors in design.

Chapter 10, "The Component Measurement Aspect," completes the Essential Model by measuring the natural rhythms and cycles of the business. It identifies peaks and averages for system services so that the designers will make informed choices about technical components capable of handling the estimated loads on the system. It provides information for doing capacity planning on a site by site basis.

Together, the Environmental Aspect, the Information Aspect, the views of the Bridge Aspect and the Behavioral Aspect are based on the *Yourdon™ Systems Method: Model-Driven Systems Development*, Yourdon Press, Prentice Hall, 1995. We again wish to thank CGI Systems (a wholly owned subsidiary of IBM) for their permission to use the case study material, and we refer the reader to the YSM book for a complete handling of the Essential Model. The book represents the collaboration and cooperation of dozens of the best thinkers in the industry on systems design, many of whom the authors have had the opportunity to work with.

We have extended YSM to enable people to apply this method to distributed systems. In that regard we have moved the Entity-Event Table and the Entity State Transition diagrams to a new aspect we call the Bridge Aspect. In addition we have added the Event Distribution Aspect, the Logical Location Distribution Aspect, and the Component Measurement Aspect to the Essential Model. Of course we have put our own spin on interpreting the existing parts of the Essential Model originally defined by YSM, based on extensive work in designing distributed systems.

In summary, the Essential Model is an often overlooked and critical part of system design. Without it, building the "right" system is largely a matter of luck. With it, client/server technology systems can be leveraged to create adaptive systems and provide sustainable competitive advantage.

4

Essential Model Overview

The Design of Adaptive Systems Must be Business Driven

Part I of this book stated the case for highly adaptive, business process-driven architectures. Part II presents an event-based method for defining business requirements. It focuses on defining the business requirements in a formal and rigorous model we call the Essential Model. No matter the tool, no matter the vendor hype of the "next silver bullet," business requirements must first be defined before any technology solution can be effective. Requirements are *the* starting point for a client/server design for a number of reasons.

First, many client/server projects either result from or provide an opportunity for some business process reengineering (BPR). In order for the system to enable the BPR effort we *must* be able to meet the business objectives intended.

Second, client/server technology enables you to design systems which closely resemble the way your business runs. We refer to these as process-driven architectures, which are desirable because they directly contribute to a return on investment to the business. This requires a thorough understanding of how the business runs, so there is alignment between the business and I/S, and so that appropriate technical choices are made.

Third, client/server technology can only adapt to meet new business requirements if the existing business requirements which have been implemented in the first iteration can be understood; otherwise there is no iteration. Instead, there is the deployment of "client/server legacy systems."

Fourth, it is these very business requirements that must be correctly partitioned across a distributed architecture of clients, servers, and mainframes. Few existing system development life cycles or multi-tier development tools tell you what and how to partition. In fact, what we partition are responses to business events. When we map the system implementation back to the business events, the system becomes easier to change and adapt to changing business needs. Therefore, a good partitioning strategy requires a good understanding of the business events.

4.1 OBJECTIVES OF THE ESSENTIAL MODEL

Requirements Modeling Ensures the System Accurately Models the Business Processes

We often get asked the question, "Why build an Essential Model?" The answer is made up of two very important parts. First, partitioning software across a distributed processor architecture in a manner that is adaptable to change and facilitates reuse, requires granularity and iteration. Granularity is achieved when the system behavior is clearly understood and documented in small, highly specialized components. Iteration is achieved when the system behavior can be incrementally deployed over time by reusing what already exists and building new functionality on top of it. It allows the designers to go back and relook at the system as more is learned about the business. Requirements modeling is the process by which system behavior is documented so granularity and iteration can happen. Second, requirements modeling verifies the pertinent business policies *before* system implementation. The requirements model makes the business rules explicit, by enabling system designers to verify with business experts that the rules are an accurate representation of how the business operates. Business and I/S each have vital roles in implementing technology to support the business. While the business analyst's job is to document the business rules, the business experts have a vital role to verify the essential rules upon which the business runs. The models aid in communication between I/S and the business to ensure the requirements are correct, complete, and unambiguous.

The product of requirements modeling is the Essential Model, which is a representation of business rules. The model becomes a contract between an I/S department and the business units. Since it is an explicit record, it aides a client/server project in several ways. First, all business rules can be checked for consistency and completeness. Second, each business event can be viewed in terms of requests for service and responses to those requests. This view maps well to the Implementation Model, where the business events are ultimately partitioned across client and server processors. Third, since the model is a comprehensive description of system capability, it can be used to measure the progress of the project. In other words, the Essential Model is a contract, a common understanding, a foundation from which partitioning can be done, and a project measurement tool. The Essential Model can do all this because it does not assume a particular technology or set of technologies will be used to deliver the system. This deferring of technology allows

- Subject matter experts to verify policy without being confused with technical details
- The model to be smaller, simpler, and more understandable
- Technology decisions to be made on the basis of business needs.

For many system developers, the idea of taking the time to create a detailed Essential Model is a troubling concept, at first. Their concern is often stated, "If the objective is to respond to user demands as quickly as possible, why not go straight into coding?" In the past, many business experts and systems analysts have experienced too many requirements modeling efforts that produced nice pictures but no real systems. We do not advocate "analysis paralysis" or elongated project times. We fully understand the need to deliver systems within the six to eighteen month time frame *and* the need for any requirements modeling to fit within these time frames. However, we would also like to caution I/S professionals to beware of rapid implementation of legacy client/server systems that cannot be easily adapted to new business needs or scaled for more business users. Large-scale enterprise distributed systems require design to reduce risk.

What we advocate is a better understanding between what constitutes analysis and what constitutes design. Most importantly, we assert that there is no such thing as "high level" analysis. Design is not a lower level of analysis. It is a distinct activity where technical constraints are applied to solving the business requirements. The question is *when* business requirements are addressed, not *if* they should be addressed. If detailed knowledge of business requirements is not worked out at the beginning of the system's life cycle, then it is done during design, and if it is not done during design, then it is done during construction, and if it is not done during construction, it is done during testing. And ultimately, what is not done during testing is done during maintenance.

While recommending requirements modeling, we are advocating shorter project duration to get systems operational. Modeling client/server requirements is not the same modeling as that which was commonly done in the 1970s and 1980s. During those years, functional decomposition was the modeling practice. System behavior was arbitrarily divided into smaller pieces based on a notion of business "departments." Our objective is to define system behavior in response to business events. The experience of those who understand this distinction have found event-based methods easier to model and far more useful during system design. They also produce systems which are more responsive to rapid and persistent change in the business, because the business rules have been clearly defined at a granular level and mapped to the distributed architecture. The goal of component-based architectures is to enable change in single components quickly and easily, or add new components with minimal impact to the overall system.

Behavior modeling according to business events organizes the Essential Model around business rules and information required to respond to those events. These map back to customer services needed to satisfy customer requests. The entire model is written in business, not technical, language. This practice separates the "what" (for example, the business operations) from the "how" (for example, the system operation). This produces an understanding of the business and its policies before dealing with the complexity of distributing and allocating those policies across a distributed processor architecture. By doing so, the Essential Model can be used over and over again during subsequent design stages by technologists who have to react to changes in the business processes and technology. Without a solid statement of the business, one cannot respond to changes in the business or design for adaptability.

The Essential Model assumes "perfect" technology. By this we mean that there are no technical issues to consider such as memory limitations, network performance bottlenecks, network latency, response time delays, required sequencing, multi-tasking, backup and recovery, or processor allocation. We know that perfect technology does not exist (yet!). However, by adopting the strategy of suppressing design considerations, we *force* the Essential Model to illuminate business policy and process. This enables business experts and systems analysts to focus on the business semantics (the meaning) contained in the model, thereby leaving the solution syntax (the structure of the design) to be addressed later, by people who are skilled in technical solutions. The resulting process-driven architecture is the ultimate objective of requirements modeling.

4.2 THE ESSENTIAL MODEL AND ITS STRUCTURE

The Essential Model Provides Different Views of the Business

The Essential Model is a comprehensive description of a system, independent of any design considerations. As such, the Essential Model creates a common understanding between end users and designers about what the system will actually do and what it will not do. In order to gain this consensus, it is necessary to verify the model with business users and experts. The Essential Model is broken into aspects, each of which represents a different dimension of the business. Figure 4–1 shows the different aspects and views of the Essential Model.

The smallest and most important portion of this model is the Statement of Purpose. In addition to the Statement of Purpose, the model contains four major aspects (descriptions) of the system. The Environmental Aspect describes how the system interacts with

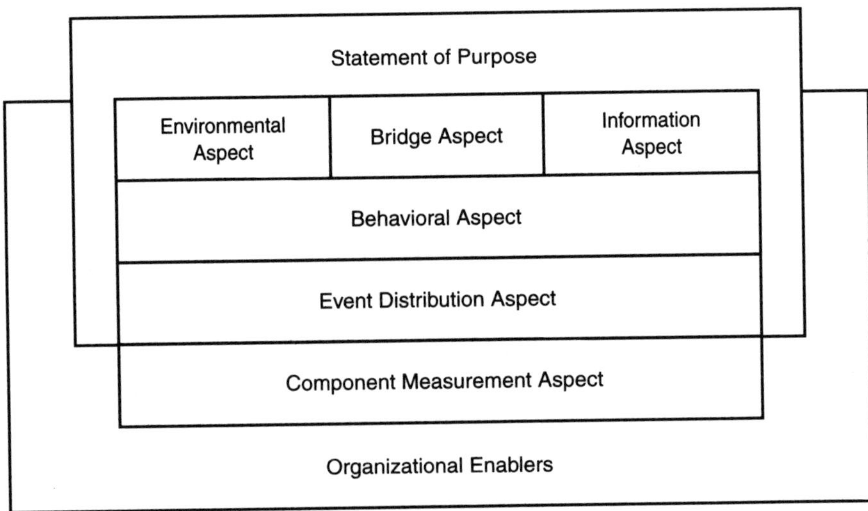

Figure 4–1 Road Map of Business Components: The Essential Model

its surroundings. The Information Aspect organizes and explains the information and the rules that drive the business. The Bridge Aspect is a mapping between the Information Aspect and the Environmental Aspect. The Behavioral Aspect is the detailed description of the system response to external events. Together, the Environmental Aspect, the Information Aspect, the Bridge Aspect, and the Behavioral Aspect provide a complete statement of essential requirements for the system. This model is like an architectural diagram of the business. It is complete and consistent, and can be verified and validated with business users. Because the Statement of Purpose is small, we have included it here. The other aspects are covered in the chapters which follow.

4.3 STATEMENT OF PURPOSE

The Statement of Purpose is the Contract With the Business

Often just a single piece of paper, the Statement of Purpose documents the business reason for the existence of the system. It states a business metric for the measurement of the system's effectiveness to the enterprise, defines what the system will do, summarizes the system's overall functional responsibilities, and explicitly clarifies what the system will *not* do. In other words, a Statement of Purpose is the over-arching context for the rest of the Essential Model, and the contract with the business sponsors as to what will and will not be included, and how success of the project will be measured. It summarizes the system's overall functional responsibilities, and then it serves as a contract on the scope of the system. The Statement of Purpose also explicitly clarifies what the system will *not* do. Just as a sculptor uncovers the final form of a work of art by chipping away at the excess of the form, so do we ultimately uncover the scope of our client/server systems by stating what will *not* be included. By forcing the project team to state the purpose on one page of paper, we enable concise thinking. There is an adage which guides this strategy, "I didn't have time to write you a short letter, so I wrote you a long one." Anyone can babble on for pages and pages about the responsibilities of the system. When attempting to be concise and summarize the main purpose, a whole new level of thinking is required. It also enables succinct communication among all interested parties regarding the system.

4.4 CREATING THE STATEMENT OF PURPOSE

The Statement of Purpose Defines the Business Reason for the Existence of the System

The Statement of Purpose drives the rest of the modeling effort. Therefore, although it is small, it is critical and deserves focused attention. In the Statement of Purpose you should document the functional responsibilities of the system as carefully and briefly as possible.

This will result in a succinct definition of the system's scope. To complete that definition, you will also have to define what the system will *not* do by clearly stating functional exclusions. It is important to keep the implementation schedule in mind when defining exclusions. Some functionality must be included in future and rapid iterations in order to deliver *any* functionality in six to eighteen months. The ultimate success of the project requires that I/S and business be aligned on the scope of the project. Figure 4–2 is an example of a clear and concise Statement of Purpose. All examples are taken from the Fleury Market Case Study. For background information on the Fleury Market, please see Chapter 21.

We have found the following guidelines to be very effective for creating a Statement of Purpose. First, define the business purpose for creating the system. This ensures all decisions regarding the system are based on business needs and priorities. Write the system's responsibilities and exclusions as lists. When creating the lists, think about

SYSTEM

Service Buyers

PURPOSE (Business Drivers)

- Provide customers with faster and more efficient service
- Provide wholesalers with the information they need to more effectively service their customers
- Provide timely and accurate information to and from other systems and decision makers

SCOPE OF RESPONSIBILITIES (Functional Scope)

1. Maintain information about retail buyers.
2. Control the receipt and refunding of funds to buyers.
3. Maintain a record of all sales made.
4. Inform the commodities system when to deliver goods to buyers.
5. Provide sales information to the wholesaler system.
6. Ensure no sales are made to buyers with insufficient funds.
7. Ensure no sales are made for items out of stock.
8. Assign a hanger to the collection of goods for the buyer.

EXCLUSIONS IN SCOPE

1. The actual movement of goods from the warehouse to the dock.
2. Payment of wholesalers for goods sold.
3. Computation and payment of taxes.
4. The maintenance of on-hand balance for stock at the wholesaler.
5. The determination of the docks at which the buyer receives goods.

METRICS

1. Decrease time between check-out and pick-up
2. Increase accuracy of Buyer information

Figure 4–2 A Statement of Purpose is a Succinct and Clear Contract Between I/S and Business Sponsors

- The essential requirements for meeting the business purpose
- The feasibility of meeting project deadlines: keep scope as small as possible.

You will actually have to think hard about these things in order to write a good Statement of Purpose. Anyone can copy down or regurgitate existing documentation, memos, or interview notes. To write a concise overview for an entire system requires assimilating and internalizing all that information and finding an effective means of communicating it. This is a much harder job, but it is a key to successful client/server projects. Your ultimate goal is align the team and the business about why the system is being created. The Statement of Purpose is the first opportunity for "defect prevention." Most importantly, it represents a contract with the users regarding what will be included and what will be excluded in the system. This is very helpful for preventing scope creep. It also defines how the success of the system will be measured.

4.5 DEFINING METRICS TIED TO THE BUSINESS

Redefining how I/S Measures Success

If I/S is going to deliver systems that meet expectations, it is critical that both the business and I/S agree on how success will be measured. Traditional I/S metrics of productivity and speed are proving to be inadequate measures. In their book, *Information Economics*, Benson and Parker discovered that I/S organizations that measure themselves based on how they directly contribute to the business are consistently the highest performers in their sector. Response time, availability, and utilization are appropriate measures when the requirements don't change. As business requirements change rapidly, the real measure of success is how I/S helps the business achieve its goals in a dynamic business climate.

Typical I/S metrics of on-time and under budget are also far more difficult to achieve with client/server systems for a number of reasons. First, we don't have the heuristics, gathered from thousands of projects and millions of lines of code that we had in the mainframe world which allowed us to enter the number of function points, number of programmers, experience of each programmer, and language, into a software tool to determine the estimated number of "manhours" the project would take. In client/server projects there are too many permutations and combinations to derive accurate project plans from these types of heuristics (not that we were all that accurate with mainframe systems either). Due dates and costs are difficult to predict with highly iterative life cycles unless project scopes are kept extremely small.

I/S should identify specific measurable business results that could not be produced in existing technology. Begin with clear project benefits, defined in business terms, then design project metrics with specific measurable results. This process has three steps:

1. Specify the metrics.
2. Operationally define each metric.
3. Normalize each metric.

First Specify Metrics. After defining project benefits in business terms, brainstorm metrics for each benefit. Then determine how well each metric measures each benefit. Consider each benefit separately. Brainstorm one or more ways in which people can measure how well that benefit has been met. When brainstorming, don't criticize or worry about evaluating the idea, yet.

The goal is to select a minimal set of metrics that cover all the benefits and are easy to implement. For example, a set of metrics for Fleury Market might be to increase customer satisfaction, lower operational costs, and improve the quality of information on customers, sales, and stock. Improving customer satisfaction may mean decreasing the amount of time it takes them to pick up their goods once they check out of the market. Lowering operational costs may mean decreasing the number of personnel required to run the market. Improving the quality of information regarding stock may be implemented by providing on-line access to stock and customer account information.

There are three fundamental types of measures that can be used to monitor the process redesign effort:

- **Benchmarking:** Define a standard figure of merit. What are the best of class results your organization wishes to achieve? Benchmark data can often be purchased from third parties. Software Engineering Institute (SEI) or ISO 9000 are benchmarking examples in normalized scales.
- **Cycle Time:** How long is the process taking to produce outcomes from both a customer and company domain? What is fast for one customer may not be for another. When analyzing customer benefits, you may have to define different metrics according to different customer categories.
- **Performance Goals:** What are we trying to achieve in terms of our ability to meet customer needs? Again, this should be from both the customer and company point of view. The company view is to minimize resources. The customer wants to maximize quality and reduce price. There's always a trade-off between these two points of view.

Operationally Define Each Metric. Create an operational definition for each metric. This includes the following:

- Name—official metric name
- Steps—procedure to measure the metric. List and number all the measurement steps. For each, define the measurement, how measurements will be taken, and who will do the measuring.
- Number—define how the measurements will result in a final number
- Units—determine the units of that number

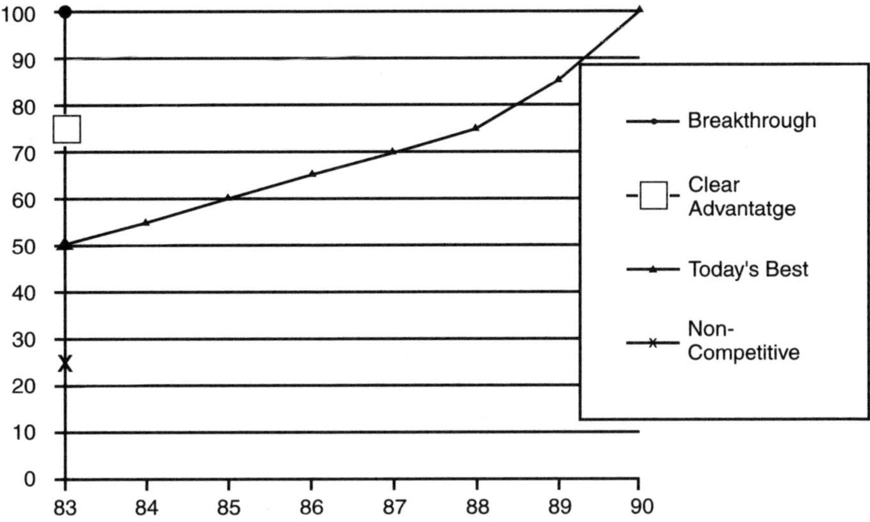

Figure 4–3 Depicting Metrics to Measure Project Success

Be sure that the metric makes sense for all the benefits that it is being used to measure.

Normalize Each Metric. Because metrics have different units and scales the goal of normalization is for each metric to generate similar results. They way you do this is to create a calibration scale for each one, which is consistent across metrics. This is done by defining the range of possible numbers and mapping them to the normalized calibration points (see Figure 4–3). For example:

- 25 = solution is unacceptable to customers
- 50 = solution is equivalent to best current enterprise solution
- 75 = solution is a clear competitive advantage
- 90 = solution is a breakthrough

4.6 CREATING THE ESSENTIAL MODEL

An Iterative and Creative Process which is Managed Through Artifacts

Unlike traditional waterfall methods where first you do analysis, then design, then code, then test, then implement, there is no standard procedure for creating the Essential Model. The waterfall methods were really a project management tool and did not represent the way systems were actually created. Information arrives in unpredictable sequences.

However, this is not bad, it is just the way knowledge naturally unfolds. Our advice is not to restrict the way information about the system comes to you. Think of creating the Essential Model as any other creative work such as writing poetry, painting, or sculpting. There is discipline behind each of these practices, yet the practitioner never restricts how the insights and innovations occur. The discipline we advise you to use can be summed up with just a few key points:

- Write a Statement of Purpose first.
- Start modeling the aspect you know best.
- Work toward discovering unknowns.
- Jump to another aspect as soon as you need to.
- Build aspects in parallel to gain insights.
- Revise an aspect as soon as you discover it needs changing.
- Keep moving: List any "stops" on an Issues List and move on to another view.

There is, therefore, much parallelism during a requirements modeling effort. Even so, our experiences on client/server modeling efforts have resulted in our identifying two common sequences by which the aspects of the Essential Model are *completed*. These completion sequences vary for the kind of system being specified. For On-Line Transaction Processing (OLTP) systems it is: 1) Statement of Purpose, 2) Environmental Aspect, 3) Information Aspect, and 4) Behavioral Aspect. Here, the environment is key, because it identifies the external events (transactions) which the system must handle. For On-Line Analytical Processing (OLAP) and Decision Support Systems (DSS) it is: 1) Statement of Purpose, 2) Information Aspect, 3) Environmental Aspect, and 4) Behavioral Aspect. Here, it is the information and its structure which is most important. Keep these factors in mind to ensure the appropriate forces are driving your analysis.

You should also keep some other very important things in mind when creating the Essential Model. As we mentioned earlier, the Essential Model assumes perfect technology. Extend this notion by thinking (for the time being only!) that the system will not generate any errors. Keep this thinking all through requirements modeling, but then let it go as soon as you commence design. If you can adhere to this discipline, you will create very succinct requirements which will be easy to design from. In addition, these requirements will tend to be quite stable, and hence require less rework or maintenance, because you will not have to consider error conditions or error handling paths (a source of great complexity!).

While you should think of the system being error free, you should consider the environment around the system to be error prone. Remember, you have no control over what happens outside the system's boundary. Therefore, much of your job will be to ensure the integrity of data which is given to the system, and this means, for example, checking for errors when data passes through the boundary.

Regarding how errors are handled, it is best to ignore the error conditions and the corresponding error handling and to instead state only the valid condition. This practice shortens the requirements modeling phase because only one condition needs to be stated.

Furthermore, in an era of graphical user interfaces, there are many ways to avoid and report on errors, and in fact the GUI design may make some error handling specifications unnecessary. For example, a GUI design may provide a scrollable list from which only valid entries may be chosen. This obviates the need to design complex error handling logic. Remember, the Essential Model is a statement of requirements which are independent of any GUI tool, data processing conventions, or user interface standards. In summary, state the valid condition only and leave the handling of how that condition is met to the GUI designer. Error handling is dealt with in the Implementation Model.

This chapter has provided an overview of the Statement of Purpose and the critical importance of rigorous requirement definition. The remaining chapters in this part of the book go into detail about the focus and purpose of each aspect of the Essential Model and give specific guidelines on how to create them.

5

The Environmental Aspect

Declaring the Scope of the System by Focusing on Business Events

Chapter 4 described the overall Essential Model and explained the Statement of Purpose (the one or two page specification of the system's responsibilities and exclusions). Once this document is complete, the project manager has the choice of which aspect to define next. For OLTP systems, a good place to continue specifying requirements is in the Environmental Aspect. For data warehousing and decision support systems, the manager may choose to first focus on the Information Aspect (please see Chapter 6).

The Environmental Aspect provides a clear and concise view of the scope of the system. This aspect describes how the system interacts with its environment and thereby declares the system's "boundaries." It addresses how to negotiate and define these boundaries as areas of responsibility within business units. It portrays what information is passed between the system and its environment, and the major sources and destinations of that information. It also defines the business events to which the system must respond. Business events represent the business activities the system must support, such as when a customer places an order. Using business events to define system requirements produces requirement specifications that map easily to distributed client/server technology which is essentially an event-driven programming paradigm (where an event could be a mouse click or a request for data to a database server). The Environmental Aspect is where all major business events are defined. Figure 5–1 depicts the Environmental Aspect in the Essential Model.

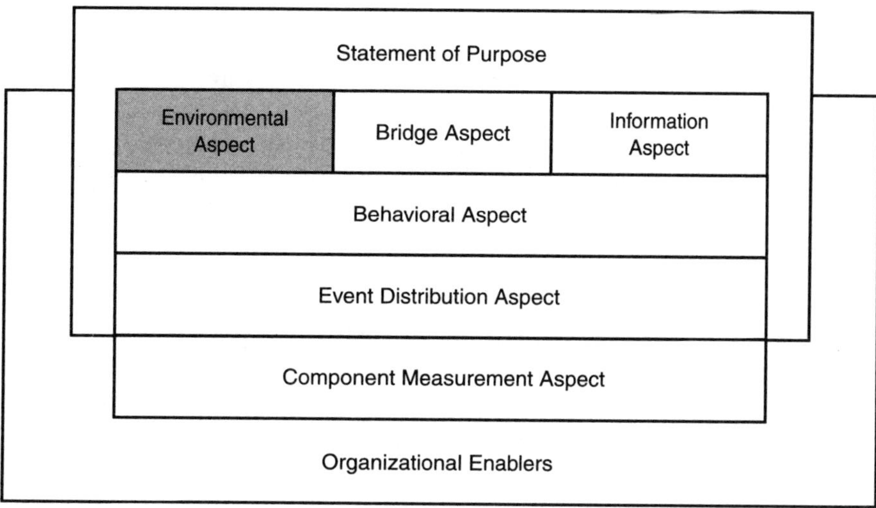

Figure 5–1 Aspects of the Essential Model: The Environmental Aspect

5.1 OBJECTIVES OF THE ENVIRONMENTAL ASPECT

Providing a Clear Definition of the System's Scope

The primary objective of The Environmental Aspect is to define the boundaries of the system in relationship to its environment. System boundaries are negotiated during the system development process. The Environmental Aspect is the portion of the Essential Model which documents the results of negotiations between I/S and the business units as to the *scope* of the system. "What's in" and "what's out" impacts how overlapping functionality between systems is dealt with, and what happens when a single business event crosses systems. Therefore, you should expect a significant amount of review and revision of this aspect.

One of the major challenges in deploying client/server systems within rapid iterative project cycles is controlling scope. In many cases the impact of the scope of the project is not *really* understood until after the project is delivered. This leads to expensive and time consuming mistakes. Time spent in fully defining the Environmental Aspect is justified because system scope impacts how the system interfaces with other systems. Errors in systems integration are expensive to fix later in the development cycle. It can lead to problems during the system development cycle and even to failure of the project.

Failure to understand the functional boundaries between systems can lead to frequent specification changes and rework. If the scope is too large, this often creates overwhelming complexity and forces the project to be late. If the scope is too small, the business will not get the system it needs. It is also critical that all business sponsors and I/S are aligned on the interpretation of the scope. For example, if the purchasing department viewed the scope of a purchasing system as printing purchase orders while the inventory department saw it as selecting goods and suppliers, then the delivery of functionality would need to be carefully negotiated, otherwise the system delivered may not meet the business needs of at least one of those departments. The Environmental Aspect provides a very precise definition of functionality and scope so all project participants, both I/S and business users, have the same understanding of how business functionality is partitioned across systems.

In our experience, defining the Environmental Aspect is extremely beneficial even when implementing purchased business application packages. The purchased application may have functionality that already exists in other systems. These applications usually must interface with legacy systems. Implementing an application package is more like open heart surgery than a plug and play turnkey operation. The Environmental Aspect helps determine functional boundaries of all systems, both custom built and purchased, and defines how systems integrate with each other.

The Environmental Aspect defines the scope by identifying the business events the system will support, detailing all inputs to the system from other systems, personnel, or customers, defining the sources of those inputs, and specifying the outputs generated and the destination of the outputs. The Environmental Aspect is considered to be sufficient when an environmental input is associated with each system output. The aspect is considered to have the necessary information when there is enough detail about inputs to determine how the outputs could be generated.

The Environmental Aspect contains several views which fully define the system boundaries and events (Figure 5–2). The Context Diagram is the graphic view which declares the inputs, sources, outputs, and destinations. Data Flow Specifications define input and output content. Data Store Specifications define information which is shared between the system and other systems. Terminator specifications define the systems and people who interface with the system under study. The Event Table defines what occurs in the system's environment to trigger the system to create outputs.

Aspect	Activity	Artifact/View	Mandatory/ Optional/ Recommended
Environmental Aspect	Identify System Boundaries	Context Diagram	Mandatory
		Data Flow Specification	Mandatory
		Data Store Specification	Optional
		Terminator Specification	Optional
	Identify Business Events	Event Table	Mandatory

Figure 5–2 Activities and Views of the Environmental Aspect

5.2 THE CONTEXT DIAGRAM

Viewing the System Boundary by Defining its Interaction with People, Business Units, Systems, Organizations, and Other Enterprises

The Context Diagram is a graphical representation of the system's boundaries (Figure 5–3). It is usually the first view that is created. The system under design is depicted as a circle, called a Context Process. The diagram depicts how the system under design interfaces with other applications and people in the environment, called terminators. The terminators are depicted as rectangles. In the Fleury Market Case Study Buyers and Wholesalers are human terminators. They are the users of the system. The Commodity

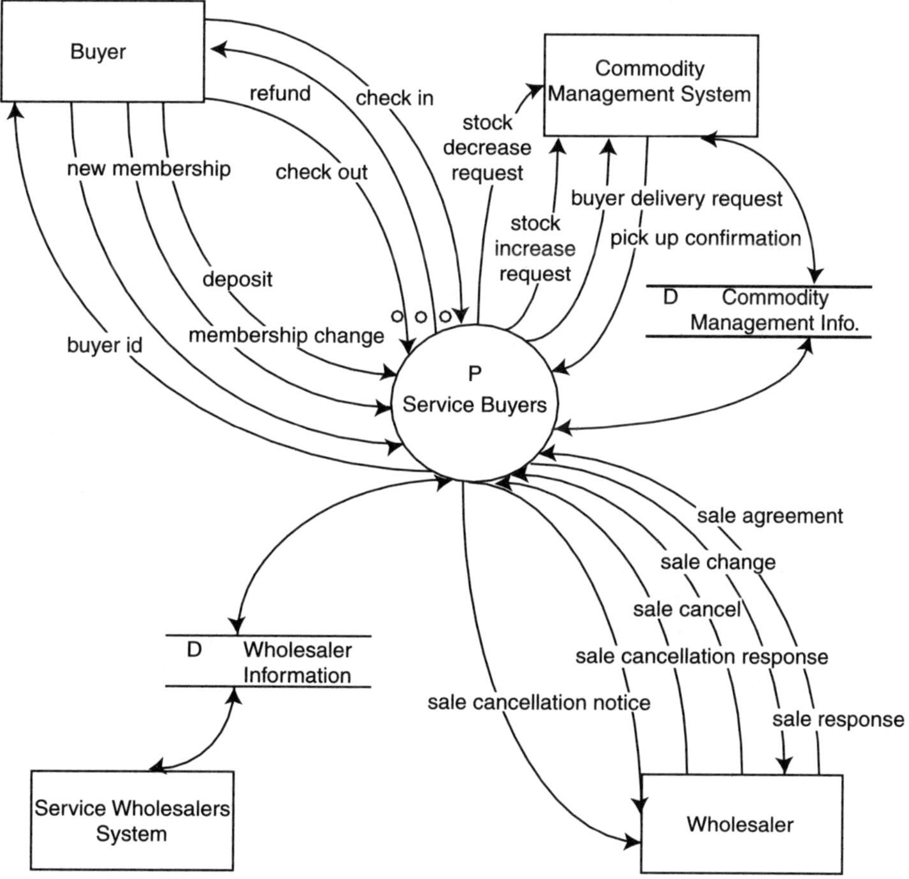

Figure 5–3 The Context Diagram for the Fleury Market System

Management System and Service Wholesalers Systems are terminators which are other applications. The Service Buyers' system interacts with all terminators through the flow of information. These are the arrows on the diagram. The open boxes are data stores, which represent the data that will be kept to record the business transactions (also called persistent data). Note that Service Buyers shares persistent data with the other systems. The context diagram does not say *how* this data is shared. It only indicates that there is data common to both systems. In fact, if the need for common data is not identified across systems, there is danger that data will be inconsistent across the systems. For more information on this example from Fleury Market, see Chapter 22, Section 22.2.1.

It is important to understand the distinction between data flows and stores. Data stores have persistence, while data flows do not. Data flows come into being when a business event occurs (thereby creating an input) or when the system responds to an event (thereby creating an output). Let us take a closer look at each of these components.

Context Process. The Context Process is the portion of the enterprise that is considered to be within the scope of the system. In other words, it defines the "area under study" during the requirements modeling phase of a client/server project. This does not mean that everything included within the Context Process will be automated at implementation time. One of the choices during implementation is to allocate system functions to people. The name of a Context Process describes main function or purpose of the system. The name should begin with a verb and the phrase must align with the Statement of Purpose. The value of the Context Process is that it focuses the requirements modeling effort on a clearly defined business process. The Context Process requires careful thought and judgment for creating the proper system boundary which will address business needs.

Terminators. A terminator represents users or producers of essential data. A terminator may represent a user, a department, an organization, a person, or another system. Terminators are either a source of input, a user of output, or both. They provide or add essential *content* to the Context Diagram. In other words, you are not interested in the *form* of the data, but instead you should consider who is responsible for the integrity of the data and who has the authority to set the value of the data. If a terminator represents a person, it is important to name terminators with the role of that person and not with the names of particular people. This is because specific people may change roles or leave the organizations. Departments, roles, customer types, and providers make for good terminator names. Defining terminators is vital, because they help define how much is inside or outside the system.

Data Flows. Data flows are either inputs which come from outside the system, or outputs from the system which go to terminators. Good data flow names should communicate the content of the flow to users and business experts. Therefore, the name should be one that business people would recognize and should succinctly represent the aggregate contents of the data. At this point we are not interested in the form of the contents. Often data flow names are singular nouns or noun phrases and stand for all the closely related data that occurs at one time from a single business event or system response. Figure 5–4 is a sample data flow specification.

Data Stores. Data stores are repositories that hold data that will be needed at a later date. A data store on a Context Diagram means there is shared data between a terminator and the system. It is important to note that this is a logical view of the need for data sharing. The decision on how to implement the capability to share data will be decided in

DATA FLOW
Sale Agreement
MEANING
The wholesaler's notice of a buyer's commitment to purchase a particular commodity
STRUCTURE
Group
COMPOSITION
wholesaler_id + buyer_id + sale_date + sale_time + 1{line_item} + total_price + hanger_id + sale_number

Figure 5–4 Sample Data Flow Specification

the Implementation Model. Shared data stores must be connected to both the context process and at least one terminator. An arrow to or from a data store shows how that store is accessed. An arrow into the store means its contents are changed in some way, and an arrow out of the store means its contents are accessed.

5.3 SPECIFYING BUSINESS EVENTS

Defining the Real World Events which the System Must Respond To

Business events define the business activities that the system must support. A business event is something which:

- Occurs in the business environment
- Occurs at a given point in time
- Must be responded to by the system.

Defining business requirements in terms of business events offers a significant advantage over other methods of specifying requirements. First, business events are easy for business users to understand, identify, and verify in a design. They represent the essential activities of the business. Second, an event-based requirements definition maps easily to the technical implementation of client/server systems that predominantly utilize event-based technology. Third, the system ends up matching the business operations very closely. This makes it much easier to change the system when the business events, or rules for responding to business events, change, because it is easy to pinpoint where changes must be made. Through further decomposition in the business component design in the Behavioral Aspect (Chapter 8), granular components are defined representing each response to each event. The artifacts produced in the Behavioral Aspect create granular business components, which become the specifications for software components and objects in the

Implementation Model. Lastly, but most importantly, a statement of the business events the system will capture and respond to, clearly defines the boundaries of the system.

A clear definition of system boundaries is essential to the success of distributed systems. Distributed systems interface with many other systems. It is essential that the boundaries between systems be defined and verified. Duplicate functionality in multiple systems can create redundant and inconsistent data. This requires additional reconciliation processes, which add complexity and inflexibility to the architecture. An enterprise application architecture clearly defines where functionality resides and how systems share data and functions. It enables future change.

For example, an order entry system needs to send orders to the warehouse system. A design that does not adhere to logical boundaries might have logic in the order entry system that determines which warehouse to send the order to. The algorithms may be based on proximity of the customer to the warehouse, or items each warehouse stocks. However, if a change occurs in the warehouse system, such as adding or closing a warehouse, the logic in the order entry system will also have to be changed. If the business can save millions of dollars by closing all the warehouses and drop shipping from suppliers, how long will it take to implement that business process change? The answer is the length of time it would take to rewrite the order entry system. If the order entry system never contains logic regarding how warehouse shipping occurs, then changes in the warehouse system will not effect the order entry system. This creates more adaptable systems.

The artifact created at this step in requirements modeling is called the Event Table (Figure 5–5). It describes the *relevant* activities that happen in the business to which the

Number	Event Name	Detection	Outputs
1	Buyer applies to become a market member	New membership	Buyer id
2	Buyer checks into market	Check in	None
3	Wholesaler proposes a sale	Sale agreement	Sale response, Stock decrease request
4	Buyer checks out of market	Check out	Buyer delivery request, Refund
5	Buyer picks up orders	Pick up confirmation	None
6	Market closes	Time	Sale cancellation notice
7	Buyer changes membership information	Membership change	None
8	Wholesaler changes sale agreement	Sale change	Sale response, Stock decrease request, Stock increase request
9	Wholesaler cancels a sale	Sale cancel	Sale cancellation response, Stock increase request
10	Buyer makes deposit	Deposit	None

Figure 5–5 An Event Table for the Fleury Market

system must respond. For more information on the business events in Fleury Market, sec Chapter 21 (background) and Chapter 22, section 22.2.3.

Events are worded carefully to ensure they communicate with business users and experts. We recommend naming an event by creating a very short declarative sentence using the name of a terminator as its subject.

There are two types of events: business events and temporal events. Business events are activities that occur in the business. Business events are detected by defining each business activity within the scope of the system. Temporal events occur at a predetermined point in time (such as market closes at noon). They are worded with some kind of temporal phrase such as, "customer fails to make payment on time" or, "time to produce monthly report." Temporal events exist because the business policy demands that certain system activities occur at certain times, or because the system produces its outputs on a timed basis (as opposed to an event basis). In our experience, all systems contain some temporal events.

At this point, it is helpful to distinguish flows from events. Data flow arrival (for example, a system input) is different from an event. The event causes the data flow arrival, which in turn triggers the system to respond to the event. The response is often the production of a system output, but could also be access to stored data. Therefore, when choosing wording for events, it is often helpful to ask the question, "What business event occurred in the environment to cause this flow to come across the system boundary?"

The Context Diagram can be used as an aid to determining events. Each input data flow occurs as a result of an event, each output is produced in response to an event, and stores are accessed because of an event. By walking through the Context Diagram with these three things in mind, you can identify most of the flow events. It is possible that the temporal events may not be evident from the Context Diagram. Identification of temporal events may require business and I/S experts. The Event Table is then verified by business users and experts.

5.4 CONSISTENCY RULES BETWEEN EVENTS AND CONTEXT DIAGRAM

Verifying the Overall Scope of the System

We end this chapter with a very brief, but very important, discussion about keeping the Event Table and the Context Diagram synchronized. In the process of building the events and the context diagram, there are three major steps:

1. Discovery
2. Update
3. Consistency

When a new event or data flow is discovered, either the table or the diagram is first updated, and then the other is brought into alignment with the change. Remember, the requirements modeling process is not linear. Discovery may happen from the context only to have the next discovery come from the events. Thus, there is much iteration. Sometimes, the discovery process gets so intense that the table and the diagram fail to get synchronized. One way to bring the two portions of the model into alignment is to hold a design review and use the following heuristics:

- There must be at least one event for each system input.
- Every system output must have been generated by at least one event.

In summary, the Environmental Aspect is a very powerful scoping tool. During the creation of this aspect your client/server project will become clearer and clearer. Through much negotiation and iteration I/S and business will align on the purpose of the system. This one aspect alone will dramatically increase the chances of success that the client/server system will meet the business objectives.

6

The Information Aspect

Defining the Business Information and its Rules of Access

In the last chapter, we looked at modeling the environment around a system. Now, we will look at modeling the information that the system uses to interact with the environment. The Information Aspect organizes and explains the information and the rules which drive the business. Information is defined by specifying a collection of unique and independent "entities." These entities give precise semantic meaning to business terminology. In essence, they are the "vocabulary" of the business. The business rules define how the entities are related to one or more other entities. These are often called "relationships." One can think of these rules as the "sentences" which describe business operations. Rules are built from the vocabulary of business terminology. Figure 6–1 depicts the Information Aspect in the Essential Model.

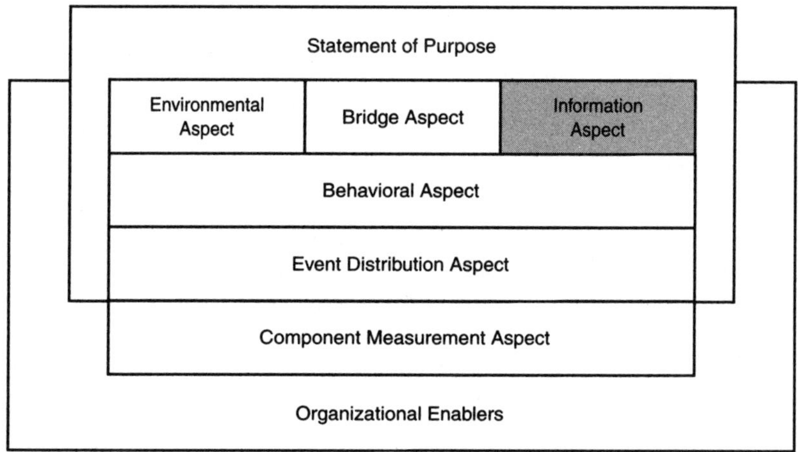

Figure 6–1 Aspects of the Essential Model: The Information Aspect

Aspect	Activity	Artifact/View	Mandatory/ Optional/ Recommended
Information Aspect	Define Business Entities, Relationships, Attributes	Entity Relationship Diagram	Mandatory
		Entity Specification	Mandatory
		Attribute Specification	Optional
		Relationship Specification	Optional

Figure 6–2 Artifacts of the Information Aspect

It is important to note the difference between the Information Aspect and a Database Model. The latter is the design for a physical information repository. In contrast, the Information Aspect can be thought of as a documented standard for the operational policy of the business. In fact, just because a particular business rule is expressed in the Information Aspect does not necessarily mean that it will be implemented in a database! For example, the rule could be implemented as an isolated procedure, or even "hard coded" into a program. Those choices will be made after the rules are understood, the technology choice trade-offs are evaluated, and the system design is finalized. Figure 6–2 depicts the activities and artifacts of the Information Aspect.

6.1 OBJECTIVES OF THE INFORMATION ASPECT

Gaining Consensus on the Definitions and Business Rules of Shared Information

The Information Aspect of the Essential Model describes the business information required to support the system in a clear, unambiguous manner so it can be verified and negotiated among all users of the information. The Information Aspect defines both the language of the business and the rules by which the business runs. The key objective of the Information Aspect is to

- Help people understand and name business information
- Help people avoid creating redundant information
- Help ensure correctness, validation and completeness.

The primary purpose of information modeling is to identify and understand shared data. Decision makers require accurate and timely information. Often, they require a cross-functional or enterprise view of the information. It is often the case that the business units, personnel, systems, and customers represented by the terminators on the Context Diagram, may not share a common business terminology or may operate under different business rules. For example, the marketing department may define a sale as a discounted price during a specific promotion, while the sales department may define a sale as any goods sold to a customer. These are called homonyms, terms which sound the same but actually mean different things. Different terminators may also use synonyms; different terms which actually have the same meaning. All large organizations that have multiple departmental systems use homonyms and synonyms. Moreover, different groups may operate under different rules. The purpose of the Information Aspect is to get consensus on terms, meanings, and rules of information that is shared across systems.

The scope of the Information Aspect is to define the information that is needed to respond to business events. It answers this question:

What information is required to respond to each business event?

6.2 THE ENTITY RELATIONSHIP DIAGRAM

Defining the Categories of Information and How They Relate

The Entity Relationship Diagram (ERD) is a graphic representation of the entities and how those entities are related to each other. As such, the ERD is the primary view of the Information Aspect. An ERD is comprised of entities, types, relationships, and associative entities. Figure 6–3 gives an example of an Entity Relationship Diagram. Please refer to it

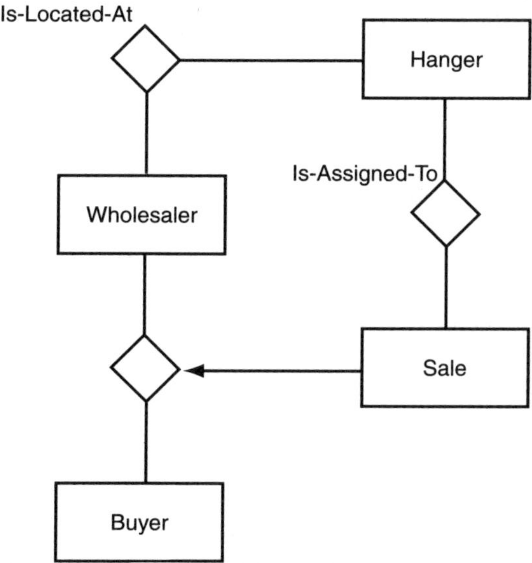

Figure 6–3 A Partial Entity Relationship Diagram of Fleury

as we briefly discuss each of the ERD components. For more information on the Fleury Market Information Model, see Chapter 22, section 22.3.

Entities. An entity represents a collection of things that are significant to the business, or it can also represent the role or classification of those things. Entities are graphically symbolized with boxes and are named as singular nouns or noun phrases (for example, buyer). The actual occurrence of an entity happens when a specific thing in the business takes on the role or has the properties of that entity (for example, M. Boucher—a man who buys cheese).

Entity Types. Entities may be defined with hierarchical classifications, called supertypes and subtypes. This hierarchy is extremely useful for propagating attributes across a set of strongly related entities. For example, a higher-level entity in Fleury may be Employee. All employees have names, addresses, telephone numbers, job titles, and salaries. There may also be part-time employees, full-time employees, and commissioned employees. All of these lower-level classifications share the attributes of Employee (all have names, addresses, etc), but the pay of each type of employee would be computed differently. This is an object-based approach to information modeling (see Figure 6–4).

Attributes. An attribute is a named property of an entity (for example, buyer_id). It is something which further describes the entity. For example, name and address are attributes of Employee. An attribute value is the measurement of the property held by one entity occurrence (for example, M. Boucher's id is 05213). Each occurrence of the entity (for example, every record for that entity) has a value for each attribute. By convention, attributes are not shown on the ERD. Instead they are listed in the Entity Specification. This helps keep the ERD less cluttered and therefore easier to understand.

Relationships. A relationship represents how business entities interact. The rules by which a business functions are inherent in the relationships. Relationships are symbolized with lines (for connecting the entities) and diamonds (for naming the relationship).

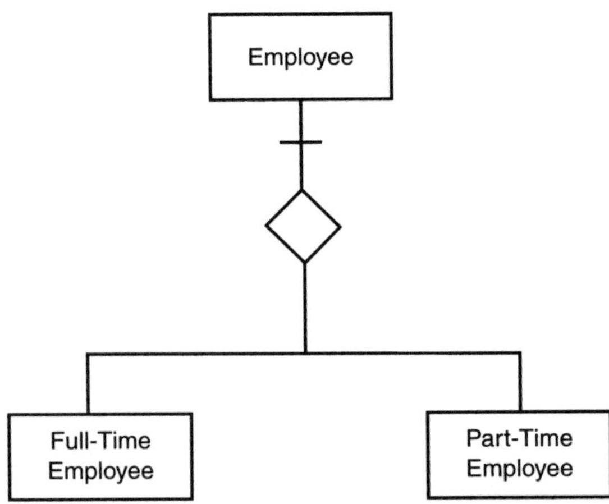

Figure 6–4 Supertype and Subtype Entities

Since relationships affect things, they are named as verb phrases that are descriptive of the relationship. For example, the relationship between Hanger and Wholesaler is that a Hanger is located at a Wholesaler's booth. The relationship between Sale and Hanger is that a Sale is assigned to a Hanger.

Business rules are often represented by relationships. They often deal with the existence of specific occurrences of either the entities or the relationship. For example, the occurrence of a sale would represent an actual sale of specific goods by a specific Buyer from a specific Wholesaler. The business rules governing the sale are represented in the relationships. For example, a sale cannot be entered unless the Buyer is a valid Buyer and there is sufficient stock available and the Buyer has a sufficient credit balance.

Associative Entities. An associative entity is an entity *and* a relationship (for example, sale). These special entities have attributes, which describe their role as real-world things (for example, a real transaction). They also associate the occurrences of other entities in their role as a true relationship (for example, Sale 946732 is the transaction between Wholesaler 26345 and Buyer 05213). As an entity, the associative relationship may take part in other relationships (for example, Hanger is-assigned-to Sale). Thus, an associative entity is represented as a box (for its role as an entity) and an arrow (for its role as a relationship). The arrow points to the diamond symbol to indicate the relationship between two entities are defined by the associative entity (see Figure 6–3 to see how this is drawn).

6.3 CONSTRUCTING THE ENTITY RELATIONSHIP DIAGRAM

Modeling Business Information and Rules so They can be Verified by Business Users

While the diagram must be kept as simple as possible so business users can understand and verify it, the complexity of real world systems often makes information modeling difficult. Therefore, we provide a set of techniques which enable people to model this complexity in a straightforward manner.

Finding Entities. Entities represent the real world things that a business needs to keep track of. An entity should be tangible. You should be able to walk around the organization and see examples (occurrences) of them. For example, we can easily identify Buyers and Wholesalers. One occurrence of an entity must be uniquely identifiable from another occurrence of an entity. No two buyers are the same and there must be a way to tell them apart.

In some businesses, there are entities (things that the business wants to keep track of) that are conceptual in nature, or abstractions. We caution you on defining intangible entities. In fact, they should be few and far between, and must be uniquely identifiable.

Naming Relationships. The names of relationships should reflect their purpose. An occurrence of a relationship is created when an event occurs. The relationship is the *memory* of the interaction among entities when that event happens. The common structure for naming a relationship is a sentence which has place holders for the entities (for example, Hanger, Sale) and the interaction (for example, is-assigned-to). The sentence can always be worded from two points of view (for example, from either entity), and it is important to determine which point of view is more appropriate. Sometimes the point of view is obvious (for example, Hanger is-assigned-to Sale), and sometimes it is not (for example, Hanger is-located-at Wholesaler versus Wholesaler is-sent Hanger). In these cases, events allow you to determine which name is most appropriate (for example, a hanger is already at a booth when a sale happens, so "is-located-at" is better). Because relationships reflect business rules, business users should be the final arbiters in naming relationships.

Multiple Relationships. Sometimes, it is possible to have more than one relationship between the same entities. In these cases, the two relationships have very different meanings to the business. Keep in mind that we are not talking about creating another relationship that is the reverse of an existing one (for example, Hanger is-located-at Wholesaler vs. Wholesaler is-sent Hanger). We are referring to distinctly different relationships. For example, there may be an additional relationship between Wholesalers and Buyers, where the Buyer is a relative of the Wholesaler. This relationship may involve different business rules, for example relatives always receive a discount.

Another type of multiple relationship is a three-way relationship. In these situations, all three entities participate in the relationship at the same time. For example, Figure 6–5a defines the business rule where a sale is transacted between a wholesaler and a buyer first, and then the sale specifies which commodity was sold. Figure 6–5b, on the other hand, defines the business rule where the wholesaler, the buyer, and the commodity must all be present in order for a sale to occur.

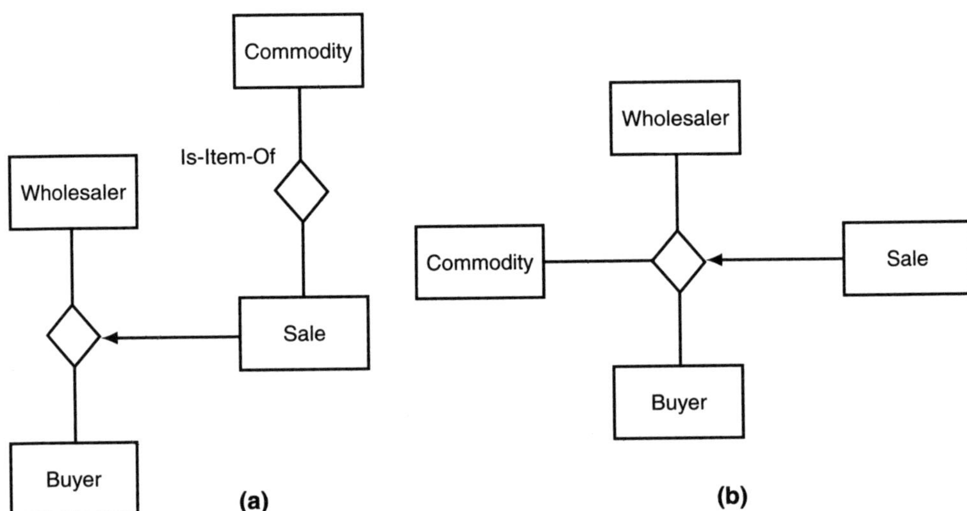

Figure 6–5 **a.** Commodity is Referenced After a Sale. **b.** Three-Way—Commodity is Required at the Time of the Sale

6.4 ENTITY, RELATIONSHIP, AND ATTRIBUTE SPECIFICATIONS

Specifying the Meaning of the Business Terminology

While we try to keep the ERD as simple and easy to read as possible, we can always use specifications to further describe entities, relationships, and attributes. These specifications serve to provide the detail necessary to fully describe entities and understand how the system will respond to events. Following is a very brief description of the specification templates for each of the components of the ERD.

Entity Specifications. Each entity has a corresponding specification that lists its meaning, its attributes, and its unique identifier (Figure 6–6). The meaning is a description of the role of the entity within the system. The attributes form a list of information which completely defines and distinguishes the entity from all other entities. The identifier is one or more attributes, whose role is to distinguish an occurrence of the entity from every other occurrence of that same entity. No two entity occurrences have the same identifier value.

Relationship Specifications. Each relationship specification lists participating entities, the meaning of the relationship, whether participation is mandatory or optional, and any upper limits to the occurrences (Figure 6–7). Meaning and entities come from the ERD. Mandatory participation is when the entity occurrence must exist (for example, Hanger assignment requires a Sale). Optional participation is when the entity occurrence is not required (for example, a particular Hanger may be at a booth but not be assigned). Upper limits define the number of existing relationship occurrences one particular entity occurrence may participate in.

Associative Entity Specifications. Each associative entity has a specification which must combine all entity and relationship components for that association. Since it is an entity, it has an identifier and attributes. Since it is a relationship, it also has participation and upper limits as well. Figure 6–8 gives a partial associative entity specification.

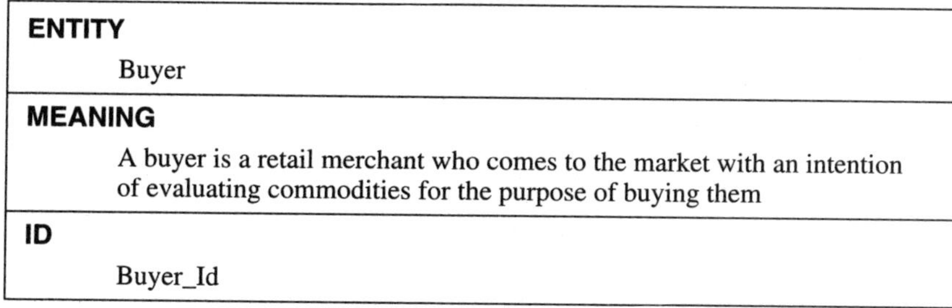

ENTITY
Buyer
MEANING
A buyer is a retail merchant who comes to the market with an intention of evaluating commodities for the purpose of buying them
ID
Buyer_Id

Figure 6–6 A Partial Entity Specification (Without Attributes)

RELATIONSHIP	
is-assigned-to	
PARTICIPATING ENTITIES	
A Hanger is-assigned-to a Sale	
MEANING	
A Hanger is assigned to hold all the goods for a Sale from the moment the Wholesaler loads it up until it is unloaded at the dock	
PARTICIPATION	
Hanger	optional
Sale	mandatory
UPPER LIMITS	
Hanger	1:1
Sale	1:1

Figure 6–7 A Partial Relationship Specification (Without Attributes)

ASSOCIATIVE ENTITY	
Sale	
PARTICIPATING ENTITIES	
Wholesaler sells-to Buyer	
MEANING	
A Sale is transacted between a Buyer and a Wholesaler, where the buyer agrees to purchase from the Wholesaler	
IDENTIFIERS	
Sale_Id	
PARTICIPATION	
Wholesaler	optional
Buyer	mandatory
UPPER LIMITS	
Wholesaler	1:1
Buyer	1:1

Figure 6–8 A Partial Associative Entity Specification (Without Attributes)

6.5 ATTRIBUTION

Assigning Information Elements to Entities, Associative Entities, and Relationships

The specifications in the preceding section all lack attributes. Attribution is the process of taking all business information elements known to be used by the system and assigning those elements to the proper components (entity, associative entity, or relationship) as attributes. To reinforce our point that the Information Aspect is not a database model, these assignments are made whether or not the data is actually stored. Each attribute has its own specification which lists the component it helps specify, its meaning, its retention property, its typing, and its range of potential values (Figure 6–9).

Retention is the property of persistence: stored, derived, or temporary. Typing uses the abstract data typing conventions of modern programming languages (for example, alphanumeric, Boolean, cardinal, character, currency, date, integer, real, string, text, time). Ranges specify either continuous (for example, deposits range from 0 to 100,000 francs) or discrete value sets (for example, cheese names can only be Roquefort, Bourzin, or Brie).

COMPONENT
Sale
ATTRIBUTE
Total Price
MEANING
The cost of a total Sale between a Buyer and a Wholesaler
RETENTION
Derived
DERIVATION
The sum of all Sale_Item.Quantity_Sold * Sale_Item.Price
TYPING
Abstract
ABSTRACT DATA TYPE
Currency
VALUE RANGE
0 to 100,000 francs

Figure 6–9 A Sample Attribute Specification

If an attribute cannot be attributed to an existing entity, associative entity or relationship, a new one must be found. Whenever an attribute is assigned to a relationship, you must determine if the assignment has changed the relationship into an associative entity. This happens when the attribute describes the occurrence, rather than the relationship.

Sometimes, it may be hard to distinguish between an entity and an attribute. We like to use the rule that an entity has an independent existence, where an attribute describes the existence of *something*. Very abstract entities and attributes having no storage requirement can be classified as qualities. If the information has retention, then it becomes an attribute.

In all cases it is important to distinguish information modeling from data modeling. The purpose of information modeling is to define the information and business rules required to respond to business events. The purpose of data modeling is to design a physical database. Physical database design involves the process of data normalization to define relational tables. Unfortunately, Entity Relationship Diagrams (ERDs) more often represent tables in a database, rather than a logical description of things in the real world. The boxes on an information model should not include tables resulting from data normalization, which makes them large, hard to read, and difficult for end users to understand and verify.

7

The Bridge Aspect

Bringing Process and Information Together to Get a Complete and Consistent Picture of Requirements

At this point in the requirements modeling process, we have fully defined the business rules (for example, the Information Aspect) and the business events to which the system must respond (for example, the Environmental Aspect). By explicitly "bridging" event processing and business rules early in a project you can ensure that the two different aspects are in fact describing a single system. The Bridge Aspect is the mapping between the Information Aspect and the Environmental Aspect that will ensure this consistency.

Lack of this aspect was one of the major limitations of Information Engineering in the 1980s, which claimed that the world is best represented as data. The Yourdon approach of the early 1980s was also guilty of another myopic approach but claimed that the world is best represented through process. Both methods kept process and data separate until implementation. Today's enlightened view is that data is an artifact of process. Data is stored to create a persistent record of the business event. It is the event, however, which creates the data. To be successful, process and data must be thought of holistically—right from the start of a client/server project. This is an object-based approach and creates systems that are "object ready," but can be deployed today in more stable and mature technology. Figure 7–1 depicts the Bridge Aspect in the Essential Model.

The artifacts of the Bridge Aspect are the Entity-Event Table and a set of Entity State Transition Diagrams. The Entity-Event Table defines the the set of information accesses required by each business event in terms of the basic entity life cycle known as MCRUD: match, create, read, update, and delete. Once this view is complete, we have the full set of data requirements for every event. Figure 7–2 depicts the activities and artifacts of the Bridge Aspect.

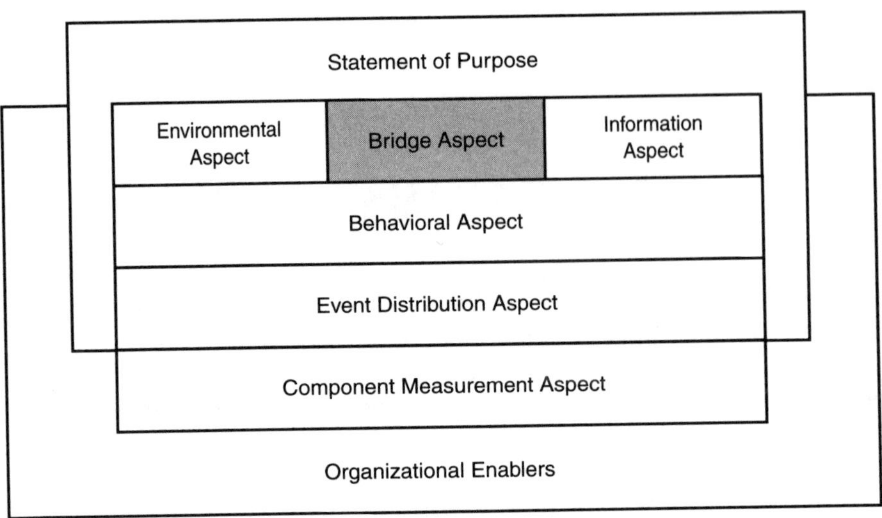

Figure 7–1 Aspects of the Essential Model: The Bridge Aspect

The Entity-Event Table is used extensively in the design stage when determining how to distribute data across processors and locations. It also provides essential information for data administration in a distributed environment because it maps what data is used in a system, how it is used, and how data is shared across systems.

Entity State Transition Diagrams are "entity lifelines," which depict the birth-to-death state changes each information entity undergoes through its life. Many business entities have complex state changes over their life that must carefully be managed. Entities change states due to the occurrence of business events. (For example the entity Person would change from a state of "single" to a state of "married" as a result of the event "Person marries Person.") The intention of this view is to explicity state which events cause which state changes to occur.

Together these two views provide the crucial details about the entities by examining which business events create, modify, and delete instances of the information and which business events cause state changes to occur in the life cyle of a single entity occurrence. This information is the final aspect that is needed to ensure that the detailed behavioral

Aspect	Activity	Artifact/View	Mandatory/ Optional/ Recommended
Bridge Aspect	Define data used by events	Entity-Event Table	Mandatory
	Define data over time	Entity State Transition Diagram	Recommended

Figure 7–2 Activities and Artifacts of the Bridge Aspect

description of the system provided in the Behavioral Aspect maintains the integrity of the information as a whole. The Bridge Aspect answers these questions:

- How does system information change with each business event?
- What information is required to respond to each business event?

7.1 OBJECTIVES OF BRIDGING PROCESS, DATA, AND TIME

Different Aspects Must Ultimately Define One Cohesive System

There are three dimensions of all systems—process, data, and time. As Figure 7–3 depicts, the Bridge Aspect links these dimensions together. The purpose of creating views which show how events use and create data, and how data is created and modified by events over time, is to ensure a consistent view of a system. It creates an object-based model which brings together process and data. In object oriented terms this would be an object, which is data plus methods. Mapping process and data to each other also prevents defects from being introduced into the system at the requirements phase. The Entity-Event Table locates inconsistencies between the Information Aspect and the Environmental Aspect. The Entity State Transition Diagram defines the impact events have on complex information entities.

We recommend you develop these bridge views before you begin major work on the Behavioral Aspect. This way, you have maximized your chances of a well-defined system scope, which has all the events and information sufficient and necessary to build the system. Once this aspect is complete, detailed examination of the system responses can take place through the Behavioral Aspect.

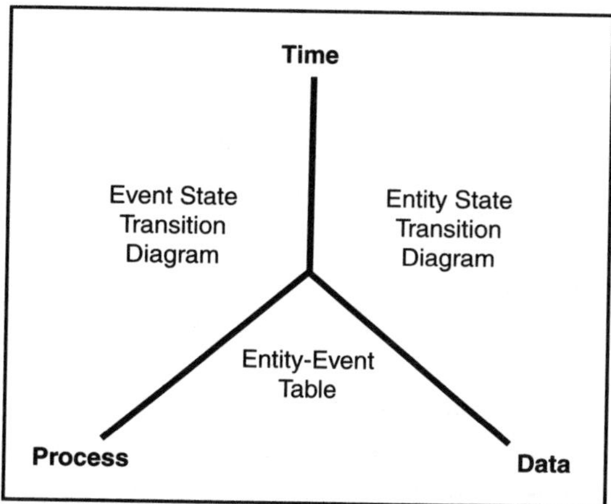

Figure 7–3 Bridge Aspect Describes the Interaction of Process and Data Over Time

7.2 THE ENTITY-EVENT TABLE

Understanding the Information Needed to Service Each Business Event

Creating the Entity-Event Table defines the data access rules for each business event and ensures that all entities defined in the Information Aspect are created, read, updated, matched, and deleted correctly; and that all relationships are created and deleted. It is also used later in the Implementation Model to define authoritative sources for data. This helps to simplify the management of distributed data, and therefore enables better consistency and integrity of distributed data. The Entity-Event Table is used extensively in the design in determining how to distribute and replicate data in the distributed environment.

The Entity-Event Table is also used for consistency checking in the Essential Model. For example, it will indicate such things as an intention to use an information entity that was never created, or it will pinpoint some information entities that are created but then never used. This consistency checking at the very highest level of the requirements specification is a vital step, because it removes errors that, if they were present, would be propagated to the remainder of the requirements model (for example, the Behavioral Aspect) as well as to the Implementation Model.

The Entity Event Table is a many-to-many view of information against events. This two-dimensional matrix puts the entities in the row headings, the events in the column headings, and the data access operations of match, create, read, update, and delete (MCRUD) in the cells. The access operations have the following meaning:

- Match—determine the existence of an entity occurrence
- Create—add an entity occurrence
- Read—obtain attribute values of an occurrence
- Update—change an attribute value in an occurrence
- Delete—remove an occurrence

The table is begun by populating row and column headings with entities and events. Once this template has been built, the cells are filled in by walking through the following steps for each event on the Context Diagram:

1. Determine the input flow for that event.
2. For each entity in that input flow:
   - Determine its attributes.
   - Determine the type(s) of access required.
   - Fill in the corresponding cell with that access.
3. Determine the output flow for that event.
4. For each entity in that output flow:
   - Determine its attributes.
   - Determine the type(s) of access required.
   - Fill in the corresponding cell with that access.

Event / Entity or Relationship	1. Buyer applies to become member	2. Buyer checks into market	3. Whole-saler pro-poses a sale	4. Buyer checks into market	5. Buyer picks up orders	6. Market closes	7. Buyer changes member informa-tion	8. Whole-saler changes sale	9. Whole-saler cancels a sale	10. Buyer makes deposit
Buyer	c,m	r,u	r,u	u	m,u	r,u	u	r,u	r,u	r,u
Wholesaler			m			r		r		
Sale <Wholesaler> sells to <Buyer>			c	r,u	u	u		r	r,u	
Sale Item <Commodity> is item of <Sale>			c	r		r		c,r,u,d		
Commodity			m					r		
Stock <Wholesaler> stocks <Commodity>			r					r		
Hanger			m					r		
<Hanger> is located at <Wholesaler>			m							
<Hanger > assigned to <Sale>			c						d	

Figure 7–4 An Entity Event Table for the Fleury Market

Determining the entities for an input or output flow requires you to investigate the relationships and/or associative entities in the Information Aspect. This is because the participation of entity occurrences in a particular flow is strongly influenced by interrelationships among entities. Once you go through the above process for every event in the Context Diagram, you obtain a table that looks similar to Figure 7–4. For more information on the Fleury Market Entity Event Table, please refer to Chapter 21 (background) and Chapter 22, section 22.4.1.

7.3 THE ENTITY STATE TRANSITION DIAGRAM

Understanding How Business Events Change the State of an Entity

The Entity State Transition Diagram (ESTD) shows the affect of time on an entity occurrence. This helps create an understanding of how information changes and under what circumstances it changes. ESTDs are also used in the Implementation Model when defining what happens to information as it crosses systems and processors. It helps in determining which events will affect the entity and what accesses are required when events occur. Each ESTD describes the state of one entity occurrence. For complex entities, a single entity occurrence may have mutliple ESTDs which represent its various states. For other entities there may be no need to model complex state changes and the entity will not have an ESTD. The ESTD is optional and is used to understand the life cyle of those entity occurrences which migrate through complex state changes throughout their life. This view is extremely helpful in understanding the meaning of the traditional "status flags" of legacy systems. The ESTD explicitly indicates what real world events cause each status (or state) to occur.

An ESTD is made up of the following components:

- State—a situation that holds for some time
- Transition—a change of state for an occurrence of the entity
- Condition—event that causes a transition to take place
- Action—the response to the event (for ESTD this would be a MCRUD access operations)
- Entity death—deletion of the occurrence

Specifying States. The life of an entity occurrence begins when it is created, and it ends when it is deleted. A state is a stage in the life of an entity occurrence. An ESTD specifies the life history, or lifeline, of the occurrence by showing which events cause the entity occurrence to change its state. A state is represented by a box with a noun or noun phrase which describes the state. Boxes without names denote the state after entity death. The states for a sale depicted in Figure 7–5 are "Pending" and "Final."

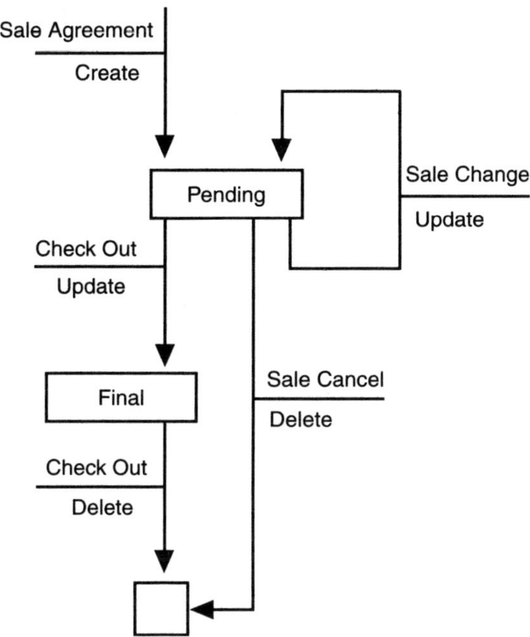

Figure 7–5 An Entity State Transition Diagram for Sales

Specifying Transitions. Transitions show which events *may* cause a state change in an entity occurrence. The arrows coming into or going out of a box symbolize a transition. If the entity is accessed during the transition, the type of access is shown just below the state, with a horizontal line separating the two. For consistency, use the same numbers for events employed in the Event Table to denote which event caused the transition. Transitions that change the state of a Sale include "Sale Agreement," "Sale Change," "Check Out," and "Sale Cancel" (see Figure 7–5). Note that actions are stated under each condition.

Special Situations. There are a few special circumstances that often arise during the creation of ESTDs. Some transitions may not cause the state to change, and therefore it is optional to depict these transitions. However, we recommend you do so for the sake of completeness, because often times, these transitions have associated access operations which do change the attributes for an entity occurrence. In this case the transition shows an arrow pointing back to the same state. The second special case is multiple events causing the same state change. The convention is to use an "or" operator and thereby placing them all next to the same arrow. We do not recommend you do this unless you are absolutely sure all the events cause the same access operations to occur.

7.4 MAINTAINING CONSISTENCY BETWEEN ENTITIES, EVENTS, AND CONTEXT DIAGRAMS

Keeping the Models in Synch

The process of creating the views in the Bridge Aspect requires many comparisons between the Entity Event Table and the Context Diagram. This process requires a high degree of iteration. We recommend you revise the Entity Event Table and the Context Diagram in parallel and use the following process for keeping the models in synch.

Compare the Entity Event Table to the Context Diagram. If an entity or relationship is being used by the system but is never created by the system then one of two things must be true. Either another system must create the information or we are missing the create event in the Environmental Aspect. First check to see if the information is being created by another system. If an entity is accessed but has no create event, then verify:

1. The entity or relationship is contained in a data store
2. The data store is accessed by the context process and a terminator (the information is shared between the two systems)
3. The terminator represents the system which creates the entity or relationship.

If the information is not created by another system then go back to the Environmental Aspect and add a new event to the Event Table which is responsible for the creation of that entity or relationship. Update all other Essential Model aspects and views to reflect the inclusions of the new event. This is a key step in ensuring that the information needed by the system is in fact available to the system.

Just as information that is used must be created, ensure that information that is being created by the system is used by some other system, even if it isn't the system under study. If no system is using the information then we should remove it from the scope. With shrinking business cycles we do not have the time to plan information that may be needed "someday." Focus on what is needed now. If a cell is created but not matched, updated, or read, then verify:

1. The entity or relationship is contained in a data store
2. The store is accessed by the context process or terminator
3. The terminator accesses the store with an operation other then create.

Compare the Context Diagram to the Entity Event Table. If a terminator requires direct access to an entity or relationship, then verify:

1. The data store containing the entity or relationship is drawn
2. The context process accesses the data store according to the table
3. The terminator accesses the corresponding data store.

If a data store appears on the diagram, then verify:

1. The table shows access to the corresponding entity or relationship
2. The access in the table matches the access implied by the diagram.

After the artifacts of the Bridge Aspect have been created, we are ready to focus on the detailed behavior of the system.

8

The Behavioral Aspect

Decomposing the System into Detailed Component Responses to Business Events

In the last chapter, we saw how to create the Bridge Aspect, which describes how events use information over time. The Behavioral Aspect is the detailed description of responses to events. The responses to the business events represent business policy. When finished, the Behavioral Aspect becomes a major input to the design of the system, because the detailed responses become granular software components.

The Behavioral Aspect brings together all the other pieces of the Essential Model created so far. It requires a thorough understanding of the business events within the scope of the system from the Environmental Aspect, the data and business rules from the Information Aspect, information necessary to respond to events, and how events effect entities from the Bridge Aspect. In the Behavioral Aspect the detailed responses to each event are documented. This process requires involvement from business experts to define business policy. All too often we have seen I/S teams unable to resolve some design issues because they were struggling with business policy. That is why we define business policy in explicit detail in the Essential Model. The Behavioral Aspect answers the question:

What are the policies and procedures we use to respond to each business event? Figure 8–1 depicts the Behavioral Aspect in the Essential Model.

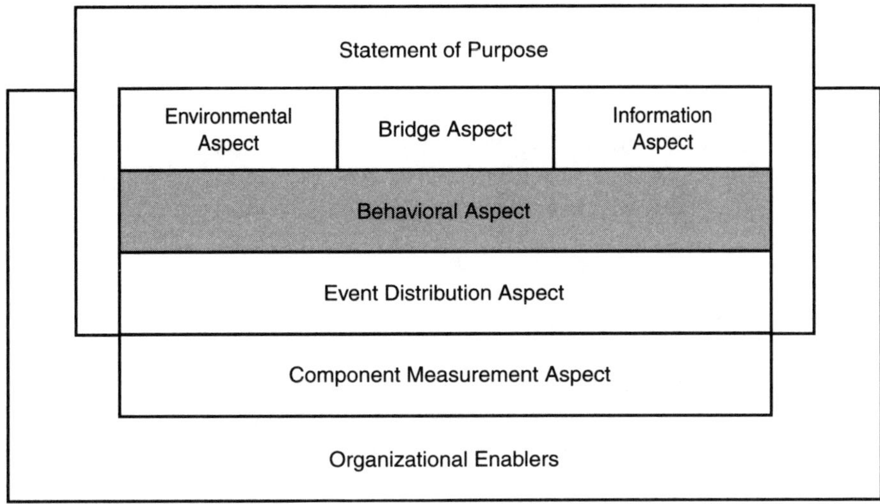

Figure 8–1 Aspects of the Essential Model: The Behavioral Aspect

8.1 OBJECTIVES OF BEHAVIORAL MODELING

Detailing All Responses to Each and Every Event

The Behavioral Aspect is the most detailed portion of the Essential Model. By defining system behavior in terms of how the system responds to events, we are really attempting to define business policy in system terms. The Essential Model always assumes perfect

Aspect	Activity	Artifact/View	Mandatory/ Optional/ Recommended
Behavioral Aspect	Define system responses	Event Response Table	Mandatory
		Event Response DFD	Mandatory
		Detailed DFD	Optional
	Define data for responses	Entity Response Table	Recommended
	Detail requirements	Minispecs	Optional

Figure 8–2 Activities and Artifacts of the Behavioral Aspect

technology so the business rules and requirements rise to the surface. Therefore, at this point we do not consider how the system will be implemented. That is the task of the Implementation Model.

The Behavioral Aspect uses all the other aspects to fully describe the event components, which include recognition of the event, the responses to each event, and the information required to respond to events. The artifacts of the Behavioral Aspect include data flow diagrams, data flow specifications, data store specifications, and minispecs (Figure 8–2).

8.2 EVENT RESPONSE TABLE

Defining Responses for Each Event

The Event Response Table defines the detailed responses for each business event. In the process of defining responses, we often discover additional business rules and additional responses required from external systems. Because the design process is highly iterative, and we continue to learn more about the business processes as we create the full Essential Model, it may be necessary to go back and expand the artifacts in the other aspects.

When defining responses, we are looking for the complete specification for business processing rules. By defining them as granular responses, we leave ourselves in a good position for designing granular software components in the Implementation Model. Granularity is a goal in software design because it increases reuse.

In the Environmental Aspect (Chapter 5), we created the Event Table (section 5.4). In Figure 8–3 we define the detailed system responses required to service each business event. We have used the convention of naming events with a number preceded by an "E" (for event) and identifying each response with the number of the event and an "R." Because a single business event may spawn multiple system responses, we number the responses for each event.

8.3 DATA FLOW DIAGRAMS

Data Flow Diagrams Provide Another View of System Responses to Events

Business policies are inculcated in systems through responses to business events. The data flow diagrams (DFDs) of the Behavioral Aspect graphically represent the responses to system events. In other words, they specify business *policy*. To accomplish this, they show:

- *Processes* that change inputs to outputs
- *Data flows* among processes or between process and terminators

Essential Event Number and Name	Essential Event Response
E1. Buyer applies to become a market member	R1.1. Check for valid buyer (credit check) R1.2. Add buyer
E2. Buyer checks into market	R2.1. Check buyer in (change status of buyer)
E3. Wholesaler proposes a sale	R3.1. Create sale R3.2. Derive <buyer> avail balance R3.3. Add sale item R3.4. Derive <sale> total price R3.5. Produce sale agreement R3.6. Assign hanger to sale R3.7. Notify Commodity System of debit to stock
E4. Buyer checks out of market	R4.1. Check buyer out (change status of buyer) R4.2. Notify dock system of buyer check-out
E5. Buyer picks up orders	R5.1. Record pick-up R5.2. Notify Service Buyers
E6. Market closes	R6.1. Cancel uncollected sales R6.2. Notify Commodity System of canceled sale R6.3. Notify Wholesaler System of canceled sale
E7. Buyer changes membership information	R7.1. Note change in membership
E8. Wholesaler changes sale agreement	R8.1. Change sale 8R2. Notify Service Buyers of account debit/credit 8R3. Notify Commodity System of change 8R4. Notify Wholesaler system of change
E9. Wholesaler cancels a sale	9R1. Cancel sale for buyer 9R2. Notify Service Buyers of account credit 9R3. Notify Commodity System of change 9R4. Notify Wholesaler system of change
E10. Buyer makes deposit	10R1. Add deposit to balance

Figure 8–3 Event Response Table

- *Data stores* that contained data shared among processes
- *Access flows* that indicate use of stored data by processes.

Using the Event Response Table, we construct a graphic view of the detailed responses to business events.

Circles represent system processes. Processes are the business events serviced by the system, and so they are named with a verb or verb phrase. A good process name will allow a subject matter expert to know what goes on in the process without having to consult other DFDs to determine its detailed operations.

Arrows represent data flows and access flows. Data flows into or out of the diagram represent essential input from or output to the environment. There are also data flows into and out of circles. These represent the input and output of processes within the scope of the system. Data flows contain the minimum data needed by an event, and each one is named so as to explain the meaning of its collection of data.

Open-ended boxes denote data stores. Data stores contain data in a steady state (as opposed to data flows). Thus, data stores contain occurrences of entities, relationships, associative entities, and their attributes and states. All data stores that appear on the Context Diagram also appear in one of the DFDs.

The Event Response Table is used to create the data flow diagram (DFD) depicting the detailed system behavior. Figure 8–4 depicts four events.

We use two levels of DFDs to fully explain system behavior. The highest level is the Event Response DFD, which identifies all business events in the scope of the system and the information required to respond to each event. We then decompose each event into a set of granular responses which we represent on a lower level DFD Figure 8–5). A

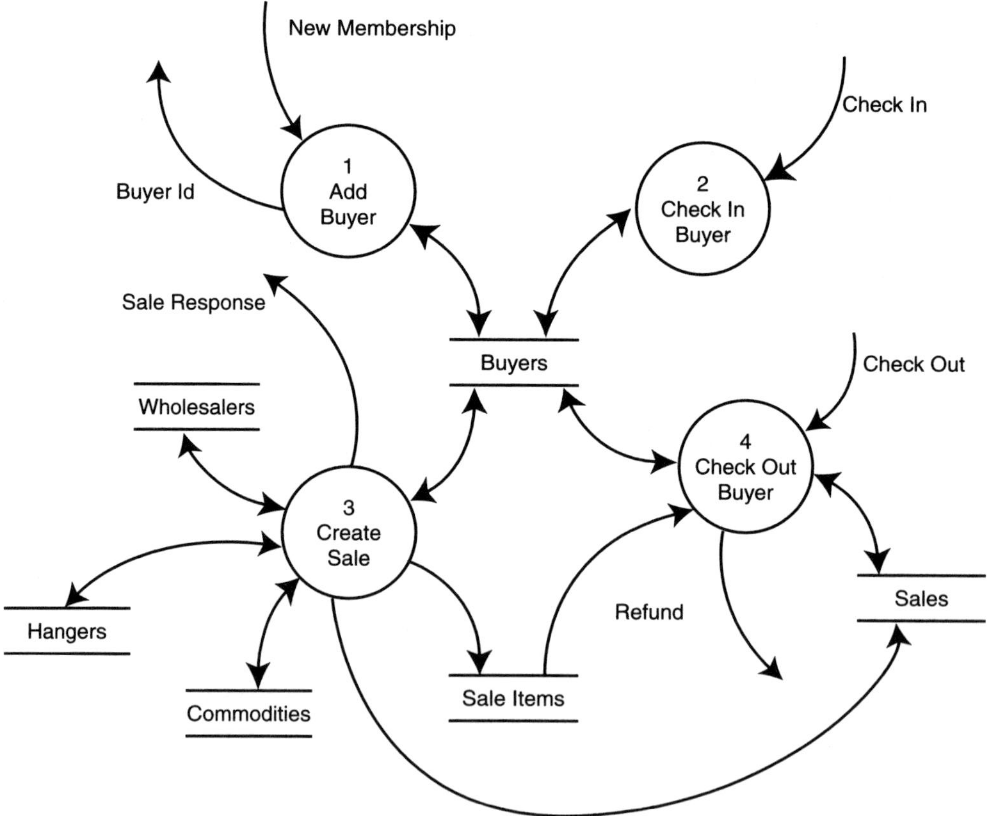

Figure 8–4 A Portion of a Data Flow Diagram for the Fleury Market

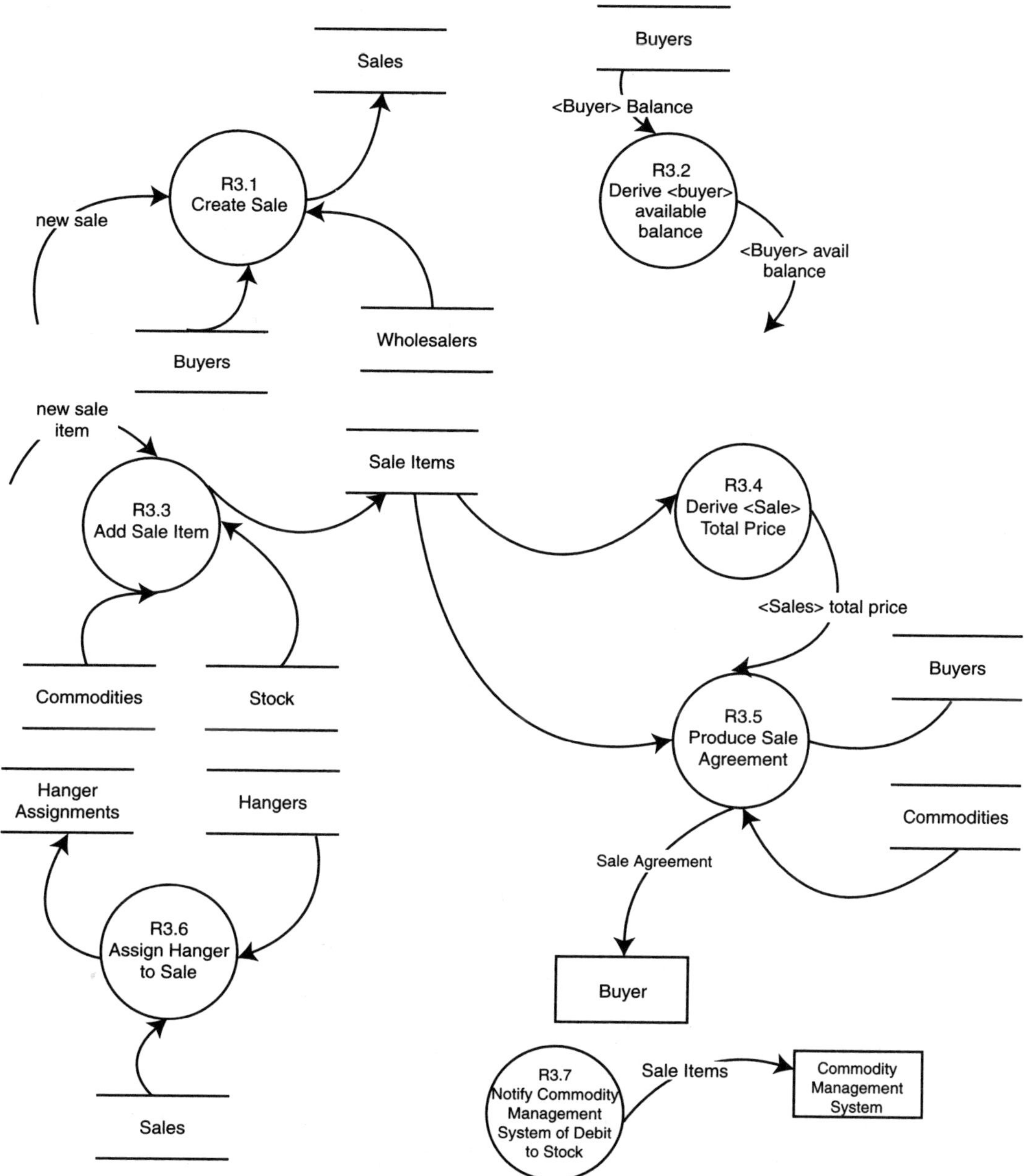

Figure 8–5 Detailed DFD for Response to "Wholesaler Proposes a Sale" (Event 3)

fully annotated Behavioral Model will contain a DFD for each event defined in the Environmental Aspect. Each DFD can be reviewed with the appropriate Business Experts to confirm that it correctly represents the business policy.

To maintain consistency in the Essential Model, the Event Response DFD is checked against both the Information Aspect and the Environmental Aspect to ensure all events and information stores have been included. Then, each event is detailed in the leveled DFD to provide additional detail. Lastly, minispecs are written for each lowest level response in each leveled DFD. Let us now investigate how an Event Response DFD is actually constructed.

8.4 CONSTRUCTING EVENT RESPONSE DATA FLOW DIAGRAMS

Detailing System Responses Through a Synthesis of the Essential Model

Constructing DFDs requires you to use every other diagram and specification of the Essential Model:

1. Using the Context Diagram, map out the events and their corresponding responses.
2. Using the Entity Event Table, add required data stores and access flows.
3. Interview business experts and end users to determine the business operations and policies for each response.
4. Use the Entity Relationship Diagram to add access and validation logic to processes.
5. Use Entity State Transition Diagrams to add entity manipulation logic.

Response Layout. When laying out responses, let the Event Table (Figure 8–3) be your primary guide. Draw a circle for each response and number it with the corresponding number. Use the detection method (specifying how the event is detected) and system output columns in the Event Table to determine the data flows and system outputs.

When there are a large number of events, first create a high level DFD which shows all events. Then create lower level DFDs detailing responses, as we have done in Figures 8–4 and 8–5. Essentially any circle on a DFD may be more fully described in a lower level DFD. The complexity of the processes being described will determine when to create a lower level DFD to make it easy to understand, review, and convert into an implementation design. One criteria to use for deciding when to stop detailing is when the minispec for a process can be written on a page or less. All detailed specifications created in the Essential Model are used during implementation. You can do it now—or later.

Low level response DFDs are used to partition the event responses into small granules. One of the design goals for the Implementation Model is to create reuseable components. It has been shown that small, functionally cohesive components, sometimes called software granules because they contain one to three function points, are far more reuseable than large chunks of code. High levels of reuse decrease costs, speed implementation, and enable better response to business needs. Therefore, time spent in breaking down the event responses into single function point processes is a worthwhile investment in the future flexibility and adaptability of the system.

Determining Data Stores. Data Stores are drawn to contain the data that must persist in time between event responses. Note again, that the data stores depicted on the DFD denote required persistent data, not how the data store will be implemented. First locate all the data stores on the Context Diagram. Each should also be represented on the Event Response DFD. Then use the Entity Event Table to find information required to respond to each event. Next, create the appropriate flow by attaching the store to the process.

Complying with Entity State Transition Diagrams. The Entity State Transition Diagram shows how events affect the way entities change their state. The event responses are the conditions that cause the state changes. The Event Response DFD must reflect all transitions depicted on each ESTD. Note that each ESTD is for one entity and will include all events that effect that entity. The lower level DFD is for one event and includes all entities affected by that event.

8.5 ENTITY RESPONSE TABLE

Defining the Information Required for Each Response

The purpose of the Behavioral Aspect is to define the detailed requirements of the system. As we previously defined the information required for each event, we now need to define information requirements at a more detailed, granular level. We do this by defining information requirements for each response. The end result of the Behavioral Aspect is a set of business event components consisting of a business event, all the responses required to service the event, and all the information required. This level of detail puts us in a very good position to design granular software components in the Implementation Model.

The Entity Response Table (Figure 8–6) is created in the same way the Entity Event Table was created (Chapter 5, section 5.4). For each response, define what information is created, read, updated, deleted, or matched.

8.6 CONSISTENCY CHECKS WITH THE ENVIRONMENTAL AND BRIDGE ASPECTS

System Responses must be Completely Consistent with the Responses Implied by the Context Diagram and the Entity Event Table

To ensure the integrity of the Essential Model, the Behavioral Aspect must be kept consistent with the Environmental, Bridge, and Information Aspects. For the purposes of

Event / Entity or Relationship	1R1 Check for Valid Buyer	1R2 Add Buyer	2R1 Check Buyer In (Status)	3R1 Create Sale	3R2 Notify Service Buyers—Debit Buyer Acct.	3R3 Assign Sale to Hanger	3R4 Notify Commodity System of Stock Debit	4R1 Check Buyer Out	4R2 Notify Dock System of Buyer Check Out
Buyer	m	c	u	r, u	u			u	r
Wholesaler				r					
Sale <Wholesaler> sells to <Buyer>				c	r	r			
Sale Item <Commodity> is item of <Sale>				c	r		r		
Commodity				r			u		
Stock <Wholesaler> stocks <Commodity>				r			u		
Hanger						r			
<Hanger> is located at <Wholesaler>						r			
<Hanger > assigned to <Sale>						c			r

Figure 8–6 Partial Entity Response Table (for Responses to Events 1–4)

making this book easy to refer to, we cover consistency between responses and information in the next section.

Consistency Checks between the DFD and the Environmental Aspect. The Context Diagram is used heavily during the creation of the DFDs. The consistency check ensures that: 1) each input flow to the context process must be an input flow to a process on the DFD, 2) each output flow from the context process must be an output flow from a process on the DFD, and 3) each store on the Context Diagram must appear on the DFD, and each access to those stores must occur at least once on the DFD. The reverse must also be true: 1) each input flow to the DFD must be an input flow to the context process, and 2) each output flow from the DFD must be an output from the context process.

Consistency Checks between the DFD and the Bridge Aspect. The Event Response DFD must also be consistent with the specification of events in the Entity Event Table. The consistency check ensures that: 1) each store on the DFD must include one or more entities or relationships in the table, and 2) each entity or relationship in the table must appear in a store on the DFD.

8.7 CONSISTENCY CHECKS WITH THE INFORMATION ASPECT

The Internal Operations of System Responses Must be Completely Consistent with the Business Rules

The definition of entities and relationships in the Information Aspect includes the rules for their existence, which represent business rules. It is imperative that these rules be upheld by the responses, which represent business policy. The Information Aspect therefore provides a source for validation logic. A consistency check between the Behavioral Aspect and the Informational Aspect ensures that the rules for creation, deletion, participation, and updating of data are adhered to in the detailed responses to events by ensuring the responses include the appropriate validation logic. This consistency check may add more detailed responses.

Creation Rules. 1) An identifier must be available to the response process, and the process must validate that there is no duplicate identifier in the store. 2) A process may not create a relationship or associative entity that references an entity occurrence which does not exist. This is a referential integrity rule. The process must first match the entity occurrence to be certain it exists in the data store. Most database management systems (DBMS) today support declarative referential integrity. This means you do not have to program the rules in the application.

Deletion Rules. 1) A process must not delete an entity occurrence if any associative entity or relationship referencing it will continue to exist. This is another data integrity rule. 2) Before deleting an entity, a process must either a) verify that there are no existing associative entities or relationships dependent upon the entity, or b) delete these associative entities or relationships as the entity is deleted. The choice here depends on the business policy for each case. In today's technology, these rules are often implemented with triggers.

Participation Rules. If an entity occurrence participates in a relationship, and that participation is mandatory, any process creating or deleting entity occurrences must obey the following rules: 1) If a process creates an entity that has a mandatory relationship, the same process must also create that relationship. 2) A process which deletes a mandatory relationship must also delete any entity occurrence whose participation in that relationship is mandatory. 3) Any process that creates a relationship having an upper limit must ensure that there is not already other relationship occurrences that reference that entity occurrence and exceed the upper limit. Again, these rules can be implemented in DBMS triggers.

```
PROCESS
    Check Out Buyer

DATA FLOW INPUTS
    Check_Out

DATA FLOW OUTPUTS
    Refund
    Buyer_Delivery_Request

STORED DATA INPUTS
    Sale Items

STORED DATA OUTPUTS
    Sales
    Buyers

LOCAL TERMS
    <Buyer_in_market> is-a-matching <Buyer> on Buyer_Id
            with state = "In market"
    <Buyer_sale> is-a-matching <Sale> for <Buyer_in_market>
            with state = "Agreed upon"

FUNCTION
    If <Buyer_in_market> then
            produce Buyer_Delivery_Request
            For each <Buyer sale> do
                    <Buyer_sale>.state = "Waiting for pickup"
            Derive <Buyer_in_market>.sales_total
            Read <Buyer_in_market>.balance
            Deduct <Buyer_in_market>.sales_total from
                    <Buyer_in_market>.balance
            If <Buyer_in_market>.balance > 0.00 then
                    Refund = <Buyer_in_market>.balance
                    <Buyer_in_market>.balance = 0
                    Issue refund
            <Buyer_in_market>.state = "Out of market"
```

Figure 8–7 A Minispec Written in Structured Language

8.8 DEVELOPING MINISPECS

Creating Detailed Specifications for Granular Components

Minispecs specify the functionality of circles on a lower level DFD which have not been detailed by another DFD. Minispecs should be kept to a single page, so that the requirements can be easily understood, reviewed, and designed. Even though they are small, they are vital components of the Essential Model because they define the detailed behavior of the system. A Minispec should be rigorous enough to be used to test systems functionality.

A Minispec can represent a system component. If the components are defined in a modular way, it increases reuse and simplifies testing. First the component itself can be tested, then each interaction with other components can be tested separately. This helps manage the complexity of testing distributed systems.

PROCESS

Check Out Buyer

DATA FLOW INPUTS

Check_Out

DATA FLOW OUTPUTS

Refund

Buyer_Delivery_Request

STORED DATA INPUTS

Sale Items

STORED DATA OUTPUTS

Sales

Buyers

LOCAL TERMS

<Buyer_in_market> is-a-matching <Buyer> on Buyer_Id with state = "In market"

<Buyer_sale> is-a-matching <Sale> for <Buyer_in_market> with state = "Agreed upon"

FUNCTION

#	PRE-CONDITION	POST-CONDITION
1	<Buyer_in_market>	Buyer_Delivery_Request
2	<Buyer_in_market>	<Buyer_in_market>.state = "Out of market"
3	<Buyer_sale>	<Buyer_sale>.state = "Waiting for pickup"
4	<Buyer_in_market>.balance> 0.00	Refund = <Buyer_in_market>.balance

Figure 8–8 A Minispec Written in Pre- and Post-Condition Style

A Minispec contains: 1) a name corresponding to the name of the process on the DFD, 2) data flow inputs, 3) data flow outputs, 4) stored data inputs (for example, the entities, relationships, or attributes read or matched), 5) stored data outputs (for example, the entities, relationships, or attributes created, deleted, or updated), 6) local terms (for example, sets of entity occurrences or functions), and 7) functions (for example, the logic of the Minispec).

Minispecs must only contain data used by the process they describe. They must use or produce all given data flows and they must detail all data accesses. Minispecs must also be unambiguous and complete so that any two people testing the same Minispec with the same data will arrive at the same answer. By convention, a Minispec is not numbered because it may be referenced by more than one lowest level process, and the numbers of those processes will be different because they come from DFD numbering conventions. As previously stated, the goal of specifying small granular components is to achieve maximum reuse.

Any style of Minispec yielding a clear and rigorous specification of a process is acceptable. Two styles most often used are structured language and pre- and post-condition specification. Structured language (Figure 8–7) is a procedural way to specify functionality. The drawback here is that people often slip into writing code instead of specifying requirements. Pre- and post-condition specification (Figure 8–8) describes the before and after conditions of the function, and thus eliminates the need for procedures. The drawback here is that some users have difficulty understanding conditions. The benefits of the pre- and post-condition style is that it usually results in far more succinct and error-free specifications.

Minispecs should communicate the functionality of the business event and response unambiguously. They become the granular business components, which are ultimately distributed across the distributed architecture in the Implementation Model.

9

The Event Distribution Aspect

Moving from a Centralized View of the System to a Distributed View of the System

At this point in the IllumiSys™ Design Method we have defined business events, the granular responses to the business events, and the data required for each response. The event management, responses, and corresponding data constitute granular Business Components. The business requirements have been studied, negotiated with business users, and documented in detail. In order to focus on the business, we first assumed that events and their responses would all take place at a single location in the business.

However, the real power of client/server systems is that they enable technology to be distributed to where the work is actually being performed. The resulting system is one that more closely resembles the business. Rather than capturing the events on intermediary forms and documents and then bringing them to a centralized system for entry (as is common in centralized systems), events can now be captured as they occur, thus increasing the performance of our systems in a world of shrinking business cycles. Therefore, a distributed design requires an understanding of where work is done.

Traditional system development life cycle (SDLC) methodologies separate logical design from physical design. The IllumiSys™ Design Method makes the separation between business and technology. Most large organizations today have distributed operations. It is not uncommon to have different business processes performed at different locations. Therefore, distributed systems must take the geographic distribution of the business into account. This was not necessary with centralized systems because regardless of where the actual work was performed, the processing only occurred in one location. Therefore, we have added the Event Distribution Aspect to the YSM Essential Model to define where business events actually occur. It defines the geographic distribution of the business events. Figure 9–1 depicts the Event Distribution Aspect in the Essential Model.

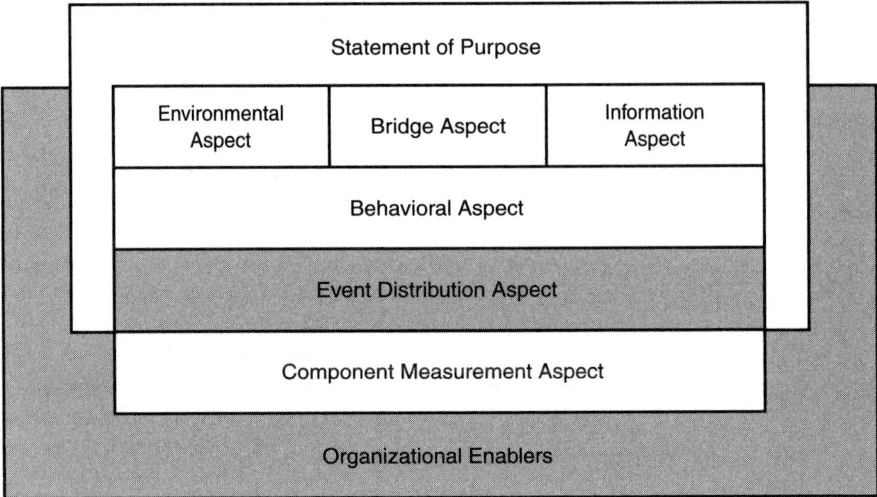

Figure 9–1 Aspects of the Essential Model: The Event Distribution Aspect

The result of the Event Distribution Aspect is an understanding of the organizational structure of the distributed business within the scope of the proposed system. Once this aspect is complete we measure the rates, volumes, and frequencies of the business in the Component Measurement Aspect. At the completion of the Essential Model the developer is in a very powerful position to recommend and design a technical solution that will truly enable the business.

9.1 OBJECTIVES OF THE EVENT DISTRIBUTION ASPECT

Understanding Where Business Events Occur

Rapid change in business processes require rapid change in the systems which support them. Today a retail store captures customer sales exclusively at their store locations, and tomorrow customers may be purchasing goods at home over the Internet. In either case the event, and the business rules and information needed to respond to the event, are essentially the same. The difference is in the location where the event takes place and the technology used to implement the sale transactions. This is why we define "logical locations." A logical location represents a point of service where one or more business events occur. Departments or roles may be represented as logical locations.

A logical location represents a set of business components that the business unit is responsible for. This includes the events, responses, and data required. The Business Components have been previously defined in the Behavioral and Bridge Aspects. Now

Aspect	Activity	Artifact/View	Mandatory/ Optional/ Recommended
Event Distribution Aspect	Determine how events are grouped by function	Event Distribution Table	Mandatory
		Event Distribution by Logical Location	Recommended
	Determine where events occur	Logical Location/ Response Distribution Table	Mandatory for Multi-sites
		Geographic Distribution Table	Mandatory for Multi-sites
		Logical Location Distribution Diagram	Optional

Figure 9–2 Activities and Artifacts of the Event Distribution Aspect

when we refer to an event, we can also assume the responses and data are attached to the event. This is what we refer to as Business Components.

The Event Distribution Aspect answers the following questions:

- What are the logical locations of the business?
- What business events take place at each logical location?
- What is the geographic distribution of these logical locations?

Figure 9–2 depicts the activities and artifacts of the Event Distribution.

9.2 EVENT DISTRIBUTION BY LOGICAL LOCATION

Assigning Business Events to Logical Locations

Event distribution is a *business* design step. Its primary objective is to define the logical locations by grouping together business events based on how system services are delivered to the customer. A number of criteria can be used to distribute events: people's jobs, existing (or new) departmental structures, or specialized locations that contain a subset of functionality of another logical location. For example, one logical location could be a customer service center that has one hundred customer service reps on phones taking orders, handling returns, and answering questions about order status. Another logical location could be a salesperson's laptop. The salesperson's system only takes orders. The other functionality is not needed. These would be considered two separate logical locations, because although they may manage some business events in common they are not entirely the same. In a purely component or object based design, each logical location would only need the business components it was responsible for. This allows for maximum flexibility and reuse. Furthermore, individual components can be customized for a particular location without impacting the rest of the organization. This makes it easier to deploy systems across diverse business units and international borders.

When choosing logical locations it is important to know the expected result of the system under study. If the new system has the freedom to reengineer the business, do not spend too much time on the current distribution of business events; instead focus on how it will occur in the future.

Because a logical location represents a set of business events that are serviced by a type or group of users, they roughly equate to Use Case Studies. If you are doing object oriented analysis with Use Case Studies instead of YSM event based modeling, you would essentially start with this grouping and work towards defining the events, responses, and information.

The Business Event Table from the Environmental Aspect is the primary input needed to start grouping events. Please refer to the Fleury Market case study, Chapter 22, section 22.2.3, or Chapter 5, section 5.4, to review the Business Event Table. Scan the table and group all the events related to one work unit or type of business location. This creates the logical locations. Keep in mind that a single business event can potentially occur at multiple logical locations.

Figure 9–3 is the Logical Location Table for Fleury Market. It takes the event numbers, names, and responses from the Event Table and defines where those responses will logically occur. For example, events three, eight, nine, and four will place at the Wholesaler's Booth. Therefore one logical location to be defined for Fleury Market is named "Wholesaler Booth."

In our experience, every system contains temporal events and cross-functional events. Therefore, an additional heuristic for distributing events is to place the handling of temporal events at a system "services" location where the information needed to trigger the event resides. For example, we have located the event "Market closes" at a logical location named "Market Services."

Some of these logical locations often bear strong resemblance to physical locations (for example, Wholesaler Booth), while others are more abstract (for example, Buyer Services or Market Services). Each logical location will ultimately occur at one or more physical locations, but at this point in the design process, do not let the physical locations cloud your thinking. For example, the event, "Buyer checks out of market" could potentially happen at many physical sites at the market, including the Bistro, the Wholesaler's Booth, the entrance gate to the market, and the Caisse Central. As a matter of fact in future releases, Buyers could check in and out from their own homes over the Internet!

In summary, your goal at this point in the Essential Model is to create logical locations which represent points of service that assume responsibility for servicing the business events.

Logical Location	Essential Event Number and Name
Dock Management	5. Buyer picks up orders
Wholesaler Booth	3. Wholesaler proposes a sale 8. Wholesaler changes sale agreement 9. Wholesaler cancels a sale 4. Buyer checks out of market
Buyer Check-in and Check-out	2. Buyer checks into market 4. Buyer checks out of market
Buyer Membership Administration	1. Buyer applies to become a market member 7. Buyer changes membership information 10. Buyer makes deposit
Service Buyers Administration	6. Market closes

Figure 9–3 The Logical Location Table

9.3 LOGICAL LOCATION/RESPONSE DISTRIBUTION TABLE

Further Detailing the Logical Boundaries

The next step is to map responses to business events defined in the Behavioral Aspect (Chapter 8) to logical locations. The Logical Location/Response Table further elaborates the Event Response Table, by detailing the logical boundaries between business units on a granular response level. Responses to business events may actually occur at other logical locations or terminators (from the Context Diagram—Chapter 5, section 5.2). Mapping responses to logical locations helps define where responses to events happen, and the logical location or terminator (person or system) responsible for the response. This step could result in a renegotiation of scope for the system, to keep the logical boundaries between systems clean. This mapping will greatly aid the design process by revealing potential risks early on.

Figure 9–4 depicts the Logical Location/Response Distribution Table for Fleury Market. Note that Event Number 4, "Buyer Checks Out of Market," can occur at any of the Check-in/Check-Out Locations or the Wholesaler Booth. This creates a very flexible and reuseable design. Buyers have the flexibility of saying, "This is my last order of the day, check me out." This means that later on, in the design phase, the business component "Buyer Check-Out" will map into the GUI screen that will control the business event, and a set of responses. The resulting code modules can be reused in every Check-in/Check-Out location, including the Wholesaler Booth.

Logical Location Event Manager	Essential Event Number and Name	Essential Event Response	Logical Location Event Response(s)
Dock Management	E5. Buyer picks up orders	R5.1. Record pick-up R5.2. Notify Service Buyers	Dock Management Service Buyers
Wholesaler Booth	E3. Wholesaler proposes a sale	R3.1. Create sale R3.2. Derive <buyer> avail balance R3.3. Add sale item R3.4. Derive <sale> total price R3.5. Produce sale agreement R3.6. Assign hanger to sale R3.7. Notify Commodity System of debit to stock	Wholesaler Booth Service Buyers Wholesaler Booth Service Buyers Wholesaler Booth Service Buyers
	E8. Wholesaler changes sale agreement	R8.1. Change sale R8.2. Notify Service Buyers of account debit/credit	Buyer Check-in and Check-out
	E9. Wholesaler cancels a sale	R9.1. Cancel sale for buyer R9.2. Notify Service Buyers of account credit	
	E4. Buyer checks out of market	R4.11. Check buyer out	
Buyer Check-in and Check-out	E2. Buyer checks into market E4. Buyer checks out of market	R2.1. Check buyer in R4.1. Check buyer out	Buyer Check-in and Check-out
Buyer Membership Administration	E1. Buyer applies to become a market member E7. Buyer changes membership information E10. Buyer makes deposit	R1.1. Add buyer R7.1. Note change in membership R10.1. Add deposit to balance	Buyer Membership Administration
Service Buyers Administration	E6. Market closes	R6.1. Cancel uncollected sales	Service Buyers Administration

Figure 9–4 Logical Location/Response Distribution Table

9.4 LOGICAL LOCATION DISTRIBUTION BY GEOGRAPHY

Defining How the Business Operates Across Geographic Boundaries

The geographic distribution of business events defines how the business operates across geographic locations. The most flexible and adaptive component design makes it possible to distribute processing and data only where it's needed and to easily manage and update distributed data and processing. The Logical Location Distribution by Geography Table defines the business events that occur at each logical location. Once again, when we distribute an event to a location, we are actually distributing the entire Business Component.

Enterprise client/server applications generally operate across physical locations. There may, in fact, be multiple physical geographic locations that perform the job of a single logical location. For example, the physical locations for occurrences of Wholesaler Booth are not only in Fleury, but also in Lyon, and in the future could expand to other markets as well.

Mapping logical locations to geographic locations creates a map of the business activities. This makes it possible to design the system for each geographic location. It also provides information for defining necessary communication across locations in future design tasks. This provides the essential requirements for wide area network support of the system. During design, this information will affect decisions such as the physical deployment of hardware and capacity planning for each location.

9.5 GEOGRAPHIC DISTRIBUTION TABLE

Depicting the Geographic Distribution of Logical Locations

The Geographic Distribution Table (Figure 9–5) shows where the business activities take place. It creates an accurate map of the geographic business architecture so portions of the design model can be correctly and consistently organized according to physicality. It indicates which logical locations operate at which geographic locations.

Some logical locations are located at multiple geographic sites. Some geographic locations may do business slightly differently. This may be especially true of global operations. We have found that events are the most reuseable components in design. That is why we emphasize creating Business Components that are comprised of the events, event responses, and data. When defining what events take place at different locations, we define the entire Business Component based on that event. The Geographic Distribution Table also indicates which logical locations work together at a physical location, and which need to communicate across locations based on the Logical Location/Response Distribution Table (Figure 9–4).

Geographic Location / Logical Location	Fleury	New Market in Lyon	Distribution Center in Bordeaux
Buyer Services	1. Buyer applies to become a member 7. Buyer changes membership information 10. Buyer makes deposit	1. Buyer applies to become a member 7. Buyer changes membership information	
Check In	2. Buyer checks into market	2. Buyer checks into market	2. Buyer checks into market
Check Out	4. Buyer checks out of market	4. Buyer checks out of market	4. Buyer checks out of market
Wholesaler Booth	3. Wholesaler proposes a sale 8. Wholesaler changes sale agreement 9. Wholesaler cancels sale 4. Buyer checks out of market	3. Wholesaler proposes a sale 8. Wholesaler changes sale agreement 9. Wholesaler cancels sale 4. Buyer checks out of market	
Market Services	5. Buyer picks up orders 6. Market closes	5. Buyer picks up orders 6. Market closes	5. Buyer picks up orders 6. Market closes

Figure 9–5 Geographic Distribution Table

Figure 9–5 shows how a flexible design can be created to accommodate different operating practices at different business locations. The different locations in the Fleury Market Association are highly autonomous operating units. Although they share enterprise information and have common business activities or events, the new market at Lyon is much smaller than Fleury, and is organized slightly differently. Bordeaux is just a distribution center and does not handle all the business events that Fleury and Lyon do. The Geographic Distribution Table defines exactly what business processes occur in each location. This provides information necessary to customize the system to each business unit at each geographic location. In the Component Measurement Aspect (Chapter 10) this table will be used to indicate numbers of users and transaction volumes at each geographic location. During implementation planning, this enables capacity planning on a site by site basis. For more information on Fleury Market, please refer to Chapter 22, section 22.6.3.

9.6 LOGICAL LOCATION DIAGRAM

Defining How Logical Locations Operate Within and Across Geographic Locations

The Logical Location Diagram creates a physical map of the enterprise depicting where system services must occur. This view gives a graphic representation of the logical locations. Later on in design, it will be used to determine how to distribute software components and how different geographic locations interoperate with each other. At this stage, we are merely defining where business events occur. The design of the Implementation Model will define how business components are implemented in the distributed system. The decisions of how to distribute data and processing are based on the business requirements defined in the Distribution Aspect and the technical processing requirements defined in the Measurement Aspect.

There are nested levels of a Logical Location Diagram. The lowest level is within one geographic location (Figures 9–6 and 9–7). The next level up would be across locations within a geographic territory, such as Europe. If necessary, still a larger view could

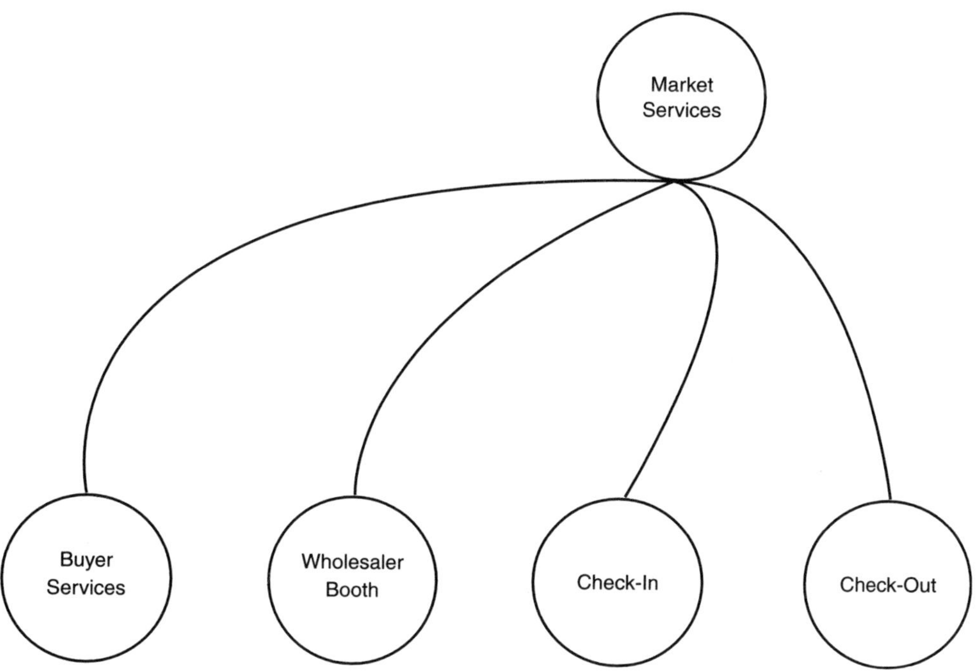

Figure 9–6 Logical Location Diagram for Fleury and Lyon

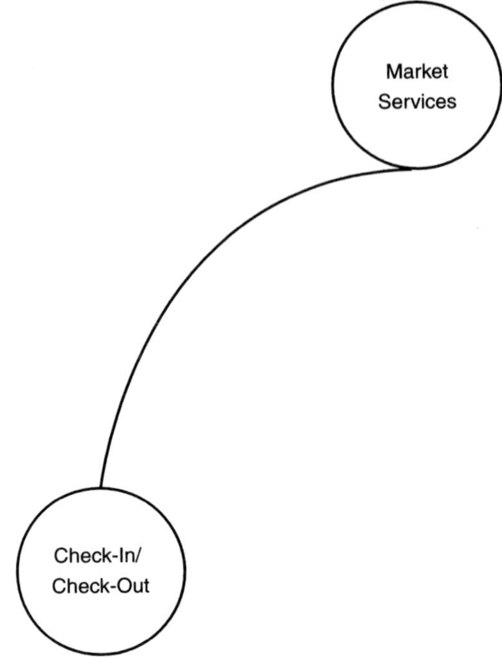

Figure 9–7 Logical Location Diagram for Bordeaux

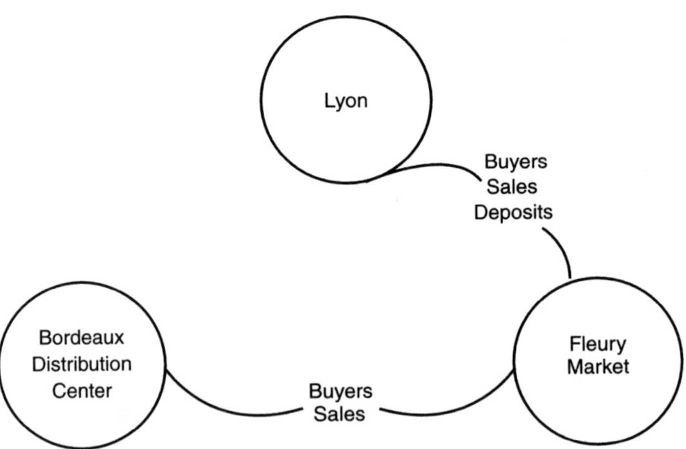

Figure 9–8 Enterprise Logical Location Diagram

be created, such as world-wide operations. Figure 9–8 depicts the Enterprise Logical Location Diagram for the Fleury Market case study.

The bulk of the geographic diagramming will occur in the design stage, where interfaces between software components across physical locations will be defined. At that time we will expand the Logical Location Diagrams.

The creation of a Logical Location Diagram for each site and the enterprise marks the end of the event distribution design step. If the scope of your system has been well-defined, and if your organizational design is not too complex, you should find this step to be relatively straightforward. Later on in the design (Part III) the Logical Location Diagrams will be used extensively when partitioning event components across processors and defining interfaces between components.

10

The Component Measurement Aspect

Understanding How the Natural Cycles of the Business Constrain Design Decisions

A comprehensive Essential Model specifies Business Components that can be partitioned in a multitude of ways across a distributed processor architecture. The partitioning can fail to produce an effective system, however, unless you fully understand all the factors which impact the design and/or implementation of that system. These factors include such things as processing volumes, performance goals, existing network infrastructure, and other critical factors which impact design and technology decisions.

The Component Measurement Aspect defines the characteristics of the natural rhythms and cycles of the business. It measures the frequency of business events by identifying the peaks and averages of transaction volumes, the data storage requirements, and the minimally acceptable system response times. Factors such as size, speed, and duration are also addressed by this aspect. To create this aspect, information is gathered about existing business conditions and expected growth over the next twelve to twenty-four months. Furthermore, the measurements are done for each geographical location to define the service requirements for each site. Figure 10–1 depicts the Component Measurement Aspect in the Essential Model.

The Component Measurement Aspect answers to the following questions:

- What is the average frequency of events at each geographic location?
- How fast must the system respond to each and every one of those events?
- What is the projected growth in the frequency over the next year or two?

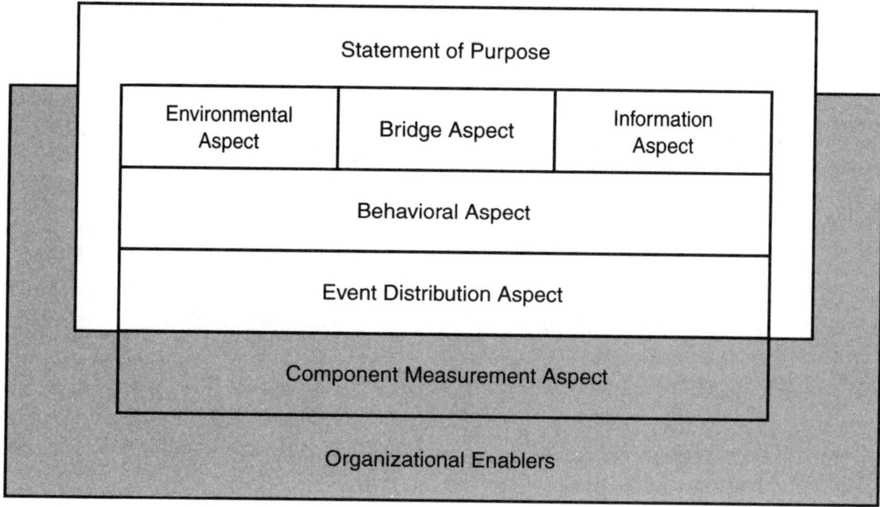

Figure 10–1 Aspects of the Essential Model: The Component Measurement Aspect

- What are the numbers of the system terminators (how many buyers, wholesalers, etc)?
- What is the projected growth rate?
- What is the projected number of occurrences of each entity?

Figure 10–2 depicts the activities and artifacts of the Component Measurement Aspect.

Aspect	Activity	Artifact/View	Mandatory/ Optional/ Recommended
Component Measurment Aspect	Determine how often and how many	Terminator Measurement Table	Mandatory
		Event Measurement Table	Mandatory
		Entity Relationship Measurement Table	Mandatory

Figure 10–2 Activities and Artifacts of the Component Measurement Aspect

10.1 OBJECTIVES OF MEASUREMENT

The Measurement Aspect Helps Define Design Constraints

The Essential Model is intentionally kept implementation free. That is, its focus is on the business requirements for the system. It is, therefore, a statement of ideal processing. The Essential Model assumes infinite memory, no processor or network delays, infinitely fast CPUs, and so on. In other words, the Essential Model assumes "perfect technology." But systems are not ideal. They do have real world properties. Though computers are now very fast, they do take time to compute answers and communicate results across networks. Once the Essential Model has been verified with business experts and end users via formal walk-throughs and inspections, the Business Components can be measured for the purpose of specifying real world constraints which will impact design decisions. The benefits of measuring the Business Components are as follows:

- It provides the information used later to size the systems for each geographic location.
- It provides the information necessary to later estimate network traffic.
- Most importantly, it can call attention to potential bottlenecks and risks *before* the system is implemented.

The Measurement Aspect specifies three sets of components from the Essential Model: terminators, events, and information. The terminators are the external people or systems that interface with the system being designed. They are defined in the Context Diagram of the Environmental Aspect (Chapter 5, section 5.2). Events are defined in the Event Table of the Environmental Aspect (Chapter 5, section 5.4). Information is defined in the Information Aspect (Chapter 6).

The measurement process should be done by first measuring terminators, then events, then information. This is because measuring the information component requires knowledge of the number of events and terminators. Measuring event components requires knowledge of the number of terminators (such as how many buyers come into the market on average and on peak days). Therefore, start with measuring the terminators from the Context Diagram.

Terminators should be measured as both current status and projected growth. It is important to explicitly decide whether to compute the event and information measurements on a current or projected basis, or both. Measuring events looks at the number, frequency distribution, and required response time of key events at each location and any critical response times. For example, eighty-nine Buyers check into the market on an average day with no buyer spending more than ten seconds to check in. Information component measurement defines the data storage required. When this entire aspect is completed, the required transaction rates, sizes, and frequencies, system response times, and system storage requirements are well-specified. When the specification is done for each geographic location the information can be used to define processing requirements on a site by site basis.

10.2 DETERMINING WHAT TO MEASURE

Measuring the Key Business Components of the Essential Model

In determining what to measure, you need to balance the effort of the task with the benefits it provides. In practice, it takes a great deal of effort to do extensive measurements. Some events will obviously not be worth the effort, especially if you know they occur infrequently and will most likely have minimal impact on the overall performance of the system. Other events will emerge as being obviously critical to the overall performance of the system. The key here is to identify any potential risk factors and the critical processing requirements. The following dimensions of the business components are measured.

1. **SIZE—The number of external entities the system must interact with.** You determine these by locating all the terminators in the environment, measuring their current numbers, and then creating an estimate of future growth or decline for each (for example, the market can support 500 buyers/day today and must support 1000 buyers/day in two years).
2. **FREQUENCY—The number of the events generated by those external entities.** You determine these by how many events each terminator occurrence can generate on a second-by-second, minute-by-minute, hourly, or daily basis (for example, 400 buyers check out each day).
3. **DISTRIBUTION—The frequency patterns of events.** At a minimum, we suggest you measure current event frequencies so you can compute average and peak frequencies (for example, ten buyers check out every hour but nearly 100 buyers check out during the last hour).
4. **RESPONSE—The maximum response time for critical events.** You determine these by understanding the business needs of each terminator (for example, most Buyers are willing to wait no more than two minutes to have their sale changed). For some events, response time is less critical.
5. **STORAGE—The disk space needed for information storage.** You compute this by finding all the data stores determining the sizes of those stores, multiplying size times the number of event occurrences, and multiplying that result by the retention needs (for example, 500 Buyers * 200 bytes/record = 100K byte file * 5 years = 500K bytes total). Note that estimating actual storage requirement is a function of the database design and depends on things such as clustered indexing. Formulas can usually be found in the Database Administrator's (DBA) manual of the DBMS.

With this set of facts about current business operations, estimates for projected growth or decline of future business, and computations on expected system performance, you will have enough measurements to reliably make important technical decisions such as sizing of servers at each location.

10.3 HOW TO DESIGN MEASUREMENTS

Defining Clear and Consistent Metrics

We recommend a simple measurement process we have found very useful during the course of developing client/server systems:

1. **State the Measure.** Stating the measure is the first and most important step. Here, you define what is to be measured with specific language. For example, "Number of Buyers" is less specific then "Number of Buyers per day." The inclusion of units in the statement is a crucial component. In fact, for some systems, the units are the hardest part to determine. For example, the Fleury Market resides in France, so the measure, "size of buyer accounts in francs" naturally specifies the French unit of currency. But what about an international cheese market? Selecting a single currency unit will cause fluctuations in account values based on the currency exchange rates. We advise you to carefully consider the units, so you are fully aware of the difficulty you may face when actually trying to take the measurement.
2. **Operationally Define the Measure.** Here, you define an exact procedure for taking the measurement. List and number all the measurement steps, and for each define how the step will be accomplished and who will do the activity. These steps must

MEASURE:
Number of deposits per day
STEPS:
1) Arrive at Cassise Centrale 30 minutes after market closing 2) Ask M. Garcon for all deposit slips for the day 3) Count the slips and write the total on a piece of paper 4) Return all slips to M. Garcon 5) Leave Cassise Centrale
NUMBER:
Integer
UNITS:
Deposit slips

Figure 10–3 An Operational Definition for a Measure

play together to produce a result, and so the definition must include a number and its corresponding units. Figure 10–3 displays a sample procedure.

3. **Calibrate the Measure.** Even for small systems, measurements often produce numbers with varying magnitudes and/or units. Sometimes, it is important to calibrate the results of these measurements to a standard scale so they can be compared to each other (for example, international bank accounts are converted to a single currency) or so ranges of results can be aggregated for future analysis (for example, the number of Sale Items is mapped to a unitless scale: 1–5 items = small, 6–10 items = medium, 11–20 items = large).

By following these simple steps, you can, without investing a large amount of time or number of people, reliably produce a solid collection of facts about current operations.

10.4 THE TERMINATOR MEASUREMENT TABLE

Measuring Each Terminator on the Context Diagram

The first table created in the Measurement Aspect is the Terminator Measurement Table. This table documents the current and projected number of entity occurrences for each terminator on the Context Diagram. For example, Figure 10–4 documents the number of Buyers during a typical week, and the current and expected number of Buyers and Whole-

Day	Mon	Tue	Wed	Thu	Fri
Buyers	**50**	**55**	**60**	**156**	**125**

**Average sales per buyer is 8.*

**Average sale items per sale is 5.*

**Average commodities stocked per wholesaler is 20.*

**16 delivery bays are planned—with a peak of 160 Buyers checking out in the last hour of business.*

**There are 125 Commodity types in the system.*

Market Members	Today	Two Years Out
Buyer	**174**	**348**
Wholesaler	**20**	**25**

**We expect a 50% increase in Buyers and a 15% increase in Wholesalers in the next two years*

Figure 10–4 A Terminator Measurement Table for Fleury Market

Day	Mon	Tue	Wed	Thu	Fri
Buyers	**28**	**27**	**28**	**76**	**35**

**Average sales per buyer is 8.*

**Average sale items per sale is 5.*

**Average commodities stocked per wholesaler is 20.*

**4 delivery bays are planned—with a peak of 80 Buyers checking out in the last hour of business.*

**There are 125 Commodity types in the system.*

Market Members	Next Year	Two Years Out
Buyer	**85**	**170**
Wholesaler	**10**	**20**

**We expect a 100% increase in Buyers and a 100% increase in Wholesalers in the next two years*

Figure 10–5 A Terminator Measurement Table for Lyon Market

salers. Measurements about terminators must be acquired, because they are used in computations to complete other tables in the Measurement Aspect. However, sometimes these measurements are hard to take. For example, imagine the difficulty in daily counting Buyers if the market had seven entrances with no turnstiles. Taking reliable measurements would require a small project team for an extended period of time! When a measurement is difficult to obtain, we recommend that you use historical measures combined with expected growth rates. Especially for these measurements, project teams often work closely with the business experts to reduce the effort needed to acquire this crucial information.

Figure 10–5 is a Terminator Measurement Table for Lyon. Note that the measurements will be different for each geographic location. Taking measurements for each location enables you to maximize the use of the new, scalable technology by sizing systems for each location.

10.5 THE EVENT RESPONSE MEASUREMENT TABLE

Measuring Business Events to Determine Processing Requirements

The Event Response Table contains all the data needed to define how often events occur and how fast the system needs to respond to those events. For example, Figure 10–6 gives the average and peak frequencies for events based on the projected (two-year) numbers in

Event No.	Average	Peak	Max Response Time
1. Buyer applies to become a market member	.35	.35	10 minutes

**250 work days per year, for 2 years = 500 work days. In the next two years we expect 178 new members. 178/500 days = an average of .35 new members per day. There is no known peak for buyer membership.*

2. Buyer checks into market	177	313	10 seconds

**In 2 years we expect to have 348 buyers. Using terminator measurements, daily check-ins average 51% of total buyers per day = 348 * .51 = 177 buyers on average. The peak for buyers is on Thursdays when 90% of buyers shop for the weekend. 90% of 348 = 313. (Percentages derived from current trends. 156 buyers check in on peak or 90% of buyers.)*

3. Wholesaler proposes a sale	1416	2784	2 minutes

**Average buyers per day is (348* 51%)= 177. See Note 1. Each buyer purchases from an average of 8 wholesalers. Total average wholesaler proposes sale = 177 * 8 = 1416. Peak = 318 * 8 = 2784.*

** Number of times event "Wholesaler Proposes a Sale" assumes all buyers who enter the market purchase goods. For this calculation a more accurate measure would be to find the historical average of the percentage of members who come into the market who buy.*

4. Buyer checks out of market	177	313	30 seconds, overall response time for picking up goods should be no longer than 15 minutes

** Same reasoning as for Event #2. That some buyers forget to check out is negligible.*

5. Buyer picks up orders	177	313	3 seconds

** Same reasoning as for Event #2. Sometimes buyers who check in do not buy, but we decided to estimate for top level sales.*

6. Market closes	1	1	Batch window constraints need further investigation

** Market closes once a day.*

7. Buyer changes membership information	1	5	3 seconds

** Complete "guesstimate" and not enough volume to care.*

8. Wholesaler changes a sale	354	626	2 minutes

** On average 5% of sales are changed.*

9. Wholesaler cancels a sale	142	250	10 seconds

**On average 2% of sales are canceled.*

10. Buyer makes deposit	177	400	10 seconds

** Estimate: Buyers normally make 1 deposit/day but can make as many as 3.*

Figure 10–6 An Event Response Measurement Table for Fleury

Event No.	Average	Peak	Max Response Time
1. Buyer applies to become a market member	**.34**	**.34**	**10 minutes**

**250 work days per year, for 2 years = 500 work days. In the next two years we expect 170 new members. 170/500 days = an average of 34 new members per day. There is no known peak for buyer membership.*

2. Buyer checks into market	**66**	**153**	**10 seconds**

**In two years we expect to have 170 buyers. Using terminator measurements, daily check-ins average 38.8% of total buyers per day = 170 * .388 = 66 buyers on average. The peak for buyers is on Thursdays when 90% of buyers shop for the weekend. 90% of 170 = 153. (Percentages derived from current trends im terminator measurement.)*

3. Wholesaler proposes a sale	**330**	**765**	**2 minutes**

**Average buyers per day is (170 * .388) = 66. See Note 1. Each buyer purchases from an average of 5 wholesalers. Total average wholesaler proposes sale = 66 * 5 = 330. Peak = 153 * 5 = 765.*

** Number of times event "Wholesaler Proposes a Sale" assumes all buyers who enter the market purchase goods. For this calculation a more accurate measure would be to find the historical average of the percentage of members who come into the market who buy.*

4. Buyer checks out of market	**66**	**153**	**30 seconds, however overall response time for picking up goods should be no longer than 15 minutes**

** Same reasoning as for Event #2. That some buyers forget to check out is negligible.*

5. Buyer picks up orders	**66**	**153**	**3 seconds**

** Same reasoning as for Event #2. Sometimes buyers who check in do not buy, but we decided to estimate for top level sales.*

6. Market closes	**1**	**1**	**Batch window constraints need further investigation**

** Market closes once a day.*

7. Buyer changes membership information	**1**	**5**	**3 seconds**

** Complete "guesstimate" and not enough volume to care.*

8. Wholesaler changes a sale agreement	**16.5**	**38**	**2 minutes**

** On average 5% of sales are changed.*

9. Wholesaler cancels a sale	**7**	**15**	**10 seconds**

**On average 2% of sales are canceled.*

10. Buyer makes deposit	**66**	**100**	**10 seconds**

** Estimate: Buyers normally make 1 deposit/day but can make as many as 3. The peak is a guesstimate, but can be more closely derived through historical averages.*

Figure 10–7 An Event Response Measurement Table for Lyon

the terminator component measurements. By juxtaposing event frequency, distribution, and response time in a tabular format, you can create a detailed specification that is very easy to read and understand. One point is worthy of note here: You may wish to create other views such as bar graphs to depict other types of information such as their distribution over time. We recommend creating the simplest table you can, making sure all measurements are accurate and sufficient, and supplementing it as needed. Note that here we have decided to measure projected volumes. We recommend you project volumes out over no more than one or two years because these are the numbers that will be used later to actually size the systems.

Create a separate Event Response Measurement Table for each geographic location. This will provide the information for capacity planning on a site-by-site basis. Figure 10–7 is the Event Response Measurement Table for Lyon. Note that the numbers are quite different from the Fleury location.

Entity/Relationship	Number of Occurrences per Year			History (years)	Total Bytes
	Number	Bytes	Total		
1. Buyer	348	170	59,160	5	295,800
2. Wholesaler	25	4	100	5	500
3. Sale <Wholesaler> sells to <Buyer>	696,000	100	69,600,000	5	348,000,000
4. Sale Item <Commodity> is item of <Sale>	3,480,000	50	174,000,000	5	870,000,000
5. Commodity	125	25	3,125	0	3,125
6. <Stock> <Wholesaler> stock <Commodity>	500	6	3,000	0	3,000
7. Hanger	2784	5	13,920	0	13,920
8. <Hanger> is located at <Wholesaler>	130	N/A	N/A	N/A	N/A
9. <Hanger> is assigned to <Sale>	2784	N/A	N/A	N/A	N/A
					1,218,316,345
Total x 2 for indexing					2,436,631,690

[2] *Buyer—Only the Wholesaler number is kept in the Service Buyers Systems.*
[3] *Sale—2784 average sales per day on peak x 250 working days per year.*
[4] *Sale Item—Average of 5 line items/sale = 696,000 * 5.*
[6] *Stock—25 Wholesalers times 20 average Commodities stocked per Wholesaler.*
[7] *Hanger—Peak total sales/day = 2784. Here we are assuming 1 hanger per sale.*
Total disk size assumes clustered indexing, which requires 2x space. This depends on the implementation database.

Figure 10–8 Entity Relationship Measurement Table for Fleury

10.6 THE ENTITY RELATIONSHIP MEASUREMENT TABLE

Measuring the Information Aspect to Determine Storage Requirements

The Entity Relationship Table, the last table in the Measurement Aspect, is a statement of storage requirements for the system. It provides specifications on record sizes for entities (for example, each Buyer record is 170 bytes), and record retention (for example, Sales are kept for five years). Every entity, associative entity, and relationship appears in the table. This is a very important specification technique, as it makes explicit the need or the lack of need of storage (for example, Commodities are retained; Hanger assignments are temporary). It is important to note that we do not purchase storage disks by the megabyte, therefore we are looking for ballpark figures here. Is it hundreds of megabytes, tens of gigabytes, hundreds of gigabytes, or terabytes?

Again, you must first determine whether you are calculating historical, current, or projected storage requirements. For sizing required disk space, we recommend you project growth for twelve to twenty-four months (depending upon your organization's budget process). The price of storage has steadily gone done over the past few years. Therefore, on the average, systems are sized for no more than one to two years out.

Create a separate Entity Relationship Measurement Table for each geographic location. This will provide the information for storage capacity planning on a site-by-site basis. Figure 10–8 depicts the data storage requirements for Fleury and Figure 10–9 depicts data storage requirements for Lyon.

10.7 USING THE COMPONENT MEASUREMENT ASPECT TO SIZE SYSTEMS

Creating the Necessary Information to Take Advantage of Scalable Technology

The Component Measurement Aspect provides the necessary information for accurately estimating the hardware requirements on a site-by-site basis. This information allows you to truly take advantage of scalable technology. For example, Lyon will have all the same processing functions as Fleury, but in the beginning will have much less volume. Therefore, it is possible to buy a smaller server for Lyon from the same vendor using the same operating system. One of the benefits of distributed architectures is highly scalable technology. However, we have rarely seen organizations take full advantage of this scalability. Most often, organizations immediately start building large Unix servers and centralized architectures with this scalable distributed technology because that is what they know how to build and what they have built in the past. This method enables organiza-

Entity/Relationship	Number of Occurrences per Year			History (years)	Total Bytes
	Number	Bytes	Total		
1. Buyer	170	170	59,160	5	144,500
2. Wholesaler	20	4	80	5	400
3. Sale <Wholesaler> sells to <Buyer>	191,250	100	19,125,000	5	95,625,000
4. Sale Item <Commodity> is item of <Sale>	956,250	50	47,812,500	5	239,062,500
5. Commodity	125	25	3,125	0	3,125
6. <Stock> <Wholesaler> stock <Commodity>	400	6	2,400	0	2,400
7. Hanger	765	5	3,825	0	3,825
8. <Hanger> is located at <Wholesaler>	38	N/A	N/A	N/A	N/A
9. <Hanger> is assigned to <Sale>	765	N/A	N/A	N/A	N/A
					334,841,750
Total x 2 for indexing					669,683,500

[2] *Buyer—Only the Wholesaler number is kept in the Service Buyers Systems.*
[3] *Sale—765 average sales per day on peak x 250 working days per year.*
[4] *Sale Item—Average of 5 line items/sale = 191,250*5.*
[6] *Stock—20 Wholesalers times 20 average Commodities stocked per Wholesaler.*
[7] *Hanger—Peak total sales/day = 765. Here we are assuming 1 hanger per sale.*
Total disk size assumes clustered indexing, which requires 2x space. This depends on the implementation database.

Figure 10–9 Entity Relationship Measurement Table for Lyon

tions to design and tactically deploy distributed solutions based on needs of each geographic location.

We do not recommend you size the system yourself, or hire a consultant to size the system. Instead, we recommend that you use the results of the Component Measurement Aspect in your Request for Proposal (RFP), and let the vendors size the system based on your specifications. That way, you can write the contract to state that if the system does not perform as specified, the vendor will supply an appropriate system that does, and you will be able to upgrade at no additional cost (the preferred solution in a hot bidding war between vendors) or at a cost equal to the price you would have paid if you bought the bigger system in the first place (no upgrade penalty). The idea is to get the vendor to assume some of the risk.

Predicting systems performance on a new system is not easy today. In the mainframe world we had decades of statistics and heuristics to guide our sizing decisions, and in that case you got the hardware, operating system, and software from the same vendor. Now you can get hardware from one vendor, the operating system from another, the software from another, and network and middleware components from still five other vendors. The possible combinations and permutations make it impossible to predict performance. Not even the vendors can do it. Therefore, it is critical to partner with your vendors, and preferably have them assume some of the risk. The Component Measurement Aspect helps reduce risk because it provides enough information so companies and vendors can make reasonably informed decisions.

Please note that this completes the Essential Model. Organizational Enablers appear on the diagram, because they profoundly impact business requirements. For example, if organizational politics rule the day, functional boundaries could be very difficult to agree upon. Similarly, Organizational Enablers profoundly affect the implementation of the system. Therefore, Organizational Enablers appear in Part IV of the book (Chapters 18, 19, and 20).

PART III

SOFTWARE COMPONENTS—THE IMPLEMENTATION MODEL

Part II covered how to specify business requirements that can be partitioned across a distributed architecture. It assumed perfect technology, so only business requirements would be addressed. Now, having specified all the requirements, it is time to turn our attention to designing for a distributed architecture. Distributed design is different from mainframe centralized design for a number of critical reasons. In traditional centralized design, all processing took place on one processor. Now we need to partition the processing across clients, servers, and distributed geographic locations. The design criteria for centralized systems was also different. Mainframe processing and storage was expensive, and systems were designed to maximize processing and storage efficiency. This led to systems which were not easy to change. Proof of this is the year 2000 problem that all major organizations are now facing. Accommodating a change in the size of the date field requires changing millions of lines of code. In some cases it is difficult to determine the impact of a change in one part of the code on other parts of the code. The design of these systems was efficient and often elegant in the maximization of computing resources, but inflexible to change.

Today's processing and storage technology is inexpensive. In order to meet the dynamic and changing needs of the business, we need to design adaptable systems that are easy to change. This means making design trade-offs between adaptability and processing efficiency. Given adaptability as our design goal, the way we design systems is going to be fundamentally different than the way we designed our legacy systems. Instead of tightly compiled executable code modules, design is moving toward loosely coupled software components that interact through clearly defined interfaces. I/S professionals who

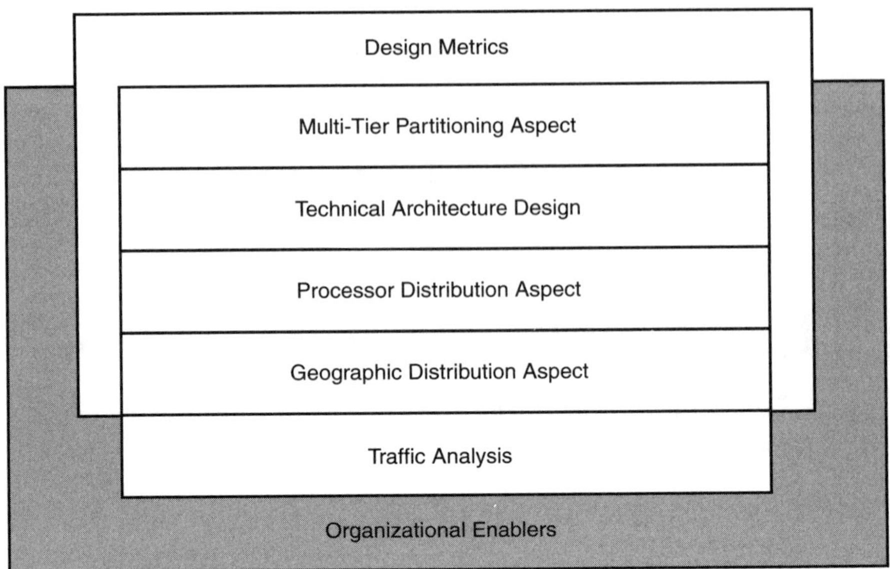

Figure III–1 Road Map for Part III—Software Components—The Implementation Model

fail to realize the design point has fundamentally shifted are continuing to build inflexible legacy systems with new technology. However, it must be noted that thus far the success rate of distributed systems has been poor. They have not been built with the robustness of mainframe systems. The infrastructure has not been built to make them cost effective to maintain and support. All of these factors are required to build successful systems, or client/server systems prove to be more costly than legacy systems and no more flexible for meeting the needs of the business. Figure III–1 depicts the Aspects of the Implementation Model of the IllumiSys™ Design Method.

Chapter 11, "Implementation Model Overview," is a summary of the process for creating the Implementation Model.

Chapter 12, "Design Metrics," defines design criteria used to guide design tradeoffs throughout the design process.

Chapter 13, "Multi-Tier Partitioning Aspect," defines the tiers of a multi-tier application architecture and how the Business Components are across a multi-tier architecture. We have found that this mapping is a straightforward process when the Essential Model is created as recommended.

Chapter 14, "Technical Architecture Design," defines all the technical components of the system. As previously stated, the Essential Model purposely assumes perfect technology. However, the choice of technology may impact design decisions. Therefore, before proceeding further in software design, we define the technology the system will be implemented in.

Chapter 15, "Processor Distribution Aspect," determines how data and processing will be distributed across the processors. This step takes each Business Component and partitions it into multi-tier technical components.

Chapter 16, "Geographic Distribution Aspect," determines the geographic distribution of the system. We previously defined the geographic distribution of the business in the Distribution Aspect of the Essential Model. We know where business events take place and the responses and data required to service the business event. At this point, we need to define how different locations will be serviced; either through distributing processing locally (replicating functionality and data) or through on-line access, or some combination of both.

Chapter 17, "Traffic Analysis," measures the impact of the design on the network. Mainframe system designs never had to consider the network before, and many early client/server systems did not either. Therefore, before determining the final design, we do Traffic Analysis, which measures the estimated network traffic any proposed design solution will generate. This information will help determine the most optimal distributed design.

As in the Essential Model, Organizational Enablers wrap around the Implementation Model because factors such as distributed support and responsibility for cross-functional systems, severely impact the feasibility of distributed systems. However, Organizational Enablers are discussed in Part IV, Chapters 18, 19, and 20.

11

Implementation Model Overview

Implementing the Essential Model With "Real World" Constraints

Part I of this book stated the case for highly adaptive, business process-driven architectures. Part II provided an event-driven, object-based process for defining business requirements, called the Essential Model. In Part III, we design the implementation of the system. In the Implementation Model we consider all the "real world" constraints including technical infrastructure, support, and processing requirements.

11.1 OBJECTIVES OF MODELING SOFTWARE COMPONENTS

Modeling the Implementation Before It is Built Reduces Risk

With today's technology, it is often assumed that the only design we need to do is prototyping. While prototyping greatly facilitates rapid application development by gathering requirements while building the user interface with the user, that is all it can do. It cannot model the design of communications between applications and geographic locations, it cannot model the partitioning across the distributed architecture, it cannot model the presentation logic (what happens after you push that button on the screen), and it cannot model network traffic. When building an application for a dozen or so users which will have a limited lifespan, a so-called tactical application, prototyping is probably all that is needed. However, there is much more complexity and risk involved in building mission-critical distributed enterprise systems. In fact, the greatest amount of risk occurs in the complexity that lies beyond the GUI.

The low success rate of client/server systems, may be attributed to the fact that these systems are often not well-designed. The implementation risks were not evaluated before the system was built. A rule of thumb is that defects are ten times more expensive to fix during development than they are during design, when they exist only on paper. When the defects are implemented they are ten times more expensive to fix than they are during development. Therefore, the purpose of design is to reduce risk, increase the success rate, and decrease the overall cost of the system.

There are always multiple ways to implement the system, using different technology and different ways of distributing data and processing. The Implementation Model helps in evaluating a myriad of alternatives to determine the optimal solution.

11.2 THE IMPLEMENTATION MODEL AND ITS STRUCTURE

> *The Implementation Model Provides a Road Map for Distributing Business Events and Responses Across the Distributed Architecture*

The Implementation Model maps the business events and responses defined in the Essential Model to the distributed architecture. The artifacts created help communicate the proposed design to all involved parties including network architects, operations and support personnel, data administrators (if they exist), reuse administrators (if they exist), developers, and end users. Enterprise-distributed systems typically involve people from across the organization. The aspects and views of the Implementation Model are designed to communicate to all of them. Figure 11–1 depicts the Aspects of the Implementation Model.

Design Metrics are created to define the criteria against which the success of the system will be measured. We defined metrics tied to the business in the Statement of Purpose. Design metrics directly relate to the technical solution and guide technical decisions.

The Multi-Tier Partitioning Aspect takes the components defined in the Essential Model and maps them to a multi-tier distributed architecture. We find that if the Essential Model is done well, this mapping is fairly straightforward. If no Essential Model is created, this step is more challenging and not yet well understood among developers.

Technical Architecture Design defines all technical components that will be used in the system. This can be done on a project-by-project basis or an enterprise level. Like all modeling techniques offered in this book, the method presented here works for both. However, we'd like to offer a few observations in this regard. When organizations allow technical architectures to be created on a project-by-project basis, they wind up with a technical infrastructure that is difficult to impossible to support. As a rule of thumb, in-

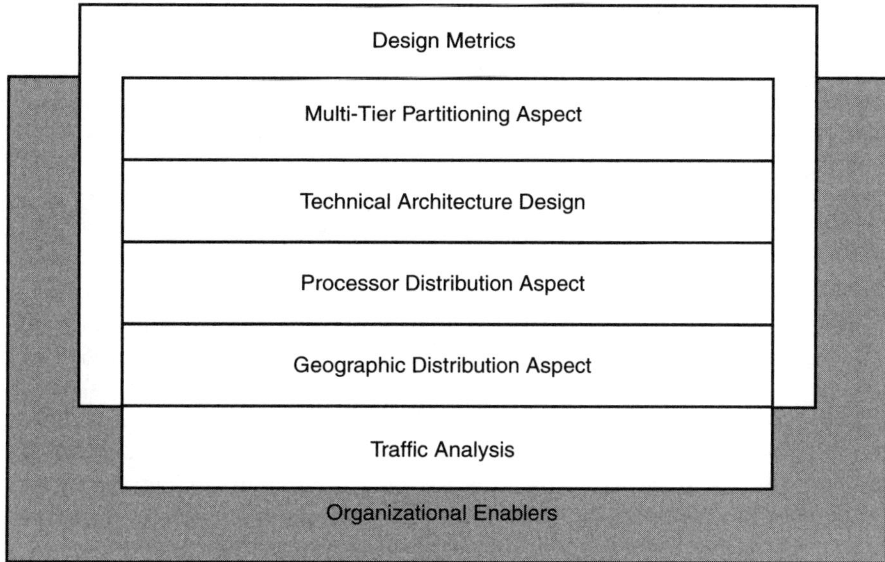

Figure 11–1 The Implementation Model

creased heterogeneity in the technical architecture increases support costs. However, at some point the permutations and combinations make support impossible. Therefore, we highly recommend a limited set of enterprise technical standards, with some flexibility allowed for particular business needs.

The Processor Distribution Aspect defines all the software components for each processor in the distributed architecture as well as communication interfaces and dialogs between processors. This aspect produces the software blueprints for the system.

The Geographic Distribution Aspect defines how software will be geographically distributed. It maps to the logical location distribution by geography created in the Essential Model. Communication dialogs between geographic locations are also defined and data access and replication across locations is decided upon.

Traffic Analysis looks at the communication dialogs between processors and geographic locations. Because networks are part of the distributed system, it is necessary to design for the network. Traffic Analysis helps determine the feasibility of the design and the optimal partitioning strategy.

Organizational Enablers include the organizational factors such as organizational architecture (the org chart), process management, and operational support which impact the feasibility of success for any system implementation. We have found this is especially true of distributed systems because few organizations have the infrastructure in place to support them. Because of the impact Organizational Enablers have on a distributed design, and because they may even impact design decisions, we wrap them around the Implementation Model. They are further discussed in Part IV of the book (Chapters 18, 19, and 20).

11.3 CREATING THE IMPLEMENTATION MODEL

An Iterative and Creative Process which is Managed Through Artifacts

Creating the Implementation Model is an iterative process, much like it is to create the Essential Model. Shrinking cycle times also demand that different design tasks be done in parallel. When designing the software components it is important to look for any opportunities for reuse. For future systems' adaptability and reuse, it is also crucial to build upon enterprise knowledge by making design artifacts available to other projects through shared repositories. This is how cross-functional software components are built over time.

As the purpose of the Implementation Model is to reduce risk, we highly recommend that you prototype any areas of risk as soon as possible. This includes such things as communications, batch updates, and data extracts from legacy systems. It also includes testing new technology as soon as possible, to ensure it will perform as expected. In general, we recommend the following process for creating the Implementation Model.

- Define Design Metrics first.
- Map the Essential Model to the multi-tier architecture.
- Define the technology that will be used to implement each tier.
- Design the software components for each processor.
- Define processing and data distribution and replication across locations.
- Do a traffic analysis of the design to determine feasibility and optimal partitioning.
- Repartition if necessary.
- Keep moving: List any "stops" on an Issues List and move onto another view.

This chapter has provided an overview of the Implementation Model and its importance in reducing the risks associated with building enterprise-distributed systems. The remaining chapters of Part III go into detail about the focus and purpose of each aspect of the Implementation Model and give specific guidelines on how to create them.

12

Design Metrics

Design Metrics Guide Design Trade-offs

In the Statement of Purpose of the Essential Model we defined business metrics to be used to determine how the success of the system will be measured against meeting business goals. Design metrics provide a succinct and complete specification comprising the principles and objectives which will guide all design decisions.

As previously noted, the principle design metrics for systems design have drastically changed. The design of legacy systems focused on maximizing expensive processing and storage technology. Programs needed to make clever and careful use of RAM and storage. These were the correct design metrics for the available technology of the time. However, the cost of processing efficiency was inflexible systems that could not be easily changed to accommodate changes in the business. Tightly coupled, compiled software modules will always execute faster than loosely coupled components (that may be bound together at run time), but they are much harder to modify. Inflexibility was also the cost of designs which maximized storage space. The case in point is the year 2000 problem. In order to save 2 bytes of storage space for all dates, now there are billions of lines of code that must be changed to accommodate the change of the millennium.

Today, the basic design metrics have changed, in part because technology has radically changed. Processing and storage technology has become extremely inexpensive. Today, the primary design goal of all systems should be to maximize flexibility so changes can be rapidly implemented. This means that when you must choose between flexibility and processing efficiency, choose flexibility, and when possible, then beef up the processing power of the system to accommodate that design trade-off. In cases when performance must win, the design should be componentized as much as possible to enable

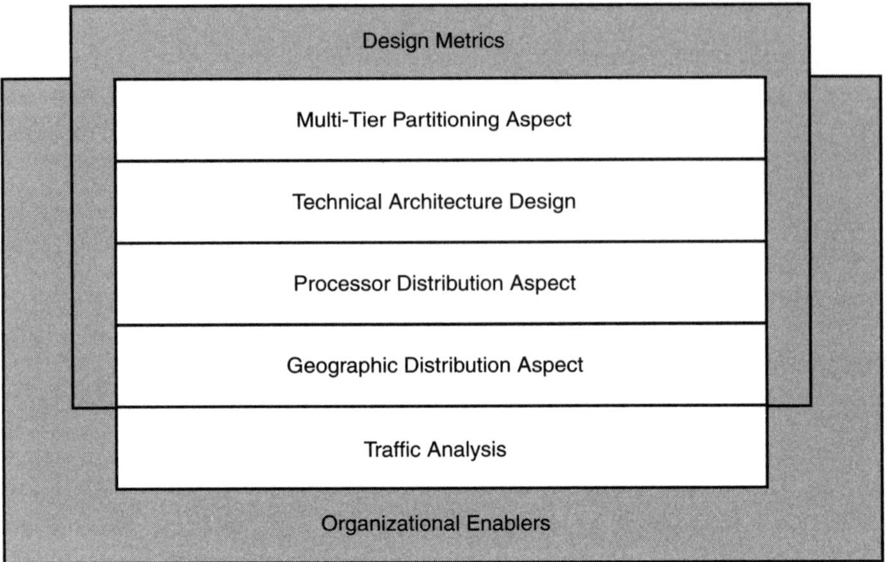

Figure 12–1 Aspects of the Implementation Model: Design Metrics

changes in business processes. Figure 12–1 depicts Design Metrics in the Implementation Model.

There are often design metrics which are particular to the system and which will impact design decisions. A few questions must be answered:

- Is "real-time" data required for decision support?
- How secure must the system be and how easy must it be to use?
- How soon must the system recover from failures?
- What extensibility must be designed into the system?

Figure 12–2 depicts the activities and artifacts of Design Metrics.

Aspect	Activity	Artifact/View	M/O/R
Design Metrics	Define Metrics to Evaluate Design	Statement of Design Goals	Mandatory

Figure 12–2 Activities and Artifacts of Design Metrics

12.1 OBJECTIVES OF DESIGN METRICS

Using Metrics to Build Software Components

A complete and measured Essential Model is required for a successful design. However, it is not, in and of itself, sufficient for guiding choices in design trade-offs. A client/server project needs commonly understood and accepted criteria for making those design trade-offs. The Statement of Design Metrics serves this primary objective. The second major objective of having explicit design metrics is using them to partition the essential requirements across the distributed processor architecture.

Design metrics are often specific to the project. We sometimes refer to them as the "abilities" of the system, because they include such things as availability, maintainability, scalability, usability, transportability, reusability, reliability, and recoverability. Metrics also include factors such as security, speed, and data "freshness." Additionally, we recommend specifying factors that can potentially impact the business through disruption of business tasks or current worklfow.

An example will serve to illustrate our point. In the Fleury Market, Buyers go from Wholesaler to Wholesaler making purchases. A design goal could be stated as, "The current Buyer's balance must be immediately available to all Wholesalers." This statement is a design goal, for it constrains the kind of design that is deemed to be acceptable. For example, designs which update balances on a nightly basis do not meet the aforementioned goal. The constraint is clear and unambiguous. Somehow, the software for processing a Sale must make Buyer Balance available to all Wholesalers.

12.2 CREATING DESIGN METRICS

Design Metrics Must be Aligned with Business Goals

Just like its counterpart in the Essential Model, the Statement of Design Metrics is a small and very succinct document—no more than one to two pages in length (see Figure 12–3). It has five sections:

1. The name and description of the system
2. Goals
3. Constraints
4. Standards
5. Performance

System Name: Service Buyers

Description: This system provides all required support for the interface of the Fleury Market with retail buyers.

Goals:

- The system will be continuously available from 12 AM to 12 PM while the market is open.
- Buyers will be allowed to check out at many locations.
- There will be an electronic bulletin board, located at the Bistro, to notify buyers that delivery is ready.
- Buyer balance must be updated in real time and available to all wholesalers.
- Buyers who shop at the market must use their Fleury Card. Purchases over the Internet also use the Fleury Card ID number.
- The system will have the ability to increase wholesalers or buyers without having to recode the software components (requirements for scalability).
- Wholesalers will have access to their sales and commodity data as needed for ad-hoc analysis through a decision support system.
- The design will accommodate the opening of another market. This system will pilot the capability of a chain restaurant to replicate orders to more than one market. This will require set order and pick-up times for replicated orders.
- Buyer sales are targeted for the Internet. The Markets want to have some portion of commerce-based transactions up in six months.

Constraints (including existing infrastructure):

- Wholesaler Payment System will remain on the mainframe. Service buyers will interface to the existing system.
- The Commodity Management System will be installing its own separate server for the data which is owned by that system. This agrees with the concept of modular server implementations.
- Although Buyers can view specials at Fleury Market via Internet, right now they must be physically located at the market to purchase goods. Plans are to have Internet commerce within six months.
- The first release of the Service Buyers system will be in operation within nine months.

Standards:

- Must conform to Electronic Data Interchange (EDI) banking standards.
- Must conform to Internet (E-mail) standards.
- Hewlett Packard, Sybase, and Microsoft are preferred vendors.
- All systems design models will be kept in LBMS.
- Refrain from designing a distributed unit of work. When unavoidable, use a TP monitor.
- The standard office suite will be Microsoft office. Office automation is being done by a separate project team and is out of scope of this project.

Performance Requirements:

- Buyers will be able to pick up their goods at the dock on average 15 minutes from the time they check out, and on peak days no longer than 30 minutes.

Figure 12–3 Design Metrics

The goals section contains a variety of common system characteristics, such as availability, maintainability, scalability, usability, transportability, reusability, reliability, recoverability, and data freshness. The constraints section defines factors deserving special attention, such as release date, system access, and interfaces to other existing or planned systems. The standards section contains the technical decisions that have already been made before the design has started, such as security mechanisms, particular middleware, programming languages, and hardware platforms. The performance section contains any specific measurable results for items in the prior three sections, such as: when data feeds from other systems must be available, system response times, mean time between failures, and mean time for repair.

Although some of these seem like system characteristics, they require the involvement of the business users because these factors can have significant impact to the business. Experience has shown, however, it is necessary to pose the question in business terms. For example, when we asked a business user about his requirements regarding mean time between failures or minimum down-time he responded by saying that's not a business issue. But when asked what the impact would be to his business if the system was down 1 hour, 2 hours, 4 hours, or 8 hours he had a very different response. When asked about 24x7 support versus 8x5 support (24 hours/day, 7 days a week versus 8 hours/day Monday through Friday) he didn't have a clue. When asked what the impact to his business would be if he could not get his critical reports first thing in the morning because of a failure in the nightly batch operations he had some definite opinions.

12.3 DEFINING DESIGN GOALS

A Set of Design Principles to Guide All Design Decisions

The overall design goals come from understanding how the system will be used and how it will operate during that usage. Regardless of the kind of system, some goals are universal to all systems. As stated above, today the primary design goal for all distributed systems is flexibility to adapt to the changing needs of the business. Some goals, however, are specific to a particular system. An example of a design goal specific to Fleury would be, "Wholesalers will have access to their sales and commodity data on an as-needed basis."

System reliability is another design goal that should be explicitly stated. The mean time between system failures, system performance degradation during partial failure, and network availability under heavy load are examples of reliability goals. It is important to state the metric in business terms. In other words, how long can the business afford not to have the system on-line? Recovery is then also part of the equation, including backup procedures and recovery mechanisms. From this metric, technical solutions can be proposed for all components to fit the specification. For example, a system could require complete redundancy, either where reliability is absolutely key, or where the geographic location is so remote it would be difficult to repair key components. In other cases partial redundancy may be adequate. Each technical solution will depend upon the business needs, business geography, and technical infrastructure.

Another goal that may heavily impact design is usability. For example, a national movie theater chain wished to implement a system where the data entry would be done by part-time employees who typically left the job within six months to a year. One of the primary design goals of the system was to minimize training. Therefore, they were willing to heavily invest in bullet proofing measures such as designing the front end of the system to ensure the integrity of the information as it was entered.

12.4 DEFINING CONSTRAINTS

Existing Factors will Impact Design Decisions

System constraints are determined by considering the special circumstances in the environment or useage of the system. For example, the Service Buyers system for Fleury will be required to interface with the Wholesaler Payment System that will remain on the mainframe. Factors such as the freshness of data (for example, Buyer balances will be updated in real time), physicality (for example, Buyers can purchase goods only at the market), or schedule (for example, version one of Service Buyers will be released in nine months) are typical constraints.

12.5 DEFINING STANDARDS

Technical Standards Impact Design Decisions

The standards to be used during the construction of the system are derived from the existing technical architecture and may be revisited during the course of the project. Standards may include all aspects of the technical infrastructure: hardware, software, operating systems, protocols, middleware, and naming conventions. Any existing standards must be adhered to in the design of the system and may impact a specific implementation decision.

Security is a commonly specified standard. For example, Fleury has adopted DCE as their middleware standard, and thus security for financial transactions will be handled with Kerberos. The design trade-offs are usually between security and ease-of-use and performance. Some security mechanisms can decrease ease-of-use and slow performance.

12.6 DEFINING PERFORMANCE

The Performance of the System Equals the Performance of the Slowest Component

In the Statement of Design Metrics, we need to define specific performance requirements from a business or customer standpoint. However, the application will perform only as fast as its slowest component. Poor performance could be due to application design, an inefficient piece of commonly used code, a heavily used network segment, an outdated batch process that must be fed or must feed a component of the system, or even a slow network interface card. Because the network is part of the distributed system, we suggest that network architects review design plans to evaluate the expected performance over the existing network infrastructure. For example, the same piece of code will perform differently if the server is on the same LAN segment as the client, than if the server is in another location and the message must be routed through the network. In fact, there are so many components in a distributed application, it may be difficult to isolate performance problems. A new type of software called an application monitor is becoming more popular for this purpose.

In order to operationalize a performance metric it is necessary to specify an acceptable maximum response time. It is also important to note that there may be multiple technical solutions for achieving the design goal. For example, short response times may be achieved with faster networks, by having the necessary data local to the user, by adding more processing power, or by some elegant software engineering. Each of these alternatives may impact other design metrics as well. That is why it is necessary to specify all design goals.

12.7 CONFLICTING DESIGN GOALS

Optimize at the Enterprise Level

When all design goals, constraints, standards, and performance requirements are specified, a situation may occur where it may be impossible to satisfy all the goals and requirements. In fact, some technical solutions to meet requirements may be in conflict with organizational standards. Some designs may optimize system performance but may negatively impact other systems that are fed from the system.

The overriding design goal of building systems that are flexible, scale easily to accommodate more users and geographic locations, and can be extended with new capabilities, necessitate that all design metrics be optimized at the enterprise level rather than the individual system. This is because the most successful organizations today are those which can easily adapt to change in business market conditions. It is not unusual for changes in the business market to result in organizational change. Reorganizations are very common occurrences in large companies. Therefore, optimizing any single system at the expense of the enterprise infrastructure is not a flexible or adaptable solution. When necessary, design trade-offs are best made at the enterprise level. However, this may be a highly political issue and require a high degree of support and commitment from executive management.

If the Statement of Design Metrics contains any potential conflicts, the conflicts need to be resolved at the beginning of the design stage, not after the system is built. In this way, the Statement of Design Metrics may be used as both a negotiation tool and contract with the business users.

13

Multi-Tier Partitioning Aspect

Partitioning Business Components Across Clients, Servers, and Mainframes

In the last chapter we looked at defining Design Metrics. We stated that the overall design point has shifted from maximizing system efficiency to maximizing system adaptability. The goal of building adaptable systems can best be achieved through a multi-tier architecture. A multi-tier architecture shields the GUI presentation, business processing rules, data access, and data tiers from changes in any other tier. This is not a new design principle. It's the design of the Open Systems (OSI) Network Architecture model, which has worked for over twenty years.

Encapsulation of tiers is accomplished via clearly defined inviolate interfaces. As long as the interface doesn't change, the functionality within the tier can easily be changed. This is also the model of a component-based architecture. Distributed component-based architectures will dominate in the future because they enable reuse and incremental, rapid change. We firmly believe that a multi-tier application architecture is the only architecture that can successfully support enterprise-wide distributed systems. Of course, not all systems are mission-critical enterprise systems. Two-tier architectures will continue to meet the needs of many applications for some time to come. They are far simpler to build and require less infrastructure. However, we predict that as more enterprise multi-tier applications are successfully built and deployed, a rich infrastructure of component-based services will be available to all applications and will greatly benefit the smaller applications as well. Figure 13–1 depicts the Multi-Tier Partitioning Aspect in the Implementation Model.

At this point in the process we have an in-depth knowledge of the business processes the system will support. From the Environmental Aspect we know all the busi-

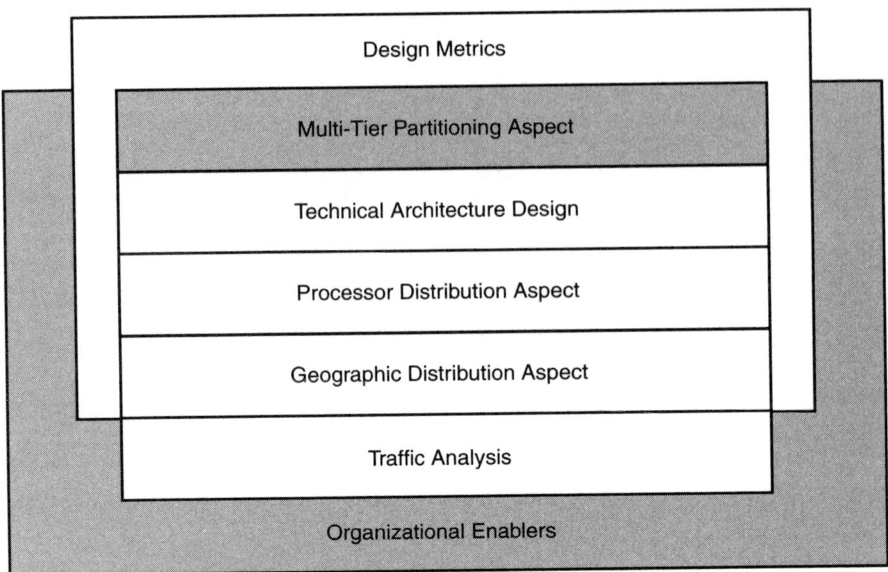

Figure 13–1 Multi-Tier Partitioning Aspect—Aspects of the Implementation Model

ness events that will be handled by the system and which other systems it will communicate with. From the Information Aspect we know about the data, the relationships between business entities, and the rules that govern the relationships. From the Bridge Aspect we know what data is needed by each event and the access required (create, read, update, delete, match). From the Behavioral Aspect we know the detailed responses to each event, which represent many of the business processing rules. In fact, the work done in the Essential Model makes the work of multi-tier partitioning much easier because we have already gathered almost all the business information we need.

The Essential Model also maps very well to defining requirements for client/server systems because it is an event-based programming paradigm. From the Essential Model we know what the events are, when events are launched, the responses to each event, and the data used by each event and response. At this point we look at how the Business Components of the Essential Model map to a multi-tier architecture.

In the Multi-Tier Partitioning Aspect we answer these questions:

- How do the Business Components map to the distributed architecture?
- Will the application architecture be two-tier or multi-tier?

Figure 13–2 depicts the activities and artifacts of the Multi-Tier Partitioning Aspect.

Aspect	Activity	Artifact/View	M/O/R
Multi-Tier Partitioning Aspect	Map business components to multi-tier architecture	Multi-Tier Model Diagram	Optional
	Define application architecture (centralized, two-tier, or multi-tier)	Application Architecture	Mandatory

Figure 13–2 Activities and Artifacts of the Multi-Tier Partitioning Aspect

13.1 OBJECTIVES OF MULTI-TIER PARTITIONING

Multi-Tier Partitioning Creates Adaptive Systems

A computer system is nothing more than a set of automated business processes. The challenge is to design the system so it can be rapidly changed when business rules change, data sources and legacy systems are replatformed, business grows and systems must accommodate more users, reorganization of business results in repartitioning of responsibilities, new technology is introduced, or any other change occurs. The ability to adapt to all these factors is achieved through modular code sets containing consistent interfaces, which communicate with other modules asynchronously whenever possible. This is multi-tier client/server. In particular, multi-tier partitioning enables:

- Data encapsulation
- Granular business rules
- Component application architecture
- Scalability.

Data encapsulation enables the front end application or GUI to access data without knowing the structure or source of the data. In other words, the application only needs to specify *what* data it needs, and not *how* to get the data. This insulates applications from changes in data sources.

Granular business rules are small, functionally cohesive software components which perform a single business function according to the given business policy. Business rules change faster than anything else in the system. Implementing them in a way that makes them easy to change without impacting other components, results in a much more flexible system. It also maximizes reuse and increases the speed of implementation. Creating software components which represent business rules results in a system that more naturally resembles the business and therefore is much easier to understand and maintain.

Business rules are also reuseable across applications. The return on investment for defining and developing business rule components comes from careful management of those rules and maximum reuse. Business rules may also spawn workflow rules, which is an area many companies are now focusing attention on.

A component application architecture is comprised of software modules that can be reused in multiple applications. Reuse is necessary to maximize return on investment (ROI) and minimize implementation time. As long as interfaces remain the same, the functionality of a service can change without affecting the applications or components that request the service. This enables maximum flexibility for designing systems. As the inventory of application components grow, it will become faster and easier to piece together an application as a set of components, adding new components as needed.

Scalability is achieved in a multi-tier architecture both through the component architecture and through asynchronous communications. In a two-tier client/server system the front end Graphical User Interface (GUI) sends synchronous Structured Query Language (SQL) calls across the network to the database. This requires an active session for each and every client. As the number of clients increase, synchronous connections can create network traffic jams and contention on the server. Asynchronous communications enable multiple requests to be submitted in a single session, thereby decreasing contention on the server. Because they require fewer live sessions, the overhead for management of those sessions is significantly decreased, thereby decreasing network traffic. This is a more scalable solution because more users can be added without requiring a linear increase in system resources.

13.2 WHAT IS MULTI-TIER PARTITIONING?

Partitioning Events and Responses into Presentation, Business Rules, Data Access, and Data

Multi-tier partitioning is the process of taking a business event and its responses and partitioning them into logical tiers of presentation, business rules, data access, and data. The presentation tier is the graphical user interface (GUI) to capture and process the business events in a logical location. It is the contact point between the user and the system. Business rules are essentially the event responses defined in the Behavioral Aspect. We have defined these down to the minispecs. The data access tier contains data access rules, defined in the Bridge Aspect in the Entity-Event Table and further detailed in the Behavioral Aspect in the Entity Response Table. The data tier is basically the data store, which has been well defined in the Information Aspect, where we specified entities, attributes, and relationships.

At this point, they are still logical tiers, because we do not define technical implementation design until the Processor Distribution Aspect, after all the technology has been chosen. The benefits of first doing logical partitioning is that it makes it possible to physically implement the tiers differently, depending on the needs of the organization. For example, if an order entry application is going to be used by hundreds of order entry clerks sitting on the phone all day taking orders, as well as on a salesperson's laptop, the same functionality may be needed in both places, but the physical implementation will be different. There should be clear and logical boundaries between the tiers of a multi-tier architecture, even if the tiers will be physically placed on one machine. This logical partitioning creates the most adaptable design.

As Figure 13–3 reveals each tier of the multi-tier architecture communicates with the other tiers either through synchronous SQL calls, remote procedure calls (RPCs), or asynchronous messaging. The communication mechanisms are chosen in the Technical Architecture Design (Chapter 14). Synchronous designs are inherently less scalable than asynchronous designs.

It is becoming increasingly imperative that the application architecture allows the business to create a phased approach to deploying its applications onto the Internet. Although there is much debate about Internet and intranet applications replacing client/server applications, the Web *is* a client/server application, with a thin, universal client called a browser. The benefit of a Web application is that you don't have to design, program, or deploy the presentation layer. You do, however, still need to do everything else. Moreover, security becomes much more critical with Internet/intranet applications. Today, the trend is to design the application with flexibility so it can be easily deployed over the Internet or an internal intranet at a future date. Much of the hoopla about Internet/intranet replacing client/server revolves around the fact that Internet/intranet applications are much more flexible and scalable. However, it must be understood that this extensibility and scalability is due to a platform-independent, multi-tier architecture. This

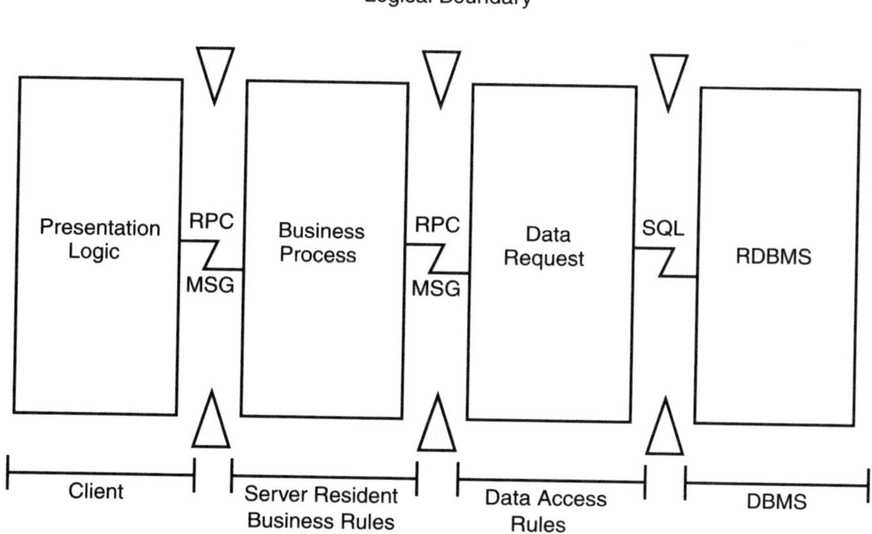

Figure 13–3 The Structure of a Multi-Tier Client/Server Application

is precisely the architecture we are recommending for *all* enterprise systems. As Figure 13–4 depicts, Internet and intranet applications have multi-tier architectures. The only difference is how the user gains access to the system, and the technology used. Therefore, the IllumiSys™ Design Method is also applicable for Internet/intranet applications. What will change is the technology used to implement it.

It is useful to understand the evolution of multi-tier applications, because many of these applications are part of the legacy systems. Bob Epstein of Sybase, defines a legacy system as, "anything that currently works." The first client/server applications, developed in the late 1980s, had a two-tier structure. The client had the GUI presentation, all the application logic, and communicated with the server via synchronous SQL calls. The server contained only the database. This is what is commonly called the "fat client" architecture (see Figure 13–5).

When Sybase released their DBMS with stored procedures around 1988 it became possible to store application logic in the database server. The client contained the GUI presentation and communicated to the server via synchronous remote procedure calls (RPCs) (see Figure 13–6). This is the so-called the "skinny client" or "fat server" architecture. It must be noted however, that most implementations of stored procedures were still "fat client" applications with most of the application logic residing on the client and some commonly used procedures stored on the server.

The third evolutionary phase came when tools such as SAP, Forte, and Dynasty enabled the business processing and data access to be on a server separate from both the

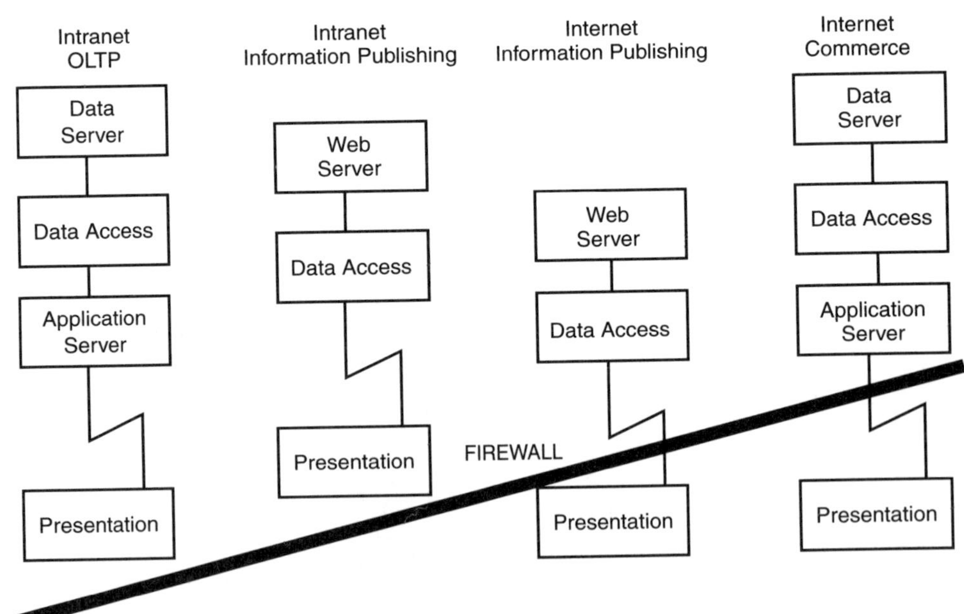

Figure 13–4 Multi-Tier Architecture of Intranet and Internet Applications

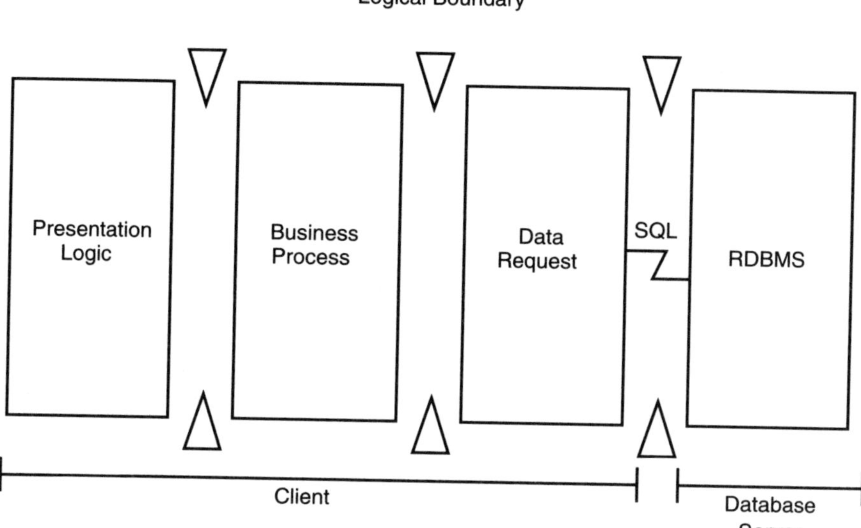

Figure 13–5 "Fat Client" Two-Tier Client/Server

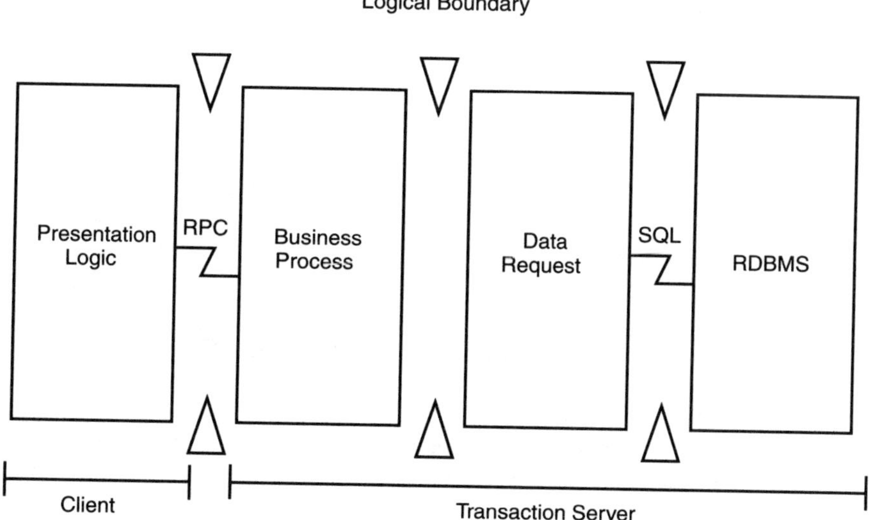

Figure 13–6 "Transaction Server" Two-Tier Client/Server

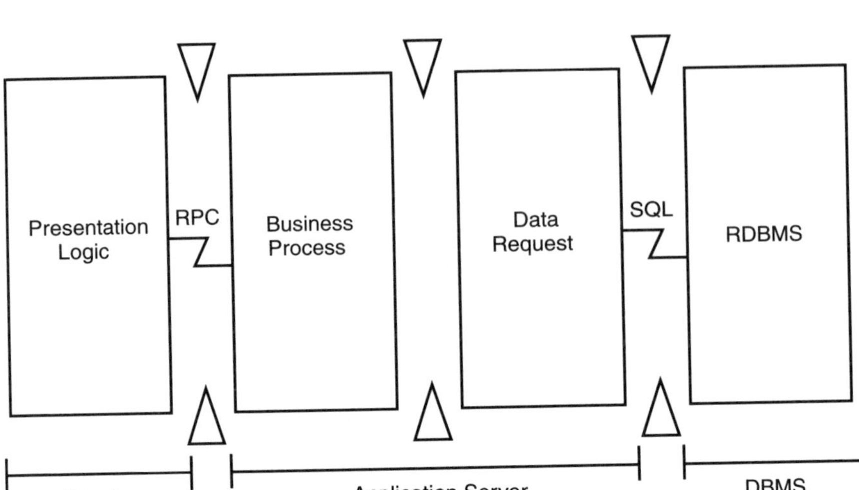

Figure 13–7 Three-Tier Client/Server

GUI presentation and database. This architecture is commonly called three-tier client/server and is displayed in Figure 13–7. (Note the aforementioned tools can now also be used to build multi-tier applications).

The advantages of a multi-tier architecture over a three-tier architecture become clear when you look to the future of distributed component architecture. In a three-tier architecture the business rules tier, or business logic, needs knowledge of the structure and source of the data. The data access rules are embedded in the business logic tier. Often, the business logic tier communicates to the database via synchronous SQL calls. As previously discussed, this creates more network traffic for management of many synchronous sessions and more contention on the database server. It is less adaptable and scalable than a multi-tier solution. In general, the three-tier solutions are being marketed by companies selling large-scale application packages and by high-end tool vendors (see Chapter 14, section 14.3.2.1). The explosion of the high-end tool market itself speaks volumes to the importance of multi-tier architectures for enterprise systems.

13.3 THE ESSENTIAL MODEL AND MULTI-TIER PARTITIONING

The Essential Model Maps Easily to Multi-Tier Architectures

Artifacts created in the Essential Model easily map to a multi-tier design, leaving us little to do until we distribute the tiers to physical processors. We believe the Essential Model has some advantages over other requirement analysis techniques because it starts with business events, which are easy for users to understand, and maps quite naturally to an event-driven design and multi-tier client/server applications.

13.4 PRESENTATION

The Presentation Tier Manages Events

The presentation tier is the user interface to the initiation and management of business events. The GUI enables the user to create an instance of a business event (such as creating a sale) and initiate system responses such as retrieving and processing data. The GUI also enables the user to manage business events by providing the ability to easily update, delete, and query event data. One of the things GUIs do effectively is trap errors before they go over the network through edit rules and exception handling. Typical GUI features such as scrollable pull-down lists, check-boxes, and radio buttons eliminate the possibility of invalid input. This simplifies error handling and results in decreased network traffic because transactions with errors never get transmitted.

At this point in the process we know which events will be serviced by each logical location. A logical location becomes a logical client in the Implementation Model because it represents a set of business events managed by a type or group of users. Therefore, we know what needs to be captured about each event at each client and the required responses to those events.

To accelerate the design process, prototyping may begin at this time if the client technology has already been selected. Please refer to Chapter 15, section 15.6 for further information on modeling the presentation design.

13.5 BUSINESS RULES

Business Rules Define Responses to Events

Many traditional design techniques separate conceptual, logical, and physical design. As previously stated, we separate design into business and technology. Multi-tier partitioning is a design step associated with technology because at this point we take the Essential Model and partition it into tiers based on technology functions of graphical user interface, business logic processing, data access and transfer, and database management. However, at this point they are still *logical* tiers. These logical tiers are mapped to technology and become a physical design in the Processor Distribution Aspect (Chapter 15).

This distinction is especially important when designing the Business Rules Tier. This tier is, in effect, a repository of the *definition* of business rules. During the Processor Distribution Aspect, however, these business rules may be implemented in multiple tiers.

For example, some business rules may be implemented on the GUI in the form of validation rules. We have already defined most of the business rules in the Behavioral and Information Aspects of the Essential Model. The DFDs, minispecs, and Entity Response Table of the Behavioral Aspect fully describe processing and data requirements for each business rule. Unless there are outstanding questions, issues, or areas of high risk or complexity that require further attention, there is nothing more to be done at this time regarding business rules.

13.6 DATA ACCESS RULES

Data Access Rules Define how Responses Use Data

Data access rules define what data each Response needs, and whether the Response creates, reads, updates, deletes, or checks for a match for each entity it accesses. The data access rules are fully defined in the Entity Response Table of the Behavioral Aspect. The access rules are represented by the CRUDM entered in each cell representing the intersection between each Response and the Entity.

The data access rules represent data requirements defined for each event response. During the Processor Distribution Aspect these rules will be used to determine the optimal physical distribution of data. There are, however, other factors which influence physical data distribution, such as geographic locations, data volatility, and the need for instant access to all data transactions. The access rules merely state *what* data is required for each response. They don't state *how* the data is provided to the response. Data could physically be on a local server or at a central server half way across the world. These decisions are made when processor decisions are made. At this point in the logical partitioning phase, we do not need to do anything further.

13.7 DATA

Data is a Persistent Artifact of Process

Many design methods focus on the data. Data is the most reuseable component of a system because it is (or should be) shared across multiple systems. The investment in defining enterprise level data is crucial to the success of data warehousing and effective data management. However, a purely data-driven design approach will not produce the most adaptive design, because it's the wrong design focus. Very little happens to change the actual meanings of data. What changes most are the business rules. The data itself represents the information that is kept as a record of the business event. In effect, data is the persistent artifact of the process. Therefore, data-driven design misses the mark for adaptive systems in a very important way. It's the events themselves that change, and the pressing need is for event processing to be designed for change. The data needs to be designed to represent a cross-functional view of the persistent information about the business.

The Information Aspect of the Essential Model defines all data entities, attributes of entities, relationships between entities, and business rules regarding relationships and entities. The next step is the design of the database. However, we cannot design the database until the database technology has been chosen and decisions are made regarding which processors will store which data. These decisions are made in Technical Architecture Design and the Processor Distribution Aspect. At this point in time we do not need to do anything further.

13.8 DEFINING THE APPLICATION ARCHITECTURE

Choosing Between Two-Tier and Multi-Tier Architectures

The decision must be made to use a two-tier or multi-tier architecture, so appropriate technology can be chosen. We have stated that multi-tier architectures are more scalable and adaptable than two-tier client/server architecture. However, multi-tier applications are also more complex. In come cases they may be overkill. Therefore, you need to decide what architecture is appropriate for the application you are building.

In general, two-tier applications are appropriate for the following types of applications:

- Table maintenance
- Decision support (especially against a local data mart)
- Short-term solutions (application will only be in use for weeks or months)
- Applications with few users (under twenty-five)
- Point solutions that do not require scalability and are not expected to adapt to business changes

Multi-tier applications are appropriate for the following types of applications:

- Mission-critical applications that are expected to grow and change with the business
- Applications that run over wide area networks
- Applications with large numbers of users, or where usage is expected to grow
- Applications with high performance requirements
- Internet and intranet applications

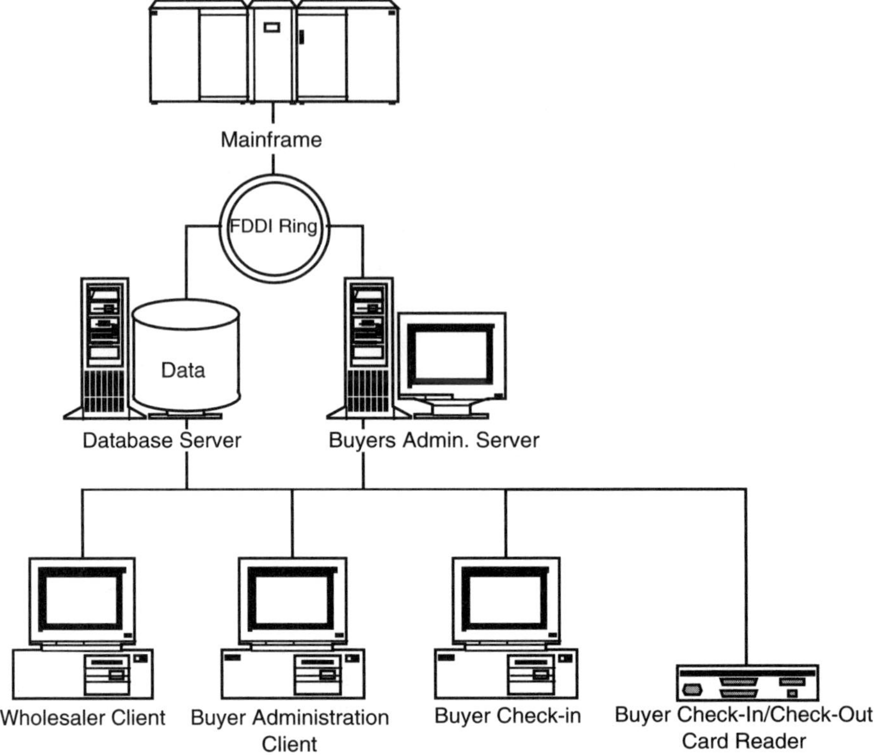

Figure 13–8 Three-Tier Client/Server Architecture for Fleury Market

When an organization must build the distributed computing infrastructure in parallel with the application, it may be preferable to deploy the application in phases; first as a two-tier application then as a multi-tier application when the infrastructure is built and the useage grows. This is possible if the application is *designed* as a multi-tier application, but then deployed in two-tier technology. This may be accomplished if attention is paid to designing granular software components with clearly defined interfaces.

In the case of Fleury Market, it was decided to design the application as a three-tier application, with each logical location becoming a client, an application server processing responses and temporal events, and a database server. For more information on the Fleury Market case study, please see Chapter 23, section 23.2.

During Technical Architecture Design (Chapter 14) the technical components will be chosen for the system and mapped to the architecture diagram shown in Figure 13–8. This includes hardware, operating systems, application development tools, connectivity tools, and management tools.

14

Technical Architecture Design

Selecting the Technology to Implement the System; Including Processors, Communications, Tools, and Components

In our work with many client/server projects, we have found over and over that the lack of a clearly defined enterprise-wide technical infrastructure slows implementation of projects. Because every distributed application must run on specific technology, the technical components can either be defined for each project or technical standards may be defined for the enterprise. Organizations that allow projects to choose technology end up with a "one of everything" architecture. These highly heterogeneous architectures make it more difficult to integrate new components and applications. The long-term support of these systems is difficult and expensive. In fact, up to a critical point increased heterogeny increases costs, then beyond that point, the number of permutations and combinations in the technical architecture makes it *impossible* to support. There will come a time when an application will fall over and you simply will not be able to isolate the fault to get it up and running again. Increased permutations and combinations in technical components always slows application deployment, thereby decreasing the ability of I/S to respond quickly to changing business needs. This point cannot be over-emphasized. It must be widely communicated to the entire I/S community as well as the business users. Process, procedures, and organizational structure must all be in place to ensure the distributed computing infrastructure is robust and supportable (see Part IV for further details). Figure 14–1 depicts the Technical Architecture design in the Implementation Model.

The process for designing the Technical Architecture has five steps (Figure 14–2). This process is appropriate for enterprise architecture planning. However, if there is no enterprise architecture, the entire process will have to be done on the project level. If there is an enterprise architecture, then projects do not have to spend time evaluating and choos-

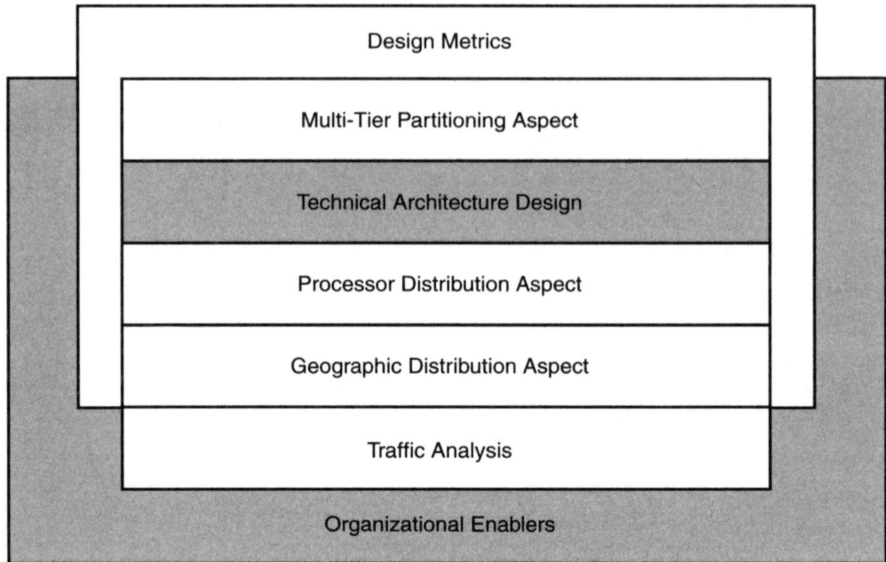

Figure 14–1 Implementation Model: Technical Architecture Design

ing technical components. Because multiple applications and groups will use the same technology, the enterprise will build more expertise in fewer technologies, further speeding implementation of business solutions.

Business Drivers are the key factors driving the business. They include factors such as shrinking cycle times, goals defined in strategic planning or business reengineering on the enterprise level, and the Statement of Purpose created for a project.

A Comprehensive I/S Inventory is required, including tools, applications, hardware, software, networks, protocols, staff, and skills.

Technology Requirements include a framework for all components of the technical architecture, including hardware, operating systems, development tools, databases, middleware, management tools, network components, and Internet/Intranet components.

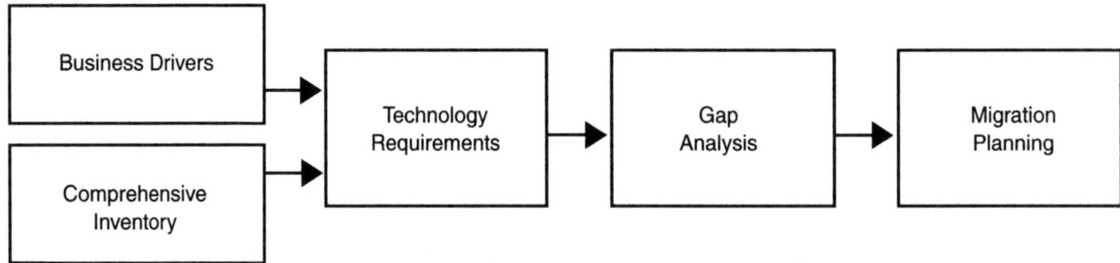

Figure 14–2 Technical Architecture Design Process

Gap Analysis is the first stage of Migration Planning. It maps key business drivers to the technology required to support those business processes. This yields a shopping list for technology that is required to meet the business needs.

Migration Planning is the process of prioritizing needs and creating a plan for implementing the technical infrastructure on a project-by-project basis.

14.1 BUSINESS DRIVERS

Adaptive Systems Require Process-Driven Architectures

The technical infrastructures that are failing today are failing because they cannot accommodate the rate of change in business processes. The "wrong relationship" is where technical infrastructure inhibits the deployment of new applications, which in turn negatively impacts an organization's ability to change. The "right relationship" occurs when the business processes drive the application architecture and technical infrastructure (Figure 14–3). In the past, it was not unusual for I/S to take the approach of buying the latest and greatest technology and then going out and finding a business use for it. Technical architectures were technology-driven, under the assumption that the latest and the greatest must be the best. The only problem with this approach was that while businesses spent millions on new technology, they were unable to demonstrate a return on investment. The new era of business downsizing and cost cutting has changed all that. Many organizations now require that technology investments show a return on investment within eighteen to twenty-four months.

The 'Right' Relationship
PROCESS-DRIVEN ARCHITECTURES

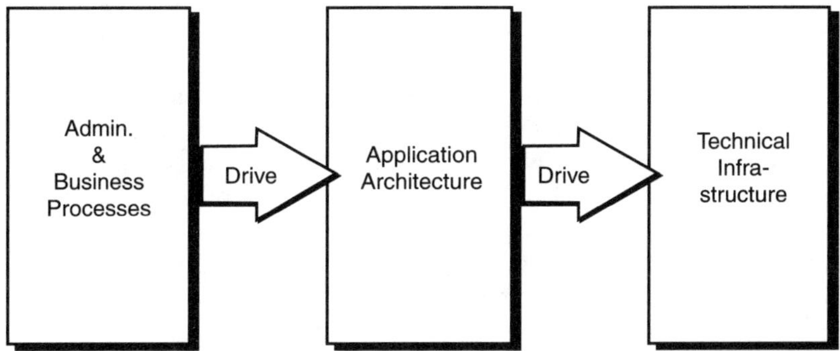

Figure 14–3 Process-Driven Architecture (By permission of Larry DeBoever, META Group)

Rapid changes in business practices and increased competition require the use of technology to sustain competitive advantage. I/S must become very focused on meeting the needs of the business and contributing to the bottom line, instead of being a cost center. Gone are the days when I/S receives a blank check to go play with the latest and greatest technology. Today, technology investments must be results-oriented. In order for this to occur, the Technical Architecture must be driven by the business it's built to support. We call this a process-driven architecture. This means that the application architecture enables rather than inhibits change. The technical infrastructure is then defined by the processing requirements and enables new application requirements to be rapidly deployed.

Because the "wrong relationship" inhibits an organization's ability to change, many executives are concluding that business needs must directly drive technology decisions, and not vice versa. This is a process driven architecture. In order to achieve a process driven architecture, I/S must become aligned with the business. This comes through understanding the core business processes and knowing the strategic plans for the future. This is also why the Technical Architecture Design process begins with understanding the business.

The first step in developing a process-driven architecture is to answer these questions:

- What are the key business processes?
- What technology is necessary to support the business?
- What currently owned technology and skillsets are available to meet the needs of the business?
- What new technology does the organization need to acquire?
- How should the organization migrate to new technology?

14.1.1 Defining Business Process Requirements

Key Business Drivers Determine Technology Requirements

The driving force for determining technology requirements is the business requirements. Business drivers include the universal business climate of shrinking cycle times. In our adaptive systems design method we fully define business requirements before any technology is considered. The method defines business processes in terms of events and responses to events, frequency and volumes of events, which business units have responsibility for each events, and where they geographically occur. We can put all this together in a way to map it to technology requirements.

To do this we use the Technical Architecture Design Document (Figure 14–4). First we define business drivers. Business drivers include the strategic initiatives of the organi-

Technical Architecture Design Document

Page ___ of ___
Date ________

Key Business Drivers (Note All Metrics)	Projects	Technology Requirements

Figure 14–4 Technical Architecture Design Document

zation. Enterprise business drivers are found in the strategic plan. Project business drivers are found in the Statement of Purpose.

14.1.2 Key Performance Requirements

Key Performance Requirements are Derived from Business Requirements

Technologists are very comfortable with defining performance requirements. But sometimes, these requirements seem similar to the beer commercial were one computer hobbyist describes his latest system configuration that has just slightly less power than an early model Cray computer. When his friend asks what he's going to do with all that power he answers, "Go on-line to pick up girls."

Although one of the major benefits of today's client/server technology is that it is highly scalable and can easily be upgraded in the future, the first inclination of many organizations is still to go out and buy a Unix machine which is the equivalent of a mainframe. This approach will negatively impact I/S's ability to consistently show a return on investment for their systems.

Key performance requirements must be business driven. Each requirement must map back to a business need. Types of performance requirements include major technical risks or challenges which may potentially impact the success of the system, high availability requirements, the need to support highly distributed business operations, large transaction volumes, and any other factors that may translate in processing requirements.

Key performance requirements are derived from the Component Measurement Aspect (Chapter 10). They are used as background information when choosing technology components. A single performance requirement may affect multiple components.

14.2 COMPREHENSIVE INVENTORY

Before You Move Forward, First Understand Where You Are

The successful introduction of new systems and technology requires a thorough understanding of what exists today. In many organizations there are *hundreds* of applications on a multitude of platforms. Robust management and systems integration in this environment is difficult to impossible. Yet many organizations do not yet have a comprehensive I/S inventory. In one large company the business users created the inventory just so they could gain a better understanding of the systems that were running their business. I/S management, however, refused to commit resources to finish and expand the inventory.

A comprehensive inventory is also the first step for addressing the Year 2000 problem. Companies are going to have to invest significant resources to ensure their systems will be viable past the turn of the turn of the century. Successful companies will be those who understand that the problem is far more reaching than fixing a date. Once you fix the date, will the system continue meet the changing needs of your business? Does it meet your needs now? Companies should carefully consider where their return on investment lies; fixing date functions in millions of lines of legacy code, or reengineering critical applications so they better support the business. We highly recommend that every organization take a complete I/S inventory, including a Technical Architecture Inventory, an Application Inventory, and a Skills Inventory.

14.2.1 Technical Architecture Inventory

Documenting All Existing Technology in the Organization

The purpose of the Technical Architecture Inventory is to document each and every piece of hardware, software, firmware, and network component. This document will be used in planning the new architecture and the Gap Analysis process. Therefore, it is also important to include whether it is an enterprise standard. Figure 14–5 is a sample of a Technical Inventory Form. It can be modified as required to better meet the needs of your organization.

Technical Component	Product Name	Configuration (Including Version #)	Standard (Y or N)	Notes
Servers				
Small				
Medium				
Huge				
Clients				
Desktop				
Mobile				
Development Tools				
Client				
Server				
Database				
Desktop Tools				
Office Suite				
Database				
Other				
Process Management				
Testing Tools				
Networks				
Protocols				
Topology				
Network Interface Card				
Modem				
LAN OS				
MAN				
WAN				
Middleware				
Naming Services				
Time Services				
Security				
Database API				
Database Gateway				
Messaging				
RPC				
ORB				
TP Monitor				

(continued)

Figure 14–5 Existing Technical Architecture Inventory

Technical Component	Product Name	Configuration (Including Version #)	Standard (Y or N)	Notes
Internet/Intranet				
Secure Web Server				
Nonsecure Web Server				
Web Browser				
Web Authoring Tool				
Web Development				
Search Engine				
Firewall/Security				
Groupware				
Database Connectivity				

Figure 14–5 Existing Technical Architecture Inventory *Continued*

14.2.2 Application Inventory

Documenting All Existing Applications and the Interaction Between Applications

Many organizations find themselves in a position today where they have *hundreds* of applications in their organization, some of which they no longer can maintain because everyone who built them is gone, or have kludgy extensions to support new business processes they were never built to support. Moreover, the information is shared across applications, either electronically or by taking reports produced by one systems and reentering them into another systems. The reverse is also true where different systems *should* share data, but instead redundantly recapture the data thereby creating data inconsistencies. Known inconsistencies must often be addressed in the batch cycle, which must include multiple reconciliation processes. Companies that face the problem of not finishing their batch cycle on time should look at the design of their application and data architecture and simplify in order to eliminate the need for multiple reconciliation processes. The first step in this process is also an Application Inventory.

The purpose of the Application Inventory is to understand the total processing environment across the organization. This will greatly aid in designing a comprehensive distributed architecture because it will help map the scope and responsibilities of current applications and information sharing across the organization (see Figure 14–6). The problem with the current architecture is that the applications weren't *designed* to integrate with each other, therefore it is not surprising that it is very difficult to get them to do so. To be effective, the new architecture must be designed to support information sharing across the organization. The existing Application Architecture also helps define migration priorities.

Application Name	Business Unit	Category (MF, PC, 2-Tier C/S, n-Tier C/S)	Data Source	Data Dest.	Platform	Language

Figure 14–6 Application Inventory

14.2.3 Skills Inventory

Documenting Existing Skillsets Within the I/S Organization

A skills inventory is important for planning support of existing applications and for choosing the new Technical Architecture. The investment an organization has in existing skills and in developing new skills should not be underestimated. Many of our clients have told us that one of the most difficult challenges they face is in keeping skills within their organization. Existing skillsets within a company may be an important factor when deciding on which technology to use. Training is time consuming and expensive. Effective utilization of skills across the organization can yield the same cost benefits as reusing other components of the technical architecture.

Figures 14–7 and 14–8 are examples of the information captured in a Skills Inventory. We actually recommend a skills database, to accommodate the many-to-many relationships that will arise because a single employee will have multiple skills, and a skill will be possessed by multiple employees. Therefore, the purpose of this table is to identify the types of information to capture in a skills inventory. We view this as a starting point of your inventory. Add more skills as you deem necessary.

14.3 TECHNOLOGY REQUIREMENTS

Components of the Technical Architecture are Chosen to Meet Changing Business Requirements

The Technical Architecture defines all components of the technical infrastructure required to meet the business needs. However, to meet changing business needs, I/S must learn the art of finding the balance between being driven by a return on investment and being driven by adaptability. This is accomplished by building systems with an adaptive range. This adaptive range translates into buying or building in an average of 15%–20% more capacity than what is immediately required, so I/S can quickly respond to business needs

Skill	**Department**	**Employee**
Programming Languages:		
COBOL		
C++		
PowerBuilder		
Visual Basic (etc.)		
Database		
Oracle:		
Design		
Performance Tuning		
Triggers/Stored Proc.		
API		
Gateway		
Sybase (etc.)		
(See categories above)		
Network		
Architecture Design		
Monitoring		
Capacity Planning		
Protocols		
Maintenance		
Security		
Backup and Recovery		
Internet		
HTML		
Server Maintenance		
Project Management		
Systems Design		
Testing		
Procurement		

Figure 14–7 Skill Inventory Listing All Skills

Employee Name	**Employee #/Dept.**	**Skill**	**Proficiency**

Figure 14–8 Skill Inventory by Employee

when they change. This adaptive range, however, is a far cry from buying the Unix mainframe equivalent without knowing what it will be used for.

The following is an explanation of the components that may be included in the Technical Architecture. These include clients, servers, development tools, databases, network components, communication protocols, middleware, Intranets, groupware, and Internet connectivity.

14.3.1 Servers

The Most Important Thing About Choosing Servers is to Standardize on Vendors, Models, Versions of Operating Systems, and Software Configurations

Server hardware choices abound; they include the mainframe, Intel, MIPS, Alpha, and RISC machines. Many organizations choose servers on a project-by-project basis and are left with a plethora of hardware platforms and operating systems from different vendors, which translates into a support and maintenance nightmare. If I/S is going to be successful it is going to have to allocate more of its shrinking resources to supporting the changing needs of the business rather than maintaining the legacy systems. The key is to standardize on servers to enable binary compatibility across platforms. Remember, MIPs are now the least expensive part of the system, and support personnel is the most expensive. It is cheaper to throw more processing power at the problem than it is to maintain a plethora of different software configurations. Hand-crafted, finely tuned servers tend to be as reliable as the old Jaguars. They require too much support. Further, adding new applications to the same server, or changing servers, is hampered by extensive custom tuning parameters.

The fast server technology is being built on 64-bit platforms, which provides 32^{32} more addressable memory than a 32-bit system. Oracle's 64-bit VLDBMS allows huge amounts of data to be cached in memory, thereby enabling very fast access to very large amounts of data. Previously the database needed to be designed and tuned for performance. Now hardware can solve many of the problems. Another hardware decision point for large systems and databases, such as data warehouses, is whether to go with a symmetric multi-processing (SMP) or massively parallel processing (MPP) architecture. An SMP machine contains multiple processors within the same chassis sharing memory. It is sometimes also called shared memory processing. In an SMP architecture, different processes are spawned to different processes, thereby enabling greater throughput. SMP is a highly scalable architecture. As the number of users grow, it is fairly easy to simply add additional processors. However, there is a physical limit to the number of processors that can be put in one box. Technology is now available to cluster SMP systems. This enables highly scalable systems to be built with commodity components. An alternative to SMP for very large systems is massively parallel processing (MPP), which is a shared nothing architecture. MPP systems do not have the same restrictions of scalability that SMP systems do. But for the most part they are proprietary technology. The trend seems to be moving towards clustered SMP architectures that can give almost the same scalability as MPP systems.

The choice for a hardware platform depends on the category of server required. Small servers (under $20,000) are often needed for a particular application—either custom built or purchased packages. Small servers are often NT or SCO Unix machines, depending upon the installed base of applications within the organization.

Mid-range servers (under $100,000) are required for departmental solutions, including data marts or departmental decision support systems. Some organizations use only small and mid-range servers. This strategy allows maximum flexibility for deploying adaptive systems. It does, however, cost more to support. Although the installed base of mid-range servers is currently Unix, we see adoption of NT rising. Microsoft's introduction of SMS for systems management, Exchange for messaging, and Internet support for all their applications is making the Microsoft strategy attractive to many organizations.

Very large servers (over $100,000) are generally used for data warehouses and enterprise systems with many users. Some companies buy very large servers and use them like Unix mainframes. However, these systems are not as easy to deploy and change as many smaller servers.

The key to a server strategy is to standardize on the platform, operating system, and configuration for each category of server. It is cheaper to upgrade a server box with more processing power than it is to do performance tuning on each server and then maintain multiple configurations on different servers. In general, heterogeneity inhibits adaptive systems.

14.3.2 Development Tools

There Are No Silver Bullets

There are different development tools for different tiers in the application architecture, including client development tools, server development tools, and database development tools. There are also tools that claim to do it all, including generating all the middleware. However, organizations should beware of the silver bullet approach, because it may leave you with a proprietary solution, which will not help you to integrate legacy systems and purchased applications. The real silver bullet is good adaptive systems design.

The key to choosing development tools is to standardize on a small set of tools for each type of platform. Many early adopters of client/server technology now find themselves with "one of everything" because their buying decisions were driven by developers who wanted to learn the hottest new technology. The problem with this approach is that after completion of the project the programmer often leaves to earn more money elsewhere. The organization is then stuck with yet another platform to support as well as the requirements to maintain that skillset within the organization as long as the application is around.

Today, the major categories are two-tier development tools, which can also be used as client development tools in a multi-tier architecture, multi-tier development tools, and Internet/intranet tools.

14.3.2.1 Two-Tier Client Development Tools

Rapid application development (RAD) is made possible through the use of new graphical application development tools. These tools require far less coding than the third generation languages such as COBOL and FORTRAN. Today, all are object oriented and enable rapid prototyping and building of graphical applications. The most popular ones include PowerBuilder from PowerSoft, a subsidiary of Sybase, SQL Windows from Centura (formerly Gupta), Delphi from Borland, and Visual Basic from Microsoft. Java is also becoming more popular as the demand for Internet and intranet applications increases. PowerBuilder gained an early market lead by putting database connectivity right in the box. Today it maintains that lead. However, Visual Basic is extremely popular due to low cost and large installed base. More recently, Delphi has gained momentum in the market.

Many organizations struggle with the decision of which development tool to buy. Often, it is developers who wish to gain new programming skills that are pushing for new tools. Many organizations find themselves with a conglomeration of development tools and a maintenance problem on their hands. Although it is unlikely that one tool will meet all needs, it is highly recommended that organizations standardize on a small set of tools and establish guidelines for choosing a tool for a particular project. Note that the current two-tier development tools are evolving into multi-tier and Internet tools. However, today they do not have the same level of functionality as the multi-tier tools.

Object-Oriented tools The popular RAD tools are all object oriented in that they support some form of encapsulation, polymorphism, and inheritance. However, for the most part, the objects being built are application objects—push buttons, pull-down menus, scroll bars, etc. These are different from business objects, such as customers or products. The RAD tools just take care of the GUI front end code. Business objects generally are stored on servers and written in object-oriented languages such as C++, SmallTalk, and application development environments that produce C++ and SmallTalk such as VisualAge from IBM. When building business objects, the issue then becomes how to give persistence to those objects, or how to store them. The choice is to disassemble them as objects and store the data in relational databases and the processing code on the server, or to use an object database. The former solution is used by organizations that are not ready to take a chance on the object database vendors, which tend to be small companies. They are waiting for object support from their preferred database vendors. Currently Informix supports an object-relational model, and Oracle and Sybase have announced support in upcoming releases.

Cross Platform Companies that have a mixture of computing environments have the problem of deploying applications across different platforms such as Windows, Mac, and Unix. The choice is to write the application for each application or use a tool that enables the company to write the application once and just recompile it for each platform. These development tools tend to be far more expensive than single platform tools but can save money in the long run for companies with heterogeneous environments. These tools include Uniface, SmallTalk, Neuron OpenInterface, Unify, Galaxy, and XVT.

14.3.2.2 Multi-Tier Tools

The new high-end tools are those which support partitioning across a multi-tier architecture. Many of these tools grew out of the cross-platform market. Some of these tools automatically generate the middleware between tiers as well as the binary code for each target platform. Another benefit of these tools is that they enable all tiers of the application to be written in one tool. We see this market exploding at the present time with offerings from Antares Alliance Group (ObjectStar), Compuware (Uniface), Forte (Forte), IBM (VisualAge), Seer Technologies (Seer/7000), Texas Instruments (Performer and Composer), Dynasty (Dynasty), Intersolv (AppMaster), Magic Software (Magic), Nat Systems (NatStar), Passport (Passport), Prolifics (JYACC), and Unify (Vision).

14.3.2.3 Internet/Intranet

An alternative to cross-platform development that many organizations are now exploring is the intranet. Intranets use Internet Web technology, and enable platform independent deployment through Web browsers that are universal clients. Technology is now becoming available to deliver on-line processing capabilities over the Web through applets that are program modules downloaded and executed only during runtime. The applets do not have to be installed on the client machines. This is the benefit of Java. As Java development tools become more sophisticated, they may become more popular for all client/server development. Microsoft is also extending the capabilities of Visual Basic to compete with Java. However, Java Active-x based development environments are far less mature than existing client/server tools. For more information on Internet/intranet Architectures see section 14.3.10.

14.3.2.4 Server Development Tools

These tools are used to develop the business rules and application processing that run on servers. They include the three-tier development tools which partition the application into client code containing the user interface, server code containing the application logic, and a database on the back end. These are also multi-platform tools that write the middleware to connect the heterogeneous platforms. Generally they carry a very large price tag compared with RAD tools.

Multi-tier applications can also be built with a component tools approach. The presentation tier can be developed using GUI RAD tools or a Web browser. An enterprise middleware infrastructure can be created with a messaging engine, transaction processing (TP) monitor, and open database connectivity software. Another tool or compiler can be used to develop server code, such as C and C++ development environments, SmallTalk, and COBOL. Business rules can also be programmed in DBMS specific triggers and stored procedures. However, this results in a database-specific solution.

We have found that the most important issue involving development tools is to minimize the number of different tools within the company. Each additional software platform increases maintenance and support costs and complexity. Today, many organizations are reducing personnel in support and maintenance roles. This strategy will only succeed if the organization is successful in minimizing the number of different environments they need to support.

A process we have successfully used with many organizations in guiding them through tool selection is to start with a list of product features, weight the features on a scale of one to four in order of importance, then rate each of the products. Figure 14–19 depicts a table we have successfully used to help teams quickly work through the process of choosing

	Your Rating	Power Builder		Visual Basic	
		Raw	***Weighted***	***Raw***	***Weighted***
Business Factors					
Vendor stability & marketshare					
Vendor support					
Product stability					
Business partner relationships					
Product Features					
Support for common look & feel					
Report writer					
Integrated development environment					
Debugger					
Ease of use/time to become proficient					
Speed of development					
Screen design/prototyping					
Performance					
Cost					
Object-oriented support					
Compiler					
DDE, DLL, OLE support					
Database connectivity					
Integration of third party tools					
Documentation					
GUI functionality & flexibility					
Cross-platform functionality					
Scalability					
Runs on target platforms					
Personnel Issues					
Ease of finding skilled personnel					
Cost of skilled personnel					
Availability of training					

Figure 14–9 Application Development Tool Selection

a tool. There are no magic numbers. But we have found the process helps build consensus. The most important thing is to choose and move on. We have found that many teams get stuck at this stage. Yet the success of the project depends less on which tool you use than on how you use it, that is, how the application is designed. We need to get accustomed to the idea that technology changes very rapidly, and no matter what level of due diligence we perform in making critical technology decisions. The best we can do is make the right decision for the time and move on. Inevitably, technology will change, and we may wish we had made different decisions. Multi-tier application designs can help, because they enable you to replace different components without redesigning other components.

14.3.3 Database

Database Technology Must Support Accelerated Decision Making

The key to choosing database technology is understanding the business requirement to accelerate decision making. The success of a company depends on the decisions it makes, and better decisions require better information. To paraphrase Sherlock Holmes, in today's competitive business climate, "To reason with inadequate information is dangerous."

To accomplish this, organizations must evolve from a PULL model of information access to a PUSH model of information leverage. In the PULL model of information access, the onus is on the knowledge worker to determine the information required and request that information. It assumes that the knowledge worker understands the data, how to use the tool, the results returned, and any incorrect results. In the PUSH model of information leverage, the database automatically initiates activity to notify the appropriate user of a recent event (typically via electronic mail, beeping, sending a fax, and so forth). The difference is the timeliness of event-driven information delivery versus report generation. The questions get stored in the database. The goal of the knowledge worker becomes one of creating new questions that will deliver new types of information and analysis. Examples include the ability to alert managers when certain thresholds are reached. This capability is implemented with database trigger technology and, of course, design.

The other key to accelerated decision making is the ability to get the information where it is needed; in the hands of the decision makers. This means distributed and replicated data will be found throughout the organization. A clearly defined data architecture, with authoritative sources defined and managed, are key to maintaining the quality and integrity of distributed data. Tools to manage distributed data are also required.

When you choose a DBMS vendor, you are also choosing a business partner. It is important to evaluate the partnership as well as the product. What kind of partnerships does the vendor have with other vendors? What kind of service guarantees can the vendor give? These questions are as important as the technical features of the product.

The relentless quest on the part of organizations for more and more information is evident in the explosion of database sizes. Whereas multi-gigabyte databases seemed extremely large just a few years ago, they are now the norm, with large databases pushing into the terabytes. There have been a number of technological developments enabling very large databases. Hardware architectures, especially SMP and MPP are highly scalable and when combined with parallel query optimization they make it possible to process requests against very large data sets. Parallel query optimization refers the DBMS's ability to take a query (particularly a complex one) and parse it so it runs on multiple processors simultaneously. Data replication and distribution technologies make it far easier to make information available to business users when and where they need it.

While relational databases have become the standard for client/server systems, multidimensional databases are widely used for "on-line analytical processing" (OLAP) systems. A multidimensional database provides much better performance for in-depth information analysis, where canned queries and reports are not useful because the user poses new queries based on the results of the previous query. Analysts looking for trends over time, regions, products, stores, and salespeople, pose the types of questions that multidimensional databases were designed to answer. Some multidimensional databases allow for pass-through SQL access to relational databases when the information is not found in the multidimensional database. It must be noted that these databases are not suitable for on-line transaction processing. In fact, the indexes often take a long time to build and the databases, therefore, take a long time to load.

As more and more organizations adopt object oriented technology the big issue is how they will store, or give persistence to, the business objects they create. Many organizations use runtime objects, but store the data in relational databases. Object databases make it possible to store and access complex objects much more quickly. Currently there are a number of object database vendors, but they are all small companies. The major database vendors are in various stages of developing and deploying object/relational technology, where the database will be able to store complex objects. The decision of which type of database technology to choose depends on the needs of the organization and the strategic vendor partnerships the organization decides upon. Figure 14–10 is a comparison of different database technologies. It is our belief that object/relational technology will solve many of the problems of complex object storage. Object/relational technology also offers the ability to create single enterprise reuse repositories that hold the enterprise data dictionary (meta data), data models, design models, project documentation, and source code (including components and objects).

Some applications, such as salesforce automation, require that data and a DBMS be on the client. The choices are growing. The former PC databases have evolved into desktop systems capable of connecting to enterprise systems. The major vendors of PC data-

DMBS/ Application	Hierarchical	Network	Relational	Object	Multi-Dimensional	Object Relational
High Performance OLTP	X	X	X	X		?
Many-to-Many (Bill of Materials)		X	X			X
Complex Data Types				X		X
On-Line Analytical Processing					X	

Figure 14–10 Comparison of Different Types of Database Management Systems

bases include Sybase with SQL Anywhere, Microsoft with both Access and FoxPro, Borland with Delphi, and 4th Dimension for the Mac.

14.3.4 Design/Process Management Tools

Choosing Between Two-Tier and Multi-Tier Architectures

In many organizations programmers hold the formal title of "Software Engineer" while continuing to practice artisan programming. Few I/S organizations have completely transformed themselves into a culture that can quickly and reliably deliver systems on-time, on-budget, which meet the needs of the business today, and can easily adapt to meet the changing needs of tomorrow. This requires a culture of reuse, design reviews, and development standards.

All of the above are supported through a growing area of tools for managing the process of building applications. Smaller, narrower focus tools called "lower case" have replaced the older "upper case" tools, which carried high price tags and often failed to achieve a return on investment. Tools for database design include ER-Win, Bachman, Info Modeler, and S-Designer. Tools for modeling system design include System Architect, Oracle CASE, and LBMS System Engineer. When choosing a modeling tool it is important to make sure the tool supports the notation to which you have standardized. The value of the models over time lies in their continued use and the information they provide to each new project.

Process Management tools enable a software engineering process to be standardized, distributed, and managed across projects. They promote predictable and repeatable results by providing process, guidelines, instructions, explanations, and templates. Project managers can customize the process to fit the project, and manage through deliverables (artifacts). These tools contribute to the success of projects because they incorporate best practices, allowing everyone to benefit from the expertise of a few. Examples of process management tools include LBMS and SECA. Some organizations are now building intranet applications for this purpose.

14.3.5 Testing Tools

Testing Event-Driven Distributed Systems is Highly Complex Because of the Different Possible Scenarios

Testing event-based GUI distributed systems are far more difficult than testing central linear programs. In the latter case, step-through testing is sufficient. In the former, it is often impossible to predict the exact sequence of events that will fire a process. Some testing tools greatly aid the process by automating test suites to simulate concurrent users across a network. The testing tool should include an excellent defect tracking system. While testing tools are often limited in their scope and do not test for everything in the distributed environment, such tools end up paying for themselves if the chosen tool supports automated test planning, validation of user interface elements, client/server performance testing, regression testing, stress testing, and defect tracking. Some of the testing tools integrate easily with the more popular development environments. There are over 1200 testing tools on the market; some a holdover for mainframe testing. The more popular client/server testing tools include SQA Team Test, Mercury Interactive, ATF, Automator QACenter, Microsoft Test, Segue—QA Partner, and Sterling TestPro.

14.3.6 Operating Systems

The Fewer the Operating Systems, the Easier it is to Deploy and Support New Systems

The most important thing about operating systems is to standardize as much as possible. Although all large organizations will continue to have multiple operating system platforms for clients, servers, and mainframes, supporting all the different systems becomes even more difficult when versions of operating systems are allowed to proliferate. We recommend standardizing on one operating system for each type of platform in the organization, including clients, small, mid-range, and large servers, and mainframes. By standardization we also mean the same version of the operating system on each and every machine. We do not recommend phased roll-outs of new operating system versions. We do recommend testing all new versions thoroughly, then once you decide to migrate to it, do it all at once. We also recognize this is a challenge when it comes to thousands of desktops, especially when a new operating system requires a hardware upgrade. Some of these problems are being addressed with new systems management tools. Vendors are also providing "evergreen" service contracts, which enable a company to upgrade desktop systems all at once and pay for it over the course of the contract. This issue is driving the corporate interest in network PCs.

On the desktop, it is clear that Windows '95 is the current winner. Unfortunately OS/2, a technically superior operating system to Windows 3.x, never gained the mind share or market share. IBM has been forced to support the Windows '95/NT path. Windows NT is a better solution for power users and complex applications. It has preemptive multi-tasking, meaning that if one process fails it will not impact the other processes running on the machine. Many organizations have Macs. It always seems that Mac users are passionate about their computers and would rather fight than switch. However, building and supporting cross-platform applications for both Mac and Windows is expensive and complex. It greatly restricts the tool choices. While it is most difficult to standardize on the desktop, some organizations are developing strict desktop standards as a matter of support survival.

14.3.7 System Management Tools

System Management Tools are Required to Support Distributed Systems

Over the past quarter of a century, I/S has learned to make mission-critical systems extremely robust so they can run 24 hours per day, 7 days per week, 365 days per year. Robust systems require a robust set of system management tools. As client/server technology matures, these tools are finally becoming available for distributed platforms. In general, distributed systems management is far more complex than mainframe operations management. The types of tools required include the following:

- Version Control
- Software Distribution
- Document Management
- Network Management
- Systems Administration
- Performance Monitoring and Capacity Planning
- Application Monitoring
- Security
- Event Management
- Backup and Recovery

These tools need to manage systems across hardware platforms and across networks. The goal is to use tools to enable a "virtual data center." A virtual center is the same concept as a "glass house" approach, where all computing resources are in one place for management. However, the virtual data center may be a locked utility on an offshore oil platform that is managed from a central location. Tools that enable the remote management of system components are necessary for creating robust distributed systems.

14.3.8 Network Components

The Network is the Most Important Underlying Infrastructure of Distributed Systems

The network is an enabling technology for client/server computing. Without the network, which is an interconnected collection of autonomous computers, there can be no physical distribution of an application. Network components allow access to a wide spectrum of information, applications, and resources. They expand the reach of organizations to customers and suppliers. The network is the essential delivery mechanism for distributed computing services. When it comes to client/server design, the network is a risk factor. The application will only perform as well as its weakest component, and sometimes this can be the network. If improperly designed, the network can perform poorly, be unreliable, impede application components from interacting, and make it very difficult to isolate faults. Even if the network is properly designed, poor or no management of it can lead to the same negative impacts previously mentioned. We now present some very basic architectural principles about networks to give you a feel for the most general design choices you will have to make to ensure the network portion of your infrastructure supports your client/server designs. It is important for network architects to be involved in the project planning as well and enterprise planning efforts, because the network is now part of the applications.

It is especially important to standardize on notebook systems and modems. Some organizations have found it cheaper to buy all their users new modems than to try to support remote access configurations for multiple modems. Standardizing on all components that connect to the network, including network interface cards, simplifies support. The number one reason for calls to the help desk is about problems gaining access to the network.

14.3.8.1 Protocols

The physical portion of the network is typically some kind of wire (twisted pair, coaxial cable, fiber optic) which connects two or more computers together. However, wiring alone will not make the computers communicate. What is also needed is an agreed upon way for the communication to occur. A protocol is a specification of that communication standard. Protocols are a communication language. They have a fixed syntax, which defines the format of data and the signal by which that data is transmitted over the wire. A good analogy is an envelope. To mail a letter, you need to put the address of the person you're sending it to in the middle, and the return address in the upper left hand corner. If you decided to switch the two, the letter would just come back to you. The protocol defines the "packets." The packets contain semantics that control and coordinate how data is transmitted.

The OSI Network Architecture model is an architecture that defines protocols for different layers of the communication process. The design principle of the OSI model is modularity. Each layer has a defined set of functions that can be accessed only by the layers directly above and below it through a defined interface. This modular architecture makes it easy to integrate new technology for a particular layer without affecting the other layers. Essentially, when an application sends a message to another application on a remote server, the message is "wrapped" in multiple protocol layers which, when combined, guarantee the delivery of the message. Then the packet is sent over the physical wire, and "unwrapped" by the receiving application (see Figure 14–11).

14.3.8.2 Topology

The way in which devices are connected to the network and how they gain access to the network is called the topology. There are three kinds of topology generally in use today: bus, ring, and star. In the United States, the most common topologies are Ethernet (a bus topology) and Token Ring. The major difference between them is the access protocol they use. Token Ring uses token passing. Tokens are continually passed

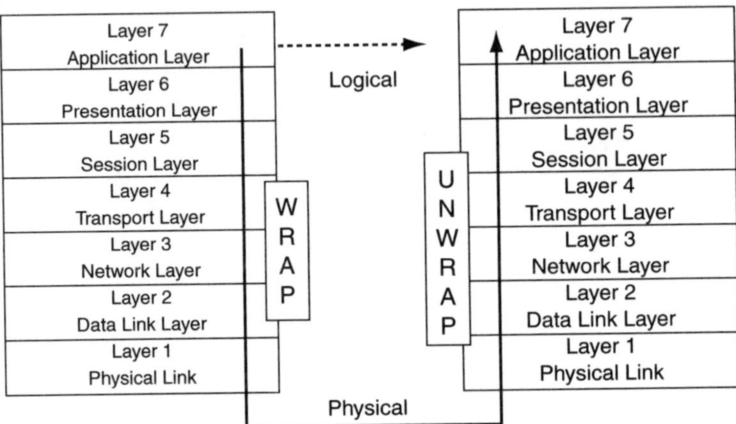

Figure 14–11 The Seven-Layer OSI Network Architecture Model

around the ring. When a computer wants to send a message, its places it into a free token. The token gets passed around the ring until it reaches the machine that is supposed to receive the message. Token Ring is a deterministic topology. Access to the network is determined by the number of tokens available and the number of users on the network. In times of heavy useage, performance degradation is far more graceful than Ethernet. The overhead for network management is constant for managing the tokens being passed.

Access to an Ethernet network is through contention. It is like the old telephone "party line," where different users share the same line, but can only send a message (make a call) when the line isn't busy. Therefore, users are in contention to gain access to the line. If two users detect a free line at the same time and both attempt to transmit a message, a collision will occur, and both messages will be damaged and need to be resent. The overhead for managing an Ethernet network comes from managing collisions. Performance on Ethernet networks degrades ungracefully under heavy loads, as contention increases. Under lighter loads, it has better throughput than Token Ring. The development of fast Ethernet that can transmit data at 100 Mbits/second is edging out Token Ring technology.

14.3.8.3 Network Interface Cards (NICs)

Gaining access to either a Token Ring or Ethernet network requires a network interface card (NIC). There are NICs specifically for Token Ring or Ethernet. In terms of distributed application performance, the NIC can sometimes create problems, especially if it is older technology or conversely, brand new technology. It can create incompatibilities with existing components and application programming interfaces (APIs). In organizations that have multiple network topologies, client workstations will require multiple NICs.

14.3.8.4 LANs, MANs, and WANs

A LAN is a local area network (LAN) which connects computers on a floor or within a building. A MAN is a metropolitan area network that interconnects LANs on a campus or a defined geographical area, larger than one building. A WAN is a wide area network that enables geographically dispersed computers to communicate.

LANs are used to connect a limited number of nodes (devices including clients, servers, printers, modems, and fax servers) within a relatively small geographic region. Multiple LANs can be interconnected with bridges, routers, or bridge/routers (brouters). A bridge connects two LANs using physical addresses (managed by Layer 1 of the OSI model), and the connection is restricted to one and only one path. A router uses special tables which contain network information (managed by Layer 3 of the OSI model). Thus, if one connection fails, the tables can be used to dynamically create an alternative path. A brouter is more intelligent than a router. It enables messages to be encapsulated so that only protocol is transmitted over the network.

A wide area network (WAN) provides communication links to geographically dispersed sites over private or public telephone lines. The wiring for this kind of a link can be one of four types:

1. Fiber Distributed Data Interface (FDDI), which provides high-speed message transfers over fiber optic cable
2. Ethernet, which (now with version II) provides 100 megabit per second transfer rates
3. Integrated Services Digital Network (ISDN), which uses regular (hence inexpensive) telephone lines for high-speed transfers of voice and data
4. Broadband ISDN, which runs on coax cable.

The message transfer methods for WANs are as follows:

1. X.253, which is the 1976 standard for transferring "switched packets"
2. Frame relay, which is a switched packet technology that can dynamically allocate bandwidth
3. ATM, which allows gigabit transfers of voice, data, and video on demand.

Today many WANs are built with frame relay technology. However, ATM technology is clearly a promising technology for the future. Many network companies have merged over the past few years to provide end-to-end ATM solutions. Solution providers are also offering pay-as-you-go networks for transmission of data. The phone companies have been laying fiber optic cable across the country. The cable companies have also been busy connecting homes with broadband coaxial cable suitable for high bandwidth transmissions necessary for full motion video. Cable modems are now being introduced. The battle lines are clearly being drawn between the cable and telephone providers.

Other components of the network architecture include the network operating system e-mail server, e-mail gateway (required if more than one e-mail system is present), mail readers which "grab" mail off the server and allow users to read and compose replies off-line, and directory services.

14.3.9 Middleware

Middleware Enables Adaptive Systems by Insulating Application Developers from the Underlying Complexities and Details of Network Connectivity

Middleware connects the software components of a distributed application. Middleware insulates the application designer from having to write to the lower level protocols of the OSI architecture, thereby providing application independence from the underlying network infrastructure. There are different types of middleware that provide a menu of services, including database connectivity, SQL translation among heterogeneous databases, interprocess connectivity, time synchronization, distributed directories, security, and transaction management. The ultimate goal is to provide adaptability, responsiveness, and leverage. Application developers code to the middleware layer. Then the application programs remain unaffected as the internals of the middleware change due to changes in the technical infrastructure.

The two basic kinds of categories for middleware are data passing and process transfer. Currently, roughly 90% of all applications employ data passing, but as more applications are built using three-tier and logical multi-tier architecture, process transfer middleware will become more widely used.

14.3.9.1 DCE

The Distributed Computing Environment (DCE) was developed by the Open Software Foundation (OSF). OSF is an industry consortium formed to solve the problem of having different Unix systems talk to each other across networks. First OSF defined the requirements for interoperable distributed systems. This resulted in a comprehensive framework they called DCE. They then put out a Request for Technology and different vendors offered solutions. OSF then chose some vendor solutions as standards. Although DCE has not been widely adoped, it is useful to look at DCE as a comprehensive middleware architecture for distributed computing. Figure 14–12 depicts the components of DCE.

Different vendors supply DCE solutions. The gray areas in Figure 14–12 indicate areas of the architecture that have been defined but which vendors have not provided solutions for. Time synchronization services provide transaction synchronization across time zones. Directory services provide location transparency for any type of network. Security services are based on MIT's Kerberos which ensures user authentication. It is the most robust security available for distributed computing, but requires more application overhead.

Although DCE provides open systems solutions, it is complex to implement, has limited language support (only "C"), and requires substantial labor and system resources, as well as an enterprise-wide commitment.

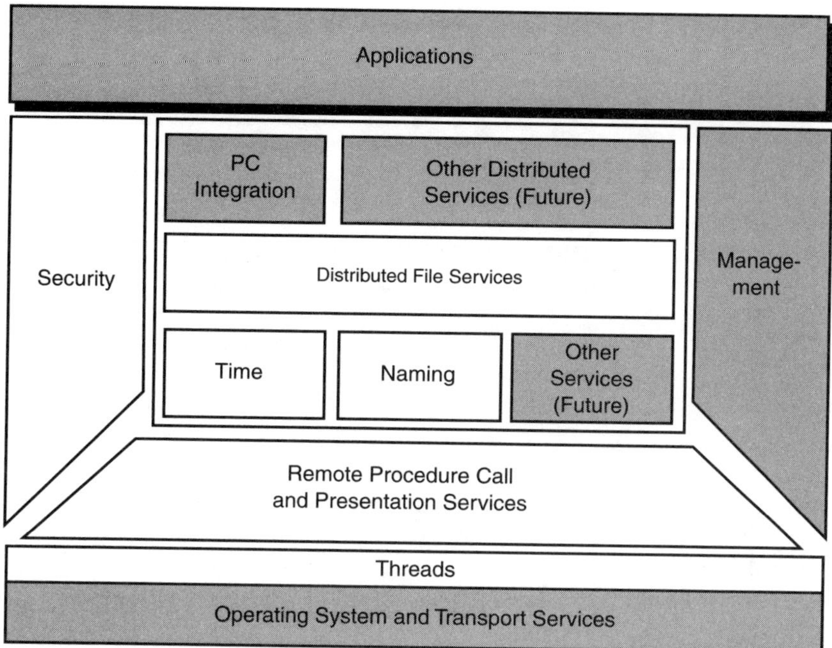

Figure 14–12 The Distributed Computing Environment Architecture

14.3.9.2 Data-Passing Middleware

Data-Passing Middleware Predominated Early Client/Server Efforts

Data-passing middleware connects clients to target server databases using SQL. The application running on a PC sends a SQL call to a database on a server via an application programming interface (API). An API is a set of function calls which allow the application to call the services of the server. Figure 14–13 is an example of how a client communicates through an API to a server using data passing middleware. APIs can either be specific to the application software or common across vendor applications. For example, Oracle, Sybase, Informix, and DB2 (to name but a few) each have their own APIs. An alternative is ODBC (Open Database Connectivity), developed by Microsoft which can connect to any database that has an ODBC driver. Data passing is an effective mechanism for simple two-tier client/server applications, for multi-tier decision support applications, and for those applications with few users or scalability requirements.

Database Gateways enable applications to connect to heterogeneous data sources via SQL calls. Some gateways even connect to nonrelational data sources. Gateway products may offer different levels of functionality. A gateway may enable read only access or full SQL support, including update capability. A gateway may be unidirectional, which means the requesting database can access the target database, but not the other way

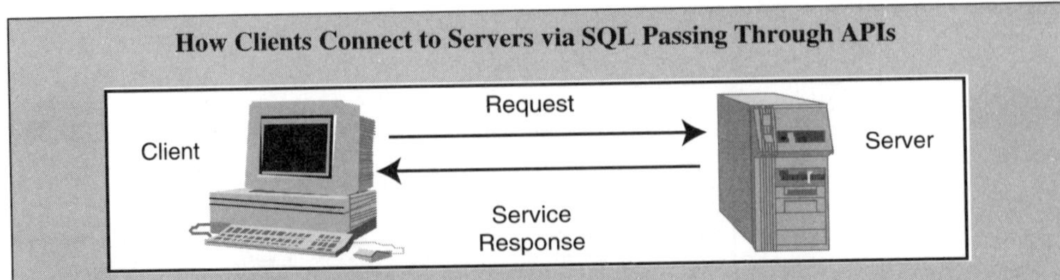

1. Client generates requests for services to a server.

This is done by invoking the functions of an application programming interface (API). A piece of the API resides on the client (the requester piece), and a piece of the API resides on the server (the listener piece). The server has a process running at all times listening for requests (in Unix terms, it's an agent).

The request for services (via SQL, RPC, messaging, ORB) is packaged via a network protocol. This is the common language the client and server speak.

2. Server processes requests for services.

Available services depends on the type of server including: database server, application server, transaction server, communication server, object server. Response is communicated back to the client via an API and network protocol.

3. Client displays and manipulates results.

Figure 14–13 Examples of How a Client Connects to a Server via Data Passing

around. A gateway may be bidirectional. Most products on the market today are unidirectional because each translation process is a separate engineering effort. In other words, a bidirectional gateway would actually be two separately engineered gateways packaged together. A gateway may offer only pass-through SQL or full SQL translation. Pass-through SQL means that the target data source must understand the SQL call, which in turn means that the programmer must program the SQL call in the native syntax. This clearly reduces the adaptiveness of the application because it is essentially programmed for only one data source. Full SQL translation means that the application is programmed in the local SQL syntax and the gateway translates the SQL to the target syntax. This creates a far more adaptive design. An issue to consider with SQL translation is how the gateway handles error code returns. It is far preferable to have the error codes translated to the appropriate code for the calling database, otherwise the application will have to have a separate error trapping procedure for each target database.

14.3.9.3 Process Transfer Middleware

Process transfer middleware was designed for multi-tier, complex applications and for applications which must handle high transaction volumes, mission-critical reliability, subsecond response times, and scalability. Process transfer technology provides application-to-application connectivity by shielding the requesting application from dependency on the underlying data source to which it makes requests. There are several different kinds of process transfer middleware: messaging, remote procedure calls (RPCs), object request brokers, and transaction monitors. Each are described below.

Messaging provides reliable asynchronous communications between application tiers and different applications. Messaging uses message queues to implement a "store and forward" mechanism, similar to e-mail, where a sent message waits in the queue until it can be serviced by the receiving application. Applications use a high-level API to send and receive messages and manage queues. Basically, the API is a high-level verb set of less than a dozen commands. The benefit of messaging middleware is that all communication internals are hidden from the application programs. The messaging system provides a consistent interface which means that changes to the underlying communication layer will not require changes to applications.

In order to accomplish the benefits of messaging, applications must be carefully designed with clear boundaries that must be recognized and respected. Staff must be trained to develop with these constraints in mind and the boundaries must be treated as the new standards of development. The design process outlined in this book helps define the boundaries and interoperations between system components.

One problem today is that most messaging products are proprietary. The Message Oriented Middleware Association (MOMA) is an industry consortium currently establishing messaging standards.

Messaging makes it easier to integrate new and purchased applications with existing systems and add functionality to back end applications inside the network, outside of the applications. The leading messaging products on the market today include IBM MQ Series, Microsoft Exchange, DEC Message Q, and Lotus Notes.

Remote procedure calls (RPCs) are another type of process transfer middleware. RPCs are easy for application programmers to understand because they work just like procedure calls, except the procedure is executed on a different computer. RPCs are generally synchronous. The application issues a request and is blocked from proceeding with other work while waiting for a reply. Synchronous RPCs are connection-oriented and perform best with high-speed communication media. Unlike messaging, which enables interapplication communications, RPCs require compiling on both sides and therefore are most useful for communication between platforms for a single application. Asynchronous RPCs are also now becoming available. Figure 14–14 is an example of how RPCs work.

Essentially, remote procedure calls hide all the network code in the stub procedures. This prevents the application programs, the client, and the server from having to worry about details such as sockets, network byte order, and the like.

Object Request Brokers (ORBs) enable interoperability with a higher level of abstraction than messaging or RPCs, in fact, the underlying transport mechanism is either messaging or RPCs. The application makes requests by using an Interface Definition Language (IDL), which automatically generates all the necessary code for cross-platform communication. Today, the Object Management Group is the body that is setting the object middleware standard. CORBA, the Common Object Request Broker Architecture, has become a standard that is still evolving and leaves room for different interpretations, but few products are fully CORBA compliant.

How Remote Procedure Calls Work

In a remote procedure call (RPC) a process on the local system invokes a procedure on a remote system. The reason that this process is even a "procedure call" is that the intent is to make it appear to the programmer that a normal procedure call is taking place. The term "request" is used to refer to the client calling the remote procedure, and the term "response" is used to describe the remote procedure returning its results to the client.

Step 1—The client calls a local procedure, called the client stub. It appears to the client that the client stub is the actual server procedure that it wants to call. The purpose of the stub is to package up the arguments to the remote procedure, possibly put them into some standard format, and then build one or more network messages. The packaging of the client's arguments into a network message is termed "marshaling."

Step 2—The network messages are sent to the remote system by the client stub. This requires a system call into the local kernel.

Step 3—Within the local kernel the system's networking routines are accessed and the network messages are converted into the appropriate network format (packets) and transferred to the remote system. Either a connection-oriented or a connectionless protocol is used.

Step 4—The network routines on the receiving system checks in the incoming packets, assembles them in the appropriate order (packets do not necessarily arrive in order), and hands the information off to a waiting server stub. The server stub retrieves the arguments from the network messages and possibly converts them.

Step 5—The server stub then executes a local procedure call to invoke the actual server function, passing the arguments it received in the network messages from the client stub.

Step 6—When the server procedure has finished its activity, the "return values" are passed back to the server stub.

Step 7—The server stub converts the return values (if necessary) and then assembles the values into one or more network messages to send back to the client stub.

Step 8—The packets with the return arguments are transferred back across the network to the client stub.

Step 9—The client stub reads the network messages from the local kernel and in the final step, after possibly converting the return values, the client stub gives the data to the client function.

Figure 14–14 Examples of How Remote Procedure Calls (RPCs) Work

Competing object interoperability mechanisms are being offered by IBM and Microsoft. IBM offers SOM and DSOM (for distributed objects) which provide a syntax-free runtime engine and interoperability across languages. DSOM will include support for MVS, including CICS and IMS. This will make DSOM a candidate for linking old and new applications, something most ORBs do not support. Microsoft is promulgating ActiveX as a defacto market standard that provides a language neutral binary interface. ActiveX does not support inheritance, and only runs on Microsoft operating systems. SOM supports full inheritance and is platform-independent. Before ORBs are robust enough for mission-critical enterprise computing, they must support high transaction volumes.

Transaction Processing (TP) Monitors manage distributed units of work. A distributed unit of work is a transaction that spans more than one platform and must be committed on all platforms or rolled back on all platforms. An example is a withdrawal from one bank account and a deposit into another. If the deposit fails, then the withdrawal must be rolled back, or your money is lost. Distributed transactions require two-phase commit protocol. In phase one of two-phase commit protocol, the controlling node sends a request to all other nodes participating in the transaction asking if they are ready to commit. All participating nodes must respond affirmatively. Otherwise, the request is repeated. If all nodes are ready, the controlling node sends a commit command, and all nodes commit synchronously, or the transaction is rolled back at all sites.

TP monitors offer additional functionality for high transaction volumes including load balancing, multi-threading to reduce severe contention, administration, and more. They support many types of communication: synchronous, asynchronous, queue-based, and publish-subscribe. There are some things to watch out for with transaction monitors, however. The most important is the platforms the TP monitor supports if a single transaction crosses processors. At this time objects are not supported.

14.3.10 Internet/Intranet

Intranets will Play a Key Role in Information Sharing within Organizations, While the Internet will Become the Information Vehicle Between Organizations and Their Customers

Recently, there has been an explosion of interest in aggressively moving applications onto the Internet as well as using Internet technology to build internal intranets. These enable platform-independent access to corporate information. A recent study by the Strategic Focus Group predicted that Internet application development will increase by 226% by 1998, and Intranet development will increase by 369%! (See Figure 14–15.)

The fastest growing part of the Internet is the Web, which provides a user friendly hypertext interface to information. Web development, and the tools to support it, are ex-

Type of Application	1996	1998	% Increase
2-Tier Client/Server	26.4%	25.3%	–4%
3-Tier Client/Server	7.8%	22.9%	+200%
Internet	2.7%	8.8%	+226%
Intranet	2.9%	13.6%	+369%
Legacy with GUI	13.3%	12.5%	–6%
Non Client/Server	46.9%	17%	–63.8%

Strategic Focus (www.strategicfocus.com)

Figure 14–15 Types of Applications

ploding. Microsoft has put a big push on making all their tools Web enabled. PowerBuilder is also becoming Web enabled as are all the other major tools. We believe that careful consideration should be given to choosing Web development tools. As stated above, the currently available development tools are adding Web capabilities, while a whole new set of Java development tools are also becoming available. This is a fast growing market, with many newcomers. Inevitably there will be a shakeout in this market, with market leaders—not the best technology—winning out.

Although the rise of the Web has prompted some pundits to pronounce the demise of client/server, Internet/intranet applications are based on client/server technology. We are advising companies to build integrated architectures. Clearly, database access plays a pivotal role in this integration. All the major database vendors are moving aggressively in the area of Internet access. In the area of Web databases we recommend an integrated solution, either with your existing database vendor, or with a Web database vendor (then using their HTML development tools). There are also tools that add Internet/intranet access to standard database and client/server applications.

Although Lotus Notes has been the groupware standard for the past few years, the growth of intranets has provided new options for companies. Browsers provide a common interface to disparate corporate information sources. In developing groupware applications, the choices are between using groupware products, such as Notes and Collabra, or building custom applications using existing client/server databases and tools and Web Browsers, or a combination of both.

Components of an Internet/intranet Architecture include:

- Secure web servers
- Nonsecure web servers
- Web browsers
- Web authoring tools (HTML generators)
- Web application development tools
- Search engine
- Workgroup
- Firewall/Security
- Groupware
- Database connectivity for dynamic information retrieval.

14.4 TECHNICAL SPECIFICATIONS

Technical Specifications Unambiguously Define and Depict the Technical Infrastructure Supporting Each and Every Software Component

Technical specifications need to communicate both the existing and planned technical architecture clearly to both a technical and nontechnical audience. The depiction of the technical architecture needs to be widely distributed and clearly understood by system designers, programmers, and business managers responsible for purchasing technology.

There are actually two different technical specifications that can be created. One is the "as is" picture. The "as is" picture can be created at any time before gap analysis because it is not dependent upon any other step.

More importantly for architecture design is the technical specification of what the planned architecture "will be." This is created by analyzing key business drivers, deriving the technical requirements to meet the business needs, and defining the technical components that meet those requirements. This leads to a business-driven architecture rather than a technologist-centric architecture.

Many of our clients clearly understand the need to define their technical architecture and communicate it to others in the organization. But they repeatedly ask, "How do we do that and what does this specification look like?". There are alternative ways to depict a system. We believe that the types of diagrams used are less important than the consistent use of *any* diagramming method. What is most important is to standardize on one way of doing it, and communicate this to all of the constituencies in the organization. It is important to stick to one method, so the diagrams are more easily understood across the organization. The way to maintain your investment in your models is to maintain knowledge of the models over time. It is also helpful if the technique is suitable to all levels of the organization, from a small project to a full-blown enterprise-wide architecture (as the IllumiSys™ Method is).

14.4.1 Types of Technical Specifications

Diagrams and Detailed Specifications Communicate the Technical Architecture to a Wide Audience

There are technical specifications for both existing technology and the design of the planned architecture. In both cases the specifications are the same. The types of technical specifications we find useful to include are Technical Architecture Diagram, Technical Architecture Specification, Logical Network Diagram, and Existing Standards Specification.

14.4.2 Technical Architecture Diagram

Communicates the Technical Architecture to Managers, Business Users, Designers, Developers, Implementors, Network Administrators, and Maintenance and Support Personnel

The purpose of Figure 14–16 is to communicate the technical infrastructure to the widest possible audience. Therefore, it should be easy to understand. This is successfully accom-

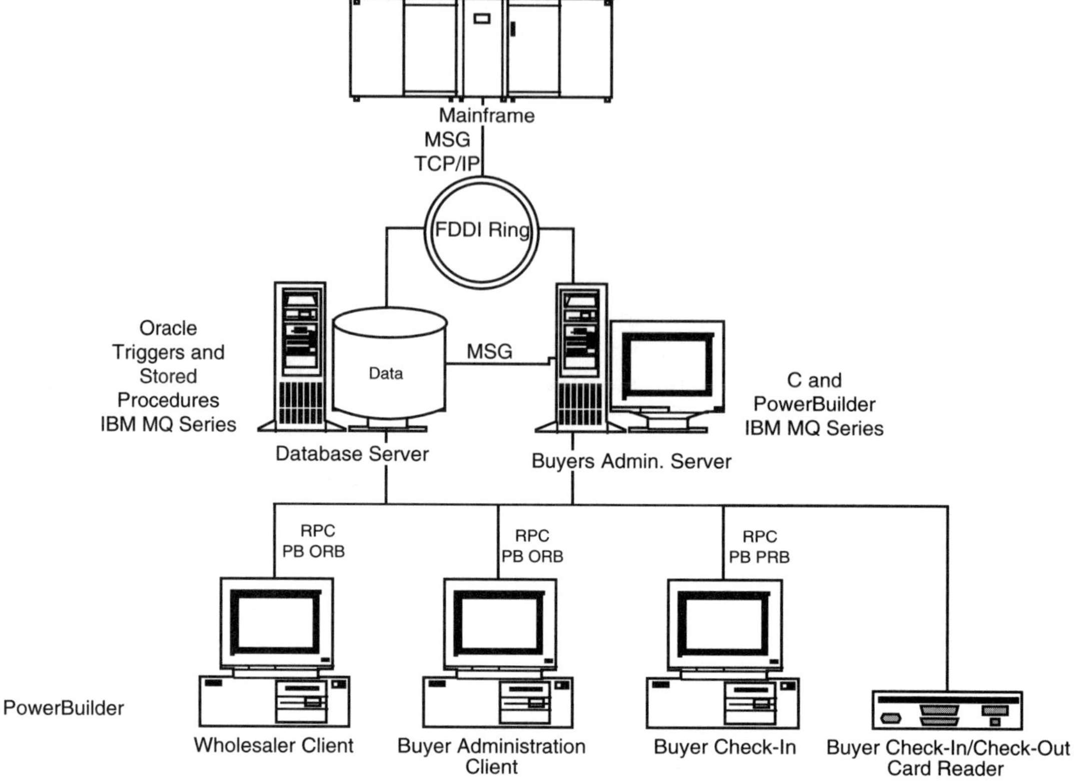

Figure 14–16 A Technical Architecture Diagram

plished by keeping it as simple as possible. Text specifications can always be used to more fully describe any and all components.

The technical architecture diagram depicts the major hardware components, textual annotations naming those components, and network connectivity. We have found that sometimes it is useful to include information on development tools and middleware for application developers because the software specifications will differ depending on the technology chosen. For example, if IBM MQ Series is going to be the middleware layer, then the software specifications will depict asynchronous messaging. If ODBC is the middleware layer, then synchronous SQL calls will be defined in the access layer.

The most adaptable designs are the most granular ones. This is true of processors as well. An adaptable design has a client and server for each logical location defined in the Essential Model. This will produce a technical implementation that closely resembles the business. Therefore, when the business changes, it will be faster and easier to change the application. Granularity in servers facilitates the partitioning of application systems, the partitioning of databases, and the preservation of logical boundaries. We recommend multiple, highly scalable, mid-size servers that have binary compatibility rather than a

Component	Product Name	Configuration (including version)	Installed	Standard	Software Installed
Service Buyers Admin. Server	HP 9000	64 MB RAM; NT; 20 GIG HD; Symmetric multi-processor. Development machine will have 2 processors. Production machine will be sized after design phase is completed. Clustered with data server.	No	Yes	Entera, IBM MQ Series, C compiler, PVCS, Encina; Multi-Tier 4GL
Database Server	HP 9000	64 MB RAM; NT; 200 GIG HD; Number of processors TBD clustered with business server.	No	Yes	Sybase System 11 with Replication Server, X-Open SQL, Omni SQL Gateway; IBM MQ Series
Wholesaler Client	Compaq	Pentium, 75-100 Mhz, 24 MB RAM, 1 GIG HD, Win 95; card reader attached. HP Printer	Yes	No	Entera RPC; PowerBuilder; SQL Anywhere; TCP/IP
Buyer Admin. Client	Compaq	24 MB RAM, 1 GIG HD, Win 95; card reader attached. HP Printer	No	No	Entera RPC; PowerBuilder; Multi-tier 4GL; TCP/IP
Buyer Check-In Client	Card Reader		No	No	
Buyer Check-Out Client	Card Reader		No	No	
Network	Ethernet		Yes	Yes	NT, TCP/IP
Middleware	Entera	RPC	No	Yes	Client to Bus Rules Server
	Omni SQL Gateway	Mainframe Gateway	On Mainframe	Yes	Server to Mainframe
	IBM MQ Series	Messaging	No	Yes	Server to Server

Figure 14–17 Technical Specifications for Fleury Market

Component	Product Name	Configuration (including version)	Installed (Y or N)	Standard (Y or N)	Software Installed
Servers					
Small					
Medium					
Huge					
Clients					
Desktop					
Mobile					
Development Tools					
Client					
Server					
Database					
Process Management					
Testing Tools					
Networks					
Protocols					
Topology					
Network Interface Card					
Modem					
LAN OS					
MAN					
WAN					
Middleware					
Naming Services					
Time Services					
Security					
Database API					
Database Gateway					
Messaging					
RPC					
ORB					
TP Monitor					

(*continued*)

Figure 14–18 A Technical Architecture Specification Form for Enterprise Architecture

Component	Product Name	Configuration (including version)	Installed (Y or N)	Standard (Y or N)	Software Installed
Internet/Intranet					
Secure Web Server					
Nonsecure Web Server					
Web Browser					
Web Authoring Tool					
Web Development					
Search Engine					
Firewall/Security					
Groupware					
Database Connectivity					

Figure 14–18 A Technical Architecture Specification Form for Enterprise Architecture *Continued*

single large server. Servers should be centrally managed and should be located in data centers (which may be 'virtual' such as a secured closet). The trade-off is that granularity in servers results in higher up-front costs (to buy a server for each application) and increased operational and support costs. Our bias is to trade increased operational costs for increased flexibility in the business. Granularity in servers can result in the lowest life cycle costs in a period of change.

14.4.3 Technical Architecture Specification

The Specification is Used to "Annotate" the Technical Architecture Diagram

A Technical Architecture Specification is a simple table, listing every component of the technical infrastructure, the configuration of every component, and any other information pertinent to the component (including status of adoption as a standard and notes regarding special information).

Because there are so many components of a Technical Architecture, it may be necessary to further categorize the components into types of components, especially when defining an enterprise architecture. These component types include: clients, servers, application development tools, databases, middleware, mainframes, network components, system management, process management, and Internet/intranet. Figure 14–17 is the Technical Specification for Fleury Market. Figure 14–18 is a sample specification form for an enterprise architecture. The purpose of the specification is to add detail information as needed, so the diagrams may be kept as clean and simple as possible.

14.4.4 Logical Network Diagram

> *The Objective of the Logical Network Diagram is to Simplify the Complexity of the Network Infrastructure so it can be Widely Communicated Through the Organization*

Because the network is a large part of the technical infrastructure, and because it is comprised of multiple components, it is often advisable to produce a separate logical network diagram. The purpose of this diagram is to describe the overall network by depicting communications between types of sites (central office, satellite office, district offices). It is meant to communicate an understanding of the network to non-network professionals. The key is to simplify.

If all network components are standardized across locations, a practice we *highly* recommend, then regardless of the number of large and small offices there are still only two test cases for the distributed application. This greatly reduces testing and implementation time.

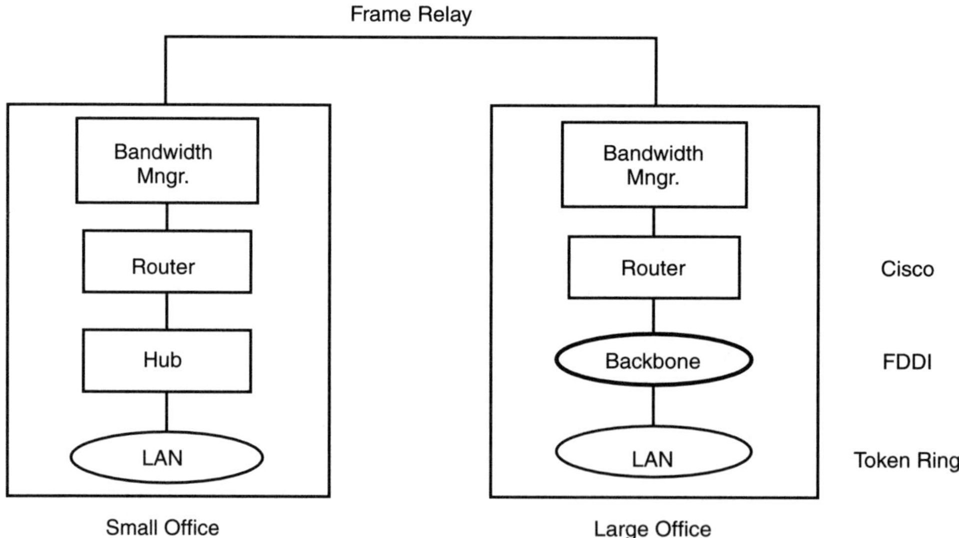

Figure 14–19 Logical Network Diagram (By permission of Larry DeBoever, META Group)

14.4.5 Existing and De Facto Standards Specification

Make an Explicit Effort to Define Any Existing and De Facto Standards

There is a column on the Technical Architecture Specification for indicating whether the component has been defined as a standard. This is a straightforward process for new technical components. Either it is being brought in as a standard or it represents a unique requirement (such as a purchased application). But what about existing technology? In many cases, you will find many de facto standards for existing technology. De facto standards may include tools for which there is a significant existing skillset within the organization; a large installed base of some technology; technology for which there is large acceptance within the user community; and others.

14.5 GAP ANALYSIS

Gap Analysis Defines the Difference Between "What Is" and "What Will Be"

Organizations moving to distributed processing architectures often find the task of building a robust distributed technical architecture daunting. In many organizations what we find are many pockets of client/server technology which do not integrate with each other. The challenge is to create an integrated and flexible architecture. Many organizations thought that open systems technology would be the key. But there are no silver bullets here. It takes planning and management to succeed. Gap analysis is the first step to planning the migration process.

The objective of a gap analysis is to look at where you are today and where you want to be in the future. Then figure out what is missing. It represents the delta between the comprehensive inventory and the planned technical architecture. It results in specific areas of the technical infrastructure that need to be focused on.

14.5.1 Gap Analysis Process

Comparing Business Requirements to Existing Technology

The gap analysis process consists of comparing the existing technical infrastructure to the technology required to meet business requirements. If the Technical Architecture Design process is followed as outlined herein, this is a straightforward process. It uses the Key Business Drivers gathered either in the Essential Model or through a strategic planning

Technical Architecture Design Document

Page ___ of ___
Date ________

Key Business Drivers (Note All Metrics)	**Architecture Requirements**	**Technical Specifications/ Options** (Technology/ Standards/Products/Etc.)

Figure 14–20 Technical Architecture Design Document

session and the analysis done above on the existing technical architecture. It also identifies what additional technology is required to meet the business requirements.

14.5.2 Technical Architecture Design Document

A Simple Tool for Tying Business Drivers to Technology

Gap analysis can be simply performed by filling in the last two columns of the technical architecture design form (Figure 14–20). The middle column lists all technology components that can be used to fulfill the business requirements. The last column is completed by using the Technical Architecture Diagrams and Specifications. Fill in which technology components exist in the organization. This process will probably yield blanks or gaps in the third column. This indicates a need for technology that does not currently exist.

14.6 MIGRATION PLANNING

Migration Planning Provides a Roadmap for Getting from "What Is" to Where the Organization Wants To Be

Migration planning is the process of prioritizing needs and creating a plan for implementing the technical infrastructure on a project-by-project basis. We recognize that few organizations can afford large-scale infrastructure projects, and no one can afford to stop all development until the infrastructure is built. Therefore, we recommend developing the full-scale design and then a plan of how to get there. It also must be recognized that Technical Architecture Design is an ongoing process. Both technology and business needs change rapidly. An enterprise architecture assessment should be at least a yearly activity. The process for defining the technical architecture for each application must also feed into the overall enterprise architecture. The key is to design the architecture for change and implement it for strategic competitive advantage.

The objects of a migration planning effort is to derive an optimal strategy for implementing a technical infrastructure that will support both the immediate strategic needs of the organization and the long-term goals. An optimal strategy enables any investment in technology to show a return on investment to the organization. Migration planning answers the following questions:

- Which components of the architecture should be implemented first?
- Which components of the architecture are necessary for multiple projects?
- What is the implementation plan for the next year, two years, three years?

14.6.1 The Migration Planning Process

Setting Technical Priorities Based on Business Needs

Migration planning is usually done on the enterprise level. It involves selecting certain projects or applications to migrate to a distributed architecture. This requires setting priorities for migration planning. The process for defining priorities can either be part of the organization's strategic planning process, a business process reengineering effort, or finding a way to incrementally build the technical infrastructure in the course of deploying new applications.

In our experience, few organizations have a lot of money for infrastructure projects. We therefore recommend building the infrastructure as part of ongoing projects; by spending 10%–20% more to build in an "adaptive range." This adaptive range includes buying a larger chassis for the server so it can be easily upgraded, building in more network functionality than the current project actually needs but that the enterprise needs, or building a robust middleware infrastructure when the application minimally could run on a two-tier data passing architecture. Generally, the money spent on the adaptive range is later recouped through reusability.

Migration priorities can be defined through the process of creating a separate Architecture Design Form for each project, then comparing them. Identify all architecture requirements that span multiple projects (such as a database gateway or an information warehouse).

If enterprise technical architecture requirements are considered in the process for funding projects, the infrastructure can be implemented more quickly. Furthermore, the funding of the infrastructure can be spread across multiple projects. Infrastructure costs can then be more easily justified.

Component	Location	Support Group
Server and client hardware	Fleury Lyon Bordeaux	Operations group in Fleury Operations group in Lyon Operations group in Fleury
Operating system upgrades	Fleury Lyon Bordeaux	Operations group in Fleury Operations group in Lyon Operations group in Fleury
Application installation	Fleury Lyon Bordeaux	Operations group in Fleury Operations group in Lyon Operations group in Fleury
Application support	Fleury, Lyon, Bordeaux	Application group
Network	Fleury, Lyon, Bordeaux	Operations group
Gateway	Fleury, Lyon, Bordeaux	Database Administration with operations group for networking
Data extracts	Fleury, Lyon, Bordeaux	Mainframe application group *OR* PC applications development group
Database installation	Fleury, Lyon, Bordeaux	Database Administration
Database support	Fleury, Bordeaux Lyon	Fleury Database Administration with Applications Development group Lyon Database Administration with Applications Development group
EDI support	Fleury, Lyon, Bordeaux	Operations? EDI administration?
E-mail support	Fleury, Lyon, Bordeaux	Operations group

Figure 14–21 Support Table for Fleury Distributed System

14.7 DEFINING SUPPORT

The Feasibility of The Technical Infrastructure Lies In Long Term Support and Maintenance

The feasibility of any technical architecture will depend on the organization's ability to support the solution overtime. Sometimes elegant distributed architectures cannot be supported in remote locations. We recommend defining how each component of the Technical Architecture will be supported in each location. In our experience, this information quickly points out potential problems and issues that must be resolved before the system is implemented. Figure 14–21 depicts the support for each component at each location in the Fleury Market case study.

15

Processor Distribution Aspect

Distributing the Multi-Tier Design to Physical Processors

At this point in the design we have defined the *logical* multi-tier partitioning and the technical components for each tier. The Processor Distribution Aspect specifies the software granules that will operate on each processor. These specifications are used by programmers to build the software components. Because the Essential Model maps so well to a multi-tier architecture, all the detailed specifications of the Behavioral and Information Aspects are used here. They provide an excellent foundation for the specifications of this aspect. In the Multi-Tier Partitioning Aspect we mapped the business components defined in the Essential Model to the Presentation, Business Rules, Data Access, and Data Tiers. In the Technical Architecture Design we defined all technical components for each tier. We are now ready to define what processing and data will occur on each processor and how processors will communicate with each other at each location. In the next chapter, "The Geographic Distribution Aspect," we define what processing occurs at each geographic location and how processors will communicate with each other across locations. As soon as a particular component is specified in sufficient detail, programming of that component may begin. Figure 15–1 depicts the Processor Distribution Aspect of the Implementation Model.

The Processor Distribution Aspect answers the following questions:

- Which business events are being responded to by each processor?
- What local functions, data, and interim data structures are required to respond to those business events?

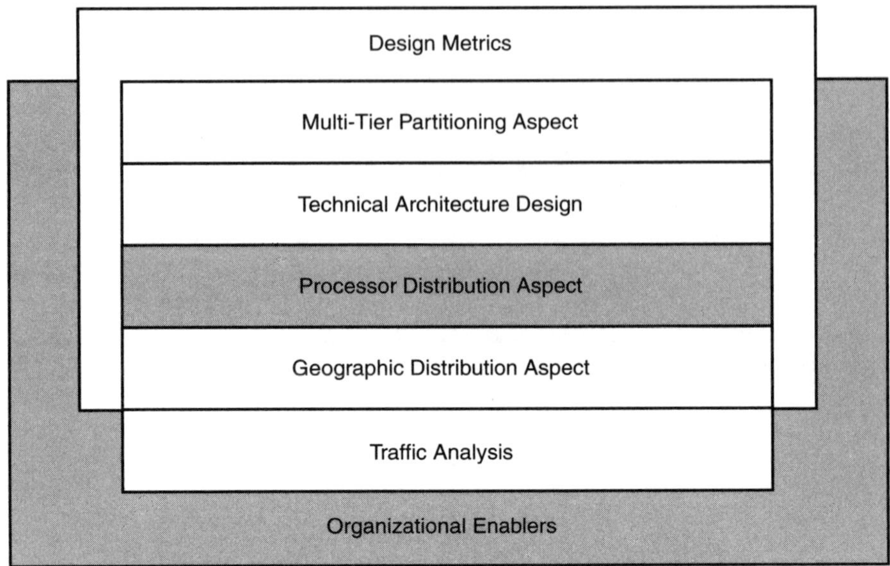

Figure 15–1 Implementation Model: Processor Distribution Aspect

- What (if any) user interface (UI) events trigger processor functions?
- What specific business and data integrity rules are enforced during the response to events?

Figure 15–2 depicts the activities and artifacts of the Processor Distribution Aspect.

Aspect	Activity	Artifact/View	M/O/R
Processor Distribution Aspect	Distribute events and responses across processors	Processor Model	Mandatory
		Processor Distribution Table	Mandatory
		Processor Data Flow Diagram	Mandatory
		Lower Level DFDs	Optional
	Model the presentation tier	Prototype	Mandatory
		State Transition Diagram	Recommend
	Distribute data across processors	Entity Processor Table	Mandatory
		Data Distribution Table	Mandatory
	Define communications between processors	Message Specification Table	Mandatory

Figure 15–2 Activities and Artifacts of the Processor Distribution Aspect

15.1 OBJECTIVES OF PROCESSOR DISTRIBUTION

Designing Reuseable, Adaptable Software Components

The major goals when designing the software components for each processor are reusability and ease of change. The smaller the software component, the more reuseable it is. For example, a scrollable window component can be used in almost every client presentation screen. An entire screen, however, will be more difficult to reuse because it is designed for a specific purpose. The Behavioral Aspect of the Essential Model defined granular responses to business events, which can be designed as small, granular software components. We will use the minispecs from the Behavioral Aspect extensively in this design phase. We will also define additional system events and responses that result from partitioning the Business Components across processors.

At this point we define data distribution across processors. The logical boundaries for processing defined in the Environmental and Behavioral Aspects produced the necessary information to define the data requirements for each system response, as detailed in the Bridge Aspect. This provides sufficient information for defining Authoritative Sources of data. An Authoritative Source is the data store of record for a particular entity. For processing efficiency we may decide to replicate data to multiple processors, or we may decide to access Authoritative Sources. Defining Authoritative Sources provides the ability to replicate and distribute data for processing efficiency, while managing the integrity of data regardless of how it is distributed. Here we must discuss data architecture and the role and structure of the data warehouse. The data warehouse architecture can impact decisions on how to distribute data across the organization for the purposes of ad hoc queries, reporting, and complex analytical analysis.

The process for defining the processor distribution is listed here:

1. Start with proposed technical architecture and define physical processors.
2. Distribute multi-tier components of business events, responses to events, and corresponding data across clients, servers, and data sources.
3. Define communication between processors.
4. Apply heuristics and guidelines for optimal distribution.

15.2 THE PROCESSOR MODEL

Creating the Processor Model from the Technical Architecture Model

In the Multi-Tier Partitioning Aspect the application architecture was defined. In Technical Architecture Design all technical components of the system were chosen. Now we must create detailed software specifications for each processor. Figure 15–3 depicts the processor model for Fleury Market. It was created from the Multi-Tier Model (Chapter 13).

The Processor Model should look much like the logical locations defined in the Event Distribution Aspect of the Essential Model. These were Wholesaler Booth, Buyer Check-In, Buyer Check-Out, Buyer Membership Administration, and Service Buyers Administration. We allocated temporal events to Service Buyers Administration. This logical location will become the Business Rules server. All the other logical locations become logical clients (there may be many physical check-out locations, but we only have to design it once). In YSM notation processors and processes are both depicted with circles. External systems, or terminators on the Context Diagram, are depicted with squares.

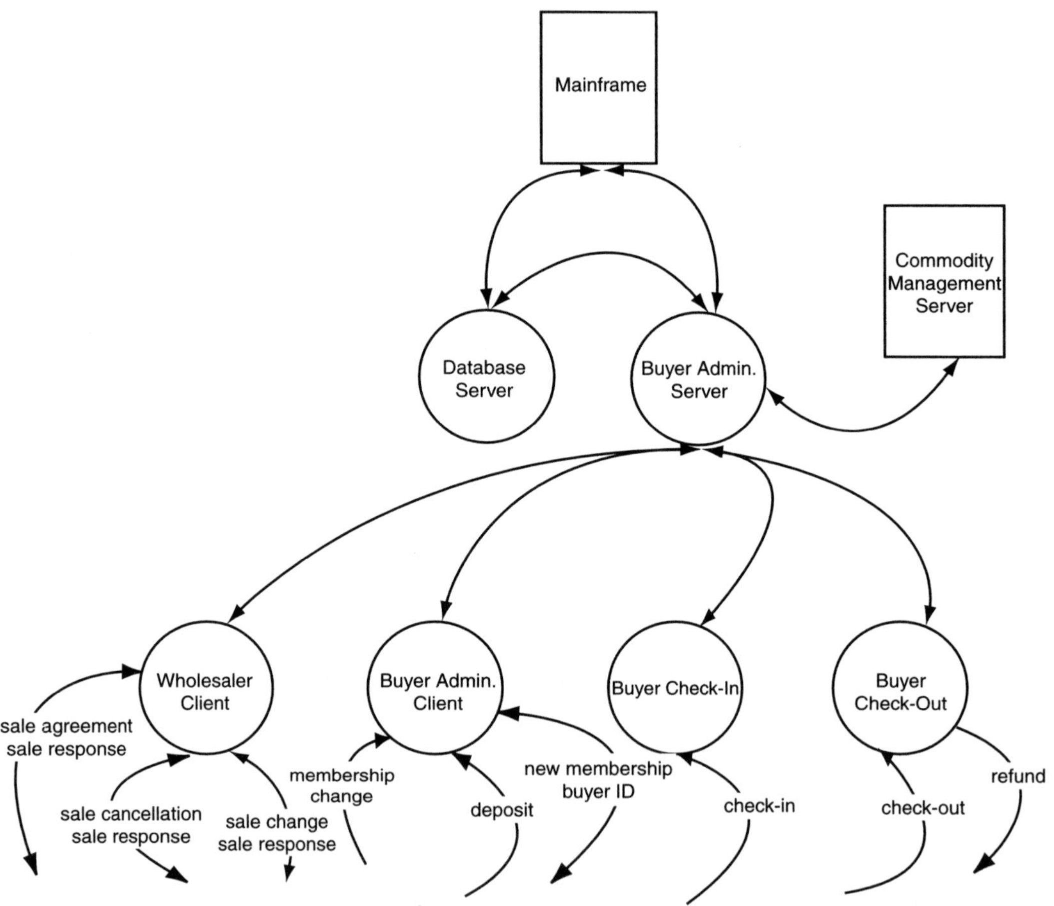

Figure 15–3 Processor Model for Fleury Market

15.3 THE PROCESSOR DISTRIBUTION TABLE

Distributing Event Management and Responses to Processors

At the heart of the IllumiSys™ Design Method is the conviction that adaptable systems require small-grained components that interact with other components in well-modeled and designed processes. These components are easiest to change when they more closely resemble the business processes themselves, because it is change to these processes that most often necessitate changes in system processing. As always, we start with the business event. Management of that business event is distributed to the client. Responses to events are mapped across processors in the distributed architecture. This mapping is done with the Processor Distribution Table.

The Processor Distribution Table (see Figure 15–5) lists all business events and responses processed on each processor. At this point in the design process, we have a great deal of information to allocate individual processing components to specific processors. The heuristics for allocating processes can produce reasonable designs, but it may take several iterations to achieve optimal distribution. This is because in the final analysis, network traffic is a critical factor, and we typically perform Traffic Analysis after the Geographic Distribution Aspect. It is important to note that if issues of network traffic arise at this point with critical processes, a limited network traffic analysis should be done in parallel with other efforts. It is essential to identify critical areas of risk as soon as possible at any stage of design. This is a risk management strategy that often prevents costly failures. At this stage, it may even be important to prototype some alternative solutions.

The Event Response Distribution Table created in the Behavioral Aspect (Chapter 9) is the major input for creating the Processor Event Table. To create the Processor Event Table first compare the Event Response Distribution Table (Figure 15–4) to the Processor Model (Figure 15–3). Assume all events will be represented on the clients as event management through the GUI. Business rule responses should be distributed to the Buyer Administration Server. Data access responses should be distributed to the Database Server. There is something important to note here. At this point there will be *additional* events and responses that must be defined. These are internal system events that occur due to the technical partitioning of the business event. For any data access, for example, there needs to be a request defined on one server and a response defined on another server. Sometimes these additional system events, which become messages, RPCs, SQL calls, ORBs, or ActiveX controls become more evident from the Processor Distribution DFD.

For example, one system internal event is the automatic triggering of canceling Sales that have not been picked up once the market closes. The temporal event "Market Closes" triggers a host of close-out routines, which include daily close-outs, weekly close-outs, monthly close-outs, quarterly close-outs, and yearly close-outs. The close-out routines themselves trigger many different events and responses, including messages to

Logical Location Event Manager	Essential Event Number and Name	Essential Event Response	Logical Location Event Response(s)
Dock Management	5. Buyer picks up orders	5R1. Record pick-up 5R2. Notify Service Buyers	Dock Management Service Buyers
Wholesaler Booth	3. Wholesaler proposes a sale	3R1. Create sale 3R3. Notify Service Buyers of account debit	Wholesaler Booth Service Buyers
	8. Wholesaler changes sale agreement	8R1. Change sale 8R2. Notify Service Buyers of account debit/credit	Wholesaler Booth Service Buyers
	9. Wholesaler cancels a sale	9R1. Cancel sale for buyer 9R2. Notify Service Buyers of account credit	Wholesaler Booth Service Buyers
	4. Buyer checks out of market	4R1. Check buyer out	Buyer Check-in and Check-out
Buyer Check-in and Check-out	2. Buyer checks into market	2R1. Check buyer in	Buyer Check-in and Check-out
	4. Buyer checks out market	4R1. Check buyer out	
Buyer Membership Administration	1. Buyer applies to become a market member	1R1. Add buyer	Buyer Membership Administration
	7. Buyer changes membership information	7R1. Note change in membership	
	10. Buyer makes deposit	10R1. Add deposit to balance	
Service Buyers Administration	6. Market closes	6R1. Cancel uncollected sales	Service Buyers Administration

Figure 15–4 The Event Response Distribution Table From the Event Distribution Aspect of the Essential Model

external systems, and batch processes (such as deleting unclaimed sales and notifying the Wholesalers system to cancel orders and increment stock).

Additional technical events happen from the interactions among the clients, servers, and mainframes. The partitioning determines the nature and content of these events. Each technical event strives to manage the integrity of an original business event by keeping it synchronized across every processor that handles that business event. (These events are the processor-to-processor dialogs, which are ultimately implemented as SQL calls (RPCs, or messages).

The minispecs from the Behavioral Aspect provide an excellent start for the processor specification, but clearly further detailed specifications are required at this point. The goal is that as soon as a component has been sufficiently defined in this aspect, it can be built, even while other design activities are still in progress. It is especially useful to build the most commonly used components first.

Processor / Response	Wholesaler Booth Client	Buyer Membership Admin Client	Check In / Check Out Client	Service Buyers Admin Server	Commodity Mngmnt Server	Service Wholesalers Mainframe
1. Add buyer		Add buyer presentation		Execute add buyer rules		
2. Check in buyer			Checkin buyer presentation	Update buyer status		
3. Create sale	Create sale presentation			Update sale status Add sale Add line item Update buyer balance Assign hanger to sale Notify service buyers of account debit	Update hanger status Check stock level Reduce stock level	Update wholsaler sales
4. Check out buyer	Buyer check-out presentation		Check out buyer presentation	Update sales status Update buyer status	Release hanger from sale Update hanger status	
5. Record pickup				Update sales status		
6. Market closes/ cancel uncollected sales				Cancel uncollected sales Update buyer status Update sales status	Release hanger from sale Update hanger status	Update wholesaler sales
7. Note membership change		Membership change presentation		Change membership info		
8. Change sale	Change sale presentation			Update buyer balance Send message to commodity mgnmt.	Check stock Reduce stock Increase stock	
9. Cancel sale	Cancel sale presentation			Update buyer balance Update sales statu Send message to commodity mgnmt.	Release hanger from sale Update hanger status	
10. Add deposit		Add deposit presentation		Add deposit to balance		

Figure 15–5 Processor Distribution Table

Figure 15–5 depicts the first "cut" of the event/response distribution for Fleury Market. It is a "reshuffling" of the event distribution by Logical Locations to event distribution by processors. After completing the processor DFD, the next iteration of this table would be to add the message events between processors. This is usually easier to do after the processor DFD is created.

The Processor Distribution Table provides a two-dimensional view of process distribution. The horizontal view, looking across a row, provides a beginning to end view of how an event is processed across distributed processors. The vertical view, looking down a column, provides a view of all processing handled by each processor. This helps identify potential areas of processing overload even before any detailed measurements have been done.

15.4 THE PROCESSOR DATA FLOW DIAGRAM

Highlighting Interaction between Processors to Define System Events

The Event Processor Distribution Table is extremely useful for "sorting" events and responses to processors. It is not as useful for seeing the interaction *between* processors. The Processor DFD provides this view of the system. After drawing the Processor DFD, additional internal system events may be identified, particularly messaging events between processors. Alternative solutions may also be proposed, until the optimal solution for the particular application and organization is determined.

In Figure 15–6, the separation between the business rules and data tiers are strictly adhered to. However, one alternative is to use stored procedures and triggers in the database to execute some business rules regarding adding new buyers and sales. These are named and precompiled modules of code which are stored and executed on the server. Stored procedures and triggers provide reuseable modules of code which have better performance than synchronous SQL calls that must be parsed and optimized at runtime.

Figure 15–7 depicts an alternative solution using a two-tier architecture with synchronous SQL calls between the client and server. One of the benefits of this solution is that it is easier to implement. The drawback is that it is not as scalable as the multi-tier solution because each request to the database server will be a separate synchronous connection to the database. It is also less adaptable if the database changes because the code modules are written in vendor specific procedural extensions to standard SQL. This locks you into a specific DBMS.

In this case, the assumption is that the business rules for adding a new buyer are fairly simple and straightforward and can easily be handled by stored procedures and triggers. The same is true for adding a deposit. However, the rules for processing sales are more complex, and therefore require intermediate processing on the "Buyer Admin. Server."

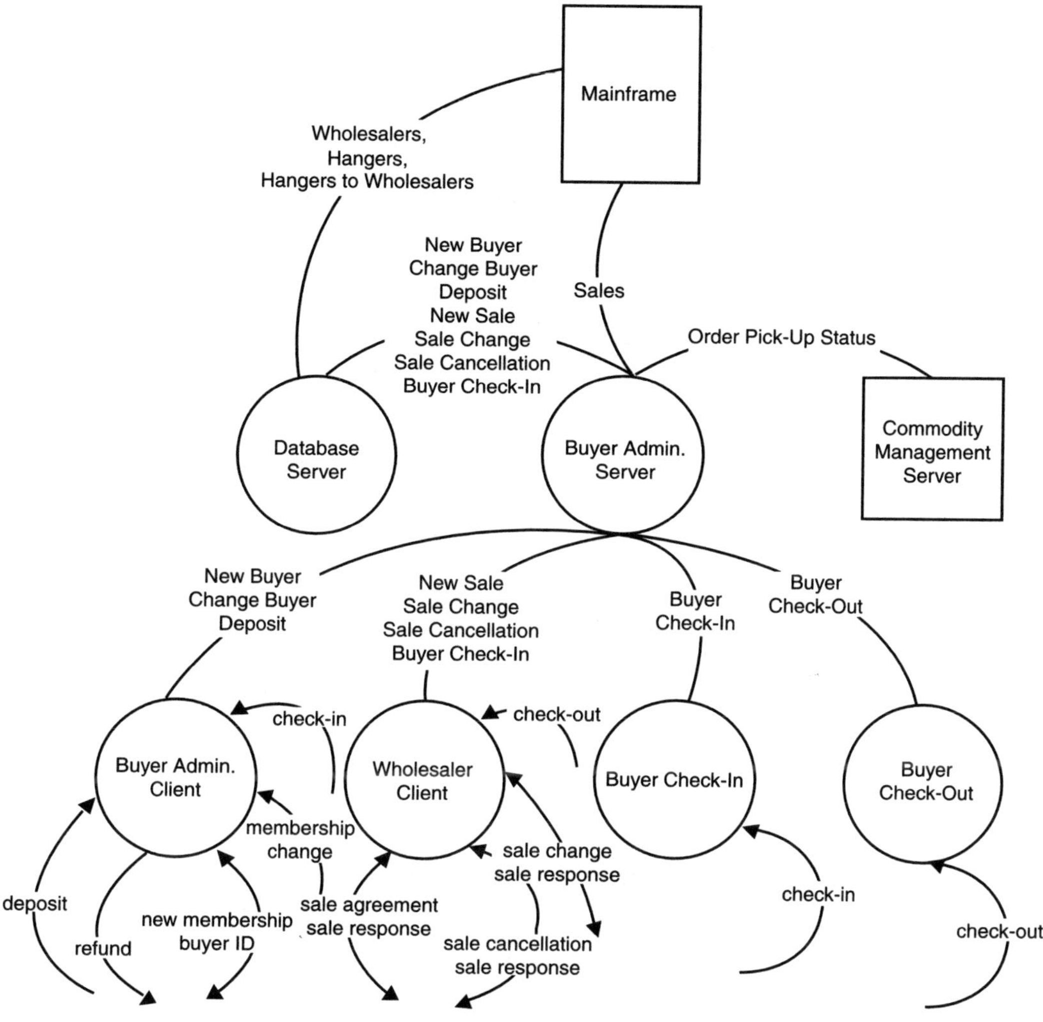

Figure 15–6 Processor Data Flow Diagram

15.5 DETAILING PROCESSES ON EACH PROCESSOR

Creating DFDs and Minispecs for Each Processor

When the process distribution stabilizes, the next step is to fully describe the processes and messages occurring on each processor, to the level of detail necessary to code the system. This is the set of blueprints that programmers will rely heavily upon. Programmers

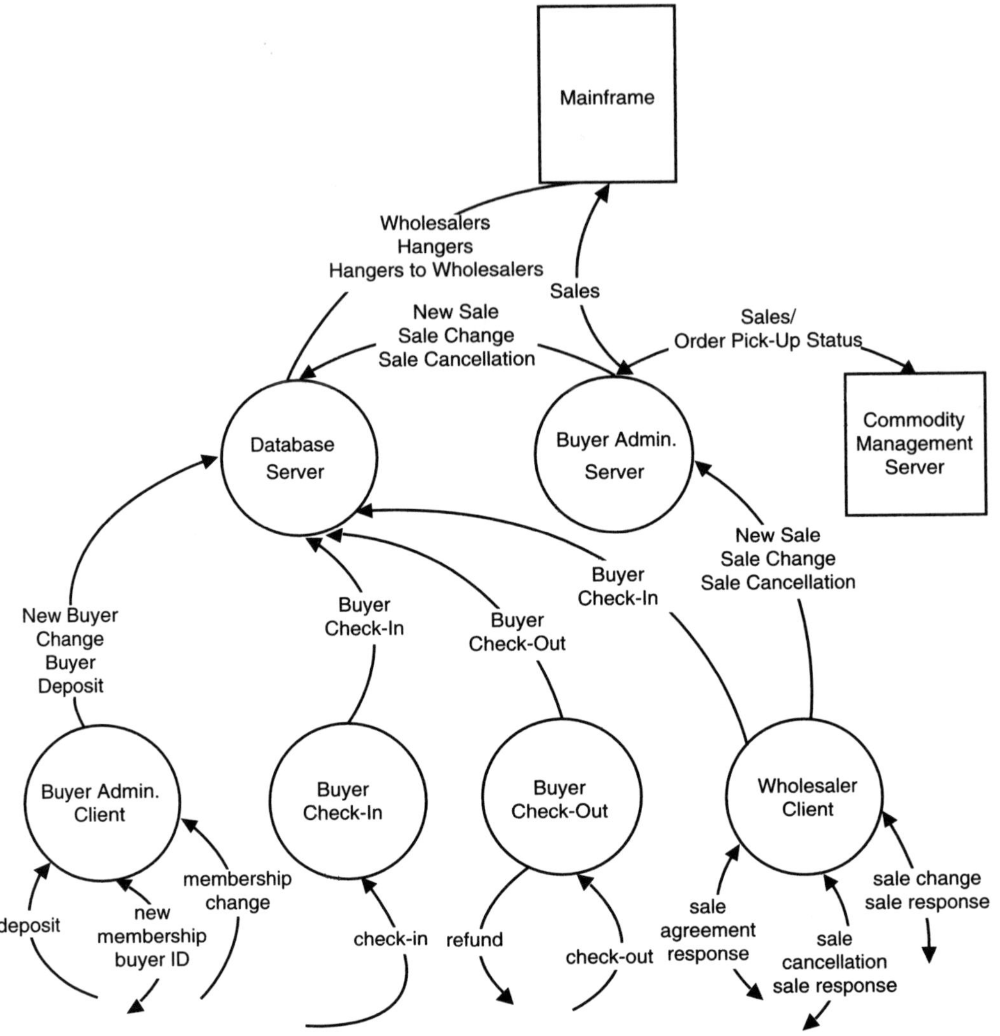

Figure 15–7 Alternative Processor DFD Synchronous Two-Tier Architecture

should also understand, as much as possible, the entire design and how each component interacts with the other components. At this point we know the events, responses, and messages each processor must handle. We have mini-specs fully describing some of the responses. We need to fully describe the new partitioning events we discover. Leveled DFDs and mini-specs can be used to further describe the processes for each processor. Figure 15–8 depicts a detailed DFD for the Service Buyers Admin. Server.

Other diagramming methods may also be used to further describe the processing logic. Figure 15–9 depicts a structure chart for breaking down the processing. The completed specifications will include all business rules as well as functions which must do com-

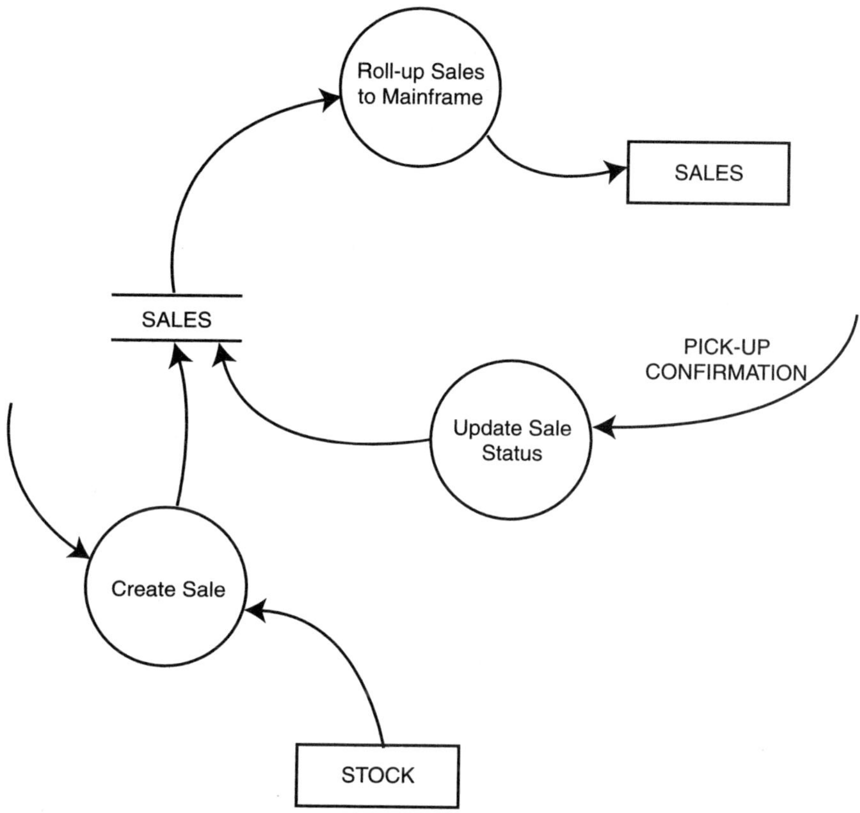

Figure 15–8 The Software Logic for Creating a Sale

putations or handle system internal events. Computations can be intermediate in nature and are done often several times during the total response to an external business event (for example, keep a running total as a sale is being created). Computations can also be done either before or after the main response logic is executed. An example of logic executed before the response is when Buyer record containing current balance must be read and checked prior to entering Sale Items. An example of logic executed after a response is the updating of the Buyer's balance after a Sale has been completed. Logic to handle system internal events must also be specified. For example, the internal event which triggers the deletion of all unclaimed sales after the market closes not only updates the already altered Commodity quantities and Buyer balances, it must make sure these operations are done in concert with the operations of the business, such as putting the stock back in the warehouse. This is a good example of where an internal event impacts multiple systems. In this case, the internal event caused responses in the Service Buyers and Commodity Management Systems.

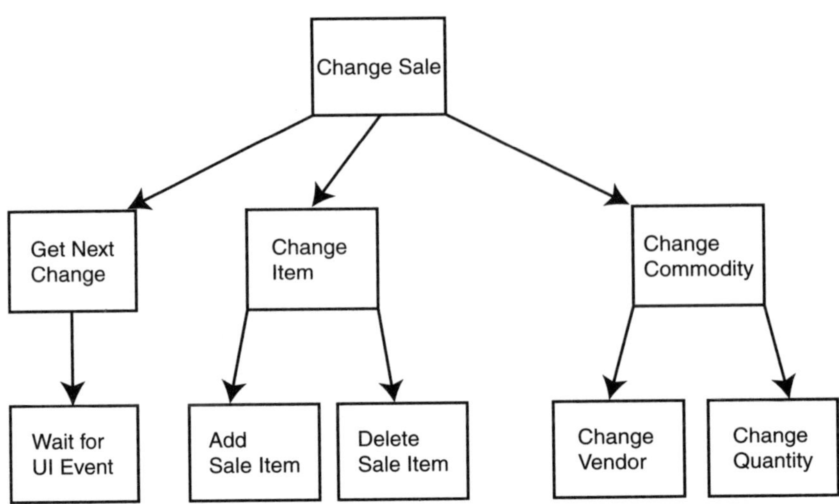

Figure 15–9 Structure Chart for Controlling Sale Change Logic

15.6 MODELING THE PRESENTATION TIER

Designing how the User Interfaces with the System to Process Business Events and how the System Responds to Those Events

Prototyping is extremely effective for working with users to determine the most effective presentation of the business event. Prototyping does not, however, show the presentation logic behind the GUI. This is what happens when the user pushes a button or chooses a menu item. The GUI events trigger the responses to the business event. These responses were defined in the Behavioral Aspect. At this point we need to design the presentation with GUI objects which trigger and manage the responses. This design can best be portrayed with a prototype of the user interface and State Transition Diagrams (STDs) to define the presentation logic.

STDs are ideal for modeling presentation logic because they model the responses to the business events that cannot be captured in a GUI. They show an initial state, the events that occur to change the state, and all the possible intervening states and events until some final state is reached. This is a very natural way to model what happens as users open and close windows, submit transactions and queries with the click of a mouse button, or print reports.

Figure 15–10 shows the components of an STD. The boxes depict states. A state is passive. It represents the memory of a sequence of events that resulted in the particular state. States can represent either an externally visible window or an internally organized transitory state. It is important to note that the process being described may be in only one state at a time. For example, a window may be open or closed, or a button may be acti-

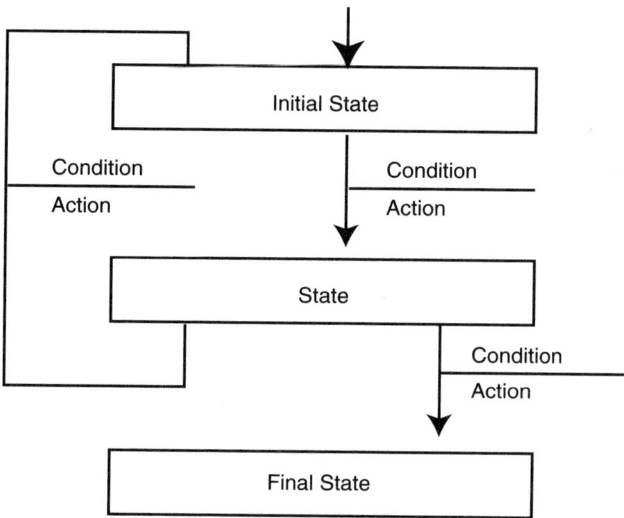

Figure 15–10 State Transition Diagram (STD)

vated or not. The conditions on the STD represent something that produces an action that effects the state. Conditions may be GUI events, such as a button being clicked or a menu item selected. A condition may also be an internal condition, which may result from the response to an event. Actions are pieces of work launched by the presentation logic. For example, when an icon is clicked it may launch the processing of some business rules or a request for data.

A presentation design is done for each logical location defined in the Essential Model. A logical location represents a set of events that are performed or initiated by users who are responsible for that business function. Note that a person may perform multiple functions and their job may cover more than one logical location. Combined logical locations may exist in some geographic locations (a small distributed office) and not others (corporate headquarters). This is part of the adaptability of the design. There should be at least one presentation screen for each logical location, which we now define as a logical client. A physical client may represent one or more logical clients.

The process for designing the presentation tier is as follows:

1. Prototype the interface.
2. Indicate the states of the GUI object. Each STD models a window associated with a single application thread. Do not model interaction between threads.
3. Indicate the conditions as window events.
4. Indicate the actions.

Figure 15–11 represents the screen for the wholesaler client. Figure 15–12 is the state transition diagram (STD) detailing the processing logic behind the screen.

Sale Form	Wholesaler	**Marcel Boucher et Cie**		Note if you have a Carte Fleury Insert it now!	Date 1 Nov	Wholesaler ID 0098 Buyer ID 0234 Hanger ID RQ1180
Line Items						
#	**Commodity**	**Description**	**Vendor**	**Qty**	**$**	**Total**
0 1	CH023	Brie	Best Class	12	1.23	14.76
0 2	CH077	Camembert	Budget	10	1.57	15.70
					Total	30.46
	Agree	**Change**	**Cancel**			

Figure 15–11 Presentation Design of Fleury Wholesaler Client

15.7 SYNCHRONOUS VS. ASYNCHRONOUS DESIGN

Designing for Adaptability and Scalability

At this stage of design, some of the most important and difficult design decisions are to determine how the different tiers of the architecture communicate with each other and with external systems. As described in the Multi-Tier Partitioning Aspect (Chapter 13), asynchronous designs are more adaptable and scalable. Synchronous communications require separate open sessions with the server for each request, and the requesting application is blocked from doing further processing until it receives a reply. Asynchronous communications can multiplex multiple requests for one open session, thereby reducing network traffic and making it easier to scale an application for large numbers of users. However, asynchronous design requires more infrastructure and a different way of thinking about systems design.

For example, let us consider an Order Entry Application. To process the business event "Customer Places an Order" the Order Entry system needs to share information with the Inventory System. A business rule may be that the sales clerk will notify the customer if an item is out of stock. A synchronous design of this business rule would be that the Order Entry System sends a request to the Inventory System to determine if the item is in stock and waits until it receives a reply. This request may be in the form of a SQL statement, which necessitates that the Order Entry System contains knowledge of the data

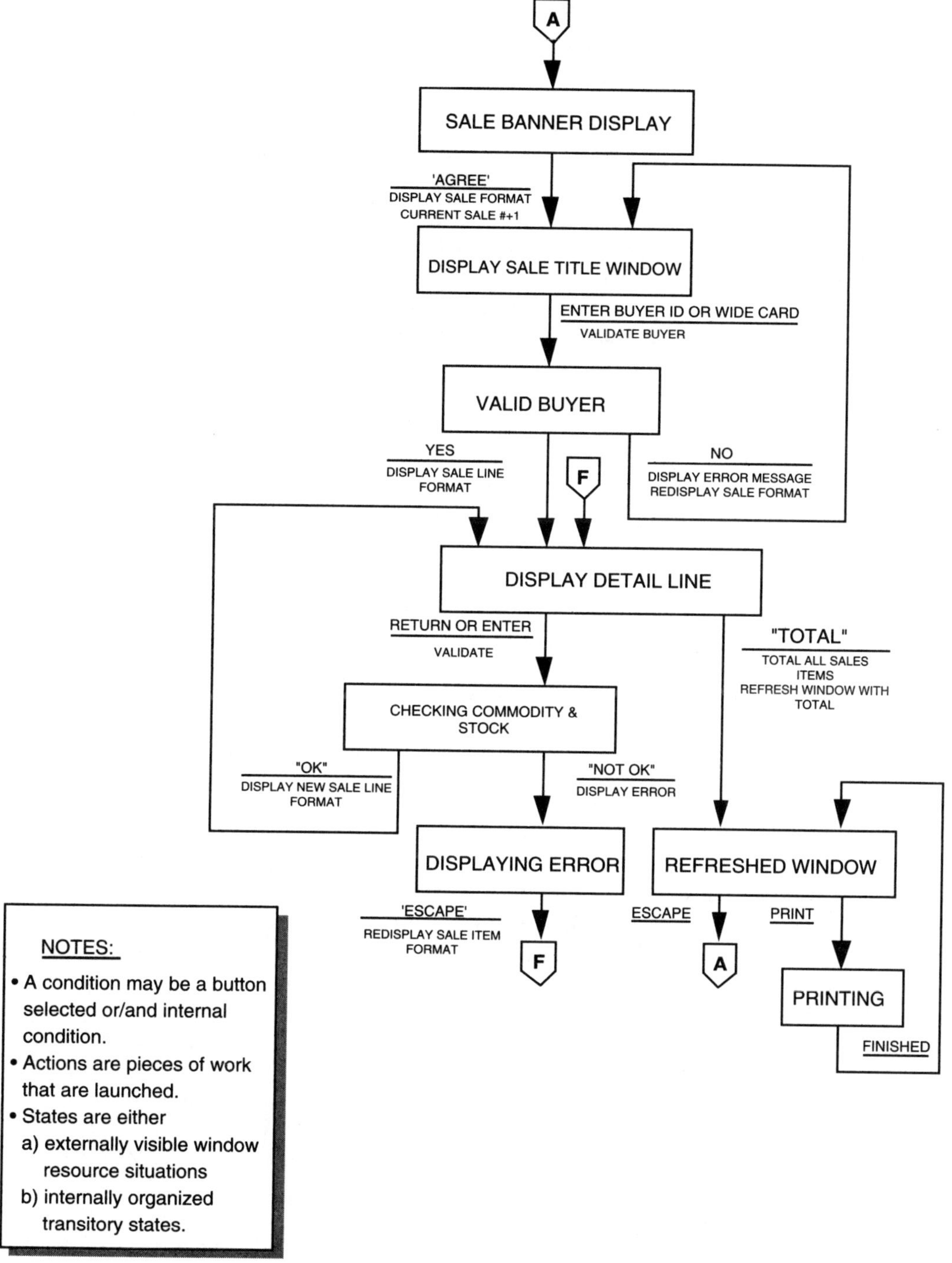

Figure 15–12 STD for Agree to Sale Presentation Logic

structures of the Inventory System. This is synchronous logic and synchronous communications. The request may also be in the form of a message to the Inventory System. The Order Entry System may still wait for a reply, but the *communications* between the systems is asynchronous. This is synchronous logic implemented with asynchronous communications.

Another option is to design the system totally differently. For example, the company may typically be out of stock on only 15% of their items at any time. Instead of checking Inventory for every item, the assumption may be that the item is in stock unless otherwise noted. In this design, a business rule may be implemented in a trigger on the Inventory database that states that if a stock level falls to a certain level, send a message to the Order Entry System. The Order Entry System contains *replicated data* of only out-of-stock items. This logic can easily be implemented with publish-subscribe replication. In this design both logic and communications between the Order Entry and Inventory Systems is asynchronous. Figure 15–13 depicts both asynchronous and synchronous designs.

Asynchronous logic preserves the logical boundaries between systems and creates the most adaptable designs. For example, if the same company has multiple warehouses, typically the Order Entry System will contain logic that determines from which warehouse the order will be shipped. If the company opens a new warehouse, the Order Entry System must be changed. If the company decided to close all their warehouses and drop ship from

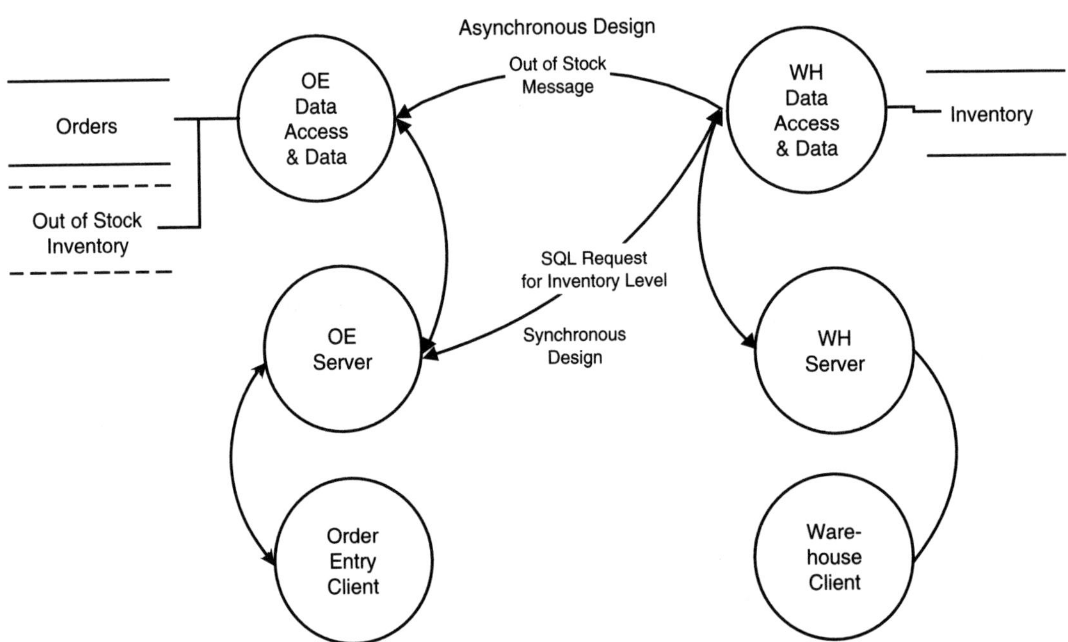

Figure 15–13 Asynchronous and Synchronous Multi-Tier Design

their suppliers, and this business decision would save the company $100,000 per month, the question is how long would it take to implement this change in the business? If the Order Entry System contains the logic of where orders are shipped from, then the system must be rewritten to implement the business change. If the Order Entry System sends an asynchronous message to the data access tier of the Warehouse System, then no changes are required to the Order Entry System. Only the data access tier of the Warehouse System would have to be changed to send orders directly to manufacturers for drop shipment.

15.8 GUIDELINES FOR PROCESS DISTRIBUTION

Applying Principles of Adaptive Designs to Software Blueprints

Decisions of where to place processing and when to use multi-tier design instead of two-tier design can be based on a set of heuristics for best practices in adaptive software design techniques. Please refer to Chapter 13 for more information on deciding between two-tier and multi-tier architectures.

In short, two-tier synchronous designs are easy to implement. They will continue to be used for small applications, decision support applications, and applications that have an expected short lifespan. Synchronous communications are suitable for systems that have a small number of users where the server(s) is located on the same LAN segment. Multi-tier asynchronous designs are more suitable for enterprise applications that have large numbers of geographically dispersed users, but require more investment in design and building infrastructure. This investment can be recouped throughout the life cycle of the application as it grows and changes.

Systems management is another important consideration for process distribution. If the system management capabilities are not yet in place, it may be preferable to *design* for multi-tier and implement on two tiers. Then, as the infrastructure is built the application can easily be distributed to a multi-tier architecture.

The other important issue in process distribution is load balancing on servers. After analyzing the processing loads on each processor (during Traffic Analysis) it may become necessary to redistribute processes. However, we always recommend a design that most closely resembles the business. This can be maintained by increasing the processing capability on a particular server, or using load balancing technology such as clustered SMPs and transaction monitors.

The IllumiSys™ Design Method provides the necessary analysis and models for defining how to distribute processing. Logical clients have been defined in the Event Distribution Aspect, by considering the events a client must handle. In the Behavioral Aspect we defined the detailed responses to each event. These responses are the processing that is distributed to the server in a multi-tier architecture, or that remains on the client in a two-tier architecture. The data model was fully defined in the Information Aspect.

This is used to create the database design. We also know where things happen. In the Geographic Distribution Aspect (Chapter 16), we design the software for each geographic location. At that point, much of the design is reuseable.

15.9 DATA DISTRIBUTION

Creating a Distributed Data Architecture That can be Managed

How data is distributed is dependent on the design decisions made in process distribution, the network infrastructure, and the data architecture and administration policies of the organization. The distribution of data can have a profound impact on the performance of the system. For example, if the data is on the local server, responses to data requests will be very fast. If the data is located on a remote server, and the request must cross a wide area network and several routers, response time could be much slower.

The key decision factors for any data distribution design are manageability and performance—in that order. Instant access to incorrect data is of dubious benefit to the organization. Therefore, it is important to create a Data Architecture that can be managed in a distributed environment. Redundant data is not a problem but inconsistent data is. Distributed data administration requires a high level of commitment from both business users and developers. This is because data that is shared across the enterprise requires a shared understanding and consistent use of the data.

Most large organizations have many systems. The number can be anywhere from dozens to hundreds. These systems were generally built to support separate specific busi-

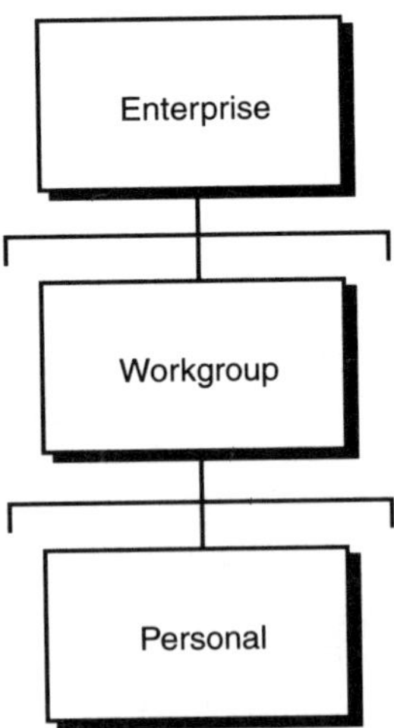

Figure 15–14 Levels of Data Distribution and Sharing in the Enterprise

ness functions. The data in these systems was generally defined according to the needs of one application, not the enterprise as a whole. It is very common to find synonyms and homonyms across systems. Synonyms are data elements that mean the same thing, but have different names and data structures in different systems. Homonyms are data elements that have the same name but which actually mean different things. For example, the data element Sale may mean an order in the Order Entry System. In the Marketing System, a Sale may be a promotional discount that is valid for a period of time and has a specific computational value. At a large railroad, there were many different definitions of a "Train." To the dispatcher a Train was a scheduled run, such as the 5:15 from Boston to New York. To the maintenance crew a Train was Locomotive #123 with five passenger cars. In our experience, these examples exist in all large companies. The most difficult issues to solve in distributing data are *not* technical. They are issues of differences in symantic meaning across the enterprise. Resolving these issues requires the participation of business managers who are responsible for the data. It is often very difficult to obtain the necessary time commitment from these high level managers.

Early efforts for building enterprise data models were generally not successful because they were too large and not directly related to a return on investment to the business. They did not focus on determining which data was shared across the enterprise. As Figure 15–4 depicts, there are different levels of data sharing across the enterprise. Some data is only pertinent in specific departments. And as long as there are hard drives on personal computers, there will be data distributed to desktops in spreadsheets and personal databases. We recommend that companies do not try to manage data down to the desktop, except for backing up over the network. However, critical enterprise data should be managed across systems. This is where enterprise data modeling and management efforts should focus.

We recommend starting with a small amount of critical enterprise data that is shared across all systems. Customers and products are often good places to start. When the scope is kept small, the effort is more manageable, and has a greater chance of success. Then incrementally build on the success, in the context of meeting the information needs of new strategic efforts. Tying the incremental building of the enterprise data repository to strategic business initiatives ensures the effort will provide a return on investment.

15.10 THE DATA WAREHOUSE

The Data Warehouse Plays a Central Role in the Enterprise Data Architecture

Managing distributed data and determining how to distribute data starts with a Data Architecture and data administration policies. The Data Architecture is based on two principles:

1. Separate operational transaction data from decision support data.
2. Only update authoritative sources of data and replicate from there.

It is critical to create separate decision support databases for a number of reasons. First, it insulates transaction systems from long ad hoc queries, which can adversely impact the performance of mission-critical transaction systems. This is an important point because there are commercially available software products to directly query transaction systems. We view this strategy as highly risky, because a poorly designed ad hoc query can adversely effect the performance of an operational system.

The separation between transaction data and decision support data also enables an enterprise view of the data. Whereas the transaction systems may in fact have synonyms and homonyms, the data can be mapped to shared enterprise definitions and be stored separately for the purposes of decision support. Decision support databases often require additional data not found in transaction systems, including summary data, historical data, and external data. Furthermore, the data structures for optimizing updates are different from the structures for optimizing data retrieval.

The Data Warehouse becomes the central focus of the Enterprise Data Architecture. It is the one place where a cross-functional definition of data can be found. This is especially important for organizations that have decided to buy rather than build applications. Commercial package applications each have their own database, designed to run the vertical application. The vendor can not easily change the database to fit within the overall enterprise information model of a particular organization. Therefore, the data in application packages should be mapped to the Enterprise Information Model for the Data Warehouse, which then becomes the authoritative source for all decision support. The same is true for legacy applications that cannot be easily changed. The data is ported and mapped to the common definitions in the Data Warehouse. This provides a cross-functional view of enterprise information with minimal impact on the operational systems.

It is important to note that the data warehouse architecture (Figure 15–15) is actually a collection of databases. The architecture can evolve from an integrated copy of transactions data used for reporting and ad hoc queries, to a Data Distribution Center. The Data Distribution Center is somewhat of a transaction processing system. The processing includes taking feeds from other systems, validating and reformatting feeds, loading the data, and sending data to other systems in a variety of formats. The Data Distribution Center stores transaction level data, and can even take real-time updates. This would enable real-time decision support. The data warehouse also stores summary data, historical data, and external data from outside the organization. The Warehouse/Distribution Center design, which includes a normalized structure for real time data feeds in addition to a multidimensional structure, is the most adaptable data architecture. It enables all information requirements to be met (including recasting of history when reorganizations occur).

Normalized data structures are designed to prevent insertion and deletion anomalies, and are necessary for transaction processing. However, they yield many small tables that must be joined together through common key columns (called primary and foreign keys) to actually answer the business questions. The join process is I/O (input/output) intensive (the slowest operation a computer performs). The more tables that must be joined, the slower the response will be to the query. Complex queries against normalized databases can become so resource intensive that they can, and have, brought a mainframe to

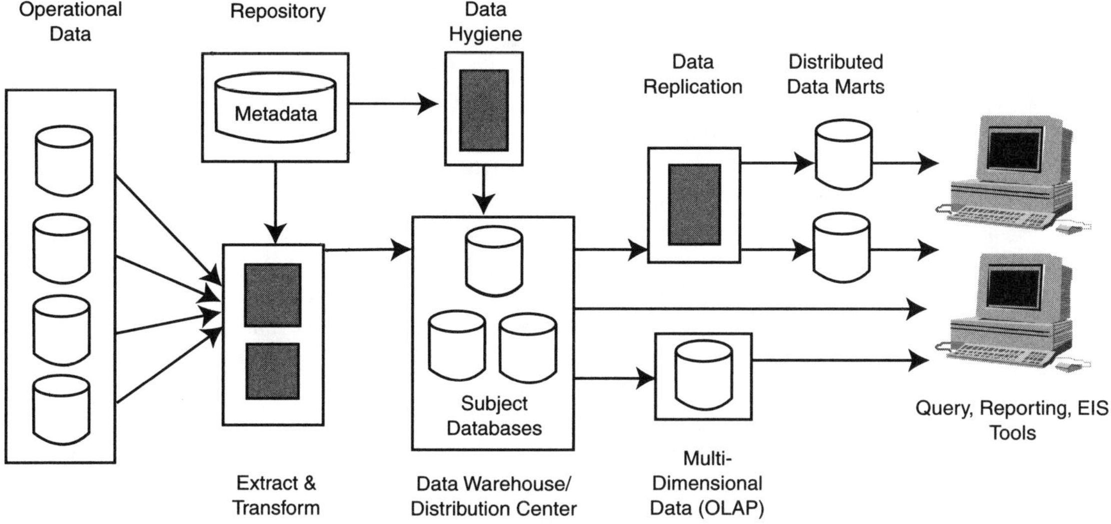

Figure 15–15 The Data Warehouse Architecture

its knees. Furthermore, they are more difficult for end users who would need to understand the table structures and how to join many tables to answer their question.

Data structures optimized for information retrieval include denormalized tables for reporting; multidimensional or star schema for on-line analytical processing (OLAP). Data Marts are denormalized databases that are distributed to the business units for querying and reporting. They contain a small subset of the information contained in the Data Warehouse. The Warehouse feeds the Data Marts. Replication tools automate this process.

The multidimensional and star schema databases provide structures for optimizing queries that analyze data along different dimensions. An example is analyzing sales by product within each region over a certain period of time. After examining the results of one query, the analyst may decide to look at slightly different dimensions such as analyzing sales of a product across multiple regions. Relational databases perform very poorly for time series and trend analysis queries. This is where multidimensional and star schema databases excel. They can improve query performance for some types of queries by a factor of 100!

Multidimensional databases have been used for many years by retail marketing analysts. The data structure is essentially a multidimensional, sparse matrix. Until recently all the products were entirely proprietary solutions. Then some of the large vendors, particularly IRI (now owned by Oracle), redesigned their products to be client/server to enable access from a variety of popular front query and reporting tools. Multidimensional databases typically do not contain transaction level data. Some, however, allow pass-through of SQL statements to relational sources. They enable drill-down through defined hierarchical roll-up structures. Loading the data into these structures is not fast. They are often refreshed weekly. However, the types of analysis multidimensional databases are good for, such as trend analysis, generally do not require frequent updates.

Star schema was developed at Xerox Labs. It is a design method that enables a multidimensional structure to be implemented in a relational database. The center of the star is the fact table. Dimension tables such as time, region, product, and customer are attached to the fact table. Specialized index structures provide very fast access to the information. Star schemas are easier to refresh than multidimensional databases. The indexes are dropped, the fact table is loaded with new transaction data, and then the indexes are rebuilt. These databases are often refreshed nightly. The major benefit of star schema over multidimensional databases is that it can be implemented in a relational database and does not require an additional proprietary database. The architecture also allows easy access from front end query and reporting tools. (For more information about star schema, we recommend the writings of Ralph Kimball.)

The Repository is another database in the overall Data Warehouse Architecture. It is the reference tool for both developers and decision makers for understanding what is available in the data warehouse. It contains information about the data, called metadata. The metadata may include such information about a data element as:

- Name (common and unique across the enterprise)
- Description
- Format
- Authoritative Source (including alias and format in Authoritative Source)
- Other systems it is found in (including aliases and formats in other sources)
- Other systems data fed from the Warehouse (subscription list)

The extract and transform tools automate some of the matching and transformation functions for getting the data into the warehouse. Data hygiene tools are used for ensuring the accuracy of the data. Data replication services automate the delivery of information.

The second principle of Data Architecture is to only update authoritative sources of data. If there is a data warehouse, that is the source for all replication. This provides a simple and effective method of managing distributed data. This practice can be easily implemented in a multi-tier architecture because the data access tier can just "point" to the Authoritative Source for update operations. The real difficulty is in defining and managing Authoritative Sources. One of the tools we use for this is the Data Distribution Table (See section 15.12 below).

There are a few things to note about the Data Architecture described in Figure 15–16. We have seen some organizations that need to make retroactive changes to certain data that crosses multiple systems. This often necessitates updating multiple systems, then running reconciliation processes to ensure the consistency of data. If the data is in a Data Warehouse/Distribution Center then it can be the single update source which sends the changes to the other systems. This greatly simplifies data management. Further, if data sources are migrating, and new multi-tier applications replace them, eventually the data distribution center can become the centralized capture point of all data. On other words, over time, it can become the capture point for some, if not all, transaction data.

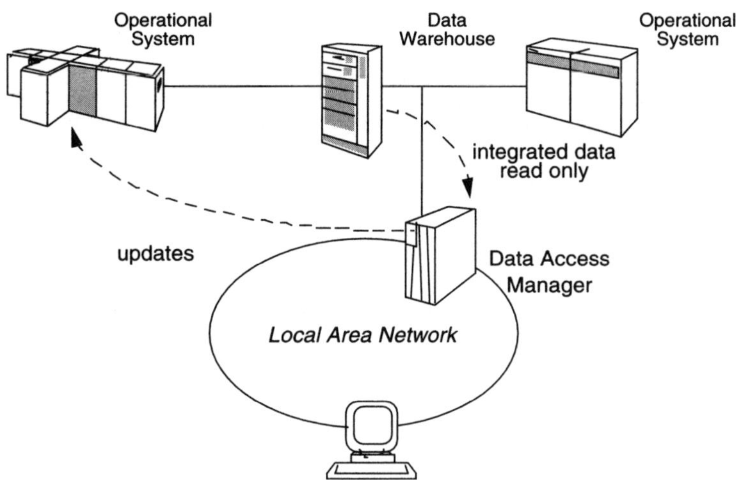

Figure 15–16 Data Architecture for Simplified Data Management

Organizations with a pressing need for real-time decision support may migrate to this architecture sooner than later.

15.11 ENTITY-PROCESSOR TABLE

Defining Data Requirements for Each Processor

It is essential that the manner in which data is distributed across processors and geographic locations simplifies data administration and ensures data consistency. The starting point is always with the business requirements. These were defined in the Behavioral Aspect (Chapter 8) in the Entity Response Table. Once we create the Processor Distribution Table (section 15.3), we can define the data requirements for each processor. This is done using the Entity Processor Table (Figure 15–17).

To create the Entity Processor Table we use the Entity Event Table from the Bridge Aspect (Chapter 7) and the Event Processor Distribution Table (Figure 15–5). Putting this information together into an Entity Processor Table defines the information required for each event and response distributed to each processor. By mapping the information access to the processors the need to share information across locations becomes apparent. For example, the <Buyer> entity is updated by processes distributed to every client. This table shows the create, update, and delete to both the clients and the database server. This is because part of the create, update, and delete process (the request) is on the client, and part of the create, update, and delete (the actual change to the data or the response to the request) is on the server.

Processor / Entity or Relationship	Buyer Admin. Client	Buyer Check In	Buyer Check Out	Whole-saler Client	Buyer Admin. Server	Data-base Server	Com-modity Mgmnt. Server	Main-frame Service Whole-salers
Buyer	c,u,m,r	r,u	r,u	r,u	m,r,u	c,u,d		
Wholesaler				m,r	r	r		c,u,d
Sale <Wholesaler> sells to <Buyer>				c,r,u,d	u	c,u,d		r
Sale Item <Commodity> is item of <Sale>			r,u	c,r,u,d	r	c,u,d	r	
Commodity			r	m,r		r	c,u,d	
Stock <Wholesaler> stocks <Commodity>				r		r	c,u,d	
Hanger				m,r		r		c,u,d
<Hanger> is located at <Wholesaler>				m		r		r
<Hanger > assigned to <Sale>				c,d		c		r

Figure 15–17 Entity Processor Table

15.12 DATA DISTRIBUTION TABLE

Defining Authoritative Data Sources and Replication Targets

The Entity Processor Table defines data requirements for each processor. The next step is to determine where data will be stored. Today's database technology includes the ability to easily replicate data to multiple sources. Some replication products include publish-subscribe capabilities, where a data source can "subscribe" to certain types of information, and when the information is updated it will automatically be sent to all subscribers. These products help automate data administration in a distributed environment. The key is to program the replication products to do the job effectively. We use the Data Distribution Table (Figure 15–18) to define Authoritative Data Sources and requirements for access or copies of data. This table is used extensively in determining the data distribution strategy.

The Data Distribution Table defines all Authoritative Data Sources and where data will be replicated to. Once the Entity Processor Table is created, this step is straightforward. All sources where data is created, updated, and deleted are Authoritative Sources (AS). We have found this charting technique also to be effective when determining data

Processor / Entity or Relationship	Buyer Admin. Client	Buyer Check In	Buyer Check Out	Whole-saler Client	Buyer Admin. Server	Data-base Server	Com-modity Mgmnt. Server	Main-frame Service Whole-salers
Buyer	Copy	access	access	Copy	access	AS		
Wholesaler				Partial Copy	access	Copy		AS
Sale <Wholesaler> sells to <Buyer>				Copy (original source)	access	AS		Copy
Sale Item <Commodity> is item of <Sale>			access	Copy (original source)	access	AS	Copy	
Commodity			access	Partial Copy		Copy	AS	
Stock <Wholesaler> stocks <Commodity>				Partial Copy		Copy	AS	
Hanger						Copy		AS
<Hanger> is located at <Wholesaler>				Partial Copy		Copy		AS
<Hanger > assigned to <Sale>				Copy		AS		Copy

Figure 15–18 Data Distribution Table for Fleury Market

administration responsibilities across business units. Generally, business users are not anxious to volunteer to be responsible for data integrity. However, if they are responsible for a system that is an Authoritative Source of data, they automatically assume responsibility for the data integrity.

After defining Authoritative Sources the next step is to decide whether to replicate data to other processors or access the Authoritative Source directly. We use a set of guidelines based on best practices when making these decisions.

15.13 GUIDELINES FOR DATA DISTRIBUTION

Guidelines for Designing Optimal Data Distribution Strategies

The optimal solution will depend upon the geographic distribution between systems, the network infrastructure, the number of instances for particular data elements (data volume), the volatility of the data, and the necessity for concurrent access to live data. The following represent some general guidelines:

- If the Authoritative Source is geographically distant from where the data is required, replicate the data if the volumes are not too large and live data access is not a requirement. This will increase systems performance.
- If the Authoritative Source is an external transaction processing system, replicate the data to the local server. This will both increase systems performance and simplify systems integration design. It also preserves the logical boundaries between applications.
- If the data is relatively stable and data volumes are relatively low, replicate the data freely. Often, this describes validation data, which may even be replicated to the client, thereby preventing extra network traffic for failed transactions.

Beyond these basic guidelines, network traffic and data volumes are the gating factors. It may be necessary to repartition data after a complete Traffic Analysis is performed. For example, an initial design may be to replicate large amounts of data on a nightly basis, but after performing Traffic Analysis it may be determined that the volume of data cannot successfully be transferred within the batch window defined. For example, Figure 15–19 defines the options for distributing data for Fleury Market.

Entity	Possible Redistribution Type	Pros	Minus Factors
Buyer	Replicate to Buyer Admin. and Wholesaler clients	Availability of buyer info for all transactions	Increased storage necessary on clients, but data volumes are manageable.
Commodity	Option 1: Copy of all the Commodities to each client machine. OR Option 2: Copy only the commodities that each Wholesaler deals in.	Easy Speedy Specific and Efficient	Requires more storage capacity on clients. Requires more processing—simplified with subscribe and publish replication.
Stock	Replicate copies to local database server. Replicate partial copy specific to each Wholesaler. Issue is when to replicate changes in stock.	Specific and Efficient	More complex processing. Preferably would like to use event triggers to update wholesaler copies.
Sale/Sale Item	Each originating sale begins on Wholesaler client then is rolled up to server.	Wholesalers need to "own" their sales	Possible "traffic jams" for uploads at check-out time.
Hanger	Each Wholesaler is issued a set of Hangers at Market opening.	Efficiency in Storage	Upload when buyer checks out.
Wholesaler	Authoritative system is commodities system—replicated copies to other systems.	Simple design	Increased storage requirements.

Figure 15–19 Data Distribution Options

From Processor Name	To Processor Name	Message Name	Message Content	Message Type
Service Wholesalers Mainframe	Database Server	Wholesalers Info	Wholesaler Record	ASCII Extract
		Hanger Assign-ment	Wholesaler ID, Hanger#	ASCII Extract
Buyer Admin. Server	Service Wholesalers Mainframe	Sales	Wholesaler ID, Buyer ID, sale total	Async. Message
Buyer Admin. Server	Commodity Mgnt. Server	Sales	Wholesaler ID, Hanger#, Sale Items	Async. Message
Commodity Mgnt. Server	Buyer Admin. Server	Pick-up Status	Hanger#	Async. Message
Buyer Admin. Server	Database Server	Add Buyer	Buyer ID, Name, Restaurant, Address, Tele#, Bank Info	RPC or Async. Message
		Change/Delete Buyer	Buyer ID, Change Info	RPC or Async. Message
		Deposit	Buyer ID, Amount	RPC or Async. Message
		Add Sale	Buyer ID, Wholesaler ID, Sale Item(s), Item Price, Hanger#	RPC or Async. Message
		Change/Delete Sale	Buyer ID, Wholesaler ID, Hanger#, Item Changes	RPC or Async. Message
		Buyer Check-In	Buyer ID, Status	RPC or Async. Message
Buyer Admin. Client	Buyer Admin. Server	Add Buyer	Buyer ID, Name, Restaurant, Address, Tele#, Bank Info	RPC or Async. Message
		Change/Delete Buyer	Buyer ID, Change Info	RPC or Async. Message
		Deposit	Buyer ID, Amount	RPC or Async. Message
Buyer Admin.	Buyer Admin. Client	Add Buyer Response	Message Status	Async. Message
		Change/Delete Buyer Response	Message Status	Async. Message
		Deposit Response	Message Status	Async. Message

Figure 15–20 Message Specification Table

15.14 MESSAGE SPECIFICATION TABLE

Specifying Messages Between Processors

The last step in the Processor Distribution Aspect can be thought of as reconnecting the pieces that were "cut up" by distributing data and processing across processors. This is done by examining the resulting processor-to-processor communications. The Message Specification Table (Figure 15–20) defines the interfaces between distributed components.

The easiest way to see the communications between processors is via the processor DFD. At this point we can name and specify the messages between systems, sometimes called dialogs. Here we have chosen not to use the term dialog because it may connote synchronous back-and-forth communications.

The message specifications are used extensively in Traffic Analysis and become the coding specs for intercomponent communications. Therefore, it is important to be as detailed and precise as possible. At this point, you may find additional messages which are necessary but which do not appear on the Processor DFD. Be sure to update the Processor DFD if you add new messages. This is part of the iterative nature of design.

The Message Specification Table can be used for any type of communications, including synchronous and asynchronous messaging, RPCs, SQL calls, messages, ORBs, or even extracts. The Message Specification Table is also one of the major inputs to Traffic Analysis.

16

Geographic Distribution Aspect

Distributing the Processors Across Geographic Locations

Once we have defined the processing and data distribution design, it must be mapped to each geographic location of the business. This step may result in repartitioning some processing and data. Basically the Geographic Distribution Aspect expands the Processor Distribution Aspect to include a set of artifacts for each geographic location, as well as an overall enterprise view of the distributed system.

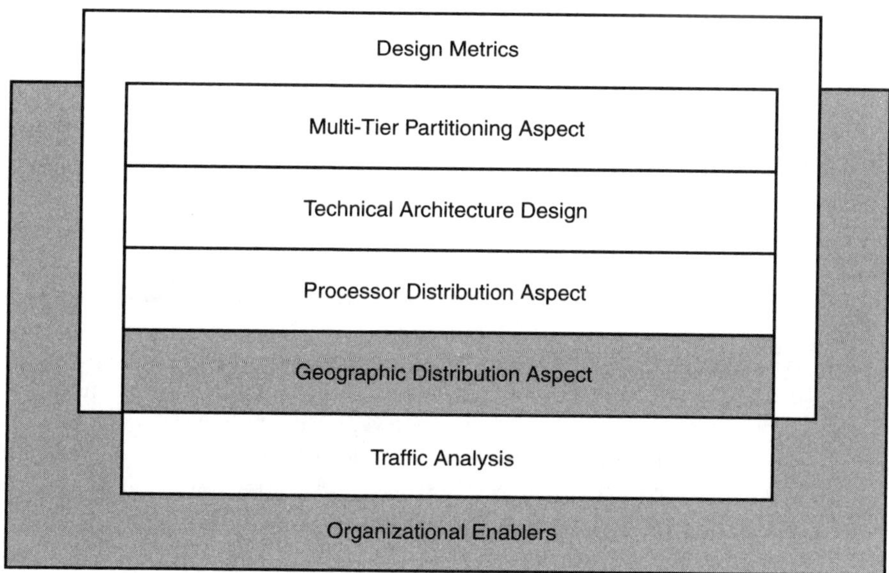

Figure 16–1 Geographic Distribution Aspect of the Implementation Model

Aspect	Activity	Artifact/View	M/O/R
Geographic Distribution Aspect	Distribute processing across geographic locations	Processor Distribution Table for Each Location	Mandatory
		Processor DFDs for Each Location	Mandatory
	Define communications between geographic locations	Enterprise DFD	Mandatory
	Distribute data across geographic locations	Enterprise Data Distribution Table	Mandatory
		Data distribution table for each location	Mandatory

Figure 16–2 Activities and Artifacts of the Geographic Distribution Aspect

In the Event Distribution Aspect of the Essential Model, we defined how logical locations are geographically distributed (Chapter 9). Now that logical locations have been mapped to physical processors, we can put the two views together and map processors to geographic locations. Figure 16–1 depicts the Geographic Distribution Aspect in the Implementation Model.

In the Geographic Distribution Aspect we answer the following questions:

- What processors will be distributed to each geographic location?
- What events will be distributed to each geographic location?
- What data will be distributed to each geographic location?

Figure 16–2 depicts the activities and artifacts of the Geographic Distribution Aspect.

16.1 OBJECTIVES OF THE GEOGRAPHIC DISTRIBUTION ASPECT

Site-By-Site Planning for Distributed Operations

The Geographic Distribution Aspect displays the software components and data that are needed at each geographic location. Each geographic location may contain one or more logical location, as defined in the Event Distribution Aspect (see Chapter 9). A geographic location can actually be a mobile site, such as a salesperson's laptop. These are the actual locations where business occurs. By applying the number of users, transactions and data volumes at each geographic location (see Chapter 10), it is possible to do capacity planning on a site-by-site basis. It is also necessary for Traffic Analysis of communication between geographic sites. This is critical because communication between sites is often over slower wide area networks.

Processor / Response	Wholesaler Booth Client	Buyer Membership Admin. Client	Check In / Check Out Client	Service Buyers Admin. Server	Commodity Mngmnt Server	*Service Wholesalers Mainframe*
1. Add buyer		Add buyer presentation		Execute add buyer rules		
2. Check in buyer			Checkin buyer presentation	Update buyer status		
3. Create sale	Create sale presentation			Update sale status Add sale Add line item Update buyer balance Assign hanger to sale Notify service buyers of account debit	Update hanger status Check stock level Reduce stock level	Update wholsaler sales
4. Check out buyer	Buyer check-out presentation		Check out buyer presentation	Update sales status Update buyer status	Release hanger from sale Update hanger status	
5. Record pick-up				Update sales status		
6. Market closes/cancel uncollected sales				Cancel uncollected sales Update buyer status Update sales status	Release hanger from sale Update hanger status	Update wholesaler sales
7. Note membership change		Membership change presentation		Change membership info		
8. Change sale	Change sale presentation			Update buyer balance Send message to commodity mgnmt.	Check stock Reduce stock Increase stock	
9. Cancel sale	Cancel sale presentation			Update buyer balance Update sales status Send message to commodity mgnmt.	Release hanger from sale Update hanger status	
10. Add deposit		Add deposit presentation		Add deposit to balance		

Figure 16–3 Processor Distribution Table for Lyon

16.2 PROCESSOR DISTRIBUTION TABLES

Distributing Events to Processors at Each Location

A Processor Distribution Table must be created for each geographic location. Note that neither Lyon or Bordeux have a mainframe, but both are assumed to have their own Commodity Management Servers. The external processors and processes are indicated in italics.

To create these tables, use the Logical Location Distribution Table by Geography (Chapter, Figure 9–6) and the Processor Distribution Table (Chapter 16, Figure 15–5). Note that Figure 16–3 is much like the Fleury, except that Lyon does not have a mainframe on site. Although much of the Fleury design is reusable, here we also note the differences between the geographic locations. This is part of the adaptability and reusability of the design.

As Figure 16–4 depicts, Bordeaux does not handle all the business events that Fleury and Lyon do. That is why there are no Wholesaler Clients, no Buyer Membership Admin. Clients. Like Lyon, Bordeaux has no mainframe. The mainframe appears on the table in italics because although it is not located there, it still performs processing for Bordeaux.

Processor / Response	Check In / Check Out Client	Service Buyers Admn. Server	Commodity Management Server	*Service Wholesalers Mainframe*
2. Check In Buyer	Check in buyer presentation	Update buyer status		
4. Check Out Buyer	Check out buyer presentation	Update sales status Update buyer status	Release hanger from sale Update hanger status	
5. Record Pick-up		Update sales status		
6. Market Closes/ Cancel Un-collected Sales		Cancel uncollected sales Update buyer status Update sales status	Release hanger from sale Update hanger status	*Update wholesaler sales*
9. Cancel Sale		Update buyer balance Update sales status Send message to commodity mgnmt.	Release hanger from sale Update hanger status	

Figure 16–4 Processor Distribution Table for Bordeaux

16.3 PROCESSOR DATA FLOW DIAGRAMS

Defining Communication Between Processors at Each Location and Across Locations

It is necessary to create a separate Data Flow Diagram (DFD) for each geographic location, showing interprocessor communication at each location, as well as an enterprise level DFD, showing communication across locations. To create the processor DFD for each location, use the Processor Distribution Table.

Note that because of the lower processing volumes at both Lyon and Bordeaux there is only one physical server for both the "Service Buyers Admin." and the "Database" (see Figures 16–5 and 16–6). We will, however, maintain the same design

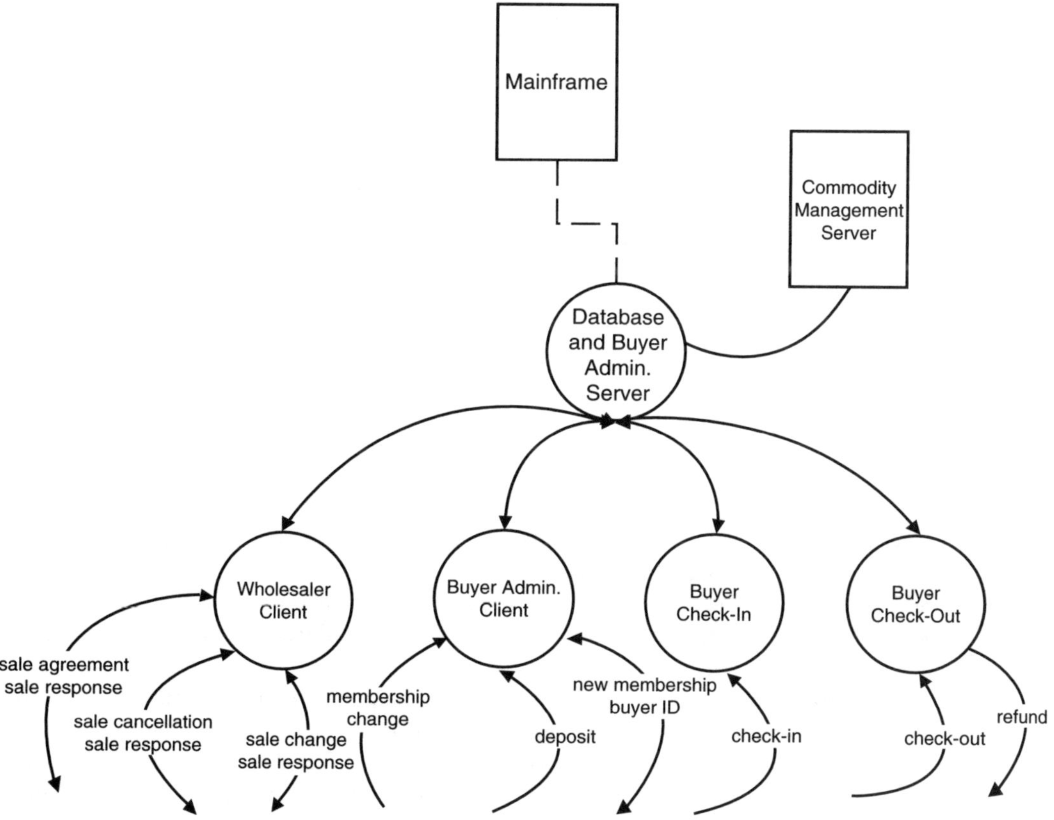

Figure 16–5 Processor Data Flow Diagram for Lyon

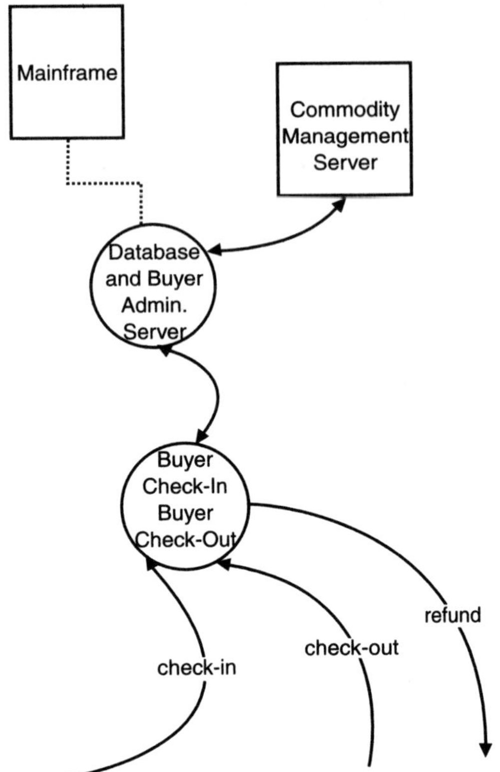

Figure 16–6 Processor Data Flow Diagram for Bordeaux

components as in Fleury and just distribute all the components for both the "Database Server" and the "Service Buyers Admin. Server" to the same physical processor. Also note that Bordeaux has only one check-in and check-out client. The granular component based design makes it easy to redistribute components to physical processors on a site-by-site basis.

The next step is to create an Enterprise Processor Data Flow Diagram (Figure 16–7) to depict communications across geographic locations. To create this view, start with the Enterprise Logical Location Distribution Diagram (Chapter 9) and elaborate to include processor-to-processor communications across locations. Here we note only server-to-server communication, because in our design clients never communicate directly with external systems or other geographic locations.

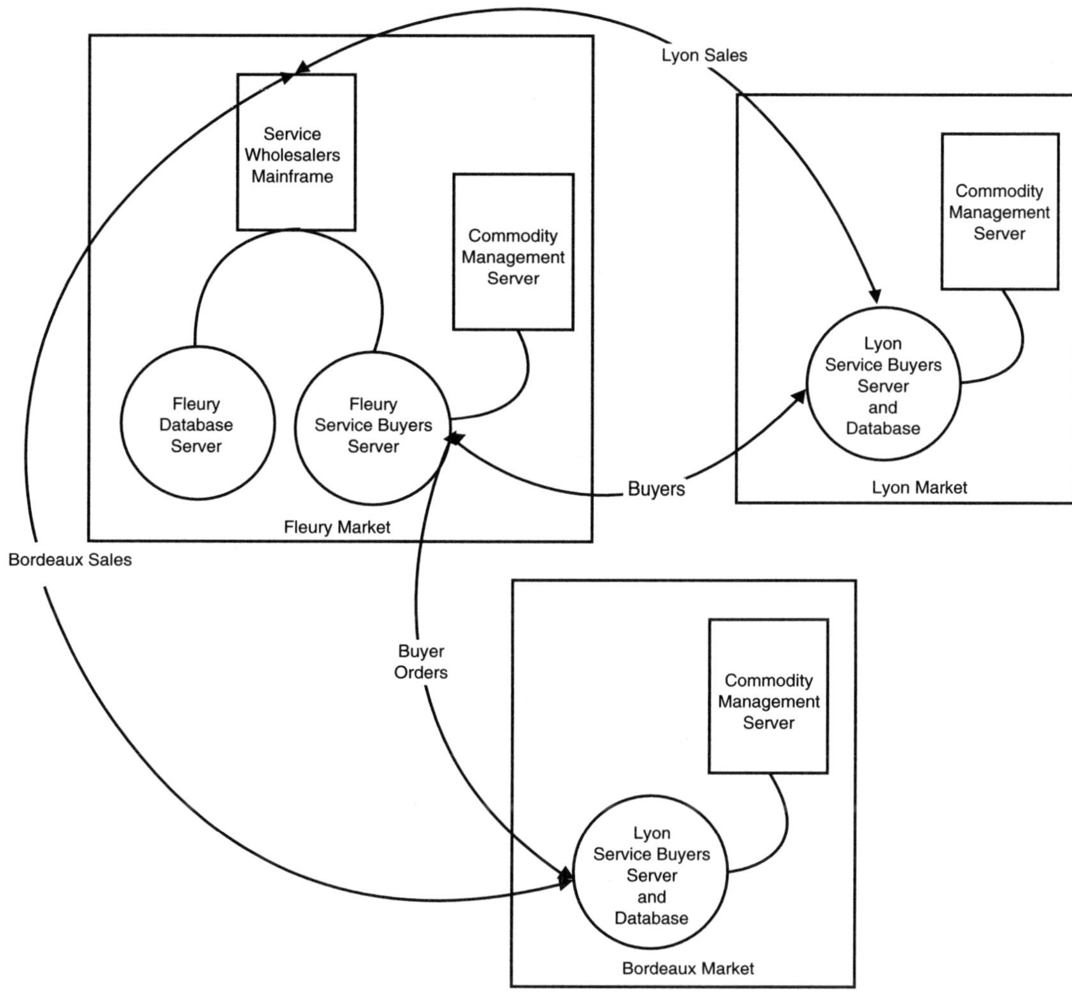

Figure 16–7 Processor Data Flow Diagram Across Locations

16.4 DATA DISTRIBUTION TABLE

Defining Authoritative Data Sources and Replication Targets

The Data Distribution Table defines all Authoritative Data Sources and where data will be replicated to. We need to create a Data Distribution Table for each geographic location (Figures 16–8, 16–9, and 16–10), as well as an enterprise view. It is useful to start with

Processor / Entity or Relationship	Fleury Database Server	Lyon Buyer Admin./ Database Server	Bordeaux Buyer Admin./ Database Server	*Commodity Mgmnt. Server*	*Mainframe Service Wholesalers*
Buyer	AS	Copy	Copy		
Wholesaler	Copy	Copy	Copy		AS
Sale <Wholesaler> sells to <Buyer>	AS (for Fleury & Bordeaux)	AS (for Lyon only)	Copy		Copy
Sale Item <Commodity> is item of <Sale>	AS (for Fleury & Bordeaux)	AS (for Lyon only)	Copy	Copy	
Commodity	Copy	Copy	Copy	AS	
Stock <Wholesaler> stocks <Commodity>	Copy	Copy	Copy	AS	
Hanger	Copy	Copy			AS
<Hanger> is located at <Wholesaler>	Copy	Copy			AS
<Hanger > assigned to <Sale>	AS (for Fleury only)	AS (for Lyon only)			Copy

Figure 16–8 Enterprise Data Distribution Table

Processor / Entity or Relationship	Buyer Admin. Client	Buyer Check In	Buyer Check Out	Wholesaler Client	Buyer Admin./ Database Server	Commodity Mgmnt. Server	Mainframe Service Whole-salers
Buyer	Copy	access	access	Copy	AS		
Wholesaler				Partial Copy	Copy		AS
Sale <Wholesaler> sells to <Buyer>				Copy (original source)	AS		Copy
Sale Item <Commodity> is item of <Sale>			access	Copy (original source)	AS	Copy	
Commodity			access	Partial Copy	Copy	AS	
Stock <Wholesaler> stocks <Commodity>				Partial Copy	Copy	AS	
Hanger					Copy		AS
<Hanger> is located at <Wholesaler>				Partial Copy	Copy		AS
<Hanger > assigned to <Sale>				Copy	AS		Copy

Figure 16–9 Data Distribution Table for Lyon

Processor / Entity or Relationship	Buyer Check-In/ Check-Out Client	Bordeaux Buyer Admin. Server	Commodity Mgmnt. Server	Mainframe Service Whole-salers
Buyer	access	Copy		
Wholesaler		Copy		AS
Sale <Wholesaler> sells to <Buyer>		Copy		Copy
Sale Item <Commodity> is item of <Sale>	access	Copy	Copy	
Commodity	access	Copy	AS	
Stock <Wholesaler> stocks <Commodity>		Copy	AS	
Hanger				AS
<Hanger> is located at <Wholesaler>				AS
<Hanger > assigned to <Sale>				Copy

Figure 16–10 Data Distribution Table for Bordeaux

the enterprise view so locations of Authoritative Sources can be identified before deciding where to replicate data. One of the guidelines of data distribution is that when the Authoritative Source is at a remote location, replicate data locally when data volumes and "live" access requirements permit. It is also helpful to replicate data from external systems.

16.5 GUIDELINES FOR GEOGRAPHIC PROCESS DISTRIBUTION

Systems Management and Performance Are Key

When defining processor distribution across geographic locations, the key issue is systems management. Some locations may not have any support personnel. It may be necessary to support the distributed system from a central location. This requires virtual data centers. Virtual data centers are secure locations, such as a locked closet, at each geographic location that is managed with the same level of monitoring as centralized data centers. Distributed management tools are required for virtual data center support. It is important to define responsibility for systems maintenance for each component on a site-by-site basis. We have often found that maintenance and support issues are key when determining the feasibility of a distributed design.

The design trade-off is between network traffic overhead for remote systems monitoring and distributed personnel. Some enterprise systems will have a combination of both; distributed personnel used at larger locations with many users and remote support used for smaller locations.

16.6 GUIDELINES FOR GEOGRAPHIC DATA DISTRIBUTION

Balancing Data Distributed Requirements with Data Integrity and Manageability as well as Network Traffic

There are a number of factors that impact the decision of how to distribute data. When the enterprise has distributed locations, it is usually more efficient to replicate and distribute data to where it is needed. When we construct the Data Distribution Table, we often find that different sites need different data. Sometimes the issue is time differences between locations. In worldwide operations one location may require access to data during the backup cycle. Data freshness requirements, defined in "Design Metrics" (Chapter 12), define whether a particular application or process requires immediate access to all data changes (often referred to as "live" access). A requirement for "live" access makes it more difficult to distribute data. Sometimes, a lag time of a few minutes is acceptable, thereby greatly simplifying the communications design for distributed copies of the data.

Other factors we often run into are ownership, control, and politics. In widely distributed enterprises different business units often prefer control of "their" data. This may require a data distribution design that is based more on politics than processing and management efficiency. We have found it helpful to spot data distribution "patterns" (Figure 16–11).

There are three sender-initiated patterns and two receiver-initiated patterns. The receiver-initiated patterns are taking extracts from multiple data sources, which can be manual extracts, distributed joins, or other implementation, and one-to-one access, which generally connotes synchronous communications between two sites. Sender-initiated patterns include sending a synchronous message to a remote site (Message 1-to-1) and replicating data from one site to multiple sites (Copy 1-to-N). We have found that the "roll-up" pattern is the most important one to pay attention to. It means that there are multiple originating sources that send copies of data to a single (centralized) location. This may imply a horizontally partitioned database, whereby different sites have similar databases but different data instances. For example, the Wholesaler Booths at Fleury Market roll-up their sales to the server. However, each wholesaler is actually an independent business entity, and has "ownership" of his/her sales data. That is why we need to keep a copy of all sales data on the Wholesaler Client, and identify it as the "Original Authoritative Source" (OAS) for Sale data. Roll-up data often involves issues of ownership and organizational politics.

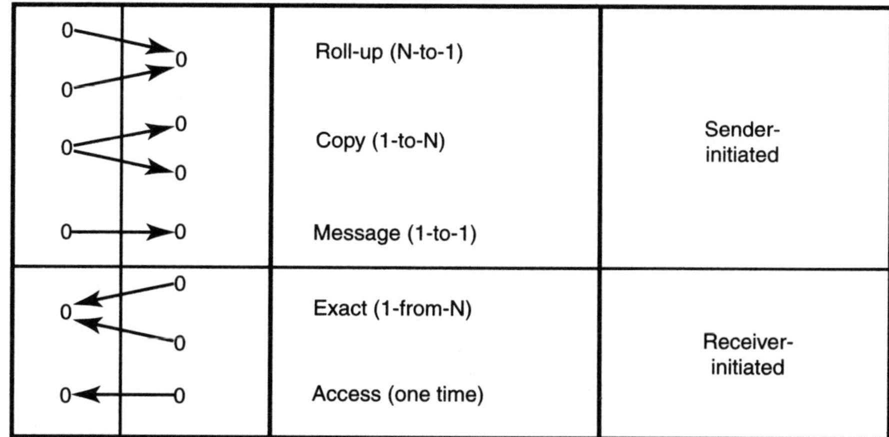

Figure 16–11 Data Distribution Patterns (by permission of Ken Schoman)

The integrity of distributed data will be enhanced through a Data Architecture that is well defined and managed. We find the key starting place for managing distributed data is defining Authoritative Sources. If all distributed copies are rectified against the Authoritative Source, integrity of distributed data becomes much easier to manage. However, it must be noted that distributed data management requires processes, design reviews, and most of all, a commitment on the part of the enterprise. Final decisions on data distribution must also take into account network traffic. This is discussed in Chapter 17, "Traffic Analysis."

17

Traffic Analysis

Traffic Analysis Measures the Impact of the Design on the Network

The network is part of the distributed application. Therefore, distributed applications must be designed for the network. After event responses and data have been distributed to processors and geographic locations and all messages have been defined between processors, the designer has sufficient information to perform Traffic Analysis. Traffic Analysis measures the message traffic between processors as well as the contention on individual processors. It helps evaluate optimal distribution of data and events. It also evaluates the feasibility of design in terms of the network infrastructure and existing network traffic. When designers provide estimates of traffic analysis to network architects, the analysis aids in network capacity planning, which is key to building a robust distributed computing infrastructure. Figure 17–1 depicts Traffic Analysis in the Implementation Model.

Traffic analysis may be done at several stages of the design process. If there are any areas of concern or risk in regard to the network, they should be exposed as soon as possible. In some cases, prototyping may also be appropriate, such as prototyping large data transfers from legacy systems. The process of Traffic Analysis uses the information from the Measurement Aspect and maps the estimates and projections to the distributed design. The results of Traffic Analysis may result in repartitioning the design.

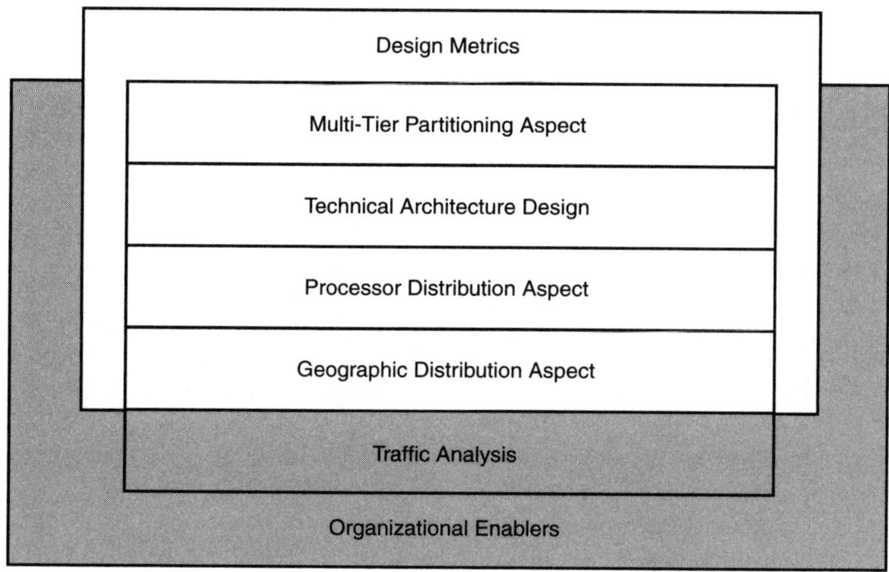

Figure 17–1 Traffic Analysis of the Implementation Model

17.1 PROCESS FOR PERFORMING TRAFFIC ANALYSIS

Designing for the Network

Traffic Analysis is an evaluation of the message traffic between processors. Figure 17–2 depicts the activities and artifacts of Traffic Analysis. The performance of the network impacts the overall performance of a distributed application. To evaluate message traffic, you need to measure messages between processors and geographic locations. The messages are defined in the Processor Distribution Aspect (Chapter 15). The frequency of

Aspect	Activity	Artifact/View	M/O/R
Traffic Analysis	Estimate network traffic	Traffic Analysis Table	Mandatory
		Traffic Flow Diagram	Mandatory
		Enterprise Traffic Table	Mandatory
		Frequency Distribution Graph	Optional
		Load Balancing Analysis	Optional

Figure 17–2 Activities and Artifacts of Traffic Analysis

each message occurrence is based on the frequency of the events. This has been defined in the Component Measurement Aspect (Chapter 10). Therefore, the two major inputs to Traffic Analysis are the Message Specification Table (Chapter 15) and the Event Response Measurement Table (Chapter 10).

17.2 TRAFFIC ANALYSIS TABLE

Estimating Message Traffic

The Traffic Analysis Table summarizes all essential information on processor-to-processor messaging, including message name, frequency, peaks, and message size. Figure 17–3 depicts sample traffic analysis between key processors. As always, in design it is important to focus on potential areas of risk. All messages should be measured for purposes of completeness in providing information for network capacity planning. Although a particular message may have insignificant impact on the overall design of the system, network traffic is cumulative, and every byte counts eventually. However, for purposes of evaluating design alternatives, it is sufficient to view critical communications. The Processor Distribution Table and DFDs are useful for identifying potential bottlenecks.

<table>
<tr><th>From Processor Name</th><th>To Processor Name</th><th>Message Name</th><th>Avg. Freq.</th><th>Peak Freq.</th><th>Peak When</th><th>Message Size</th><th>Avg. Traffic</th><th>Peak Traffic</th></tr>
<tr><td rowspan="2">Service Wholesalers Mainframe</td><td rowspan="2">Database Server</td><td>Whole-salers Info</td><td>nightly batch</td><td>none</td><td>none</td><td>250</td><td>6250</td><td>none</td></tr>
<tr><td>Hanger Assignment</td><td>nightly batch</td><td>none</td><td>none</td><td>5</td><td>12500</td><td></td></tr>
<tr><td colspan="9">For Wholesaler Info multiply message size of 250, taken from Entity Relationship Measurement Table (Figure 10–7) by number of Wholesalers (25) (Figure 10–3).
For Hanger Assignment multiply number of wholesalers (25) by average number of hangers per wholesaler (100), by size of message (5).</td></tr>
<tr><td>Buyer Admin. Server</td><td>Service Wholesalers Mainframe</td><td>Sales</td><td>480</td><td>1248</td><td>Thur.</td><td>100</td><td>48000</td><td>124800</td></tr>
<tr><td colspan="9">Multiply number of peak buyers (156 on Thursday as per Figure 10–3) by number of average sales per buyer (8).</td></tr>
<tr><td>Buyer Admin. Server</td><td>Commodity Mgnt. Server</td><td>Sales</td><td>1416</td><td>2784</td><td>Thur</td><td>50</td><td>70800</td><td>139200</td></tr>
<tr><td>Commodity Mgnt. Server</td><td>Buyer Admin. Server</td><td>Pick-up Status</td><td>177</td><td>313</td><td>Thur</td><td>5</td><td>885</td><td>1565</td></tr>
</table>

Figure 17–3 Partial Traffic Analysis Table for Fleury

From Processor Name	To Processor Name	Message Name	Avg. Freq.	Peak Freq.	Peak When	Message Size	Avg. Traffic	Peak Traffic
Fleury Buyer Admin.	Bordeaux	Sales	200	500	Thur.	100	20000	50000
		Buyers	30	60	Thur	200	600	1200

Figure 17–4 Partial Enterprise Traffic Analysis Table

17.3 TRAFFIC FLOW DIAGRAM

Depicting the Estimated Network Traffic

Data flow diagrams are the most descriptive and easily understood artifacts for depicting the movement of data across networks. Each arrow on the Processor Model represents a flow of data across the network. Because we measured the frequency of the events that trigger the messages across the network (Component Measurement Aspect, Chapter 10), we can now derive the estimated network traffic for the system. Although these are ball-park numbers and do not account for protocol overhead, they are at least a fairly accurate description of the business and a pretty good estimate for the purposes of network capacity planning.

There are more sophisticated methods for more accurately modeling dynamic processes, such as network traffic. They require simulation engines, which until recently were available only on very large-scale systems. There are now simulation engines available for mid-range servers and even some high-end workstations. Such a tool would enable a designer to perform sophisticated "what if" analysis. An ideal, but as of yet fictional distributed design tool would enable the designer to fully describe each component. Presentation and processing components could be measured by the number and frequency of requests they generate. Data components are measured in terms of size. The network architecture and protocols would also be fully defined to the tool. The user could then drag and drop the components on the Processor Model. The user would then let the model run and generate results. After analyzing the results, the user could repartition as necessary by dragging and dropping components to other processors.

Figure 17–5 is a Traffic Data Flow Diagram depicting the estimated traffic for Fleury Market. It was derived from the Processor Data Flow Diagram (Chapter 15) and the Traffic Analysis Table. When evaluating different designs from the viewpoint of network traffic, alternative Traffic Flow Diagrams can be created. Although this is not quite as easy or fast as the fictional traffic analysis tool above, at least it's derivable and communicates well with Network Architects, who are the primary reviewers of this aspect.

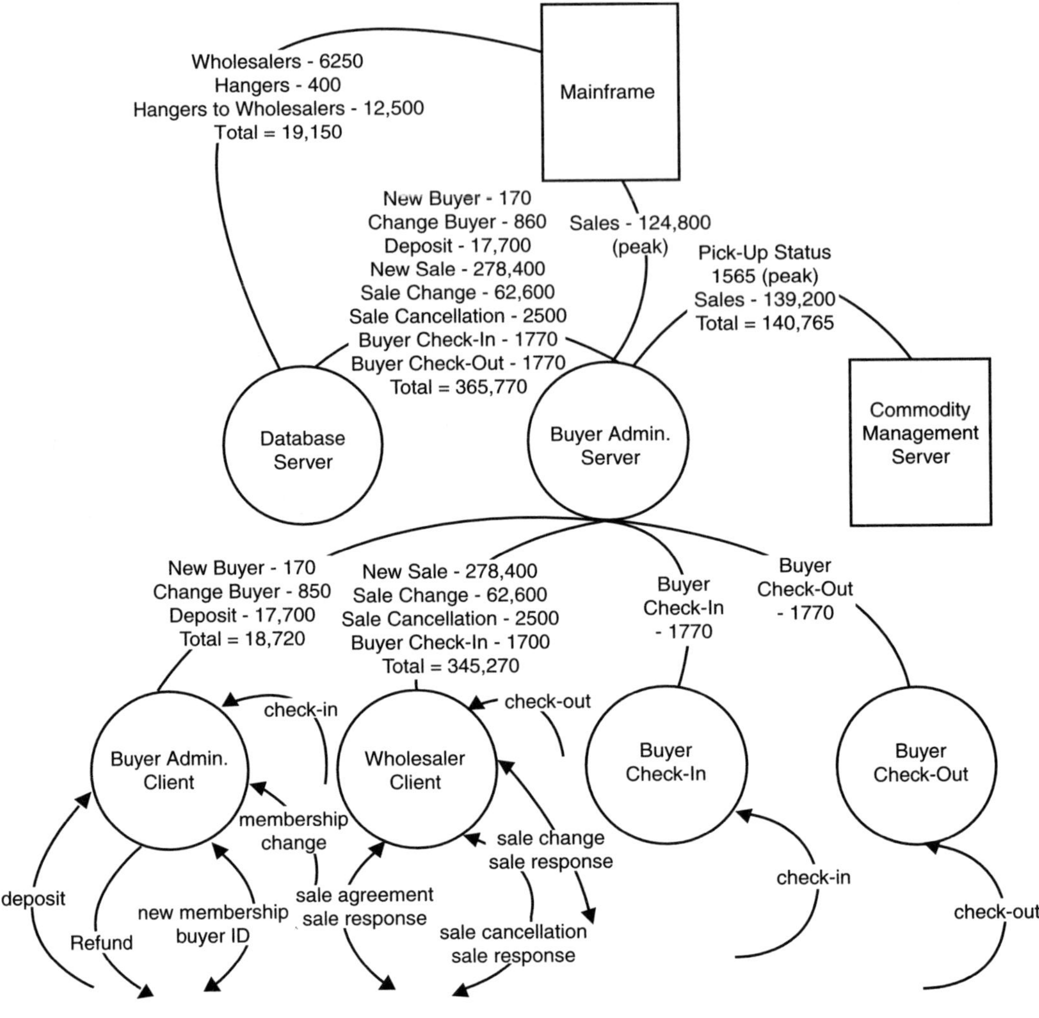

Figure 17–5 Traffic Flow Diagram

17.4 FREQUENCY DISTRIBUTION GRAPH

Determining Event Frequency Over Specific Intervals of Time

In some businesses, defining an average and peak does not sufficiently describe the complexity of the environment. Therefore, it may be necessary in some cases to determine event frequency over specific intervals of time. Usually, this information is best displayed

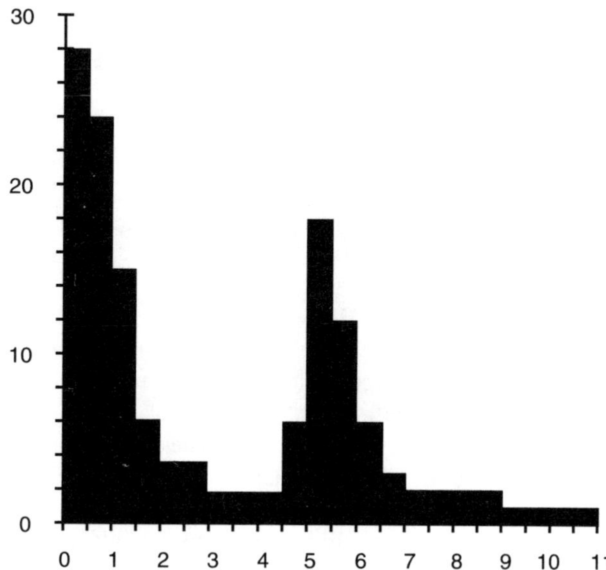

Figure 17–6 The Average Frequency of Buyer Check-In Between the Open and Close of a Market Day

in graphic form. For example, Figure 17–6 depicts the Buyer Check-In frequency during an average day at the market. Here we see two "spikes" in the number of Check-In dialogs conducted on the "Service Buyer Admin. Server"; the first during the first ninety minutes and the second during the fifth hour.

The Frequency Distribution Chart graphically calls attentions to peaks. This alone helps prevent fatal design flaws, such as not being able to handle critical peak loads. The Traffic Analysis Table may be expanded to include more columns for frequency distribution when necessary.

17.5 LOAD BALANCING

Analyzing the Design for Processing Overloads

When making design decisions such as putting the Service Buyers Admin. Server and Database Server on one processor, it is necessary to estimate the processing loads on each processor. This is done by looking at the processing volume for each server, the internal processing load each message generates, and the critical peak processing times.

For example, to determine the processing load on the Service Buyers Admin. Server, determine the message volume for each message type (Figure 17–7). That server

Server	Critical Peak Loads when	Critical Peak Loads	Solution
Buyer Admin. Server	Market Closes	# Messages = 5,500 #Transactions =50,000	Stagger processing—Update database and commodity management servers real time, batch sales to mainframe.

Figure 17–7 Processing Load Analysis Table (for the Service Buyers Admin. Server)

simultaneously handles *six* dialogs: Buyer Check-In, Buyer Check-Out, Wholesaler Booth, Buyer Membership, Service Wholesaler, and Buyer/Commodity. The sum total of all these dialogs must be mapped into the same time scale in order to do a thorough and accurate analysis of message loads of critical peak times. This analysis is recommended for critical areas of potential risk. It may be necessary at times to redesign processing and data distribution to solve some load balancing issues. It is also possible with today's technology to implement the system with clustered processors and software, including some transaction monitors, which provide automatic load balancing.

17.6 EVALUATING DESIGN ALTERNATIVES

Choosing an Adaptable, Implementable, and Supportable Design

Choosing an optimal distributed design is a process of defining alternatives and making decisions based on design trade-offs. The IllumiSys™ Design provides the information, artifacts, design goals, and heuristics to make informed decisions on complex enterprise design issues. The artifacts enable decision making through a series of facilitated work sessions. The final design may be a hybrid of multiple alternatives. This process is very effective for reaching a high quality design. The method provides information for optimally distributing data and events across processors and geographic locations. The analysis highlights potential areas of risk, such as network and processor overload points during specific time intervals. Exposing potential risks *before* the system is implemented makes it easier and cheaper to fix problems. The evaluation of each design alternative is guided by the Business Drivers, Design Goals, and Architecture Goals.

Business Drivers have driven the requirements and design at every stage of the process. As previously stated, Business Drivers include strategic enterprise initiatives plus the Drivers defined in the Statement of Purpose.

Design Goals are the "abilities" of the system. They include adaptability, manageability, feasibility, reliability, integration capability, and data consistency, availability, and freshness. The Statement of Design Goals captures the goals most pertinent to the system. Additional Design Goals may be identified in the course of the project. In that case, update the Statement of Design Goals. For example, the Design Goals for Fleury

Market include reliability (must be available from 12 P.M. to 12 A.M.), data freshness (real-time buyer balances), and availability (must operate within the given response times). Designs that do not meet these goals must be rejected.

Architecture Goals include all factors that lead to the optimization of the design across all architecture dimensions. Architecture dimensions include Data Architecture, Application Architecture, Technical Architecture, Network Architecture, and Organizational Architecture. The Data Architecture is optimized when Authoritative Sources are defined for all enterprise level data, all changes are made to and propagated from the Authoritative Source, and there is a Data Warehouse providing a separate data sources for reporting, ad hoc queries and OLAP. The Application Architecture is optimized through multi-tier partitioning, clear logical boundaries between applications, and granular reusable software components that represent Business Components. The Technical Architecture is optimized through minimizing the number of permutations and combinations through the definition and enforcement of standards. The Network Architecture is optimized when message traffic is minimized. The Organization Architecture is optimized when the organizational structure enables cross functional teaming, utilization of expertise across the enterprise, and standardization of process and technology across the enterprise. (See Part IV, Organizational Enablers.)

17.7 GUIDELINES FOR EVALUATING DESIGNS

Guidelines Based on Best Practices

Each design alternative has inherent benefits and risks associated with it, and a design decision in this area means balancing those benefits and risks. It is for these reasons that we present a few important heuristics regarding making design trade-offs during a traffic analysis activity.

Provide traceability back to the requirements. A successful client/server project delivers a system that meets the needs of a business without exceptions. The IllumiSys™ Design Method allows you to create a Design Model from an Essential Model. In other words, the method allows you to design a distributed application from a statement of business needs. Make sure your design is always tied back to the requirements. Without exception, use the same words in the design as they appear in statements of requirements. We also recommend you prefix requirements with codes that provide a higher degree of traceability. For example, we have used the letter "E" followed by a number to identify all events. You can do the same with responses ("R"), data stores ("D"), and so on. If each requirement is tied to each design element, you can evaluate those ties to see if a requirement was overlooked during the design stage. Traceability is an extremely useful technique for ensuring requirements satisfaction.

Plan for iteration. Some client/server projects fail because they do not create a project schedule which includes time for iteration. Iteration takes many forms and happens frequently on client/server projects. Throughout the book we have pointed to issues uncovered in the design process that could cause iteration in the design. For example, as mentioned earlier in this chapter, a traffic analysis could uncover the need for an alteration to the technical infrastructure, which could relax a constraint from another portion of the design, which could lead to a new design alternative, which could mean reversing a prior design decision, which would mean a new traffic analysis. This analyze-change-redesign-reanalyze cycle can (and usually does!) happen several times during a development effort. Any project that does not plan for iteration is setting itself up for failure. At the same time, we must be careful not to fall into the analysis paralysis trap. Our assumption is that good design speeds implementation rather than slow it down.

Build only what you can maintain. The organizational impact of a client/server design is crucial, because it identifies the human resources needed to maintain the system once it is deployed. An elegantly designed system that cannot be supported in distributed locations cannot be maintained over time. We recommend you build a client/server system you know you can maintain. Plan to evolve it in well-defined increments to handle more and more business events, users, and distributed locations. In this way, you will ensure the success of the project.

PART IV

ORGANIZATIONAL ENABLERS

The ability of an organization to support rapid application development and deployment of adaptive systems rests on an enterprise-wide infrastructure built for change. Adaptive organizations require the ability to meet new challenges through effective cross-organizational teaming. Most organizations have no infrastructure in place for distributed systems in the early days of migration. That means each and every development team must solve support and integration problems for themselves. This can lead to the creation

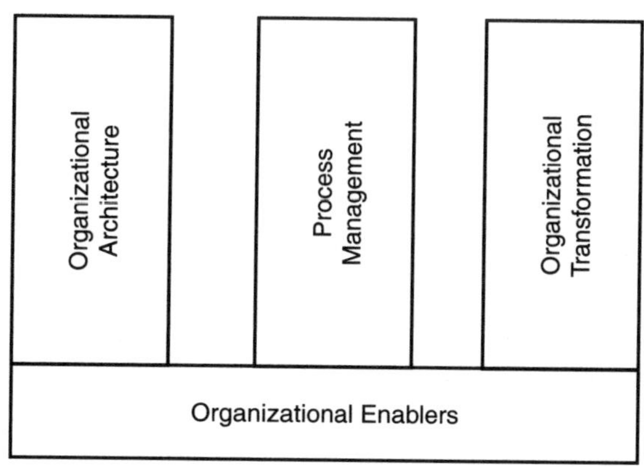

Figure IV–1 Organizational Enablers, the Pillars of Change

of stovepipe infrastructures that do not support the overall migration effort. While the actual restructuring of the organization itself can be incremental and iterative, just like the development process, it requires an overall plan and vision to enable change.

Organizational enablers include organizational architecture, process management, and organizational transformation. We call these the pillars for change. **Organizational Architecture** refers to an organizational structure optimized for cross-functional teaming and change, so the organization itself can respond to change in the marketplace. This includes the leadership structures, team structures, and support services. **Process Management** includes the propagation of best practices to enable rapid deployment of business solutions. **Organizational Transformation** includes the necessary vision, skills, training, and motivation and rewards to create adaptive organizations.

18

Organizational Architecture

In Order to Respond to Change, the Organization Must be Organized to Enable Change

The IllumiSys™ Design Method creates component-based systems that can lead to a high degree of reuse and adaptiveness to change. However, realizing those goals requires more than good coding techniques. It requires an organization that is modeled for change. Time after time we have seen the success of a project put in jeopardy because of a lack in the necessary organizational infrastructure. On the individual project level, services and resources are often required that are the responsibility of other organizational units. The priorities of one organizational unit may be in contention with the priorities of another organizational unit that controls the resources necessary for the first to succeed. This is the new cross-functional nature of a customer-driven organization.

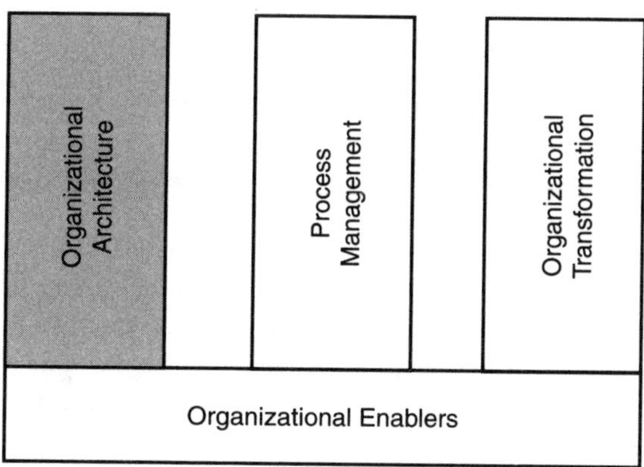

Figure 18–1 Organizational Enablers: Organizational Architecture

Organizations with rigid hierarchical structures designed around fragmented areas of responsibility cannot support this new way of working. Many organizations realize this and are undergoing massive reorganizations to better meet the needs of their customers. Many of our clients tell us that "reorgs" have become a regular fact of life. The most successful organizations have very fluid organizational structures, which change as necessary to accommodate continuous process improvement. Some organizations, trying to achieve this adaptiveness, get lost along the way without clear goals and process. Organizational transformation points to the need for organizational structures that can easily adapt to change. This is the purpose of Organizational Architecture (Figure 18–1).

18.1 OBJECTIVES OF ORGANIZATIONAL STRUCTURE

The Organizational Structure Must Enable Alignment Between Business and I/S and Cross-Functional Teaming

Success in client/server requires leadership, teamwork, and direction. I/S departments often approach client/server projects using the management structures that have been successful for developing traditional systems. Unfortunately, these structures are inadequate for client/server in three ways. First, the leadership structure is hierarchical, which inhibits effective communication and collaboration across business units. Second, each team must find its own resources for specialized expertise and support services. The expertise is not necessarily available to other projects. Lack of support services and infrastructure drive down I/S productivity and their ability to respond to rapid business change. Third, the direction of a traditional project is set from the technical vantage point of the I/S department, instead of being driven by the business. Let us see how these structures must change for client/server.

18.2 LEADERSHIP STRUCTURE

The Leadership Structure Must Ensure Alignment Between the Business and I/S

A leadership structure that aligns business and I/S has a much better chance of ensuring that technology enables the business (Figure 18–2). This is commonly the goal of an I/S Steering Committee. The Steering Committee is responsible for ensuring all I/S projects provide a return on investment to the business. It controls the I/S budgets by approving all (or all major) I/S projects and establishes or approves business metrics for each I/S project it funds. It is headed by the CIO or CTO (Chief Information Officer or Chief Technology Officer) and is comprised of a Business Council (or equivalent group) and an I/S Council. To further ensure business and I/S alignment, the CIO should also serve on the Strategic Planning Committee. The CIO should be a catalyst for business innovation by making the

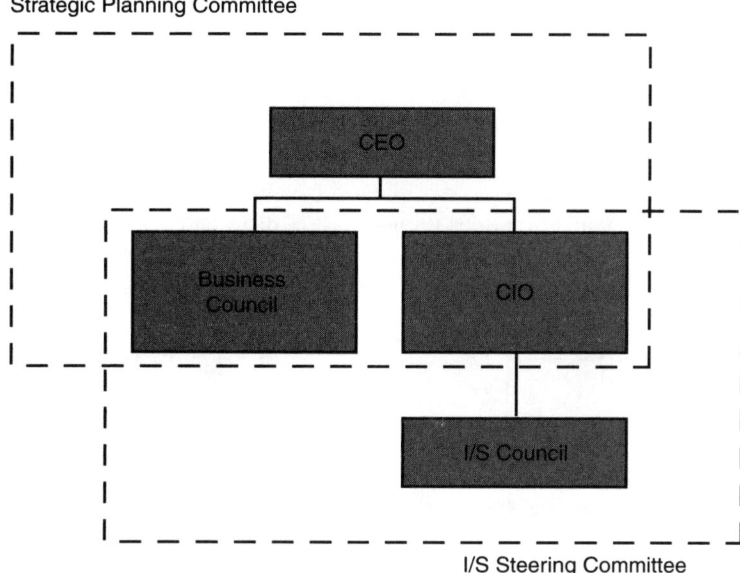

Figure 18–2 Leadership Structure for Alignment Between I/S and Business

Planning Committee aware of the possibilities technology creates and the new types of business processes it enables.

The Business Council is comprised of line managers from every business unit. Even though the client/server project may support only a subset of the whole enterprise, there is always the potential that it could impact other areas of the company. Those on the Business Council share their particular perspectives, provide feedback on the direction of the effort, and participate in critical decision making, including how to change business processes to better meet the needs and demands of their customers. The Business Council directly reports to the CEO and serves on the Strategic Planning Committee.

The I/S Council is comprised of representatives of the enterprise architecture groups, and network and systems administration. The I/S Council directly reports to the CIO or CTO.

18.3 ORGANIZATIONAL STRUCTURE

The Team Structure Must Cause Alignment with the Enterprise and Enable Maximum Utilization of Expertise

The organizational structure must enable reuse and utilization of expertise across projects. The enterprise architecture groups, including Data Architecture, Application Architecture, Technical Architecture, and Network Architecture (or their equivalents) provide consulting to project teams and ensure the projects remain aligned with the enterprise vision. This is accomplished through design reviews. This structure effectively operationalizes the alignment between I/S and business. Successful client/server projects create an effective blend of business and technical roles, which include cross-functional teams, sometimes called "virtual" teams. Cross-functional teaming requires a redefinition of roles and reporting structures.

In practice, we have seen many different implementations of organizational structures. Each organization does things slightly differently. Figure 18–3 represents our summary view of the total necessary roles, responsibilities, and infrastructure for an adaptive organization. It should be noted that few organizations today have a robust organizational

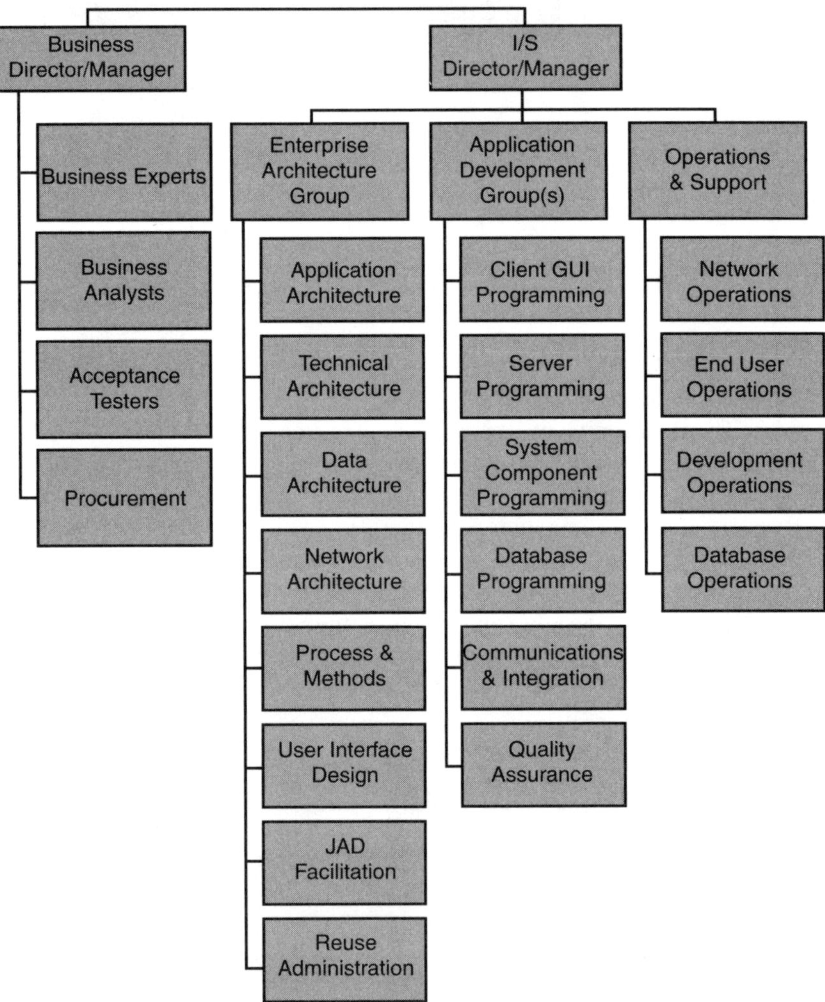

Figure 18–3 Organizational Structure for Effective Technology Solutions

infrastructure for distributed systems. As a result, projects suffer and rapid deployment of business solutions is hampered.

Note that the boxes in Figure 18–3 indicate roles, not people. A single person may perform many roles, and many people may perform a single role. For example, depending upon the size of the organization, there may be several or many Data Architects who consult to projects. A single developer may program the GUI, business roles, and database stored procedures. This chart is meant to illustrate the types of roles and skills necessary to effectively utilize technology to solve business problems. Note that User Interface Design and JAD Facilitation are in broken line boxes. That is because these roles, although necessary, can just as easily come from outside the organization. The next sections explain in more detail the roles and responsibilities for each of the branches on the chart.

18.4 BUSINESS ROLES

Active Business Involvement is Crucial to Success

Business and I/S must share responsibility for the overall success of the business. Today, few businesses can function without technology. Technology is absolutely crucial to the success of the business. But if technology is to successfully enable the business, the business must be actively involved in the deployment of technology. This is accomplished by having both an I/S manager and a business manager responsible for each project.

A **Project Sponsor** is responsible for championing the project and acquiring necessary funding. A project sponsor is usually a senior level manager who sits on the steering committee.

A **Business Project Manger** (or Leader) shares responsibility for success of the project with the I/S project manager. Many of our clients are implementing this co-management structure to ensure development projects keep in lock-step with the business. The business project manager is responsible for business project budgets, scheduling personnel resources such as business experts and design reviewers, and tracking business metrics for the project. If the organization actively practices data administration to ensure the quality of data shared across the enterprise, business project managers by default become the natural data stewards. If their system is deemed to be the authoritative source for any data, it is usually because that system is the capture system. Capture systems require additional validation features and procedures. The business is considered responsible for the correctness of the data in the system (they put it in there!).

Business Experts are subject matter experts. They are generally senior level people with a great deal of experience. They must have both the knowledge and the authority to define business rules, processes, or definitions for business information.

Business Analysts may be housed in either the I/S or the business organization. We have seen business analysts who are paid by the business unit "live within" the I/S organization and vice versa. In either case, a business analyst interacts with end users and subject matter experts to help understand and model the business to create effective technology solutions. They need good interviewing skills and must be able to work with all levels of users. They must be able to effectively model and present the information they gather. They also require some software engineering design skills.

Acceptance Testers have knowledge of the business and perform the final acceptance testing on the system. Some organizations prefer the testers to have no previous knowledge or interaction with the project, so they can provide an unbiased judgment.

Procurement Specialists help with the purchasing of the production hardware and software. We have found in our experience that coordinating the procurement of systems that may cross geographic and business unit boundaries is a nontrivial matter. We have run into some Byzantine procurement processes that seem to be designed to prevent the company from ever spending money (even after the project and budget had been approved!). The procurement process often does not support the view that technology enables the business. It can become a problem rather then part of the solution. Rapid deployment of systems requires a coordinated procurement system, which enables rather than hinders projects. Procurement should be a centralized function that supports all business units.

18.5 ENTERPRISE ARCHITECTURE GROUP

A Structure for Providing Enterprise Integration

The Enterprise Architecture Group provides an enterprise outlook and specialized expertise to all projects. This structure provides consistency across the organization. Consistency enables easier integration, more reuse, and lower maintenance and support costs. By working with all projects across the organization, the Enterprise Architecture Group becomes the natural home for enterprise infrastructure planning. Their goal is to support the continuous evolution of the technical infrastructure by building the required infrastructure over time, with the business driving implementation priorities.

Application Architecture refers to the design of the application components. The emphasis is on reusing what already exists and building new components that may be reused in the future. The Application Architect must have knowledge of objects and components, understand how to model business events, have knowledge of existing systems, and understand the workflow between systems. Depending upon the size of the organization and Enterprise Architecture Group, this person will either be from the enterprise group or will be a project team member who will work closely with them to define any opportunities for reuse.

Technical Architecture is responsible for defining and enforcing standards for every technical component in the organization. Working with project teams, the Technical Architect defines the hardware and software the system will be implemented with and evaluates purchased applications from a technical architecture vantage point. Having a centralized function for technical architecture helps ensure the implementation of standards and can more easily recognize cross-functional needs for particular infrastructure pieces. The Enterprise Technical Architecture Group (or Architect, as the case may be), is also responsible for evaluating new technology for use in the organization.

Data Architecture determines the source and destination of all data that crosses systems and helps define how different applications share data. Data architects model business data in terms of entities (or business objects) and relationships between entities which contain many of the rules governing how the business operates. In many organizations, data architects from the Enterprise Data Architecture Group work with project teams to define and model the business from an information perspective. Data Architects would therefore help create the Information Aspect. It is common in some organizations for database programmers to perform this role. However, projects go astray when a data modeling effort is not closely aligned with the Enterprise Data Architecture (or Data Repository) Group. Programmers may not choose the correct data sources for their systems or may redundantly capture information that already exists elsewhere, thereby creating the likelihood of inconsistencies in data across the organization. Failure to coordinate common data definitions in different projects leads to synonyms (different systems store the same data with different names and/or different data structures) and homonyms (different systems have data elements with the same name, but they're actually different). This greatly impedes the ability to provide decision-makers with accurate enterprise level information.

It is important to note that while the Data Architecture Group is responsible for helping projects choose appropriate data sources, the business is responsible for maintaining data consistency on an enterprise level. Most organizations have many systems (hundreds) with redundant out-of-sync data in many places. The "many places" include different applications running on different servers, legacy systems, PC applications, and reporting systems as well as different geographic locations. Resolving the differences across system and organizational boundaries is an extremely difficult process. It requires the time and commitment of top managers who have the knowledge and responsibility for the actual values of the data contained in the systems. This is the role of the Data Board. The Data Board is comprised of senior line managers who have responsibility for business operations, and therefore "own" the systems that support them. Their function is to agree on enterprise definitions of shared data, and define authoritative sources to enable managing data integrity across the enterprise. This is a business function, not an I/S function, because the issues are those of politics and control—not technology. The Data Architecture Group helps facilitate this process.

If data administration is to succeed, it is important that there be a Data Administrator who manages the board and who is on a level in the org chart higher than the members of the Data Board. Data Board members are essentially cross-functional "peers" within the organization, and therefore the Data Administrator must have the appropriate authority to ensure participation and resolve disputes. Data Architecture and data administration practices directly affect the operational support required. A well-designed Data Architecture and a strong data administration process and practice would reduce the number of database administrators needed, increase data sharing, data reuse, and data quality and enable easier access to enterprise data.

Network Architecture can encompass a wide range of enterprise services including planning and architecture of local area networks, wide area networks, middleware components, security, backup and recovery, and distributed systems management over the network. The Network Architecture Group provides an infrastructure for systems integration across the organization. Network Architects inform projects of corporate network architecture standards. They participate in design reviews to ensure the design can be adequately supported by the network architecture. Participation in design reviews also provides the Network Architecture Group with valuable information for network capacity planning. It is important to separate network architecture from network operations. The latter is concerned with the tactical day-to-day running of the network and has little concern working with project groups. The Network Architecture Group (or Network Architect) works with projects, evaluates new network technology, and acts as a liaison between network operations and business groups.

Process and Methods refer to standard procedures that make it much easier for different business units to work together efficiently. On any project, there will be varying levels of expertise. Standard processes and methods enable team members with different skillsets and skill levels to reliably produce a desired result, regardless of who is on the team. All the team members must have some familiarity with the organization's method. However, each project will also need one team member to be responsible for producing and managing the models. This person must have skills in CASE tools and model management. Depending upon the size of the organization and Enterprise Architecture Groups, this person will either be from the Enterprise Group or will be a project team member with interest and experience in methods who will work with the Enterprise Group to ensure consistency in the method.

Reuse Administration is an essential enterprise role if organizations are going to accelerate responsiveness to change in their systems. Although many of our clients recognize this, few have implemented the role. We think there are a number of reasons for this. The first is lack of critical mass at this point in time. Few organizations have a large inventory of reuseable components or a clearly defined process for creating, reusing, and changing these components. Moreover, we have not yet seen a single repository product for managing models, text, documents, data, and source code. These functions are managed on a project-by-project and tool by tool basis, which inhibits reuse. It is our strong belief that a Reuse Administrator and an integrated, easily accessible reuse library, or even multiple libraries, is absolutely necessary for achieving the goals of adaptive systems. This is not something the organization can outsource. The Reuse Administrator participates in all design reviews at all stages of the project to look for opportunities to reuse components and to "grow" the library.

User Interface (UI) Designer should be separated from GUI programming. The UI design is often left in the hands of GUI programmers who understand how to create graphical event-driven programs, but may know little about the science of usability. Most of us take very little notice of a good user interface. We just know the program is easy to use. We do, however, immediately notice a bad design when it impedes the way we want to work. User interface design has become a valid field of study in its own right. It includes such considerations as who uses the program, how often, in what type of setting, and for what purpose. A UI Designer should participate in design decisions, or at least design reviews, and act as mentor to GUI programmers. Organizations may choose to develop or hire this expertise in-house, hire a UI consultant to perform design reviews, and/or hire a UI consultant to create GUI templates. GUI frameworks are also now available for many application development tools. UI templates should be managed for reuse.

JAD (joint application design/development) facilitator is a nontechnical skill, but absolutely critical to the success of the project. JAD facilitators conduct meetings between the project team and business users and experts, reviewers, and all other audiences during the project life cycle. A facilitator works with key participants to set the meeting agenda and is responsible for facilitating the meeting in a way that accomplishes the agenda. Facilitators must not have any "stake" in the system and must remain impartial to the outcome while ensuring the most productive process. Therefore, the JAD facilitator should not be a team manager or member. There could be a centralized JAD facilitation service group (or person) who is available to work with any team, or the organization may use consultants for JAD facilitation.

18.6 APPLICATION DEVELOPMENT ROLES

Development of Multi-Tier Systems Requires Many Different Skills

Rapid application development does not come in a box. There is no silver bullet that can get the applications deployed faster. It is a combination of tools, techniques, skill, infrastructure, and support. Multi-tier applications require a number of different skills. It is unusual for one individual to possess all skills required, especially since the technology hasn't been around that long. Therefore, it will be mandatory to assemble the skills necessary for each project.

GUI Programmers build the graphical user interface using a particular application development tool such as PowerBuilder, Visual Basic, or Delphi. The programmer must work with the UI designer to ensure the application conforms to organizational standards.

Server Programmers program business rules in server-based programming languages including C++, Smalltalk, Java, Visual Basic, and new Internet development tools. This skillset can be separate from the GUI programming skillset.

System Component Programmers are experts in the tool sets being used. They build common services, reuseable components, and specialized tools, for application developers.

Database Programmers implement the database design in a particular database product and implement data access rules through triggers or procedures. Database programmers must work with Data Architects to identify opportunities for reuse and ensure integrity of authoritative data sources is maintained.

Communications and Integration Specialists focus on technologies that enable different application components in the same applications (client, server, database, and legacy) and across applications to communicate. This may be a separate programming role involving a programmer with expertise in middleware and networking or it could be a combination of server programmers, system programmers, and/or network administrators.

Quality Assurance Personnel test event-driven applications, which is far more complicated than testing linear programs. The old linear programs could be loaded into a separate region, stepped through, and stress tested. An event-driven program presents many more possible execution scenarios, especially when it runs over a network. Testing tools tend to pay for themselves in distributed environments. Quality assurance personnel must understand the business and/or work with business users to generate test suites. They must know how to use testing tools to adequately stress test the applications over a network. They also need to work with Network Architects to simulate the network environment of the application being tested. This may include setting up development networks or performing tests during OLTP "downtimes."

18.7 CROSS-FUNCTIONAL TEAMS

The Purpose of Creating Cross-Functional Teams is to Provide Seamless Service to the Customer

Responding to changes in the marketplace often results in reorganizing how work is done. Many organizations have undergone multiple reorganizations within the past few years in order to become more responsive to their customers. These reorgs often result in cross-functional teams that can better provide seamless service to the customer. Effective delivery of seamless service, however, requires a culture that supports cross-functional teamwork. A cross-functional teamwork culture first requires clarity of mission and strategy, which the aforementioned Organizational Architecture is designed to provide. Second, it requires organizational attitudes and beliefs that value giving teams and individuals the decision making authority they need to do their work without interruption. This must come from the very highest executives of the company. Third, it requires managing and coordinating how all the various groups work together. This is a combination of policies, procedures, measurements, and rewards. Lastly, cross-functional teams require the proper blending of expertise, such that a more participatory work culture is formed. Let us now look more closely at this latter aspect of cross-functional teams.

Cross-functional teams operate very differently from their traditional counterparts in several unique ways. Cross-functionality requires a shift from working independently to working with others to cooperatively get the job done. This opens the door for collaboration across the business units on a day-by-day basis. Such workgroup activity can only come about if communication is used to not only report status but to also create specific measurable results that add to the whole. This way of communicating can only happen when every member of the cross-functional team is keeping the overall mission and strategy at the forefront of their minds as they work.

We will use two case studies to illustrate why traditional and cross-functional teamwork is different. The first case study involves a software development organization inside a large computer manufacturer. They practiced traditional teamwork. People were expected to contribute according to their role, and the innovation process centered around passing judgment on ideas. A secretary proposed a process for resolving technical issues between software development projects. Even though her idea was sound, and was similar to ideas put forth in current technical journals, she was ignored, and no issue resolution process was ever created.

The second case study involves a technical division inside a large electrical utility company, which practiced cross-functional teamwork. People were not restricted in contributing ideas and the innovation process was centered on open brainstorming. A secretary proposed the idea of using helicopters to blow the snow off power lines. This was the only nontechnical idea generated during a problem solving session. Each of the technical ideas would have taken years and many millions of dollars to implement. Her idea was listened to, and the company saved valuable time and money by doing so. As of the writing of this book, the electric utility continues to be profitable while the computer company continues to lose market share.

Cross-functional teams for client/server blend business experts, I/S professionals, and infrastructure specialists. The previous section of this chapter discussed how business experts and I/S professionals work together. People often think that if this much is done, they have built a cross-functional team. Not quite! The equal participation of infrastructure specialists is a vital ingredient, because these people make not only direct contributions, but (when allowed) they provide crucial guidance as well. For example, infrastructure specialists contribute directly to the project in their roles as network administrator, data warehouse administrator, software reuse administrator, technical program coordinator, and software process engineer. But they can also provide very valuable and timely insights into the possibilities and limitations of current technology in such areas as network architecture and database administration. It is for this latter reason that the inclusion of infrastructure specialists, as equal members of a client/server project team, is a key to success.

18.8 OPERATIONS AND SUPPORT

Minimizing Operational Costs, Maximizing Efficiency, and Making Client/Server as Robust as the Mainframe

Organizations pursuing the migration path to distributed systems rarely have a support infrastructure in place. We have charted this over and over again by defining who in the organization, at each location, will support each and every component of the distributed system. In many cases there will be no one to support a particular component or components.

In some cases, the answer is different in different locations, and support becomes complicated because different locations have different technical infrastructures. Very often, this exercise exposes the fact that support for distributed systems is a cross-functional activity. Moreover, we have often had to redesign a distributed solution because of the lack of an adequate support infrastructure.

A comprehensive Operational Support Infrastructure enables distributed client/server systems to be as robust as traditional centralized data centers which support applications running 7 days a week, 24 hours a day, 365 days a year. To accomplish this, the support infrastructure must be broad reaching and provide centralized services for decentralized operations. The support issues this creates can be numerous and complex. For example, the number of unique support situations that could arise when multiple hardware platforms, different operating systems, and several versions of applications combine could reach in the millions! Support may also need to cross organizational boundaries (for

Network Operations	Network Monitoring
	Backup and Recovery
	Problem Determination/Resolution
	Messaging and E-Mail
	Availability Reporting
End User Operations	Single Number Help Desk
	Print Job Support
	Service Level Reporting
	Document Management
	Procurement
	PC Hardware/OS Configuration & Support
	PC Package Installation
	Systems Monitoring & Reporting
	Capacity Planning
Development Operations	Configuration Management
	Version Control
	Testing
	Integration
	Installations & Upgrades of Custom Apps
Database Operations	Install Databases
	Build Database Tables
	Optimize Databases
	Create and Manage Indexes
	Monitor Database Operations
	Manage Database Security

Figure 18–4 Operational Support Roles

example, when a single OLTP system touches multiple business units). In these cases, the design and implementation of the system itself may be heavily influenced by the pervasiveness, comprehensiveness, depth, and responsiveness of the support infrastructure. Clearly, minimizing operational costs and maximizing the efficiency and robustness of deployed systems are chief goals of the Operational Support Infrastructure.

The Operational Support Infrastructure must provide a myriad of support solutions for end user operations. This includes: developer operations, network operations (LAN, backbone, and WAN), application (including cross-application) operations, and database operations. To simplify the complexity of supporting numerous operational permutations and to provide the needed responsiveness when problems do arise, the Operational Support Infrastructure must be a centralized, enterprise-wide operation, even if physically distributed. We call this the "virtual data center." The goal is to create robust data centers that exist for mainframes, and replicate these environments across the organization while providing centralized management of the distributed support infrastructure. Accomplishing these goals in a distributed environment is far more complex than the centralized mainframe data center. Figure 18–4 defines the roles for operations and support.

Network Operations refers to the day-to-day operations of the network, rather than network architecture and design. It includes network monitoring of all nodes: problem determination and resolution; backup and recovery of key sites, all sites, or small distributed sites which do not have systems administration skills on-site; keeping the messaging and e-mail systems up and running; availability reporting; and monitoring and administering security. It should be noted that network security is a growing concern, especially with the growing interest of doing commerce on the Internet. Figure 18–5 depicts the profile of security exposure of client/server systems.

End User Operations support the users of the application, network, and or systems. We strongly recommend a single number Help Desk where all problems are first reported, then referred to the appropriate party for resolution. Other end user support ser-

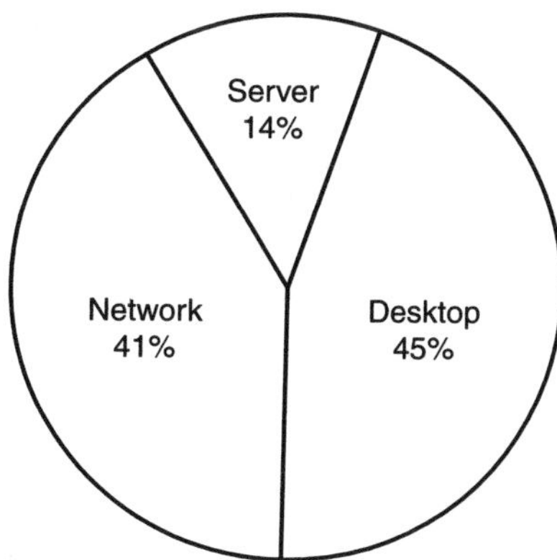

Figure 18–5 Typical Client/Server Security Risk Profile

vices include print job support; document management (unless it's part of Reuse Administration); procurement, PC package installation, PC hardware/OS configuration and support, and service level reporting. PC support costs are drastically reduced if standard configurations are strictly maintained. This is sometimes called a "sealed case" PC, which contains operating system management controls to disallow any nonstandard configuration. End User Operations also includes systems monitoring and reporting and capacity planning.

Development Operations support the development environment, which should be separated from the production environment. It includes support for configuration management and version control, which may be performed by the central Reuse Administrator who manages all project libraries or manages on a project-by-project basis (which significantly reduces reuse). Integration programming includes middleware services such as RPCs (remote procedure calls), messaging, ORBs (object request brokers), database access (ODBC, native APIs), Internet access, and legacy extracts and updates. Whereas End User Operations is responsible for PC package applications, Development Operations is responsible for PC installations and upgrades of custom applications.

Database Operations support all the database platforms in the organization. This includes installing databases and upgrades, building tables, optimizing databases through denormalization when necessary, creating and managing indexes, and managing database security through rights and permissions. Other important roles are the continuous monitoring of database operations to ensure that databases are running, performance is acceptable, and bottlenecks are not occurring.

18.9 METRICS FOR CRITICAL SUPPORT AREAS

Metrics Keep the Organization on Track

We cannot overstate the importance of having metrics as part of the Operational Support Infrastructure. We recommend keeping metrics on every important aspect of your technical infrastructure, including network traffic, storage usage, transaction volumes over time, and server availability. We caution you to design your metrics very carefully and to keep only the minimal number of metrics you need to ensure the infrastructure is being properly monitored.

An essential metric for ensuring a robust infrastructure is server availability as a percentage of overall up-time. This is represented as a single line graph that shows the difference between 100% availability and the sum total availability of all servers (Figure 18–6). When the line shows a dramatic dip, it can be exploded into a bar chart of availability for each server making up the composite value. Tracking the data in this way allows you to immediately spot times of low server availability and quickly identify any trend which may have contributed to those times (for example, a particular server continues to fail at the end of each month).

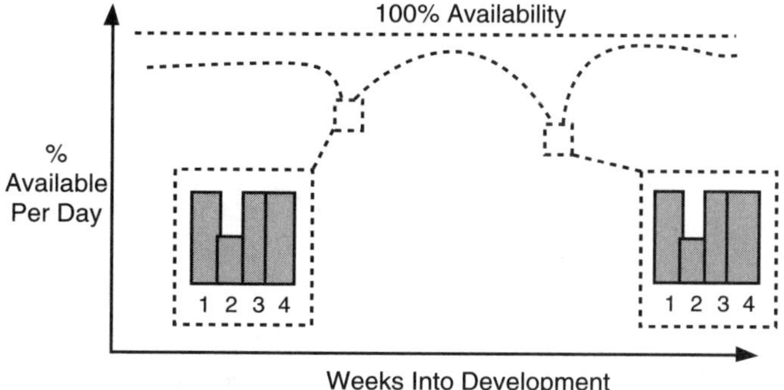

Figure 18–6 Chart Server Availability to Identify an Unreliable or Overloaded Server

To monitor network traffic, server and database utilization requires sophisticated tools, which are now becoming available for distributed and heterogeneous environments. These tools are a vital investment in the health of the corporate infrastructure.

18.10 BUILDING THE ORGANIZATIONAL ARCHITECTURE

Which Comes First, Infrastructure or Return on Investment?

In some cases, building the Organizational Architecture becomes a chicken or egg proposition. Some organizations feel they can not go forward with building distributed systems until the infrastructure is in place. But this requires a substantial investment in I/S infrastructure without an immediate ROI for the business. Increasingly, we are seeing that businesses are not making such investments.

I/S cannot stop all new development until the necessary infrastructure is in place. Most I/S shops today are already doing more with less. It is often much harder to bring in new personnel than hire contractors. Therefore, the organizational infrastructure and skills are not developed along with the distributed systems, and everyone suffers as a result. It is clear that we need to evolve necessary organizational infrastructures, as we implement new systems. This is certainly difficult and challenging. However, the process is facilitated by an overall plan that can be implemented incrementally. Meanwhile, we need to understand the impact and risk factors involved in going forward without a support infrastructure. In many cases, this may mean some interim contingency planning. When the business members are involved in this planning, they will better understand the need for investment in infrastructure.

19

Process Management

Successful System Design Efforts Require a Formal Well-Managed Approach

The design of a distributed client/server solution is created from multiple, interconnected models from a variety of different, yet complementary views. It also involves multiple business units and technical disciplines. In the last chapter, "Organizational Architecture," we discussed the necessity of providing an organizational structure that enables cross-functional teaming. The IllumiSys™ Design Method provides models that enable unambiguous communication of the design to all involved participants. In this chapter we discuss how to manage a large-scale, multi-tier design effort. The success rate for early client/server projects was just a little over sixteen percent. Multi-tier design and implementation is far more complex than two-tier client/server. Success requires a process that enables multiple tasks to be performed in parallel and with iteration. Managing this complexity requires a process that addresses these and other issues particular to distributed systems. A defined process answers the following crucial questions:

1. What kind of process is most effective for coordinating teams and producing the design?
2. What should be measured to ensure the project remains on track?

Figure 19–1 depicts Process Management as one of the pillars of change in Organizational Enablers.

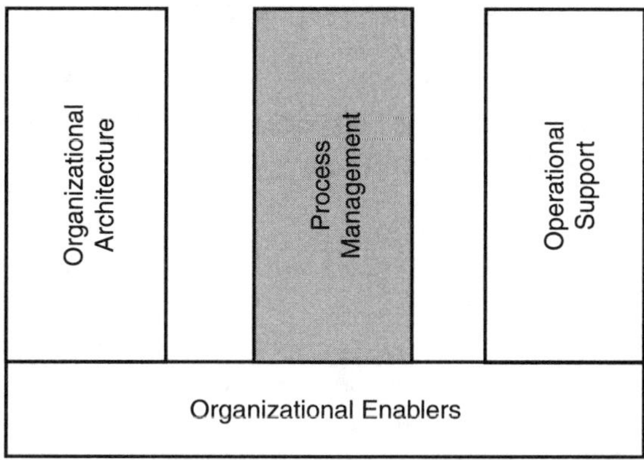

Figure 19–1 Organizational Enablers: Process Management

19.1 OBJECTIVES OF PROCESS MANAGEMENT

Prevent Defects, Produce Anticipated Results, and Maximize Reuse at Every Level

Coordinating a multi-tier client/server modeling effort is no small task. Unlike designing traditional technology, designing client/server requires a plan that can identify and manage concurrent activities. For example, a core group of designers might develop the overall design while several individuals develop prototypes for investigating design feasibility or fully understanding the critical human factors of the proposed system. All of this concurrent activity must be synchronized in order to prevent defects and ensure the system delivers the required functionality. In addition, it is typical for client/server projects to deliver small portions of the system over time. This requires coordinating the design effort with iterative delivery of operational subsystems, which need to be managed for maximum reuse. Moreover, the iterative system releases provide real-world feedback that often influences subsequent design.

Producing timely results calls for new management styles. At the most basic level, the process must validate the design. This is done through different types of design reviews. Structured interviews and facilitated work sessions are often used to gather information and validate design models. Over time, the community of reviewers expands, thereby creating a larger scope of consensus on the correctness of the design.

Lastly, but of equal importance, the process should include the development of a set of metrics for determining the quality and correctness of the design. You can measure the growing size of the models or the number of review cycles each portion of the design requires to reach stability. These types of metrics allow you to identify technically sensitive or unstable portions of the design and to predict completion times for various portions of the design or the project as a whole.

19.2 AVOIDING ANALYSIS PARALYSIS IN MODELING

Defining the Scope and Sufficiency of the Modeling Effort

Without guidance, a client/sever modeling effort runs the risk of making too many models (some of which end up being useless) or modeling the wrong subjects (which waste valuable project time). This happens for two reasons. First, at its essence, client/server technically optimizes three things: 1) flexibility of physical placement of computing resources, 2) compliance to enterprise organizational geography, and 3) adaptability to changing business needs. Second, the design of a client/server solution must serve many masters: 1) the ever-changing business requirements, 2) overall performance requirements, 3) data quality requirements, 4) the constraints imposed by the existing technical infrastructure, and 5) the operational context defined by the existing organizational design. That is the reason for carefully setting scope during the design process. Further, the complexity and projected life cycle will determine how extensive the modeling effort should be.

To determine the scope of the modeling, first evaluate the complexity of the system. In particular, we recommend you evaluate the following issues:

- The numbers of users and locations
- The number of other systems it must integrate with
- The availability of information
- The availability of resources

We have also provided a list of design activities and artifacts (see section 19.8). Note that some artifacts are mandatory, some are optional, and some are recommended. We suggest that Project Managers select the set of artifacts most suitable to each individual project.

19.3 ROLES AND RESPONSIBILITIES FOR THE MODELING PROCESS

Team Members May be Authors, Experts, Readers and Approvers

Members of the project team (defined in Chapter 17) play different roles in the modeling process. They are authors, experts, readers, approvers, or model managers. Our experiences have shown that a successful client/server modeling effort follows a process that coordinates all these roles to develop work products on time and on budget. Successful efforts also get off to a good start, make useful work products, develop only the models and diagrams needed, and support models with just the right kinds of supplements. This requires the coordination of individuals and teams (Figure 19–2).

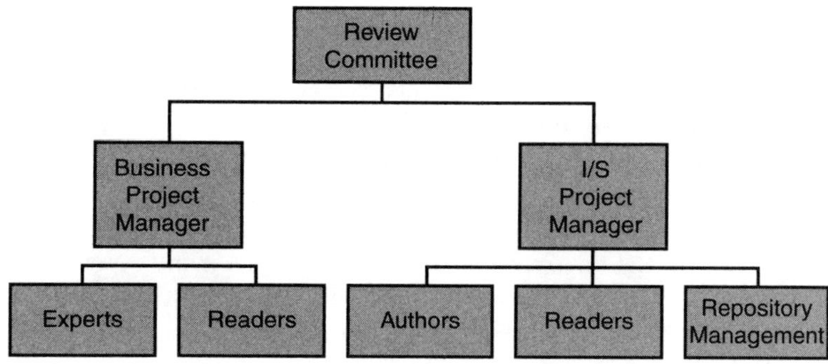

Figure 19–2 Roles for a Typical Client/Server Modeling Effort

Once again, it should be noted that the boxes in Figure 19–2 represent roles, and roles do not necessarily correspond on a one-to-one basis with people. One person may be an expert, reviewer, and approver. In smaller efforts, it stands to reason that fewer people will be involved, and one person may fill multiple roles.

The Review Committee is responsible for ensuring the design models accurately represent the business requirements. There may be different review committees for different aspects of the design. The final review committee is comprised of the Project Sponsor plus all line managers who will either receive the new system or will be impacted by it. The Review Committee must be comprised of people who are empowered to make decisions. This is necessary because, for example, if cross-departmental issues arise during the review and approval process, policy decisions can be immediately made.

The Project Manager assumes all the traditional responsibilities of project management, but the nature of managing a concurrent and rapid design effort adds some additional responsibilities to the role. The Project Manager schedules all project tasks, resources, and design reviews, and coordinates cross-functional teaming. Note that the Business Project Manager controls the resources of Experts and Readers. The I/S Project Manager controls the resources of Authors, Readers, and Repository Management.

Experts come from the business units. They are line managers, clerks, tellers, machine operators, and auditors. They are, in other words, the people who actually service the business events. The role of the expert is to explain the business process, define the business rules, and describe the various work artifacts and the reason why they are created. If time allows, some experts may double as readers because they are in the best position to determine the accuracy of the models.

Readers review the models for consistency and accuracy. The role of the reader is to identify defects as early as possible, when they are easiest to fix. Note that there may be both Business Readers and I/S Readers.

Authors have the role of producing the artifacts that comprise the Essential and Implementation Models. In this role, they are responsible for accurately describing the rules and operations of both the business and the system. They must actively work with business experts to correctly understand the business and to convey their design intentions to the business community at large. Authors require expertise in analysis and design methods. Authors are often readers for other authors.

Repository Management refers to managing the repository of project artifacts. A repository is necessary for any efforts of reuse. Many organizations use "lower case" tools to generate the models. These are modeling tools that only span part of the modeling effort such as a data modeling tool, a graphic design tool, or a configuration management tool for source code. Each tool has its own repository, which does not integrate with the others. This means that reuse requires managing as many repositories as there are tools. Many of our clients are looking for a single reuse repository that can manage models produced by any tool, source code, and all other project documentation. We believe the future of object/relational databases looks promising for this purpose. This function should be part of Reuse Administration, which acts as the organizational memory.

19.4 MANAGING THE MODELING PROCESS

Managing through Tasks, JAD Sessions, and Metrics

The management process for modeling has been described in large part by clearly defining the tasks and design deliverables at each stage of the project (see section 19.8). There are process management tools, which allow managers to define tasks and deliverables, assign resources, and track progress over the network.

Group work methods are essential for effective functioning of cross-functional teams. Joint application development (JAD) sessions are often used to discuss and negotiate design trade-offs and decisions. A trained facilitator who can either come from within the company, or be a consultant, leads the session. Good participation in these session(s) is essential so all viewpoints will be heard and considered. Trained facilitation skills are required to skillfully negotiate between different perspectives and to ensure the meeting objectives are met.

Metrics help to manage the efficiency of the process. Figure 19–3 displays a sample of modeling metrics to be used as a yardstick in beginning modeling efforts. Over time, as more reuse becomes possible, the organization will gain the experience to develop a more accurate set of metrics.

Task	Brand New	New Version
Create	15–60 minutes	10–30 minutes
Review your own work	10–30 minutes	10–30 minutes
Review someone else's work	10–40 minutes	5–20 minutes
Diagrams made per day	2–5	5–10

Figure 19–3 Sample Metrics for Modeling Tasks

From our experience, the best metric to keep is the time spent on a major modeling activity (for example, time to create a brand new diagram). By reviewing these times, an author and/or project manager can determine which activities are being done efficiently, and which are done less than optimally. If an author goes well beyond the times indicated in this chart, the following questions should be asked:

- Is the subject too large to model effectively?
- Does the author have sufficient facts to complete this part of the model?
- Are the facts inconsistent with the current understanding of the system?
- Has the author strayed outside the scope of the intended system?

The rate at which quality modeling artifacts are created are an important factor for keeping a project on track and out of analysis paralysis. Project managers should be on the lookout for modeling efforts that are overextending themselves, or not progressing at the pace necessary to deliver the project on time. Some early warning signs are large review kits (larger that two to five diagrams); too many review cycles on a particular kit (more than three); and models that have too many diagrams (see section 19.8).

19.5 THE BENEFITS OF REVIEW CYCLES

> *Review Cycles Prevent Defects and Contribute to the Expansion of Organizational Knowledge*

A review is a formalized inspection of a portion of a model by business experts or readers. The purpose is to validate and verify the models to prevent defects. Review cycles accomplish a number of things, including 1) the utilization of knowledge which exists in the minds of every worker and manager; 2) the contribution of new knowledge directly into the design of new systems; and 3) the dissemination of specific knowledge throughout the enterprise. This process thereby contributes to the expansion of organizational knowledge (see Figure 19–4).

19.6 TYPES OF REVIEWS

> *Different Types of Reviews Serve Different Purposes*

There are three basic types of reviews: 1) author-review-revise, 2) walkthrough, and 3) playthrough. An author-review-revise cycle is a group review process, with varying levels of formality. During this kind of review, an author sends out a model component to

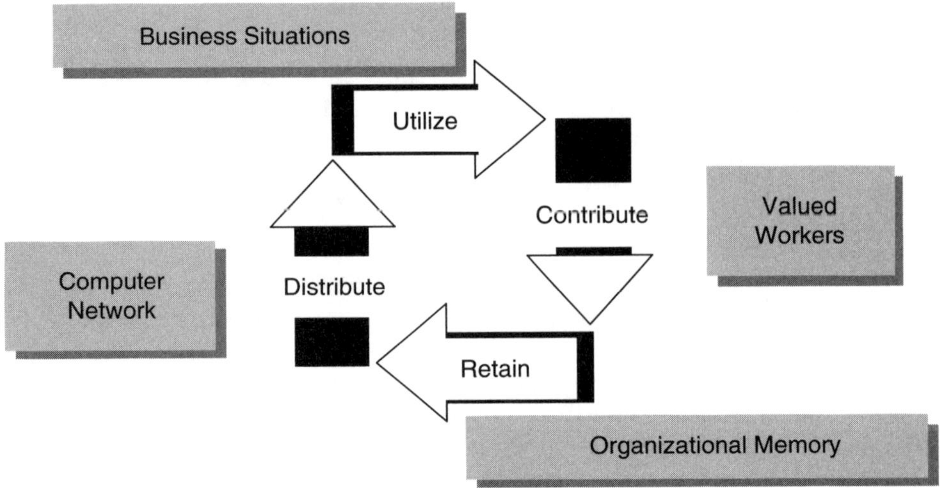

Figure 19–4 The Cycle of Expanding and Disseminating Business Knowledge

one or more reviewers. This distribution step can involve either faxing or mailing paper versions of the component or e-mailing electronic versions across the network. Readers review component(s), annotate the artifacts with pertinent comments, and return the annotated components back to the author. The author then consolidates the feedback from all reviewers and revises the original component accordingly. Though usually done among members of a team, an author-review-revise cycle can have an ever-widening community of reviewers, depending on the project's need for model validation. This community can expand over time, thereby creating a larger scope of consensus on the correctness of the design (Figure 19–5).

A walkthrough is another kind of group review process, but it differs from the author-review-revise cycle in several ways. First, a walkthrough is a face-to-face gathering of a group. It is a meeting. The objective of the meeting is to step through a modeling component and allow people to ask clarifying questions and raise issues about the component. The authors attend the meeting to answer questions of clarification and to listen to the issues raised by the review group. The reviewers attend the meeting to give specific feedback on the product under inspection. Two additional roles, which can be played by non-team members, are necessary. A Facilitator conducts the walkthrough and a Recorder captures notes and issues.

The third type of review is called the playthrough. This is a simulation of the processing or behavior of some part of a system. The simulation can be a manual or human simulation (such as use cases of business processes) or a demonstration of a prototype. In a manual playthrough, a model, or portion of a model, is distributed among the members of a group, and each person is charged with enacting their portion. An enactment starts with a specific external business event. Then, each person in turn follows their "script" as defined by their portion of the model. In this way, test cases are established and design errors, omissions, or inefficiencies are discovered. The same process can be used to review

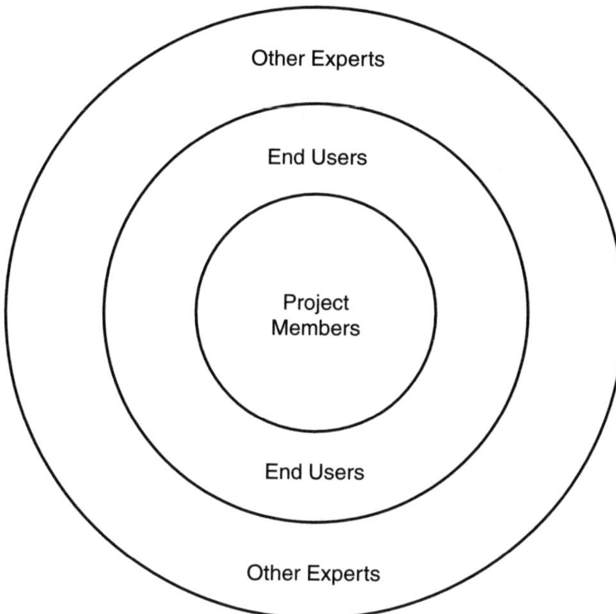

Figure 19–5 Expanding Scope of Review Communities

a prototype of a design. When done early in the analysis phase, these test cases can be used throughout the development project.

There are some important guidelines to follow in the review process, regardless of the type of review being conducted. It is essential that the *products,* not the people, are reviewed. All review sessions should start by stating that the purpose of the review is to find and correct defects before they are built into the systems, when they will be much more difficult and expensive to fix. It is good to find defects in a review, not bad. However, it is also natural for an author to want to defend his/her work. Therefore, many of our clients have instituted formalized procedures for reviews. One has even told us that the author is not allowed to speak at all, except to answer a direct question. This is to prevent defensive behavior.

19.7 MANAGING THE REVIEW PROCESS

Optimizing Review Cycles to Streamline the Process

One way to streamline the review process to make the most of everyone's valuable (and always limited!) time is by creating "kits" for review and approval. A kit is a collection of modeling artifacts (for example, tables, diagrams, aspects, and charts), selected and organized to convey one concise subject or message. This way, readers can quickly look at the contents of the kit and determine its correctness and completeness. This goal may imply that kits are small, and usually they are. We recommend you do not apply that general notion to all modeling situations. Instead we suggest you evaluate your immediate situation to determine how kit size will impact your project's productivity. The following points may assist you:

- Projects involved with new technology often require extensive review of every new idea. Because so much new information is being discovered, authors make better progress if their kits are kept small.
- Projects that model well-known systems or systems that are small or have little complexity can move more rapidly when larger kits are made.
- Projects comprising many novice authors make better progress when kits are small, because gross mistakes on one diagram or chart can be easily corrected before they corrupt other views and aspects.
- Projects comprising just a few senior authors often progress better and faster if their kits contain many diagrams, tables, or charts. Sometimes, even a complete aspect is appropriate for a kit.

Kit size is one important project concern. The number of kits distributed on a particular subject is equally important. We recommend that not one, but a series of kits be dis-

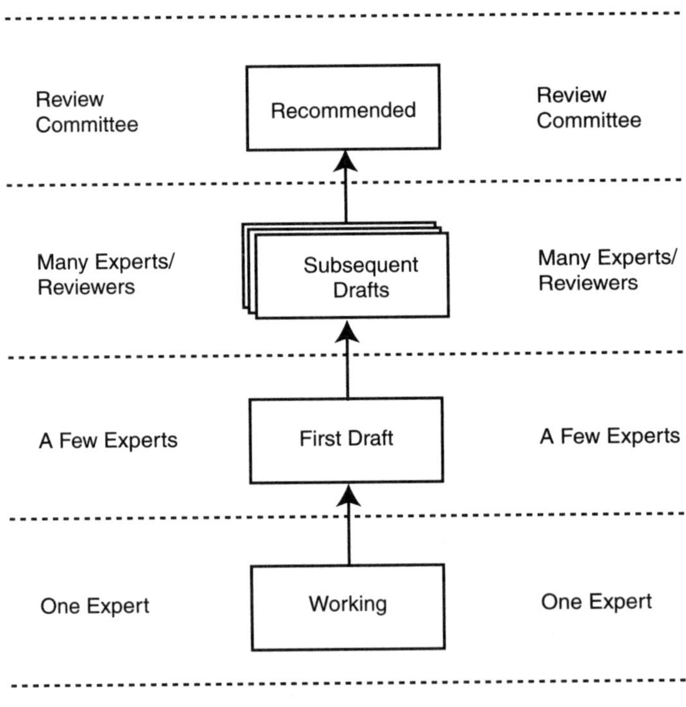

Figure 19–6 Ever-Widening Levels of Consensus

tributed for one particular reviewable unit of information. To do this, first issue a kit to a very senior expert and reach consensus with just that person. Then, issue a second kit on the same topic to a few more experts, and reach consensus with them. Third, distribute a third kit to the entire reader community. Once consensus is reached by this readership, send a final kit to the review committee for their approval. This process is what we call obtaining an ever-widening level of consensus. As Figure 19–6 shows, it is typical to go through a single review at each consensus level. The complexity and/or controversiality of what is being reviewed determines how many levels of consensus are required. A highly complex or contentious issue may require general consensus, thereby necessitating additional review cycles.

19.8 ESSENTIAL AND IMPLEMENTATION MODEL ACTIVITIES AND ARTIFACTS

Tasks and Deliverables for Each Aspect

Aspect	Activity	Artifact/View	Mandatory/ Optional/ Recommended
Statement of Purpose	Define business purpose, metric	Statement of Purpose	Mandatory
Environmental Aspect	Identify system boundaries	Context Diagram	Mandatory
		Data Flow Specification	Mandatory
		Data Store Specification	Optional
		Terminator Specification	Optional
	Identify business events	Event Table	Mandatory
Information Aspect	Define business entities, relationships, attributes	Entity Relationship Diagram	Mandatory
		Entity Specification	Mandatory
		Attribute Specification	Optional
		Relationship Specification	Optional
Bridge Aspect	Define data used by events	Entity/Event Table	Mandatory
	Define data over time	Entity State Transition Diagram	Recommended

(*continued*)

Figure 19–7 Activities and Artifacts of the Essential Model

Aspect	Activity	Artifact/View	Mandatory/ Optional/ Recommended
Behavioral Aspect	Define system responses	Event Response Table	Mandatory
		Event Response DFD	Mandatory
		Detailed DFD	Optional
	Define data for responses	Entity Response Table	Recommended
	Detail requirements	Minispecs	Optional
Event Distribution Aspect	Determine how events are grouped by function	Event Distribution Table	Mandatory
		Event Distribution by Logical Location	Recommended
	Determine where events occur	Logical Location/ Response Distribution Table	Mandatory for multi-sites
		Geographic Distribution Table	Mandatory for multi-sites
		Logical Location Distribution Diagram	Optional
Component Measurement Aspect	Determine frequency of business events; number of human terminators; and size of data stores	Terminator Measurement Table	Mandatory
		Event Measurement Table	Mandatory
		Entity Relationship Measurement Table	Mandatory

Figure 19–7 Activities and Artifacts of the Essential Model *Continued*

Aspect	Activity	Artifact/View	M/O/R
Design Metrics	Define metrics to evaluate design	Statement of Design Goals	Mandatory
Multi-Tier Partitioning Aspect	Map Business Components to multi-tier architecture	Multi-Tier Model	Optional
	Define Application Architecture (centralized, 2-tier, or multi-tier)	Application Architecture	Mandatory
Technical Architecture Design	Define the Business Drivers	Business Drivers section of Architecture Data Form	Mandatory
	Create a Comprehensive Inventory	Current Technical Architecture Inventory	Mandatory
		Application Inventory	Recommend
		Skills Inventory	Recommend

(continued)

Figure 19–8 Activities and Artifacts of the Implementation Model

Aspect	Activity	Artifact/View	M/O/R
	Define the technical components	Tool Selection Form	Optional
		Technical Processor Model	Mandatory
		Technical Architecture Specification	Mandatory
		Support Table	Recommend
		Logical Network Diagram	Optional
	Do Gap Analysis	All sections of Architecture Data Form	Mandatory
	Create Migration Plan	Architecture Data Form for each project to fund	Optional
Processor Distribution Aspect	Distribute events and responses across processors	Processor Diagram	Mandatory
		Processor Distribution Table	Mandatory
		Processor Data Flow Diagram	Mandatory
		Lower Level DFDs	Optional
	Model the presentation tier	Prototype	Mandatory
		State Transition Diagram	Recommend
	Distribute data across processors	Entity Processor Table	Mandatory
		Data Distribution Table	Mandatory
	Define communications between processors	Message Specification Table	Mandatory
Geographic Distribution Aspect	Distribute processing across geographic locations	Processor Distribution Table for Each Location	Mandatory
		Processor DFDs for Each Location	Mandatory
		Enterprise DFD	Mandatory
	Distribute data across geographic locations	Enterprise Data Distribution Table	Mandatory
		Data Distribution Table for Each Location	Mandatory
Traffic Analysis	Estimate network traffic	Traffic Analysis Table	Mandatory
		Traffic Flow Diagram	Mandatory
		Enterprise Traffic Table	Mandatory
		Frequency Distribution Graph	Optional
		Load Balancing Analysis	Optional

Figure 19–8 Activities and Artifacts of the Implementation Model *Continued*

20

Organizational Transformation

Organizational Transformation is Required to Enable Business Change

To effectively respond to the rapid pace of change in the business, many organizations need to transform themselves. New organizational architectures are part of this transformation, but there is more. It is human nature to resist change. Change is disruptive. Keeping things the same offers the least path of resistance. Overcoming resistance and enabling the organizational transformation necessary to compete in today's global economy requires the vision and active support of management, a knowledgeable and skilled work force, and a reward structure that motivates the workforce to change its old, known, comfortable processes which inhibit change. Let us now examine each of these dimensions more closely. Figure 20–1 depicts Organization Transformation as one of the pillars of change in Organizational Enablers.

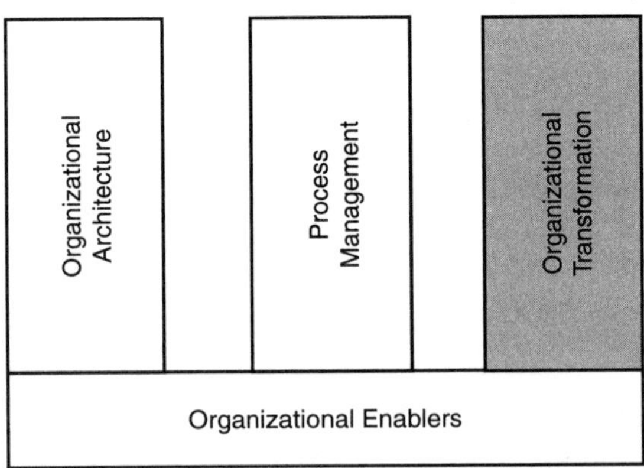

Figure 20–1 Organizational Enablers: Organizational Transformation

20.1 PROMOTING THE VISION

The "Vision" Provides the Conceptual Framework to Guide All Other Decisions

Organizational transformation requires everyone in the organization, including senior managers, line managers, programmers, and end users, to understand the business drivers and strategic goals of the company. Overall success depends on doing what is best for the organization. Sometimes this means that what is best for the organization is suboptimal for a particular project. Successful organizations optimize at the enterprise level.

When business processes and technology decisions are optimized at the enterprise level, the organization as a whole wins, but individual business units may suffer because the solution is less than optimal for their needs. How do you get managers to swallow this bitter pill, when their natural inclination, and perhaps their existing reward structure, motivates them to optimize their own operations? This requires that everyone in the organization understand the "vision." The vision is the driving force behind change and the direction the organization is moving in.

In our work, we have found that "promoting the vision" is essential to successful transformation. Most importantly, it requires the full understanding and support of I/S and business executives, who communicate the vision to the line managers, who then carry the message to everyone else in the organization. This is done through education, training, distribution of information, and most importantly, the decisions they make on a day-to-day basis. If senior management does not fully enroll the active support and participation of line managers and those who report to them, organizational transformation will falter because line managers will always be inclined to optimize their own operations.

Promoting the vision is done most effectively when senior management for both business and I/S actively and repeatedly communicate it throughout their organizations, and line managers are measured and rewarded according to alignment with this vision. Methods for distributing the vision include presentations, videotapes, personal visits by senior management to operations, e-mail, and Web sites.

Let us take, for example, a large company, which has decided that all future systems will be purchased, instead of developed in-house. Each business unit buys the package they think will best meet their needs, with little or no coordination with other business units. Each package requires its own specific technical platforms. Without strict control of standards a large organization can easily wind up with *millions* of possible configurations, permutations, and combinations. Up to a certain point, this multitude of technical environments becomes more and more expensive to support. At some point, the number of permutations and combinations make it impossible to support. Each business manager must fully understand this, or they will insist upon nonstandard solutions that they perceive will better meet their needs, because they don't have the full enterprise picture in mind. Figure 20–2 is an exercise for estimating the possible permutations in your organization. Try it!

We have seen, over and over, that I/S personnel understand this problem and are striving for a way to communicate to their managers. They face the day-to-day frustration

To determine the number of combinations that your support department may need to contend with, perform the following simple calculation:

- Determine the number of client platforms you have. A distinct platform is defined as having a different hardware manufacturer, or a different operating system, including any version of an operating system.
- Determine the number of server platforms you have.
- Determine the number of LAN operating systems you have (Unix, NT, Novell, Banyan, etc.)
- Determine the number of different routers you have. Count the routers from different manufacturers.
- Determine the number of different middleware products you have. These include all database middleware (ODBC, native database APIs, other database middleware such as SequeLink), database gateways, messaging systems (such as MQ Series), RPC products, TP Monitors, and ORBs.
- Determine the number of different DBMSs in your organization
- Determine the number of different application development environments/programming languages.
- Multiply all of the above.

Figure 20–2 Determining the Number of Different Configurations that Must be Supported in the Organization

of not being able to do their jobs effectively because of the lack of enterprise vision. It is absolutely crucial that top management play a strong leadership role in effecting change in the organization.

20.2 EDUCATION AND TRAINING

Building the Necessary Skillsets within the Organization

Distributed client/server solutions are far more complex than legacy mainframe systems and require diverse skills and expertise. Many of our clients have told us that one of the most difficult issues they face is building and maintaining the skills they need. Here we will talk about building the necessary skills. In the section on motivation and reward we will further discuss maintaining skills.

There is a great deal of education that is necessary in order to successfully create a workforce capable of providing seamless service to their customers. Everyone needs to have a conceptual understanding of the driving business forces and how technology may be applied most effectively to meet business needs. Beyond this, different people will pursue different areas of expertise and will require further education and, in many cases, hands-on training. In Chapter 19 we discussed different roles and skills required by project team members.

There will necessarily be varying levels of expertise in the organization. When forming effective project teams, the skill level of each member should be considered. The benefit of the Enterprise Architecture Group is that it provides a high level of skill in each of the architecture areas of networking, technology, data, applications, and process and methods to all project teams. Over time, the organization must continue to build expertise in critical areas, by skillfully crafting the composition of teams.

On each project there will be different levels of competence in each of the necessary skill sets. The defined levels of expertise are as follows:

- Neophyte: beginning users of technology
- Aware: have some knowledge of how technology works and how it can be utilized
- Active Apprenticeship: personnel in training programs
- Practitioner: currently utilizes the technology in day-to-day operations
- Mastery: has a high degree of skills in that area
- Expert: a leader in the field, writes books, articles, speaks at conferences

Any single person may have mastery or expertise in some area(s), be a day-to-day practitioner in another discipline, and a neophyte in yet another area.

Developing mastery and expertise within the organization requires an understanding of how people gain expertise. To effectively utilize the information gained in education and training individuals need to develop as full-fledged team members. There are five major areas of development: self-management, knowledge, participation, goal setting, and problem solving.

Self-management is the ability of a person to operate effectively in the workplace. Each person is unique. For example, they have their own levels of self-awareness, self-esteem, and self-control. They also have unique characters that allow them, to varying degrees, to take independent action, take charge, and defend possibly unpopular stands. As a person's self-management evolves, they grow in their ability to understand the larger context for their work, they are better able to negotiate priorities, and they become more facile at circumventing barriers. At the same time, they evolve in the way they manage their well-being. They become more proficient at maintaining commitments over time and they are better able to listen to and utilize, other people's feedback to continue improving. All of these dimensions of self-management need to be cultivated, because when they are, the enterprise will have a mature workforce, with people who are able to take on multiple projects and simultaneous work responsibilities.

Knowledge is the knowing one has about one's work. Again, as computer professionals, we normally gravitate to thinking our knowledge is mostly in the technical arena, but there are many dimensions to our knowledge. Over time, we build financial knowledge as we gain a better understanding of the detailed cost-value equation. We grow our awareness of the goals within which we work and the metrics that measure our performance against those goals; and we become more skilled at forecasting and managing project budgets and expenditures. From this financial knowledge we build economic knowledge. We become aware of the macro equations of investment-return, profit-loss, and productivity-quality. Most importantly, we gain knowledge of the business mission and strategy. Lastly, as our careers lengthen, we gain knowledge about our industry: its history, the competition, and future trends.

Participation takes many forms. Effective communication involves listening carefully, speaking clearly and responsibly, and appreciating other people's points of view. Active learning may involve an apprenticeship or taking on a mentoring role, and in that process learning from experiences and developing mental structures for accessing and applying those learnings. Decision making forces one to become aware of the kinds of decisions made on a moment-by-moment basis, and to vary involvement in the decision making process. Standards by which people participate are crucial and include the kinds of participation deemed as legitimate, and the kind and amount of support they give to others.

Proficiency in meeting goals requires the ability to analyze, design, implement, deploy, and maintain goals. Though goals are quite different than the computer artifacts most I/S professionals work with, goals do follow a strikingly similar process in the way they are created and maintained. Over time, people gain an increased ability to identify problems, analyze the circumstances within which problems occurred, brainstorm possible solutions, eliminate unlikely alternatives, and take action commensurate with the final decision. Overall success requires the ability to apply discipline to the process by which we design our work and solve problems.

Expertise cannot be acquired through a five day course. Expertise comes from practicing skills during the course of projects. We suggest that companies identify areas of expertise they need to develop, then identify staff who will become the experts within the organization. Particular attention and resources should be given to developing experts who can lead the organizational transformation, especially in the areas of process and project management and enterprise architecture development.

Other skills that are crucial to the success of the organization include in-depth knowledge of technologies within the company. When there are so many new technologies to learn, it is not possible to have in-depth knowledge of all of them. To start, there should be *someone* with in-depth knowledge of the operating systems and hardware platforms. There should be someone with in-depth knowledge of each and every database within the organization. There should be someone with in-depth knowledge of the programming environments used. There should be someone with in-depth knowledge of the middleware. It is easy to see that building this knowledge will be much easier if there are fewer of each. We must emphasize that lack of knowledge puts the enterprise at risk. The applications cannot be properly supported. Problems will be difficult to pinpoint and correct if there is no one with this in-depth knowledge. Both users and I/S become extremely frustrated because of poor support.

In the Technical Architecture Design (Chapter 14), we recommended completing a skills inventory. This inventory will reveal any gaps in the skill base of the organization. Filling these gaps can be prioritized and cost-justified by looking at the needs of the entire organization. The skillset within an organization is an important criteria when considering bringing in new technology. The overriding question should always be, "Can we support it?"

20.3 DESIGNING A TRAINING CURRICULUM

Effective Migration of Mainframe Programming Skills Requires an Understanding of the Paradigm Shift

Over the past few years, we have helped many organizations design training curriculums to transition their mainframe COBOL programmers to client/server. We have seen what has succeeded and what has failed. It is important to note that programming skills alone are not enough. This is evidenced by the high failure rate of client/server systems. We have found that successful organizations provide a comprehensive education and training program for both I/S and business users.

Education for Business Users. In order for business users to effectively participate in projects, they require a basic understanding of the new technology, design goals, and most importantly, data and application architectures. They also require training in the applications they use. Failure to educate users can result in higher support costs. Because business users are active participants in the development process, they should also be educated in the process and methods that will be used during the project. Again, this can be an overview course.

Education for I/S Managers. I/S managers require the same education as business users, plus a better understanding of industry trends. The former can be accomplished with overview courses offered to both I/S and business managers. The latter is best accomplished by attending industry conferences.

Education for Programmers. We often talk about the need for programmers to understand the "paradigm shift." What is this paradigm shift, and how can we get programmers to understand it? The most important paradigm shift is the need for programmers to understand that their job is to provide technical solutions to meet the needs of the business. Their job is not to program. The most effective use of the programmer's time, in fact, is to reuse what has already been programmed. This is a shift from artisan programming to component building and reuse. Successful transition depends on motivation and reward.

Programmers must also understand that the basic design goals have shifted. The most important design goal today is adaptability as opposed to minimizing CPU utilization. This may lead to less efficient code that is easier to change.

Programmers must also understand the technology, application architecture, data architecture, network architecture, process and methods, and have at least some basic concepts of user interface design. These may be the same overview courses available to I/S and business managers and users.

Of course, programmers will also need hands-on courses in the technologies they will be required to use to build and implement systems. These hands-on courses may be vendor-certified courses, computer-based courses, or customized courses that take project teams through a case study and implement a small-scale client/server system.

20.4 MOTIVATION AND REWARD

Organizational Transformation Requires a Change in the Way I/S Personnel are Measured

Organizations may find they need to transform their motivation and reward structures in order to accomplish their goals. Programmers who were once measured by the amount of code they wrote now need to be measured by their ability to quickly provide effective business solutions. This means they must understand the new business metrics that will be applied to I/S projects, and how those will influence the way they work. To effectuate this paradigm shift, it is often necessary to change the motivation and reward structure. A common complaint we hear among our clients is that they have trouble maintaining their people once they have been trained because they can easily walk out the door and make more money elsewhere. In order to be successful, organizations must be able to maintain the expertise they develop.

The question we often hear from our clients is, "How do we transition our traditional COBOL legacy programmers to the new distributed technology?" Beyond education and training, organizations need to change the way programmers work. It is human nature to wish to continue to do things in a familiar way. Change is never easy. Therefore, programmers must be compensated in a way that motivates them to change from an individual artisan approach to programming to a reuseable component-based approach to application building. There are a number of ways to make this happen.

Motivate Through Profit Sharing. One client reported a very successful profit sharing plan that motivated business units to focus on the overall success of the organization by tying bonuses to overall profit. If the profit goal was met for the corporation, all eligible employees received a percentage of their base pay as a bonus. There was also a sliding pay-out scale based on zero profit. If the company doubled their profit, the employees would receive double their bonus. Weekly reports showed how each division was progressing toward the goal. Any division could choose to expend resources to assist in the improvement of low performers. This improved the effectiveness of the division and organization as a whole, and motivated cooperation and coordination.

Reward Reuse. Programmers need to be rewarded for reuse rather than for writing new lines of code. Some organizations have instituted reward structures to effect this paradigm shift, which can be as simple or elaborate as the organization wishes it to be. It can be time off, tickets to a sporting event, gift certificates for a dinner, or cash rewards. Organizations who have implemented such reward systems have reported that simple compensations can be quite effective. In order for this to happen, however, the organization must have in place a repository for managing reuseable application components. The organization must have a Reuse Administrator who manages the repository (or object architecture group or other equivalent group) and a development process that includes design reviews. Programmers need to understand what is available in the repository and must have easy access to its contents, so it is not easier to just write a new module than to use what already exists.

The repository is built through having programmers submit reuseable components to the Reuse Administrator. The programmer who submits a reuseable component receives a reward. When that component is reused, the original author is also compensated.

The other part of the reward structure is to reward programmers who reuse code rather than rewrite it. Otherwise, they will be motivated to keep writing code and creating new "reuseable" modules. The whole key to a reuse strategy is to actually achieve reuse. Some organizations legislate reuse, applying the stick rather than a carrot. Through design reviews they identify which requirements can be met through existing components, and which require new components that can either be purchased or custom built. We believe the most effective approach is to combine a reward structure with a process to enforce reuse. Sometimes the reward structure is based on target goals for reuse (such as 75%–80% reuse). At the beginning, all reuse should be acknowledged and rewarded. These rewards can be on a point system (such as five points equals a day off or a sporting event ticket, etc.). This system can be simple and low cost.

Maintaining Personnel. Maintaining skills in-house is one of the most daunting and challenging problems many organizations face. Some of our clients have told us that they wish to retrain their legacy programmers because their business knowledge and experience is a valuable resource to the company. Maintaining personnel requires compensation packages that make it attractive for the employee to stay (such as equity building, profit sharing plans) and opportunities for professional development enabling them to stay current in their field. Most of all, we find that the best programmers are looking for challenge and acknowledgment. It is far easier to provide both in organizations that enable cross-functional teaming, so that programmers are not forever "stuck" in maintenance roles.

One of the major challenges facing many organizations as we approach the turn of the millennium is that many programmers will indeed be relegated to maintenance roles to fix the Year 2000 problem. How do organizations keep these programmers satisfied? We have found that in large organizations there is usually a group of COBOL programmers that will never make the transition of object oriented programming, and who do not want to. These are people who are adverse to change, are not interested in learning new skills, and are not looking for new challenges. Certainly there will be enough legacy code around for the rest of their careers to maintain. Programmers in this group should not be overly worried. COBOL programmers who don't want to get left behind, but are still needed to perform legacy maintenance because of their knowledge and experience, can be effectively utilized for legacy integration with new distributed systems and application packages.

In order to ensure success of distributed systems, it is necessary to clearly define how success will be determined. Often, when we ask the question, "How do you measure success?" we hear one of two responses. The traditional I/S metric is, "On time and on budget." However, unlike legacy systems, we do not have the experience or heuristics to accurately project time or budget. These numbers are often determined by when a project needs to get done and how much money the organization is willing to spend on it. It may have nothing to do with the reality of how long it will actually take or how much it will cost. The second common response is, "the users were satisfied." In some organizations, however, the users are never satisfied, and never will be until measurements of success are explicitly defined and commonly agreed to by both I/S and the business. That is why in the Statement of Purpose, we include at least one business metric that becomes the measure of success. The other benefit of using business metrics is that the return on investment can show up in the business rather than in I/S. Business managers need to understand the implications of their investment in technology, and metrics help quantify it.

It is clear that technology enables the organization to effectively compete today. Few, if any, could survive without technology. But gaining true strategic advantage through technology requires planning, design, and effective organizational practices. We have developed the IllumiSys™ Design Method to help organizations achieve their goals. We sincerely hope it helps you achieve yours.

PART V

FLEURY MARKET CASE STUDY

Part V is an example of how the IllumiSys™ Design Method would be applied to a business situation. The models from the case study are used as examples throughout the book. The purpose here is to bring all the models together to illustrate how the design would work, beginning to end.

We wish to thank CGI Systems (a wholly owned subsidiary of IBM) for their permission to use their case study and other material for the Essential Model. We also wish to thank Phil Sully and Corrine Brandi for their contribution to the case study.

Chapter 21 is the background for the Fleury Market Case Study. We recommend you begin the book by reading Chapter 21 so you can better understand the examples throughout the book.

Chapter 22 contains all the artifacts for the Essential Model for the Fleury Market Case Study. We recommend you look through Chapter 22 before reading Part II so you gain familiarity with the examples of the Essential Model.

Chapter 23 contains all the artifacts of the Implementation Model for the Fleury Market Case Study. We recommend you look through Chapter 23 before reading Part III so you gain familiarity with the examples of the Implementation Model.

21

The Fluery Market Case Study

An Example of a Distributed Systems Design Project

This last section of the book, presents a detailed example of how the IllumiSys™ Design Method is used to develop a distributed system. The ficticious business used in this example, called Fleury Market, was originally developed by CGI Systems, a wholly owned subsidiary of IBM, and is used in their analysis and requirements courses based on the Yourdon Systems Method of event-based modeling. We chose it to demonstrate how the IllumiSys™ Design Method extends current systems modeling practices, so as to fully address the particulars of distributed client/server design. Here then, is Fleury Market, broken into separate descriptions for the Essential Model and Implementation Model respectively. This chapter provides the background information on Fleury Market.

21.1 BACKGROUND ON FLEURY MARKET

The Purpose and Major Components of Fleury Market

In the early 1960s, the French Ministry of Commerce established a network of national markets serving each of the country's metropolitan areas. These markets facilitate trade between wholesalers and retailers in agricultural commodities (for example, meats, vegetables, flowers, fabrics, wines, and dairy produce). A typical example of a commodity market is situated in the town of Fleury le Deux Eglises (Fleury of the Two Churches), just outside Lyon. The Fleury Market is small but sophisticated. It contains a central bank (Cassise Centrale), wholesaler booths, docks, bistros and "Le Grande Monstreux," an elaborate conveyor system which moves goods between the docks and the wholesalers. The following discussion is a brief look at the major components of the market.

21.1.1 Buyers

Buyers are retailers such as butchers, grocers, bakers, and restaurant owners who buy their fresh goods early in the day. A retailer who wishes to make purchases in this market must be a member. A nonmember may join by applying for membership and receiving a buyer identification card. They can do this at any time by mail, or by visiting the Cassise Centrale. After becoming a member, buyers are responsible for notifying the market of any changes in membership information such as change of address. Members are never cancelled. (The Cassise Centrale must have an extensive mailing list!)

21.1.2 Wholesalers

A wholesaler is licensed to trade goods within Fleury Market. For security reasons, each wholesaler has a unique ID. To ensure fairness, each wholesaler is assigned only one rented booth (see Figure 21–1) during trading hours.

21.1.3 Cassise Centrale

The central bank does all the market business with the buyers. They record their membership, change membership information, check the buyer in at the start of the day, and check them out at the end of the day.

21.1.4 The Conveyor System

The conveyor system, affectionately known as "Le Gros Monstreux" (The Big Monster) by merchants, dates from the late nineteenth century. It consists of tracks, hangers, destination points and junction points (Figure 21–1). A track is a moving chain between two points. This track is set up to have hangers hooked on it. The hangers hold baskets where goods are placed for movement between locations in the market. When goods are to be moved between two destinations, the goods are placed into a hanger basket, and the hanger is shunted onto a track. A destination point is either a wholesaler booth or a dock in the Fleury Market. Each destination point is assigned a code. This code is a pattern that can be replicated by placing metal beads in certain positions in a matrix of rubber racks. Each hanger has one of these matricies. Before the hanger is put on the track, the beads are set for the appropriate destination. A junction point is a place where a hanger can change directions. Mechanical fingers at the junction points read the metal beads of the hanger and determine the direction it needs to go to reach its destination. Despite the complexity of 200 tracks, 200 junction points, and 900 destinations, less than one hanger in 5000 fails to reach its correct location.

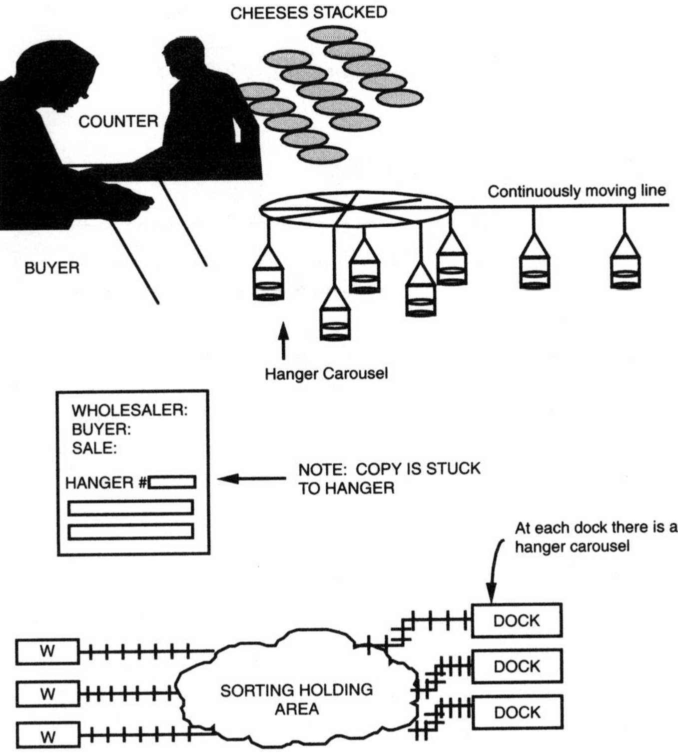

Figure 21–1 The Current (and Mostly Manual) System at the Wholesaler Booth

21.1.5 Docks

The docks at the market hold goods from truckers for delivery to the wholesalers, and collect goods from wholesalers for delivery to the buyers. One trucker may deliver goods to many different wholesalers. The dock manager will put the goods on appropriate hangers and direct the goods to the appropriate wholesaler via the conveyor system. As buyers buy goods, wholesalers place items in the basket of an available hanger. The wholesaler keeps them in his booth until he is told which dock to send them to. A buyer will pick up all his goods, which may have been purchased from different wholesalers, at one dock. When the bank tells the dock manager that the buyer has checked out, the dock manager will determine the most efficient dock, and direct the wholesalers to send any sold items to the appropriate dock via the conveyor system. The wholesaler then sets the appropriate metal bead pattern and puts the hanger on the rack.

21.1.6 The Pneumatic Tube System

A pneumatic tube network, called "la vente vite" (the fast wind) exists between the wholesalers, the Cassise Centrale, and the docks, to allow movement of the sales forms and other papers between all areas of the market.

21.2 A TYPICAL DAY AT THE MARKET

Understanding How the Market Operates

Looking at a typical day at the market may help you understand how all these components are used. The Cassise Centrale is staffed twenty-four hours a day. The Fleury Market is officially open from midnight to noon. Figure 21–2 represents the activity within the market on a typical day and approximate times within which those activities occur. (The only truly fixed times in this are market opening and closing.) A brief description of some of the activities follows.

21.2.1 Check-In

Buyers check in with M. Garcon at the Cassise Centrale. Usually, a buyer will make a deposit just after checking in, but if he just wants to window shop, a deposit is not required. Once a buyer has checked in, it is customary for the buyer to shake hands with some wholesalers before talking with them over a short breakfast of onion soup and a baguette or a few glasses of red wine in the market bistro.

21.2.2 Making Purchases

Suitably fortified, the buyer begins his rounds at the market. He begins to move from wholesaler to wholesaler. He negotiates the sale (price and number of items) of each com-

Time	Activity
Midnight	Market opens. Deliveries to wholesalers are accepted at the docks.
Midnight–3AM	Wholesalers stock their booths with goods from the docks.
3AM–7AM	Buyers begin to arrive and ***check in***.
5AM	Buyer/Wholesaler ***trade*** begins.
7AM	Buyers begin to ***check out***. Goods are moved from wholesalers to the docks.
9AM–11AM	Buyers ***pick up*** their goods.
11AM	Market closes to buyers.
11AM–Noon	Goods left at docks are returned to Wholesalers.

Figure 21–2 Typical Market Activities and Time Frames

modity, possibly buying several different commodities from any one wholesaler. He may return and change or cancel these sales. A wholesaler fills out a sales form for each sale. He then sends two copies of each sales form to the Cassise Centrale, one for their records, the other to be sent to the dock at check-out.

21.2.3 Check-Out

When a buyer has finished making purchases, he must check out at the Cassise Centrale. M. Garcon totals the buyers sales and deducts that amount from his balance. Any remaining balance is refunded. M. Garcon then sends a copy of the sales form to the dock manager so Mme. Claire Voyant, the manager, may dispatch goods from the wholesaler to a dock.

21.2.4 Pick-Up

The buyer stops by the dock manager's office to find out when and where he should pick up his goods. Traditionally, buyers end their visits to the market with a visit to the bistro, for another glass of wine, or if negotiations have been particularly successful, a glass of Pernod. Finally, at the appropriate time, a buyer drives up to the allocated dock. With luck he arrives just as his purchases are arriving from the different wholesaler booths. The dock manager marks the buyers receipt "delivered" and bids the buyer "au revoir." The manager then marks the dock copy "delivered" and sends it to the Cassise Centrale.

21.3 BACKGROUND FOR THE ESSENTIAL MODEL

Creating Automated Systems for Fleury Market

The Fleury Market is overwhelmed with paperwork. Multiple copies of sales forms create losses and inaccuracies. The pneumatic tube system is getting old and unreliable. When it fails, the market cannot deliver goods to the buyer in a reasonable time. Market management has agreed to automate the system on modern day computers, where reasonable. They have decided to charter three systems. The systems are: Service Buyers, Commodity Management, Service Wholesalers. Detail on each of these systems follows:

21.3.1 Service Buyers

The Service Buyers system will:

- Register new buyers
- Check buyers in and out of the market
- Accept deposits and refund credit balances

- Prevent sales to a buyer with insufficient funds
- Prevent sales of items with insufficient stock (this information is kept by commodity management)
- Record, change, and cancel sales
- Maintain a sales history
- Tell commodity management which hangers have sales and when to deliver goods
- Provide sales information to the Service Wholesalers system.

The Service Buyers System is the focus of our design effort, and the rest of the models in the book.

21.3.2 Commodity Management

The Commodity Management system will:

- Determine which commodities will be sold at the market
- Maintain commodity stock levels for each wholesaler
- Determine which dock to send purchased goods to and notify the buyers
- Direct the movement of goods from a wholesaler to a dock
- Correct misdirected hangers
- Maintain the status of the hangers
- Manage all deliveries from the truckers to the wholesalers.

21.3.3 Service Wholesalers

The Service Wholesalers system will:

- License and maintain information about wholesalers
- Rent booths
- Pay wholesalers for goods sold on a weekly basis
- Compute and pay taxes.

21.4 GATHERING REQUIREMENT DETAILS FOR THE ESSENTIAL MODEL

Interviews with Market Personnel

The following is a set of interview notes that provide useful information about the detailed operations of the Fleury Market.

21.4.1 Check-In and Deposits

Interview with M. Garcon, Cassise Centrale

"When a buyer comes into Cassise Centrale, I mark my log. He or she has to be a member. If not, I first register the person as a member, then I start to the check-in. Once he or she has been logged in, I see if there is any money on account. If that is so, I ask if the person wishes to add more. If so, I accept the deposit. If not, I know I'll probably hear from that person later. If he or she does not have any money on account, I point out that no purchases can be made until money has been deposited to cover the sale. Window shopping is frowned upon by the wholesalers. But it is the buyer's choice. Usually, the buyer will make a sufficient deposit to cover his estimated purchases for the day. A buyer may have deposited money before he or she checks in. I find it is a good policy to accept money whenever someone offers it, even if the market hasn't opened yet! Also, there may be a balance from a previous market day, as some buyers never pick up the goods they pay for. When that happens, we reclaim the goods and credit the account."

21.4.2 Sales

Interview with M. St. Etienne, Fromages du Midi

"As soon as the buyer comes in the booth, I take a blank form (see Figure 21–3) and fill in our ID, the date, and the buyer ID. Buyers are more reluctant to walk out if paperwork has started. It's a type of commitment, a sale where no items have been decided yet."

SALES FORM	**Fromages du Midi**
Date:	
Time:	
Sale Number:	
Wholesaler ID:	
Buyer ID:	
Hanger ID:	

Commodity ID	**Description**	**Quantity Sold**	**Price per Item**

Figure 21–3 The Sales Form

"Then we start looking at the first type of cheese the person wants. I tell them how excellent it is and suggest a price. They tell me how ugly it is and offer a lower price. I tell them about my hungry children, they tell me about the increased cost to do business, and so on, and so on. Usually we agree on a price. Then we sort through the cheeses selecting those they want. If they want more than I have, I apologize but tell them I am expecting a shipment tomorrow if they wish to stop by then. As the buyer selects the goods, I grab my empty hanger and load the cheeses into the basket. I mark the hanger number on the sales form, and note the line item details. We move from cheese to cheese until they have selected all they want."

"When the sale is complete, I total the line items and determine the total sale price. Then I call the Cassise Centrale to make sure the buyer has a sufficient balance to cover this sale and all the others that are already on file at the bank. If the buyer has sufficient funds, I give the buyer a copy of the sales form as a receipt. If there are insufficient funds, and we cannot renegotiate, I mark the form 'insufficient deposit." If later on, the buyer puts more on deposit, they have to come back and start over. If the sale is successful, I give the buyer a copy of the form as a receipt and send two copies to Cassise Centrale by pneumatic tube."

"Unfortunately, that doesn't guarantee money in my pocket. Every once in a while, I get a buyer who, right after drinking the red wine, decides to spend all his money in my booth. However, after the wine wears off, the buyer returns demanding changes. Sometimes we lower the number of cheeses, sometimes we renegotiate the price, sometimes we delete all the cheeses of one kind, and sometimes, sadly, we cancel the sale entirely. Fortunately, my luck can go the other way, too. Perhaps the person found, by the end of the day, that my goods were indeed the best in the market. The person might increase the amount, or add another type of commodity. I never have known one to come in and offer to increase the price per item, though!"

21.4.3 Check Out

Interview with M. Garcon, Cassise Centrale

"Checking out buyers is much more complicated than checking them in. It wouldn't be so bad if wholesalers would let me know about changes and cancellations when they occur! Don't they realize that I could be authorizing sufficient funds not knowing that the amount of a sale has increased? Or denying a sale not knowing it has decreased or been canceled? Well, enough complaining! First, I check my log to be sure the buyer had checked in. If so, I mark the log to show he has checked out. Then I make sure my copies of the sales forms with his ID match his copies. I need to do this because the wholesalers don't tell me about changes and cancellations. I'm only interested in sales that are still agreed upon. When I find a difference, I bring my copy up-to-date with any changes. For any sale for that buyer that is agreed upon, I add up all the sales totals to determine the buyer's total sales for the day. This is deducted from his balance. Then I refund any left-over balance to the buyer. For that rare occasion where a change increases the sale and the buyer owes the bank money, I demand a deposit right then and there, or I cancel the sale, and I send the dock receipt back to the wholesaler. I presume you'll prevent this from happening in the new system. Lastly, I send a copy of the sales form to the dock manager so they can notify the wholesaler to send the goods to the selected dock."

21.4.4 An Unusual Situation

Interview with Mme Clair Voyant

"Normally, everything goes as planned. But every once in a while, buyers don't pick up their goods. There was M. Boucher, for example. He was so rude to M. St. Etienne when he came to cancel his huge sale! M. St. Etienne pointed out to him that he wouldn't be able to sell those cheeses to anyone else since the market was about to close. M. Boucher said that was not his problem. M. St. Etienne knocked M. Boucher out, emptied the hanger basket of cheese, placed M. Boucher on the hanger, and sent him to a dock, sales form in hand! Now what should I do? M. Boucher was in no condition to check out, much less pick up his goods. I had no idea who else he had bought from. I called the Cassise Centrale, and M. Garcon told me that he would cancel all his sales for the day, credit M. Boucher's balance for the price of the sales, and send him a cancellation notice for each. I was to send M. Boucher to the hospital. I'm glad most buyers are better behaved. Sadly, the bistro tends to do a great business after check out. Sometimes the buyers forget that they have to go to the dock before the market closes. Pernod will do that to you! If I discover goods on a dock after the market closes, I mark the forms, "canceled due to failure to pick up" and send them to the Cassise Centrale. M. Garcon credits the buyer for the sales and sends out sales cancellation notices in the mail. I send the goods back to the wholesalers."

21.4.5 Sales History

Interview with M. Garcon

"Ah the paperwork around here! I am so glad you are going to relieve us of all these forms! Let me tell you what I have to do with the sales forms. First, I get two sales forms from wholesalers when they and their buyers agree upon a sale. I place those in the 'agreed upon' file. They stay there until the buyer checks out. Then I match their copy of the form to mine and, if necessary, change mine. If theirs indicates the sale was canceled, I place the forms in the 'canceled' file. If it shows changes, I correct the line items on the forms. If it matches, I rejoice. I then send a copy of any sales that were not cancelled to the dock manager, so they can get the goods to a dock. My form is then filed under 'waiting for pick-up.' The buyer then gets their form back. When I receive a form marked 'delivered,' from the dock, I match it to the 'waiting for pick-up' file and move the form to the 'delivered' file. After the market closes, I look and see if there are any forms left in the 'waiting for pick-up' or 'agreed upon' files. If there are, I know that someone didn't make it to the check-out or that the dock will be sending me a cancellation on the sale due to the buyer's failure to pick it up. I mark the sale 'canceled,' and place it in the 'canceled file.' Once a week, I go through the 'delivered' pile and determine the proper amount of funds that go to the wholesaler and the amount of taxes that go to the government. Then the sales form goes into the 'sales history' file. When the 'canceled' cabinet fills up, I destroy the oldest cancellations. But I hate to do this, because every time I do it, some buyer wants to know why they never got their goods. I'd like to keep cancellation history. As the wholesalers rely on me to keep sales history, I never destroy any sales forms. They just keep piling up. I hope you come up with a better system!"

21.5 BACKGROUND FOR THE IMPLEMENTATION MODEL

Designing the Distributed System

The market town of Fleury le Deux Eglises is being dragged "kicking and screaming" to support the market with more advanced technology. The market is to retain its rustic charm but with new up-to-date client/server technology.

The whole market system actually comprises three interlocked systems: Service Buyers, Service Wholesalers, and Commodity Management. Each of these systems has a definite role to play in the overall market. For the purposes of this book, our focal point will be the Service Buyers System. Some new technology is being proposed for Fleury Market such as office automation and a new-fangled *Le Fleury_cardTM*.

21.5.1 The Design Team

The systems development team did an excellent job with the Essential Model in a series of *JED* (French for JAD!) sessions which were held in the back room of the local bar (*La Vie en Rose*). The team spread work out over the billiard table and enjoyed lively lashings of *Vin de Anne-Marie Louise* from an adjacent wine growing region.

Mme. Clair Voyant's son Merise, who completed his Polytechnique studies and then served an internship with CGI (Camping Gaz Internationale), is leading much of the effort.

Buyer activities have been represented by Boris Boucher who has taken on the role of helping run his father's stall and assisting in the development of the market infrastructure.

Maurice Garcon is representing the wholesaler activities and was the instigator of the Fleury Card (*Le Fleury Carte*). As you will see, nepotism is not yet dead, so the genes of the last generation live on! Maurice and Merise have painted a scenario which may become the basis of the new Processor Model for Fleury.

21.5.2 Types of Computer Processors

The mainframe will be used for centralized accounting. Some of the servers are intended to accommodate activities such as checking in and checking out buyers. Another server will be used for the Commodity System. Buyer and Wholesaler activities will take place on clients located at each wholesaler's booth (see Figure 21–4).

21.5.3 Changes in Physical Building

The Fleury Market is also undertaking a big architectural change, where the whole market is to be situated under one roof in a building in the style of *Fin de Cycle,* with all the appropriate amenities located within. It is envisioned that this will make Fleury Market a more attractive prospect to wholesalers in nearby regions, especially during the wintry months. It also includes a new docking area with sufficient bays for sixteen trucks to disgorge and engorge market produce simultaneously.

21.5.4 The Fleury Card

Le Fleury_Carte is envisioned to assist in the checking in and out of the market. It will hold the basic information such as the name of the holder, his/her password, a current balance, and a status flag to indicate presence in the market. The design logo and color scheme has yet to be worked out.

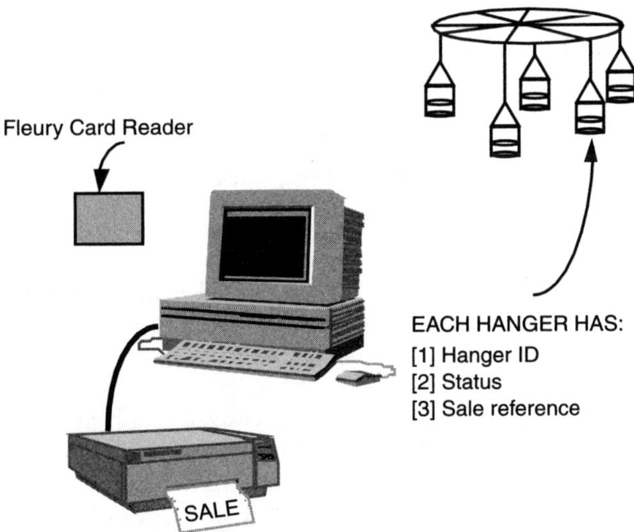

Figure 21–4 The (Proposed) Client System at the Wholesaler Booth

This card can also be used at a booth for agreement of a sale, change, and deletion of a sale. This ensures a higher degree of security and it is anticipated that it will reduce errors.

21.5.5 Processing

This is envisioned as happening just as defined in the Essential Model. The processing will be placed as near to the geographic point of exchange as possible.

- Check out could occur at the bar (*La vie en Rose*) with appropriate machinery.
- A buyer could be advised by an electronic visible bulletin board when his/her sale may be picked up (similar to how airlines display flight departure information in the airports).

21.5.6 New Intended Uses of the System—The Cream on the Cheese

The Wholesalers intend to use the electronic mail feature to offer *Spot Deal Bulletin Board* to potential buyers. It is envisioned that this will allow Wholesalers to improve their commodity turn-over, as well as improve service for the Buyers.

Although all trading will still take place at the market, the *Spot Deal Bulletin Board* could be accessed from outside the market by means of a personal computer or Antiope (French View Data System). Antiope has existed in Europe for fifteen years. It allows people to use their television set to access public information and act as a read-only screen. This would enable hotel or restaurant chains to survey what's hot at Fleury Market on a given day and send agents to the market to close sales.

The wholesalers are very excited about the e-mail automation. They can imagine many uses for ad hoc needs of e-mail communication with other wholesalers.

Everyone's imagination is active. Mme. Claire Voyant and Msr. Etienne have developed an interest in creative writing, and they envision writing a satire (soap opera) concerning life in Fleury before automation and with the lid off. They both intend to use the comprehensive word processing and electronic mail features that become available.

21.5.7 Effects on the Current Implementation

The **pneumatic tube** will sadly go, this is mixed blessing. Even though it was fast, it did cause much hot air from time to time!

The **conveyor system** is being replaced with a network that avoids much of the clanking and puffing. It is based on *swish rail* and works as smooth as silk! It will electronically encode a hanger based upon the completion of a sales agreement session with a Buyer.

The **Cassise Centrale** has been downsized (oops, rightsized!) to a monitoring function. It is a rare occasion these days that a person checks in to the market and hands over cash. The local banks in the Fleury region may update the card with the value of a cash deposit being drawn from the buyer's business account. This makes *Le Fleury Carte* a transfer media and improves efficiency, too.

Day	Mon	Tue	Wed	Thu	Fri
Buyers	55	34	56	156	45

Figure 21–5 Average Number of Buyers per Week

21.5.8 The Future—Market Growth Predictions

The market is expected to grow, and at this point in time the volumes look this:

- 53 registered wholesalers in the market
- 174 currently registered buyers with the Fleury Market

Figure 21–5 displays typical weekly traffic.

Fleury Market hopes to "raise the bar" for service for their competition by installing this new client/server platform Once the word gets out, it is envisioned that within two years there will be a 100% increase in Buyers; and being drawn in from adjacent regions, a 15% increase in Wholesalers.

Additionally, Fleury Market is planning to open an additional market in Lyon, and a distribution center in Bordeaux. Apparently, the trend of restaurant chains is spreading throughout France as well, and the large buyers want an option of placing large orders for their wholly owned chains in other parts of France. In the first implementation, the orders will be placed at Fleury and picked up in Bordeaux.

22

The Fleury Market Essential Model

A Model of Business Requirements

The first task for the design team was to create the Essential Model, which defines the requirements of the system in terms of business events, responses to events, and data produced or required in the servicing of business events. This model was used to verify the business with the users, design team members, and data administrators. It represents the shared and negotiated understanding of what the system will do. The models created in the Essential Model were used extensively in designing the technical implementation of the system (the Implementation Model: Chapter 23). The team also tracked all issues and problems in an Issues List (see Appendix G). The *artifacts* (the models, tables, and text) of the Essential Model provide an easy-to-read graphical statement of the requirements, which later serve to document the system.

22.1 STATEMENT OF PURPOSE

Negotiating Scope to Rapidly Deliver Business Solutions

The Statement of Purpose (Chapter 4) is a succinct definition of the system's scope. After much discussion and back-and-forth negotiations in JAR (Joint Application Requirements) sessions, the design team and business users jointly created and agreed to the Statement of Purpose displayed in Figure 22–1. The most important concessions the de-

SYSTEM

Service Buyers

PURPOSE (Business Drivers)

- Provide customers with faster and more efficient service
- Provide wholesalers with the information they need to more effectively service their customers
- Provide timely and accurate information to and from other systems and decision makers

SCOPE OF RESPONSIBILITIES (Functional Scope)

1. Maintain information about retail buyers.
2. Control the receipt and refunding of funds to buyers.
3. Maintain a record of all sales made.
4. Inform the commodities system when to deliver goods to buyers.
5. Provide sales information to the wholesaler system.
6. Ensure no sales are made to buyers with insufficient funds.
7. Ensure no sales are made for items out of stock.
8. Assign a hanger to the collection of goods for the buyer.

EXCLUSIONS IN SCOPE

1. The actual movement of goods from the warehouse to the dock.
2. Payment of wholesalers for goods sold.
3. Computation and payment of taxes.
4. The maintenance of on-hand balance for stock at the wholesaler.
5. The determination of the docks at which the buyer receives goods.

METRICS

1. Decrease time between check-out and pick-up
2. Increase accuracy of Buyer information

Figure 22–1 Statement of Purpose for Service Buyers System

sign team received from the business was in the responsibilities and exclusions of the system. The responsibilities and exclusions sections define the scope and boundaries of the system, which was a critical factor for overall success of the system. The design team kept the scope as small as possible, believing that nothing succeeds like success. There was much discussion regarding finding the right balance between implementing a solution as quickly as possible, and giving the users all the features and functionality they needed and wanted. The compromise came in a short, initial implementation time frame, with plans for the next iteration to follow soon thereafter. The plan is to deliver the full functionality of the system in short, iterative cycles. The metrics are used to measure the success of the system. For more information on creating the Statement of Purpose, see Chapter 4 (sections 4.3, 4.4, and 4.5).

22.2 THE ENVIRONMENTAL ASPECT

Defining the System Scope within the Context of the Overall Environment

In the Environmental Aspect, the design team determined the scope of the system in terms of processing business events. The terminators were defined either as people or other systems external to the Service Buyers System (which at this point just appears as a circle in the center of the diagram). They include Buyers, the Commodity Management System, the Service Wholesalers System, and Wholesalers. Of particular concern in this case is the fact that the Commodity Management System and the Service Buyers System both share responsibility for managing sales on Hangers. The functional boundaries between systems were not defined as cleanly as they might have been. However, we find this to be the case in many places, where functions happen on one system because of history or politics, instead of optimal design considerations.

22.2.1 The Context Diagram

The Context Diagram (Figure 22–2) was created by depicting our system, Service Buyers, as a circle in the center, interfacing with other applications and people in the environment, called terminators. The terminators are depicted as rectangles. In Fleury Market Buyers and Wholesalers are human terminators. They are the users of the system. The Commodity Management System and Service Wholesalers Systems are terminators that are other applications. The Service Buyers system interacts with all terminators through the flow of information. These are the arrows on the diagram. The open boxes are data stores (identified by a "D"), which represent the data that will be kept to record the business transactions (also called persistent data). Note that the Service Buyers System shares persistent data with the other systems. The context diagram does not say *how* this data is shared. It only indicates that there is data common to both systems. In fact, if the need for common data is not identified across systems, there is danger that data will be inconsistent across the systems. For more information on constructing the Context Diagram, see Chapter 5, section 5.2.

22.2.2 Data Flow Specifications

The information flow between Service Buyers and each terminator in the environment is further detailed in a set of Data Flow Specifications (Figure 22–3). A specification is created for each type of information shared between Services Buyers and system or human terminators. For more information on creating Data Flow Specifications, see Chapter 5, section 5.3.

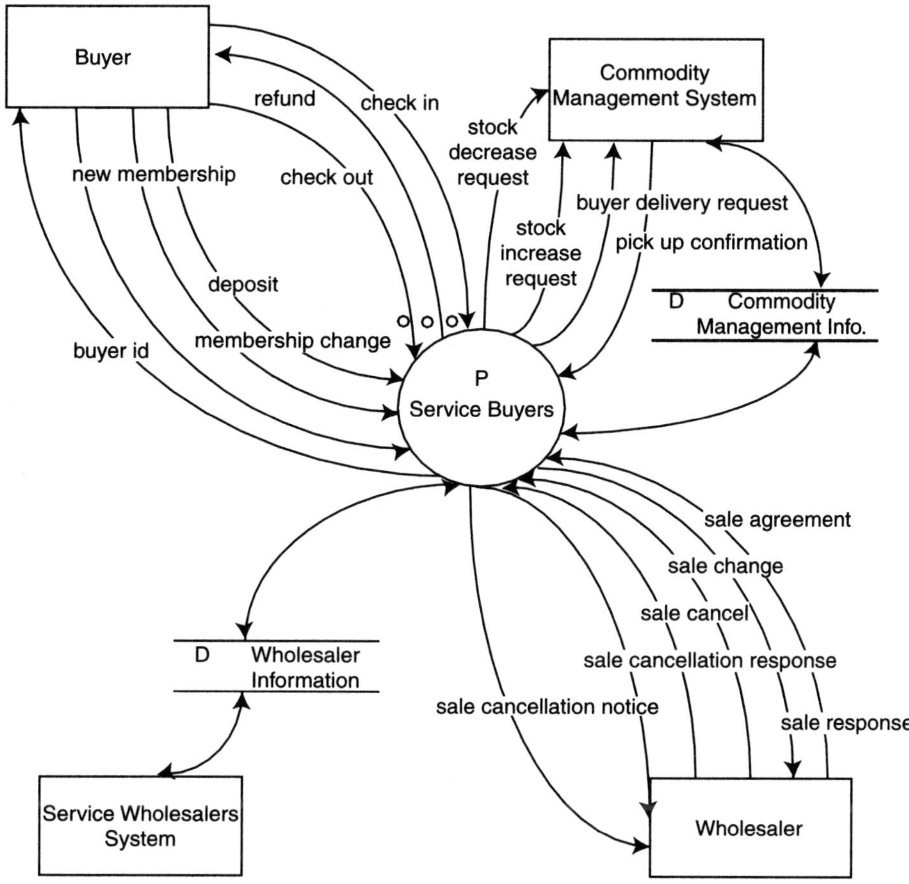

Figure 22–2 Context Diagram for Service Buyers System

DATA FLOW Sale Agreement
MEANING The wholsaler's notice of a buyer's commitment to purchase a particular commodity
STRUCTURE Group
COMPOSITION wholesaler_id + buyer_id + sale_date + sale_time + 1{line_item} + total_price + hanger_id + sale_number

Figure 22–3 Data Flow Specification for Sale Agreement

22.2.3 Event Table

One of the most important things the design team did with the business users was to define what business events would be handled by the system. This process first required that the team understood the business processes, then negotiated which events were in scope and which events were out of scope for the first implementation of the system. Understanding system requirements in terms of business processes was new to some of the design team members, who typically preferred to focus on data, and then understand the processes in terms of inputs and outputs. However, by focusing on business processes, the Fleury design team was able to better ensure they understood the business, and users were better able to describe what they do. The discussion about business process also led to some fruitful discussions about whether the implementation of the new system created opportunities to do things differently and more effectively. By describing what they do, the users brought to light some inefficient processes that could be done better in the new system. Figure 22–4 depicts the events the Service Buyers System will support. For more information on creating the Event Table see Chapter 5, section 5.4.

Number	Event Name	Detection	Outputs
1	Buyer applies to become a market member	New membership	Buyer id
2	Buyer checks into market	Check in	None
3	Wholesaler proposes a sale	Sale agreement	Sale response, Stock decrease request
4	Buyer checks out of market	Check out	Buyer delivery request, Refund
5	Buyer picks up orders	Pick up confirmation	None
6	Market closes	Time	Sale cancellation notice
7	Buyer changes membership information	Membership change	None
8	Wholesaler changes sale agreement	Sale change	Sale response, Stock decrease request, Stock increase request
9	Wholesaler cancels a sale	Sale cancel	Sale cancellation response, Stock increase request
10	Buyer makes deposit	Deposit	None

Figure 22–4 Service Buyers Event Table

22.3 THE INFORMATION ASPECT

Modeling the Information, Relationships, and Business Rules Concerning Data

Although an adaptive approach to systems design demands more focus on business process, that does not mean the design team could ignore the data. They still needed to focus on the business information, relationships between business entities, and the business rules contained in those relationships. The difficult part for some members of the team was understanding that process, and not data, drives the design of the system. They were somewhat relieved when they found that information modeling was still an important part of the process. For more information on constructing an Information Model, please see Chapter 6.

22.3.1 Partial Entity Relationship Diagram

The team created an Entity Relationship Diagram (ERD) to model the information requirements of the system and the business rules inherent in the relationship between business entities. Figure 22–5 is a partial representation of the Information Model for the Service Buyers System of Fleury Market.

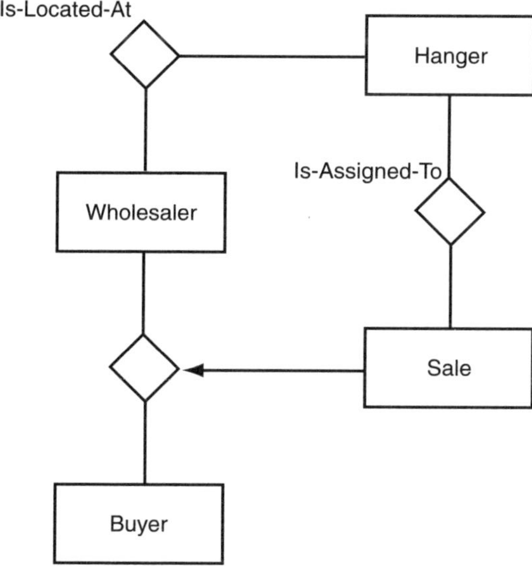

Figure 22–5 Partial Information Model for Service Buyers System

ENTITY
Buyer
MEANING
A buyer is a retail merchant who comes to the market with an intention of evaluating commodities for the purpose of buying them
ID
Buyer_Id

Figure 22–6 Entity Specification for Buyer (without attributes)

22.3.2 Entity Specifications without Attributes

After creating the ERD, the team created detailed specifications of each business entity (Figure 22–6). These detailed specifications captured the business meaning of each entity and were verified by all business users to ensure they represented the shared understanding of the meaning of the business information.

22.3.3 Relationship Specification without Attributes

Each relationship on the ERD was also specified to state the meaning, and whether participation of an entity in the relationship is mandatory or optional (Figure 22–7). This information will be used during implementation to determine how to program database triggers to ensure the integrity of relationships in the Information Model.

RELATIONSHIP	
is-assigned-to	
PARTICIPATING ENTITIES	
A Hanger is-assigned-to a Sale	
MEANING	
A Hanger is assigned to hold all the goods for a Sale from the moment the Wholesaler loads it up until it is unloaded at the dock	
PARTICIPATION	
Hanger	optional
Sale	mandatory
UPPER LIMITS	
Hanger	1:1
Sale	1:1

Figure 22–7 Relationship Specification for Hanger <is assigned to> Sale

ASSOCIATIVE ENTITY	
Sale	
PARTICIPATING ENTITIES	
Wholesaler sells-to Buyer	
MEANING	
A Sale is transacted between a Buyer and a Wholesaler, where the buyer agrees to purchase from the Wholesaler	
IDENTIFIERS	
Sale_Id	
PARTICIPATION	
Wholesaler	optional
Buyer	mandatory
UPPER LIMITS	
Wholesaler	1:1
Buyer	1:1

Figure 22–8 Association Entity Specification for Sale

COMPONENT
Sale
ATTRIBUTE
Total Price
MEANING
The cost of a total Sale between a Buyer and a Wholesaler
RETENTION
Derived
DERIVATION
The sum of all Sale_Item.Quantity_Sold * Sale_Item.Price
TYPING
Abstract
ABSTRACT DATA TYPE
Currency
VALUE RANGE
0 to 100,000 francs

Figure 22–9 Attribute Specification for Total Price (Attribute of Sale)

22.3.4 Associative Entity Specification

To make the Information model complete every associative entity on the ERD must also be specified. Figure 22–8 is an example of an Associative Entity Specification for Sale.

22.3.5 Attribute Specification

For the sake of completeness, every attribute of each business Entity must also be fully defined. Attributes are facts that are captured about an Entity. Figure 22–9 is an Attribute Specification for the attribute Total Price, which is an attribute of the Entity Sale.

22.4 THE BRIDGE ASPECT

Bringing Together Business Events, Data, and Time

An important step in the requirements definition, which was not part of top-down decomposition, is bringing together the system dimensions of process, data, and time. The design team will use the artifacts created in the Bridge Aspect extensively in the Implementation Model. This understanding of how processes use and create data provides a much more robust, multidimensional view of the business requirements and provides methods for checking the consistency and accuracy of the design to date.

22.4.1 Entity Event Table

First the team defined which events created (c), read (r), updated (u), deleted (d), or matched (m—denote existence check) entities defined in the Information Model (Figure 22–10). This information represents the data access rules for each event. It will be used to determine data distribution in the design phase as well as database access rights and permissions. For more information on creating the Entity-Event Table, please see Chapter 7, section 7.2.

22.4.2 Entity State Transition Diagram

The design team created Entity State Transition Diagrams (ESTDs) to model what happens to information over time. This helps create an understanding of how information changes, and under what circumstances it changes. These are also used in the Implementation Model when defining what happens to information as it crosses systems and processors. ESTDs also help in determining which events will affect the entity and what accesses are required when events occur. Each ESTD describes the state of one entity occurrence. Figure 22–11 is an ESTD for a Sale Agreement.

The Data Administrator reviewed the ESTDs and maintained a copy in the repository, which contributed to the overall understanding of how enterprise data is used by different systems. For more information on creating Entity State Transition Diagrams, please refer to Chapter 7, section 7.3.

Event / Entity or Relationship	1. Buyer applies to become member	2. Buyer checks into market	3. Wholesaler proposes a sale	4. Buyer checks into market	5. Buyer picks up orders	6. Market closes	7. Buyer changes member information	8. Wholesaler changes sale	9. Wholesaler cancels a sale	10. Buyer makes deposit
Buyer	c,m	r,u	r,u	u	m,u	r,u	u	r,u	r,u	r,u
Wholesaler			m			r		r		
Sale <Wholesaler> sells to <Buyer>			c	r,u	u	u		r	r,u	
Sale Item <Commodity> is item of <Sale>			c	r		r		c,r,u,d		
Commodity			m					r		
Stock <Wholesaler> stocks <Commodity>			r					r		
Hanger			m					r		
<Hanger> is located at <Wholesaler>			m							
<Hanger > assigned to <Sale>			c						d	

Figure 22–10 Entity-Event Table

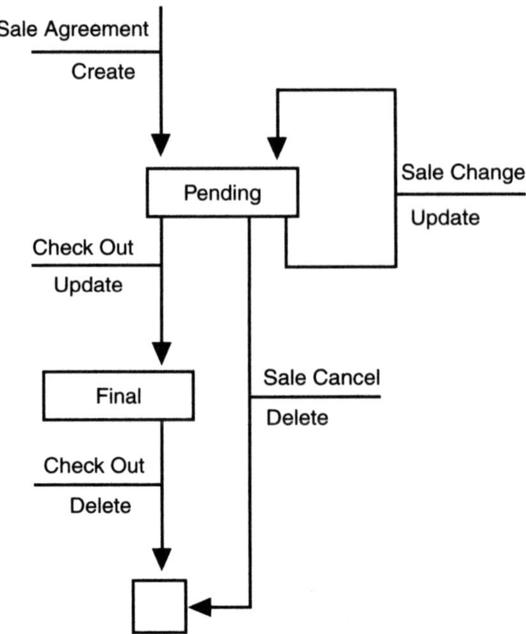

Figure 22–11 Entity State Transition Diagram for Sale Agreement

22.5 THE BEHAVIORAL ASPECT

Defining Granular Responses to Business Events

At this point in the modeling process, the design team has a clearly defined scope for the business events which will be handled by the system, the information required by the system, how the information is used by the business events, and how the information is changed over time. Now the team is ready to clearly define the detailed responses to the business events.

22.5.1 Event Response Table

In the Environmental Aspect we created the Event Table (section 22.2.3). Now we define the detailed system responses required to service each business event. We have used the convention of naming events with a number preceded by an "E" (for event) and identifying each response with the number of the event and an "R". Because a single business event may spawn multiple system responses, we number the responses for each event. Figure 22–12 is the Event Response Table for all events that will be managed by the Service Buyers System. For more information on creating the Entity Response Table, please see Chapter 8, section 8.2.

Essential Event Number and Name	Essential Event Response
E1. Buyer applies to become a market member	R1.1. Check for valid buyer (credit check) R1.2. Add buyer
E2. Buyer checks into market	R2.1. Check buyer in (change status of buyer)
E3. Wholesaler proposes a sale	R3.1. Create sale R3.2. Notify Service Buyers of Account debit R3.3. Assign Sale to hanger R3.4. Notify Commodity System of debit to stock
E4. Buyer checks out of market	R4.1. Check buyer out (change status of buyer) R4.2. Notify dock system of buyer check-out
E5. Buyer picks up orders	R5.1. Record pick-up R5.2. Notify Service Buyers
E6. Market closes	R6.1. Cancel uncollected sales R6.2. Notify Commodity System of canceled sale R6.3. Notify Wholesaler System of canceled sale
E7. Buyer changes membership information	R7.1. Note change in membership
E8. Wholesaler changes sale agreement	R8.1. Change sale 8R2. Notify Service Buyers of account debit/credit 8R3. Notify Commodity System of change 8R4. Notify Wholesaler system of change
E9. Wholesaler cancels a sale	9R1. Cancel sale for buyer 9R2. Notify Service Buyers of account credit 9R3. Notify Commodity System of change 9R4. Notify Wholesaler system of change
E10. Buyer makes deposit	10R1. Add deposit to balance

Figure 22–12 Event Response Table

22.5.2 Partial Data Flow Diagram

The Event Response Table is used to create the Data Flow Diagram (DFD) depicting the detailed system behavior. The diagram in Figure 22–13 depicts four events. Any circle on the diagram can be further detailed with a lower-level DFD.

22.5.3 Detailed Data Flow Diagrams

Figure 22–14 is a detailed DFD for Response to Wholesaler Proposes a Sale (Event 3). It shows all the responses to the single event. This entire diagram is represented as a circle on the higher-level DFD. For more information on creating the different levels of Data Flow Diagrams please refer to Chapter 8, section 8.4.

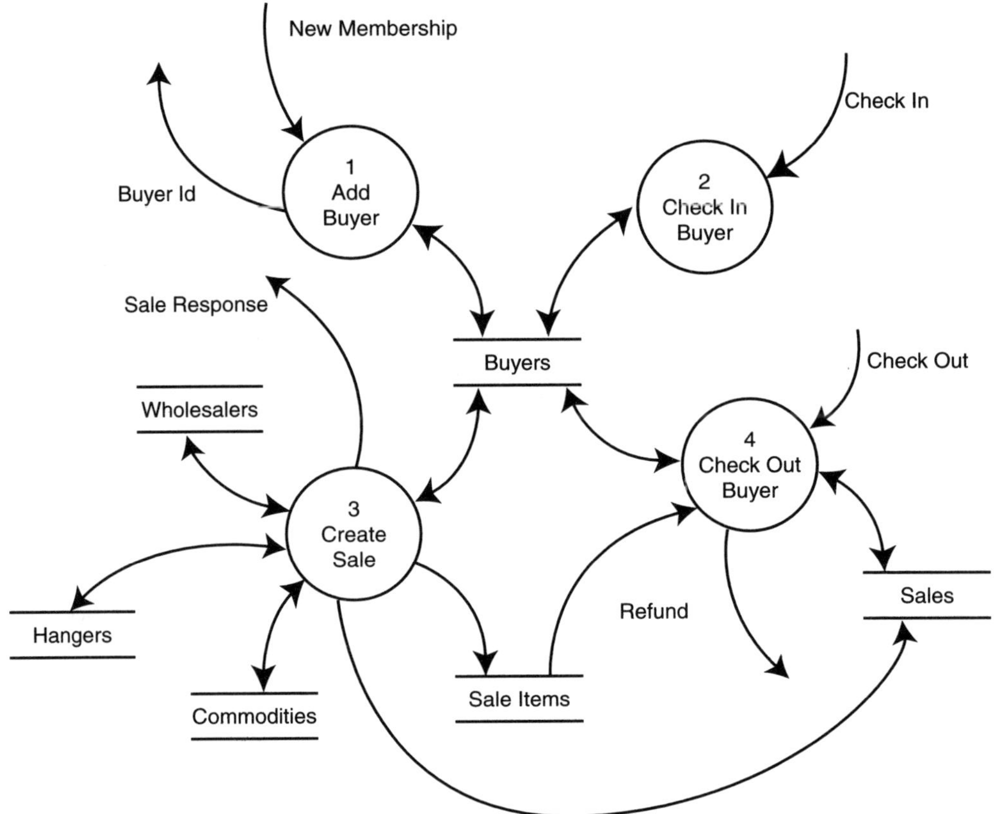

Figure 22–13 Data Flow Diagram for Events One through Four

22.5.4 Entity Response Table

We previously defined the information required for each event. We now need to define information requirements at a more detailed, granular level. In the Entity Response Table (Figure 22–15), we define information requirements for each response. For more information on creating the Entity Response Table, please see Chapter 8, section 8.5.

22.5.5 Minispec Written in Structured Language

To fully define each process on the Response DFDs, the design team created Minispecs for each process. The Minispecs written in structured language will be used later in the Implementation Model as part of the software specifications for each processor. Figure

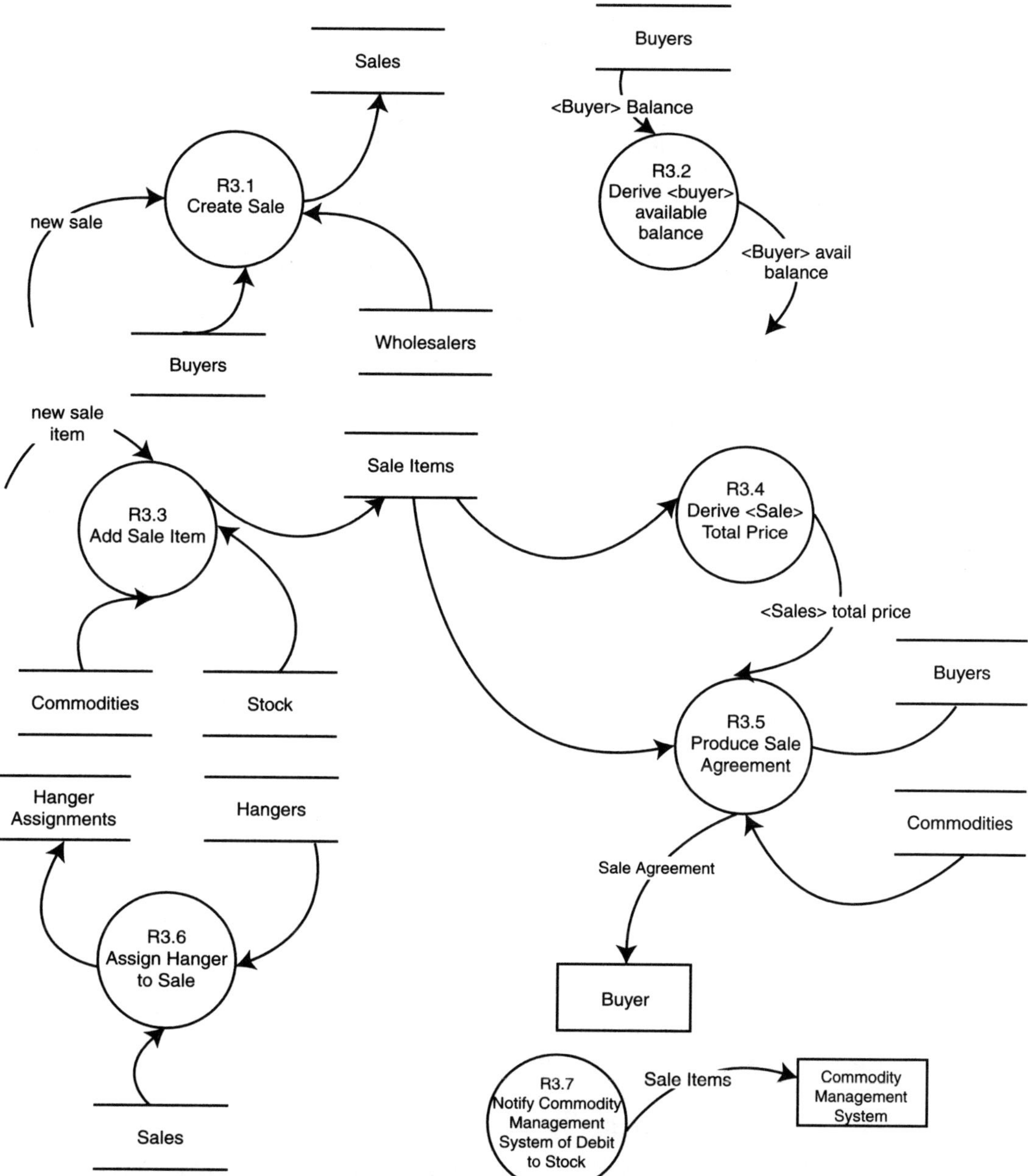

Figure 22–14 Detailed Data Flow Diagram for Wholesaler Proposes a Sale (Event 3)

Event / Entity or Relationship	1R1 Check for Valid Buyer	1R2 Add Buyer	2R1 Check Buyer In (Status)	3R1 Create Sale	3R2 Notify Service Buyers —Debit Buyer Acct.	3R3 Assign Sale to Hanger	3R4 Notify Com-modity System of Stock Debit	4R1 Check Buyer Out	4R2 Notify Dock System of Buyer Check Out
Buyer	m	c	u	r, u	u			u	r
Wholesaler				r					
Sale <Wholesaler> sells to <Buyer>				c	r	r			
Sale Item <Commodity> is item of <Sale>				c	r		r		
Commodity				r			u		
Stock <Wholesaler> stocks <Commodity>				r			u		
Hanger						r			
<Hanger> is located at <Wholesaler>						r			
<Hanger > assigned to <Sale>						c			r

Figure 22–15 Entity Response Table

22–16 is a Minispec for the Check Out Buyer process. For further information on creating Minispecs, please see Chapter 8, section 8.8.

22.5.6 Minispec Written in Pre- and Post-Condition Style

There are alternative methods for writing Minispecs. Because Minispecs become the software blueprints of the system, different styles are suitable for describing different processes. Figure 22–17 is a Minispec written in Pre- and Post-Condition Style. Pre- and post-conditions are suitable for describing trigger events.

PROCESS

Check Out Buyer

DATA FLOW INPUTS

Check_Out

DATA FLOW OUTPUTS

Refund

Buyer_Delivery_Request

STORED DATA INPUTS

Sale Items

STORED DATA OUTPUTS

Sales

Buyers

LOCAL TERMS

<Buyer_in_market> is-a-matching <Buyer> on Buyer_Id
    with state = "In market"

<Buyer_sale> is-a-matching <Sale> for <Buyer_in_market>
    with state = "Agreed upon"

FUNCTION

If <Buyer_in_market> then
    produce Buyer_Delivery_Request
    For each <Buyer sale> do
        <Buyer_sale>.state = "Waiting for pickup"
    Derive <Buyer_in_market> sales_total
    Read <Buyer_in_market>.balance
    Deduct <Buyer_in_market>.sales_total from
        <Buyer_in_market>.balance
    If <Buyer_in_market>.balance > 0.00 then
        Refund = <Buyer_in_market>.balance
        <Buyer_in_market>.balance = 0
        Issue refund
    <Buyer_in_market>.state = "Out of market"

Figure 22–16 Minispec for Buyer Check Out Written in Structured Language

PROCESS

Check Out Buyer

DATA FLOW INPUTS

Check_Out

DATA FLOW OUTPUTS

Refund

Buyer_Delivery_Request

STORED DATA INPUTS

Sale Items

STORED DATA OUTPUTS

Sales

Buyers

LOCAL TERMS

<Buyer_in_market> is-a-matching <Buyer> on Buyer_Id with state = "In market"

<Buyer_sale> is-a-matching <Sale> for <Buyer_in_market> with state = "Agreed upon"

FUNCTION

#	PRE-CONDITION	POST-CONDITION
1	<Buyer_in_market>	Buyer_Delivery_Request
2	<Buyer_in_market>	<Buyer_in_market>.state = "Out of market"
3	<Buyer_sale>	<Buyer_sale>.state = "Waiting for pickup"
4	<Buyer_in_market>.balance>0.00	Refund = <Buyer_in_market>.balance

Figure 22–17 Minispec Written in Pre- and Post-Condition Style

22.6 EVENT DISTRIBUTION ASPECT

Understanding Where Events Occur

The purpose of event distribution is to determine where business events and responses actually occur. The result of the Event Distribution Aspect is an understanding of the organizational structure of the distributed business within the scope of the proposed system.

Now that the design team defined events, information, and how events use information, they needed to define how the events are distributed in the real world environment. This was done by defining logical locations. A logical location represents a point of service where one or more business events occur. Departments or roles may be represented as logical locations. These logical locations are distributed to geographic locations, providing a complete view of distributed business operations.

22.6.1 Logical Location Table

The Logical Location Table groups events by business units or types of business locations. Once we map events to logical locations we also know the responses to those events, the data required by each of those responses, the business rules contained within relationships between entities, and rules of creation, deletion, update, and read access. When we distribute an event to a logical location, we distribute the complete Business Component. Figure 22–18 depicts the logical locations for the Fleury Market Case Study. For further information on creating the Logical Location Table, please see Chapter 9, section 9.2.

22.6.2 Logical Location/Response Distribution Table

The Logical Location/Response Table further elaborates the Event Response Table, by detailing the logical boundaries between business units on a granular response level. Responses to business events may actually occur at other logical locations or terminators (from the Context Diagram—Chapter 5). Mapping responses to logical locations helps define where responses to events happen and the logical location or terminator (person or system) responsible for the response. This step could result in a re-negotiation of scope for the system, to keep the logical boundaries between systems clean. This mapping will greatly aid the design process by revealing potential risks early on. Figure 22–19 depicts the Logical Location/Response Distribution Table for Fleury Market. For more information on creating this table, refer to Chapter 9, section 9.3.

22.6.3 Geographic Distribution Table

The geographic distribution of business events defines how the business operates across geographic locations. The most flexible and adaptive component design makes it possible

Logical Location	Essential Event Number and Name
Dock Management	5. Buyer picks up orders
Wholesaler Booth	3. Wholesaler proposes a sale 8. Wholesaler changes sale agreement 9. Wholesaler cancels a sale 4. Buyer checks out of market
Buyer Check-in and Check-out	2. Buyer checks into market 4. Buyer checks out of market
Buyer Membership Administration	1. Buyer applies to become a market member 7. Buyer changes membership information 10. Buyer makes deposit
Service Buyers Administration	6. Market closes

Figure 22–18 Logical Location Table

Logical Location Event Manager	Essential Event Number and Name	Essential Event Response	Logical Location Event Response(s)
Dock Management	5. Buyer picks up orders	R5.1. Record pick-up R5.2. Notify service buyers	Dock Management Service Buyers
Wholesaler Booth	3. Wholesaler proposes a sale	R3.1. Create sale R3.3. Notify service buyers of account debit	Wholesaler Booth Service Buyers
	8. Wholesaler changes sale agreement	R8.1. Change sale R8.2. Notify service buyers of account debit/credit	Wholesaler Booth Service Buyers
	9. Wholesaler cancels a sale	R9.1. Cancel sale for buyer R9.2. Notify service buyers of account credit	Wholesaler Booth Service Buyers
	4. Buyer checks out of market	R4.1. Check buyer out	Buyer Check-in and Check-out
Buyer Check-in and Check-out	2. Buyer checks into market	R2.1. Check buyer in R4.1. Check buyer out	Buyer Check-in and Check-out
Buyer Membership Administration	1. Buyer applies to become a market member 7. Buyer changes membership information 10. Buyer makes deposit	R1.1. Add buyer R7.1. Note change in membership R10.1. Add deposit to balance	Buyer Membership Administration
Service Buyers Administration	6. Market closes	R6.1. Cancel uncollected sales	Service Buyers Administration

Figure 22–19 Logical Location/Response Distribution Table

to distribute processing and data only where it's needed, and to easily manage and update distributed data and processing. The Geographic Distribution Table defines the business events that occur at each logical location. Once again, when we distribute an event to a location, we are actually distributing the entire Business Component.

Figure 22–20 depicts the planned expansion of Fleury Market. Another market just like Fleury is planned to open in Lyon once the new system is finished. The only difference is that the new market will not have banking services when it first opens. Also, a new distribution center is planned for Bordeaux in the South of France. The trend towards restaurant chains has reached France as well. Fleury plans to service their largest customers by making it possible to replicate orders for all their branch locations. The south of

Geographic Location / Logical Location	Fleury	New Market in Lyon	Distribution Center in Bordeaux
Buyer Services	1. Buyer applies to become a member 7. Buyer changes membership information 10. Buyer makes deposit	1. Buyer applies to become a member 7. Buyer changes membership information	
Check In	2. Buyer checks into market	2. Buyer checks into market	2. Buyer checks into market
Check Out	4. Buyer checks out of market	4. Buyer checks out of market	4. Buyer checks out of market
Wholesaler Booth	3. Wholesaler proposes a sale 8. Wholesaler changes sale agreement 9. Wholesaler cancels sale 4. Buyer checks out of market	3. Wholesaler proposes a sale 8. Wholesaler changes sale agreement 9. Wholesaler cancels sale 4. Buyer checks out of market	
Market Services	5. Buyer picks up orders 6. Market closes	5. Buyer picks up orders 6. Market closes	5. Buyer picks up orders 6. Market closes

Figure 22–20 Geographic Distribution Table

France will have a distribution center in Bordeaux that can stock and distribute nonperishable goods, especially wines and grains.

The different locations in the Fleury Market Association are highly autonomous operating units. Although they share enterprise information and have common business activities or events, the new market at Lyon is much smaller than Fleury, and is organized slightly differently. Bordeaux is just a distribution center and does not handle all the business events that Fleury and Lyon do. The Geographic Distribution Table defines exactly what business processes occur in each location. This provides information necessary to customize the system to each business unit at each geographic location.

After distributing logical locations to geographic sites, the design team reviewed the table with business users at each site to determine if they all operate in the same way. They found that similar logical locations at different geographic sites serviced a slightly different set of events. For example, Lyon does not take deposits. All banking will be done through Fleury in the first iteration. For more information on creating the Geographic Distribution Table, please refer to Chapter 9, section 9.4.

22.6.4 Logical Location Diagram for Fleury and Lyon

The Logical Location Diagram creates a physical map of the enterprise depicting where system services must occur. This view gives a graphic representation of the logical locations. Later on in design, it will be used to determine how to distribute software components, and how different geographic locations interoperate with each other. At this stage, we are merely defining where business events occur. The design of the Implementation Model will define how business components are implemented in the distributed system. The decisions of how to distribute data and processing are based on the business requirements defined in the Distribution Aspect and the technical processing requirements defined in the Measurement Aspect. Figure 22–21 depicts the Logical Location Diagram for both Fleury and Lyon, because the two locations perform the same functions. For more information on creating Logical Location diagrams, please refer to Chapter 9, section 9.6.

22.6.5 Logical Location Diagram for Bordeaux

Bordeaux is only a distribution center and therefore is different than Fleury and Lyon. Therefore, it requires a different Logical Location Diagram. Figure 22–22 shows that Bordeaux will have no Wholesalers or Buyer Services. There will only be a Check-In/Check-Out facility, and a Market Services location for managing the distribution center.

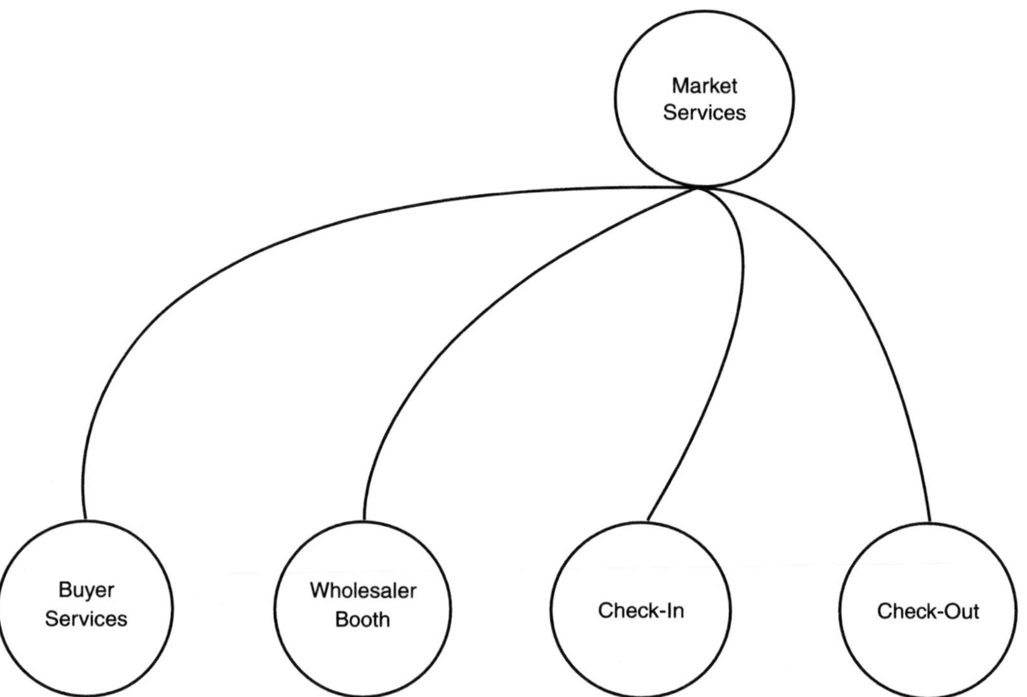

Figure 22–21 Logical Location Diagram for Fleury and Lyon

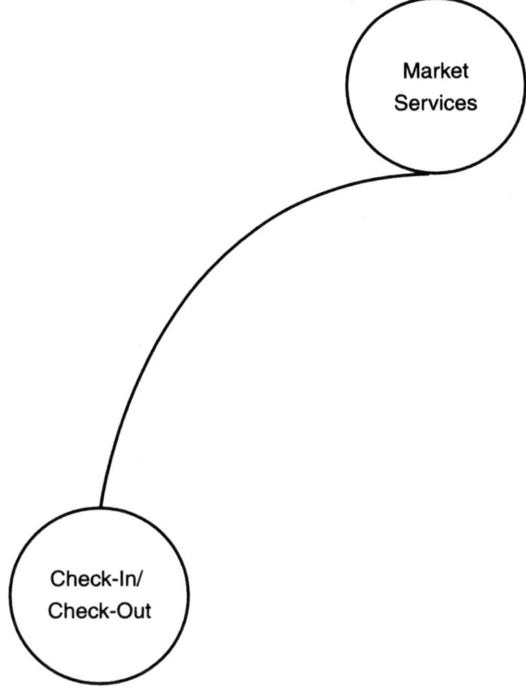

Figure 22–22 Logical Location Diagram for Bordeaux

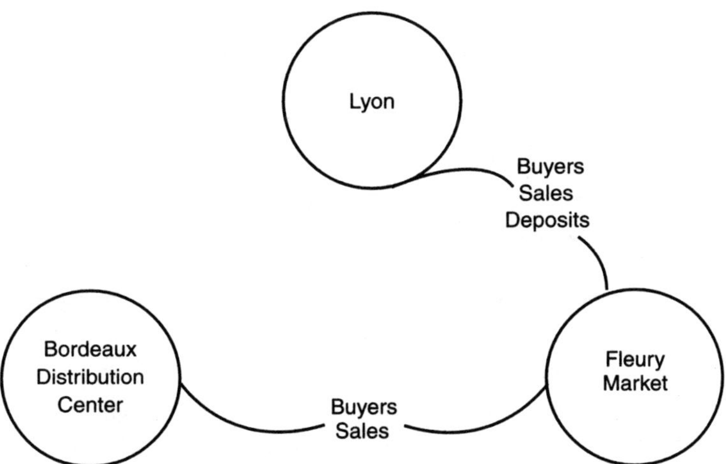

Figure 22–23 Enterprise Logical Location Diagram

22.6.6 Enterprise Logical Location Diagram

Once each geographic location is depicted, an Enterprise Logical Location Diagram is created to show how the different sites will communicate. Figure 22–23 is the Enterprise Logical Diagram showing that Buyers and Sales will be shared between Lyon and Fleury and between Fleury and Bordeaux, but not between Lyon and Bordeaux (at least in the first implementation). Additionally, deposits may be shared between Fleury and Lyon, but not Bordeaux, because Buyers do not actually make purchases at Bordeaux.

22.7 COMPONENT MEASUREMENT ASPECT

Measuring the Business Components to Inform and Guide Design and Implementation Decisions

At this point, the design team has fully defined the business requirements for the system by creating Business Components. Because the Business Components represent activities of the business, they are measurable. The benefits of measuring the Business Components are as follows:

- Measurements provide the information used later to size the systems for each geographic location.
- Measurements provide the information necessary to later estimate network traffic.
- Most importantly, measurements can call attention to potential bottlenecks and risks *before* the system is implemented.

22.7.1 Terminator Measurement Table for Fleury

The number of occurrences of human terminators is defined in terms of the current state and estimated growth over the next two years. The number of terminators drives many other processing and data requirements. For example, the number of Buyers in the market drives the number of sales, which drives the transaction volumes, which drives the processing requirements. A Terminator Measurement Table is created for each geographic location. Note that assumptions and computation formulas in Figure 22–24 are included in notes. This is essential for documenting how the numbers were estimated.

22.7.2 Terminator Measurement Table For Lyon Market

Figure 22–25 is a Terminator Measurement Table for Lyon. Note that the measurements will be different for each geographic location. Taking measurements for each location enables you to maximize the use of the new, scalable technology by sizing systems for each location. For more information on creating the Terminator Measurement Table, please refer to Chapter 10, section 10.4.

Day	Mon	Tue	Wed	Thu	Fri
Buyers	50	55	60	156	125

Average sales per buyer is 8.

Average sale items per sale is 5.

Average commodities stocked per wholesaler is 20.

16 delivery bays are planned—with a peak of 160 Buyers checking out in the last hour of business.

There are 125 Commodity types in the system.

Market Members	Today	Two Years Out
Buyer	174	348
Wholesaler	20	25

We expect a 50% increase in Buyers and a 15% increase in Wholesalers in the next two years

Figure 22–24 Terminator Measurement Table for Fleury

Day	Mon	Tue	Wed	Thu	Fri
Buyers	28	27	28	76	35

Average sales per buyer is 8.

Average sale items per sale is 5.

Average commodities stocked per wholesaler is 20.

4 delivery bays are planned—with a peak of 80 Buyers checking out in the last hour of business.

There are 125 Commodity types in the system.

Market Members	Next Year	Two Years Out
Buyer	85	170
Wholesaler	10	20

We expect a 100% increase in Buyers and a 100% increase in Wholesalers in the next two years

Figure 22–25 Terminator Measurement Table for Lyon

Event No.	Average	Peak	Max Response Time
1. Buyer applies to become a market member	**.35**	**.35**	**10 minutes**

**250 work days per year, for 2 years = 500 work days. In the next two years we expect 178 new members. 178/500 days = an average of .35 new members per day. There is no known peak for buyer membership.*

2. Buyer checks into market	**177**	**313**	**10 seconds**

**In 2 years we expect to have 348 buyers. Using terminator measurements, daily check-ins average 51% of total buyers per day = 348 * .51 = 177 buyers on average. The peak for buyers is on Thursdays when 90% of buyers shop for the weekend. 90% of 348 = 313. (Percentages derived from current trends. 156 buyers check in on peak or 90% of buyers.)*

3. Wholesaler proposes a sale	**1416**	**2784**	**2 minutes**

**Average buyers per day is (348* 51%)= 177. See Note 1. Each buyer purchases from an average of 8 wholesalers. Total average wholesaler proposes sale = 177 * 8 = 1416. Peak = 318 * 8 = 2784.*

** Number of times event "Wholesaler Proposes a Sale" assumes all buyers who enter the market purchase goods. For this calculation a more accurate measure would be to find the historical average of the percentage of members who come into the market who buy.*

4. Buyer checks out of market	**177**	**313**	**30 seconds, overall response time for picking up goods should be no longer than 15 minutes**

** Same reasoning as for Event #2. That some buyers forget to check out is negligible.*

5. Buyer picks up orders	**177**	**313**	**3 seconds**

** Same reasoning as for Event #2. Sometimes buyers who check in do not buy, but we decided to estimate for top level sales.*

6. Market closes	**1**	**1**	**Batch window constraints need further investigation**

** Market closes once a day.*

7. Buyer changes membership information	**1**	**5**	**3 seconds**

** Complete "guesstimate" and not enough volume to care.*

8. Wholesaler changes a sale	**354**	**626**	**2 minutes**

** On average 5% of sales are changed.*

9. Wholesaler cancels a sale	**142**	**250**	**10 seconds**

**On average 2% of sales are canceled.*

10. Buyer makes deposit	**177**	**400**	**10 seconds**

** Estimate: Buyers normally make 1 deposit/day but can make as many as 3.*

Figure 22–26 Event Response Measurement Table for Fleury

Event No.	Average	Peak	Max Response Time
1. Buyer applies to become a market member	**.34**	**.34**	**10 minutes**

**250 work days per year, for 2 years = 500 work days. In the next two years we expect 170 new members. 170/500 days = an average of 34 new members per day. There is no known peak for buyer membership.*

2. Buyer checks into market	**66**	**153**	**10 seconds**

**In two years we expect to have 170 buyers. Using terminator measurements, daily check-ins average 38.8% of total buyers per day = 170 * .388 = 66 buyers on average. The peak for buyers is on Thursdays when 90% of buyers shop for the weekend. 90% of 170 = 153. (Percentages derived from current trends im terminator measurement.)*

3. Wholesaler proposes a sale	**330**	**765**	**2 minutes**

**Average buyers per day is (170 * .388) = 66. See Note 1. Each buyer purchases from an average of 5 wholesalers. Total average wholesaler proposes sale = 66 * 5 = 330. Peak = 153 * 5 = 765.*

** Number of times event "Wholesaler Proposes a Sale" assumes all buyers who enter the market purchase goods. For this calculation a more accurate measure would be to find the historical average of the percentage of members who come into the market who buy.*

4. Buyer checks out of market	**66**	**153**	**30 seconds, however overall response time for picking up goods should be no longer than 15 minutes**

** Same reasoning as for Event #2. That some buyers forget to check out is negligible.*

5. Buyer picks up orders	**66**	**153**	**3 seconds**

** Same reasoning as for Event #2. Sometimes buyers who check in do not buy, but we decided to estimate for top level sales.*

6. Market closes	**1**	**1**	**Batch window constraints need further investigation**

** Market closes once a day.*

7. Buyer changes membership information	**1**	**5**	**3 seconds**

** Complete "guesstimate" and not enough volume to care.*

8. Wholesaler changes a sale agreement	**16.5**	**38**	**2 minutes**

** On average 5% of sales are changed.*

9. Wholesaler cancels a sale	**7**	**15**	**10 seconds**

**On average 2% of sales are canceled.*

10. Buyer makes deposit	**66**	**100**	**10 seconds**

** Estimate: Buyers normally make 1 deposit/day but can make as many as 3. The peak is a guesstimate, but can be more closely derived through historical averages.*

Figure 22–27 An Event Response Measurement Table for Lyon

22.7.3 Event Response Measurement Table for Fleury

The Event Response Measurement Table (Figure 22–26) defines the component processing requirements. The events are real world business events, so we can observe and record how often they occur. By defining the current volumes and projected growth, the design team can provide a fairly good estimate of the processing requirements of the system. These processing requirements were used in the RFP. All vendors used the same set of requirements to size the system in their proposal. Again, all assumptions and calculations are noted.

22.7.4 Event Response Measurement Table for Lyon

Although Lyon services all the same business events as Fleury, separate Event Response Measurement Table is created because the transaction volumes are different at each location. Figure 22–27 depicts the expected transaction volumes for Lyon. Understanding the differences at each geographic location enables capacity planning on a site-by-site basis. For more information on creating the Event Measurement Table, please refer to Chapter 10, section 10.5.

Entity/Relationship	Number of Occurrences per Year			History (years)	Total Bytes
	Number	Bytes	Total		
1. Buyer	348	170	59,160	5	295,800
2. Wholesaler	25	4	100	5	500
3. Sale <Wholesaler> sells to <Buyer>	696,000	100	69,600,000	5	348,000,000
4. Sale Item <Commodity> is item of <Sale>	3,480,000	50	174,000,000	5	870,000,000
5. Commodity	125	25	3,125	0	3,125
6. <Stock> <Wholesaler> stock <Commodity>	500	6	3,000	0	3,000
7. Hanger	2784	5	13,920	0	13,920
8. <Hanger> is located at <Wholesaler>	130	N/A	N/A	N/A	N/A
9. <Hanger> is assigned to <Sale>	2784	N/A	N/A	N/A	N/A
					1,218,316,345
Total × 2 for indexing					2,436,631,690

[2] *Buyer—Only the Wholesaler number is kept in the Service Buyers Systems.*
[3] *Sale—2784 average sales per day on peak x 250 working days per year.*
[4] *Sale Item—Average of 5 line items/sale = 696,000 * 5.*
[6] *Stock—25 Wholesalers times 20 average Commodities stocked per Wholesaler.*
[7] *Hanger—Peak total sales/day = 2784. Here we are assuming 1 hanger per sale.*
Total disk size assumes clustered indexing, which requires 2x space. This depends on the implementation database.

Figure 22–28 Entity Relationship Measurement Table for Fleury

22.7.5 Entity Relationship Measurement Table for Fleury

After the Terminator and Entity Response Measurement Tables have been created, we have the necessary information for creating the Entity Relationship Measurement Table. This table requires knowing the volume of terminators and transactions to determine the storage requirements for the system. Figure 22–28 depicts the expected storage requirements for Fleury Market.

22.7.6 Entity Relationship Measurement Table for Lyon

A separate Entity Relationship Measurement Table was created for Lyon. Because Lyon is initially expected to have fewer Buyers and fewer transactions, it will initially have lower storage requirements. As Figure 22–29 depicts, Lyon will have a little over half a gigabyte of data, while Fleury is expected to have almost two and half gigabytes of data. For more information on creating the Entity Relationship Measurement Table, please refer to Chapter 10, section 10.6.

	Number of Occurrences per Year			History (years)	Total Bytes
Entity/Relationship	**Number**	**Bytes**	**Total**		
1. Buyer	170	170	59,160	5	144,500
2. Wholesaler	20	4	80	5	400
3. Sale <Wholesaler> sells to <Buyer>	191,250	100	19,125,000	5	95,625,000
4. Sale Item <Commodity> is item of <Sale>	956,250	50	47,812,500	5	239,062,500
5. Commodity	125	25	3,125	0	3,125
6. <Stock> <Wholesaler> stock <Commodity>	400	6	2,400	0	2,400
7. Hanger	765	5	3,825	0	3,825
8. <Hanger> is located at <Wholesaler>	38	N/A	N/A	N/A	N/A
9. <Hanger> is assigned to <Sale>	765	N/A	N/A	N/A	N/A
					334,841,750
Total × 2 for indexing					669,683,500

[2] *Buyer—Only the Wholesaler number is kept in the Service Buyers Systems.*
[3] *Sale—765 average sales per day on peak x 250 working days per year.*
[4] *Sale Item—Average of 5 line items/sale = 191,250*5.*
[6] *Stock—20 Wholesalers times 20 average Commodities stocked per Wholesaler.*
[7] *Hanger—Peak total sales/day = 765. Here we are assuming 1 hanger per sale.*
Total disk size assumes clustered indexing, which requires 2x space. This depends on the implementation database.

Figure 22–29 Entity Relationship Measurement Table for Lyon

23

The Fleury Market Implementation Model

Partitioning the Essential Model Across the Distributed Technical Architecture

The Essential Model provides much information for making decisions regarding how to partition events and responses across the distributed architecture. At this point in redesigning Fleury Market the design team knows the business events within the scope of the system, the responses to the business events, what information is needed for events and responses, external systems which require or supply information, geographic locations where the business events occur, and how often the events occur. Because client/server software is predominantly an event-driven programming paradigm, defining system requirements in terms of events and responses makes it easier to turn the requirements into software specifications. Because the entire implementation model is driven by business events, the resulting system maps well to the actual business processes, and creates a design which is much more adaptable to changes in the business processes themselves.

During the design process the team continued to keep a list of issues, anomalies, and design trade-offs in an Issues List (see Appendix G). This became an important part of the documentation when design iteration caused some decisions to be revisited.

23.1 DESIGN METRICS

Establishing Criteria for Evaluating the Design for Business Optimization

The Design Metrics are the criteria against which the technical implementation will be judged. Metrics must be specific enough to help guide decisions when alternatives are evaluated. In Fleury Market, the process for defining Design Metrics was a joint effort of both the business users and the I/S development team.

System Name: Service Buyers

Description: This system provides all required support for the interface of the Fleury Market with retail buyers.

Goals:

- The system will be continuously available from 12 AM to 12 PM while the market is open.
- Buyers will be allowed to check out at many locations.
- There will be an electronic bulletin board, located at the Bistro, to notify buyers that delivery is ready.
- Buyer balance must be updated in real time and available to all wholesalers.
- Buyers who shop at the market must use their Fleury Card. Purchases over the Internet also use the Fleury Card ID number.
- The system will have the ability to increase wholesalers or buyers without having to recode the software components (requirements for scalability).
- Wholesalers will have access to their sales and commodity data as needed for ad-hoc analysis through a decision support system.
- The design will accommodate the opening of another market. This system will pilot the capability of a chain restaurant to replicate orders to more than one market. This will require set order and pick-up times for replicated orders.
- Buyer sales are targeted for the Internet. The Markets want to have some portion of commerce-based transactions up in six months.

Constraints (including existing infrastructure):

- Wholesaler Payment System will remain on the mainframe. Service buyers will interface to the existing system.
- The Commodity Management System will be installing its own separate server for the data which is owned by that system. This agrees with the concept of modular server implementations.
- Although Buyers can view specials at Fleury Market via Internet, right now they must be physically located at the market to purchase goods. Plans are to have Internet commerce within six months.
- The first release of the Service Buyers system will be in operation within nine months.

Standards:

- Must conform to Electronic Data Interchange (EDI) banking standards.
- Must conform to Internet (E-mail) standards.
- Hewlett Packard, Sybase, and Microsoft are preferred vendors.
- All systems design models will be kept in LBMS.
- Refrain from designing a distributed unit of work. When unavoidable, use a TP monitor.
- The standard office suite will be Microsoft office. Office automation is being done by a separate project team and is out of scope of this project.

Performance Requirements:

- Buyers will be able to pick up their goods at the dock on average 15 minutes from the time they check out, and on peak days no longer than 30 minutes.

Figure 23–1 Statement of Design Goals for Fleury Market

The Design Goals reflect business requirements for system availability, availability of data for end users, conveyance for customers, and planned growth and expansion. Each of these have implications for the design of the system. For example, the requirement for systems availability at all times when the market is open will require a design for redundancy and fail-over. The Constraints and Standards include items identified by the I/S team which they will have to "design around." The Performance Requirements were defined by the business users, in conjunction with I/S. These were carefully negotiated as a balance between what the users want, and what I/S felt they could reasonably deliver.

23.1.1 Statement of Design Goals

Figure 23–1 is the Statement of Design Goals defined by the team. It impacts the design and selection of technology for the system. For example, there is little tolerance for the system going down when the market is open. These availability and recoverability requirements will necessitate system redundancy and fail-over options. Wholesalers will need on-line access to customer information, especially buyer balance. The application should be designed to easily adapt to implementation on the Internet with the next iteration. Card readers will eventually be distributed to various locations throughout the market (including the bistro). The system will interface with the mainframe. In other words, the design goals constrain the implementation options and guide design decisions. For more information on creating the Statement of Design Goals, see Chapter 12.

23.2 MULTI-TIER PARTITIONING ASPECT

The Essential Model Maps Easily to a Multi-Tier Architecture

Because an entire Essential Model was created, the only real decision in the Multi-Tier Partitioning Aspect that the design team had to make was whether this would be a two-tier, three-tier, or multi-tier application, so the appropriate technology could be chosen during the Technical Architecture Design.

The team decided it would be a multi-tier architecture, because it met a number of the criteria for multi-tier applications. It is a mission-critical application that is being implemented in phases, so it must be adaptable to change. It will be distributed to a number of locations that will communicate over a wide area network. The Service Buyers System must accommodate expected rapid growth over the next year. Finally, within the next six months it must be accessible over the Internet. For these reasons, a multi-tier application was chosen. For more information on mapping the Essential Model to a multi-tier architecture, please see Chapter 13.

23.2.1 Processor Model for Fleury Market

Figure 23–2 is the Processor Model for Fleury Market. The logical locations have now become clients, including the Wholesaler Client, Buyer Administration Client and Buyer

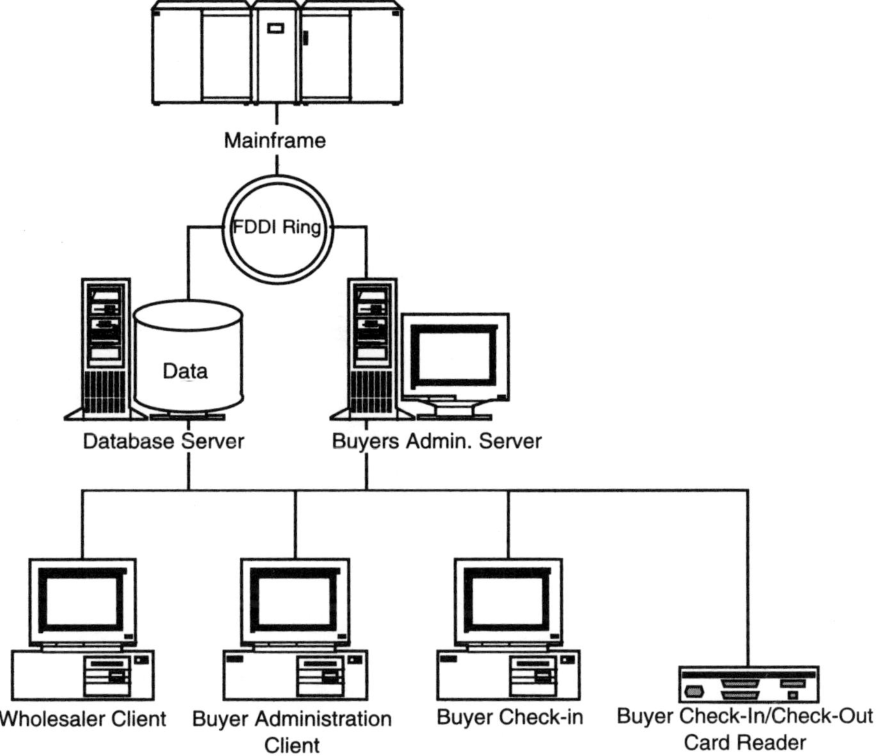

Figure 23–2 Processor Model for Fleury Market

Check-In Client. There is also a card reader that will be installed at kiosks throughout the Market, including the Bistro, for Buyers to check themselves in and out. The Buyers Admin. Server will contain all the responses and temporal events. There is a database server for data storage and management. The central accounting system will remain on the mainframe, so it is also in the diagram.

23.3 TECHNICAL ARCHITECTURE DESIGN

Defining All Technical Components of the System

The Buyers Administration System is the first major client/server project for Fleury Market. The only standards in place are EDI, client operating system, and desktop software. Therefore the Technical Architecture Design was a major effort for Fleury. They appointed a separate Technical Architecture Team, which started evaluating products and alternatives early on in the process, while the development team was still developing the

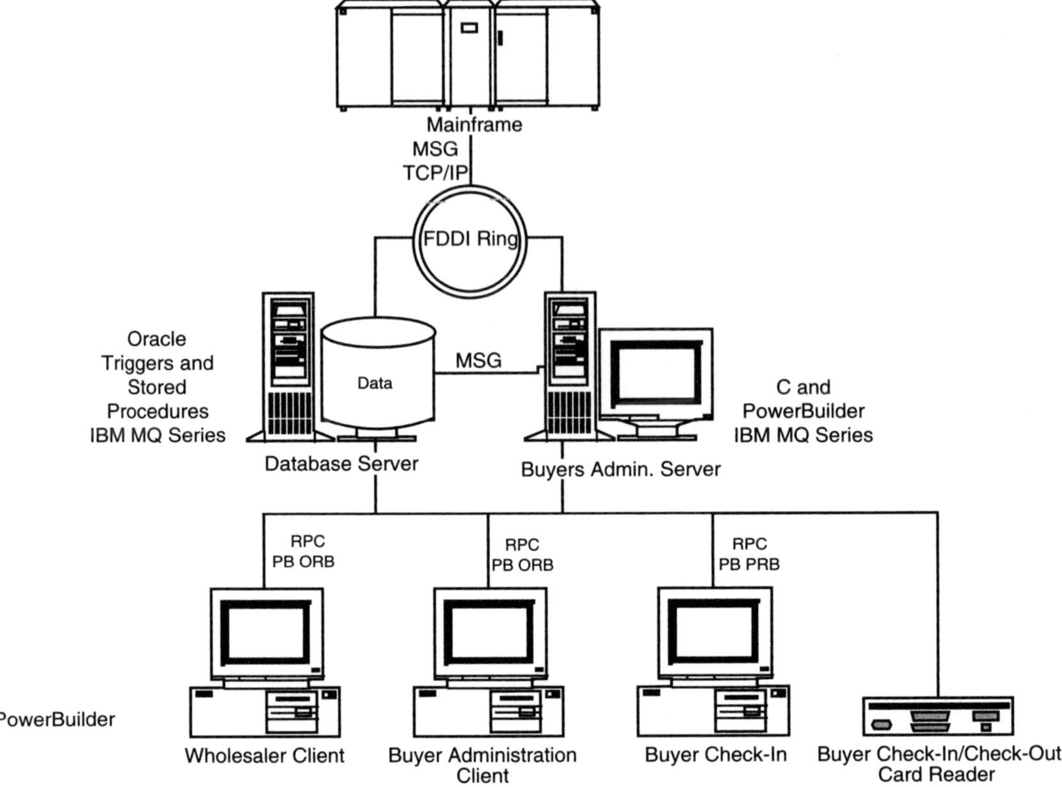

Figure 23–3 Technical Processor Model for Fleury Market

Essential Model. They did this so the technical architecture design would be complete before the team was ready to do processor distribution.

23.3.1 Technical Processor Model for Fleury Market

Figure 23–3 was developed to depict the chosen technical architecture to the design team and programmers. It shows the Processor Model with added text to depict the technology chosen for each processor. It also depicts how the different tiers in the architecture are expected to communicate.

23.3.2 Technical Specifications

Detailed specifications were defined for each component in the Technical Architecture (Figure 23–4). Some of these detailed specifications, such as configurations, were developed with the help of the vendors. The technical architecture team was able to give the vendors fairly good estimates of transaction and data volumes because of the work done

Component	Product Name	Configuration	Installed	Standard	Software Installed
Service Buyers Admin. Server	HP 9000	64 MB RAM; NT; 20 GIG HD; Symmetric multi-processor. Development machine will have 2 processors. Production machine will be sized after design phase is completed. Clustered with data server.	No	Yes	Entera, IBM MQ Series, C compiler, PVCS, Encina; Multi-Tier 4GL
Database Server	HP 9000	64 MB RAM; NT; 200 GIG HD; Number of processors TBD clustered with business server.	No	Yes	Sybase System 11 with Replication Server, X-Open SQL, Omni SQL Gateway; IBM MQ Series
Wholesaler Client	Compaq	Pentium, 75-100 Mhz, 24 MB RAM, 1 GIG HD, Win 95; card reader attached. HP Printer	Yes	No	Entera RPC; PowerBuilder; SQL Anywhere; TCP/IP
Buyer Admin. Client	Compaq	24 MB RAM, 1 GIG HD, Win 95; card reader attached. HP Printer	No	No	Entera RPC; PowerBuilder; Multi-tier 4GL; TCP/IP
Buyer Check-In Client	Card Reader		No	No	
Buyer Check-Out Client	Card Reader		No	No	
Network	Ethernet		Yes	Yes	NT, TCP/IP
Middleware	Entera	RPC	No	Yes	Client to Bus Rules Server
	Omni SQL Gateway	Mainframe Gateway	On Mainfrm	Yes	Server to Mainframe
	IBM MQ Series	Messaging	No	Yes	Server to Server

Figure 23–4 Technical Specifications

by the design team in the Measurement Aspect. The team required that the vendor guarantee the configuration would handle the processing and data volumes, or the vendor would upgrade the system at no penalty. Because of the work done by the technical architecture team, the design team had a development environment in place by the time they began the implementation design. This enabled them to begin prototyping the GUI presentation tier as part of the design effort.

23.3.3 Support Table

Once the technical architecture team defined all the components, the design team coordinated an effort which included negotiations with the operations group, database administration, network group, and PC group, to define how the system would be supported. The operations group negotiated two additional support personnel to support the system. As Figure 23–5 depicts, it is important to define support for each component at each location.

Component	Location	Support Group
Server and client hardware	Fleury Lyon Bordeaux	Operations group in Fleury Operations group in Lyon Operations group in Fleury
Operating system upgrades	Fleury Lyon Bordeaux	Operations group in Fleury Operations group in Lyon Operations group in Fleury
Application installation	Fleury Lyon Bordeaux	Operations group in Fleury Operations group in Lyon Operations group in Fleury
Application support	Fleury, Lyon, Bordeaux	Application group
Network	Fleury, Lyon, Bordeaux	Operations group
Gateway	Fleury, Lyon, Bordeaux	Database Administration with operations group for networking
Data extracts	Fleury, Lyon, Bordeaux	Mainframe application group *OR* PC applications development group
Database installation	Fleury, Lyon, Bordeaux	Database Administration
Database support	Fleury, Bordeaux Lyon	Fleury Database Administration with Applications Development group Lyon Database Administration with Applications Development group
EDI support	Fleury, Lyon, Bordeaux	Operations? EDI administration?
E-mail support	Fleury, Lyon, Bordeaux	Operations group

Figure 23–5 Technical Support Table

23.4 PROCESSOR DISTRIBUTION ASPECT

Distributing Business Process, Rules, and Information to Physical Processors

The technical design team did an excellent job by not delaying the project (an important success criteria for all technical architecture teams!). The design team was ready to distribute the components of the Essential Model—the business process, rules, and information—across the physical processors.

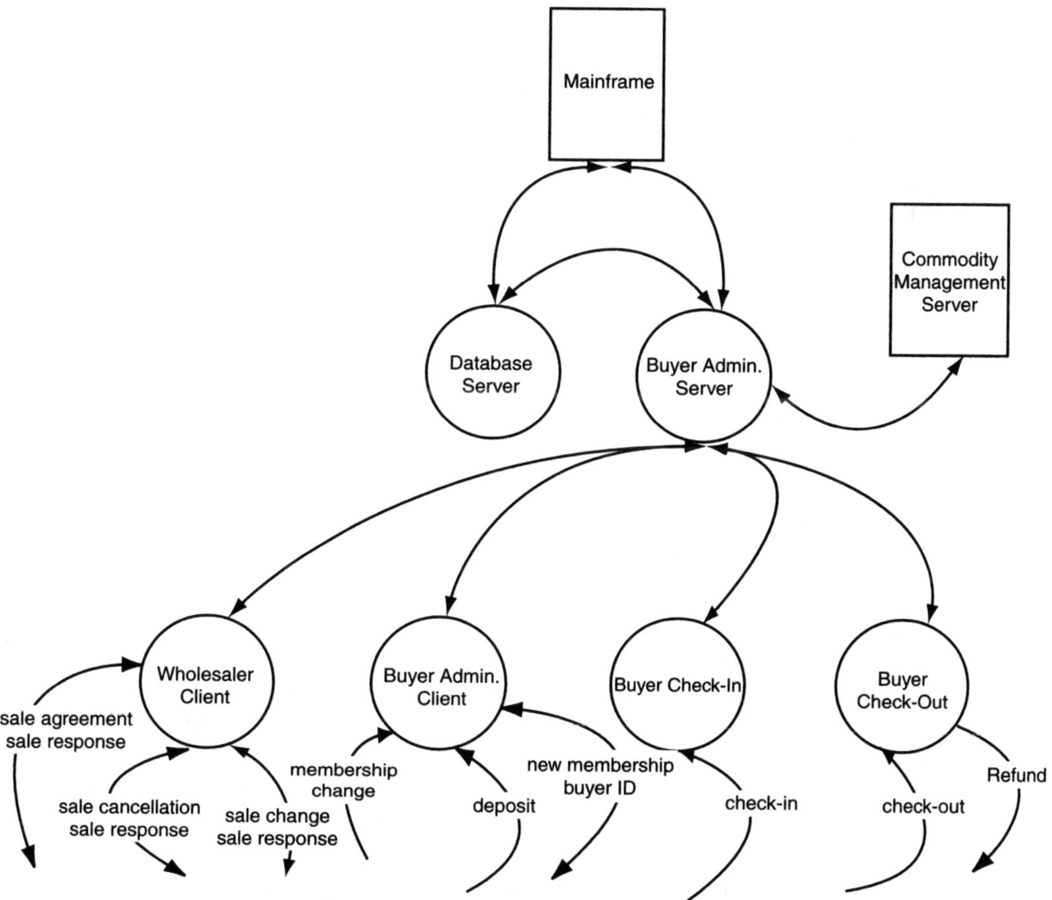

Figure 23–6 Processor Model for Fleury Market

23.4.1 Processor Model for Fleury Market

The design team created a Processor Model in YSM notation (Figure 23–6) which was essentially the same as the Technical Processor Model, except it portrays logical connectivity instead of network connectivity. That is because at this stage of design, the logical connections must be defined as requests, messages, or responses between and among processors.

23.4.2 Processor Distribution Table

The design team relied heavily on a general multi-tier design in creating the Processor Distribution Table (Figure 23–7). They distributed the presentation of the event to the client, responses to events and temporal events to the Service Buyers Admin Server. Note that Figure 23–7 includes processors external the Service Buyers System. That is because some events in the system cause responses on the Commodity Management Server and the mainframe. For more information on creating the Processor Diagram, please refer to Chapter 15, section 15.3.

23.4.3 Processor Data Flow Diagram

From the Processor Distribution Table the design team created the Processor Data Flow Diagram. It includes the information sent between processors. This DFD is derivable from the Processor Distribution Table and the Entity Response Table from the Essential Bridge Aspect. This diagram (Figure 23–8) was created to depict the messages between processors. For more information on creating the Processor Data Flow Diagram, please refer to Chapter 15, section 15.4.

23.4.4 Alternative Processor Data Flow Diagram Using Direct Communication Between Buyer Administration Client and Database Server

When the design team looked at the processor data flow diagram they noticed that the information sent between the check-in, check-out, and buyer admin. client were all just database updates. There was no intermediate processing required. Figure 23–9 depicts an alternative design, where these clients directly accessed the database in a two-tier architecture. This design would be much simpler to implement, although it would not scale as well. They determined that the design was feasible because there was only one or two Buyer Admin. Clients and a few Check-In clients. The only potential problem was the numerous Check-Out locations, because Buyers could check-out at Wholesaler booths and even the Bistro. They therefore decided to modify this design even further, and have just the Check-In and Buyer Admin. Clients go directly to the database server.

23.4.5 Detailed Data Flow Diagram Showing Logic for Creating a Sale

The next step for creating the software blueprints was to further describe the detailed processing of the system. The team developed lower-level DFDs and specifications for all

Processor / Response	Wholesaler Booth Client	Buyer Membership Admin Client	Check In / Check Out Client	Service Buyers Admin. Server	Commodity Mngmnt. Server	Service Wholesalers Mainframe
1. Add buyer		Add buyer presentation		Execute add buyer rules		
2. Check in buyer			Checkin buyer presentation	Update buyer status		
3. Create sale	Create sale presentation			Update sale status Add sale Add line item Update buyer balance Assign hanger to sale Notify service buyers of account debit	Update hanger status Check stock level Reduce stock level	Update wholesaler sales
4. Check out buyer	Buyer check-out presentation		Check out buyer presentation	Update sales status Update buyer status	Release hanger from sale Update hanger status	
5. Record pickup				Update sales status		
6. Market closes/ cancel uncollected sales				Cancel uncollected sales Update buyer status Update sales status	Release hanger from sale Update hanger status	Update wholesaler sales
7. Note membership change		Membership change presentation		Change membership info		
8. Change sale	Change sale presentation			Update buyer balance Send message to commodity mgnmt.	Check stock Reduce stock Increase stock	
9. Cancel sale	Cancel sale presentation			Update buyer balance Update sales status Send message to commodity mgnmt.	Release hanger from sale Update hanger status	
10. Add deposit		Add deposit presentation		Add deposit to balance		

Figure 23–7 Processor Distribution Table for Fleury Market

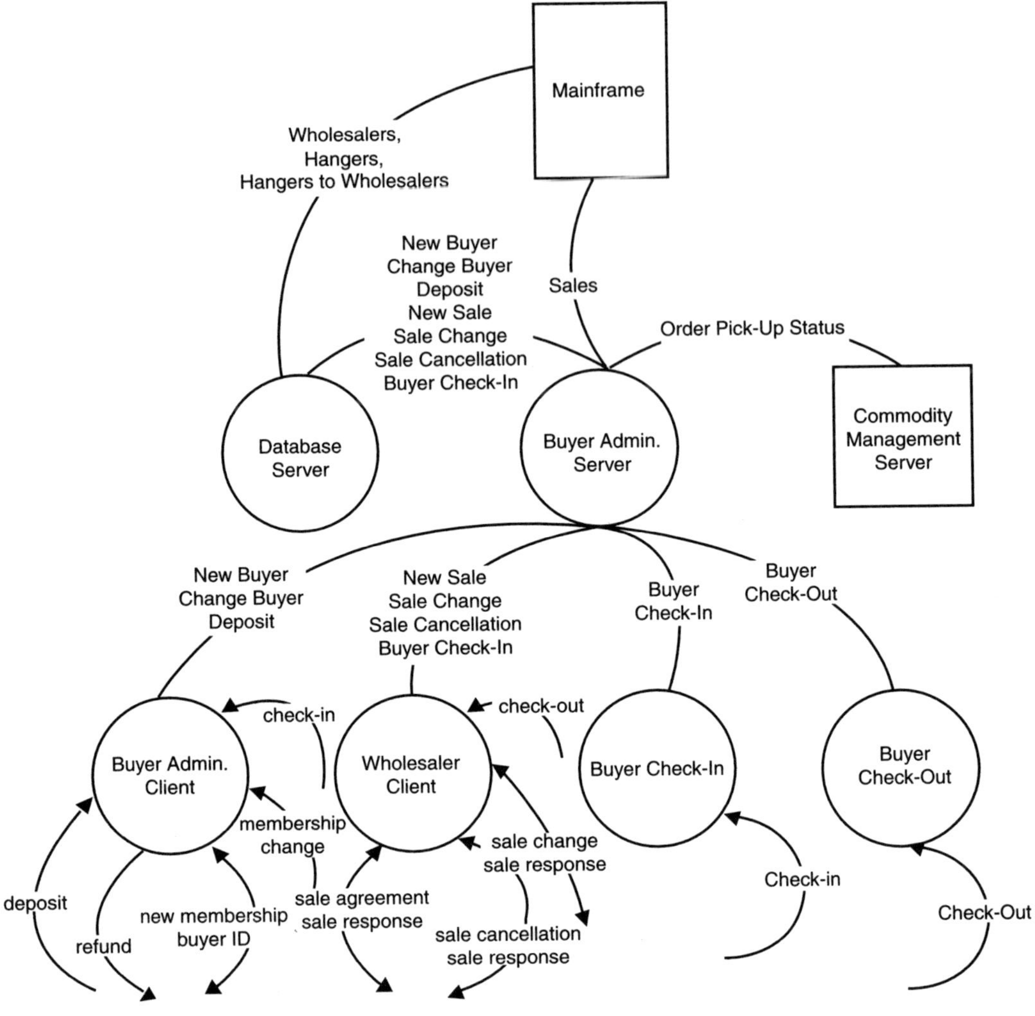

Figure 23–8 Processor Data Flow Diagram for Fleury Market

processes where complexity or performance requirements warranted further detailed study. Figure 23–10 shows the detailed processing that takes place on the Service Buyers Admin. Server when creating a sale.

23.4.6 Structure Chart for Controlling Sale Change Logic

Because of the complex logic involved in changing a sale, the team created a structure chart as a way of describing the logic. In general, structure charts do well in describing subfunctions, such as would be found in pull-down menus. Figure 23–11 is a structure chart depicting the processing for changing a sale. For further information on Structure

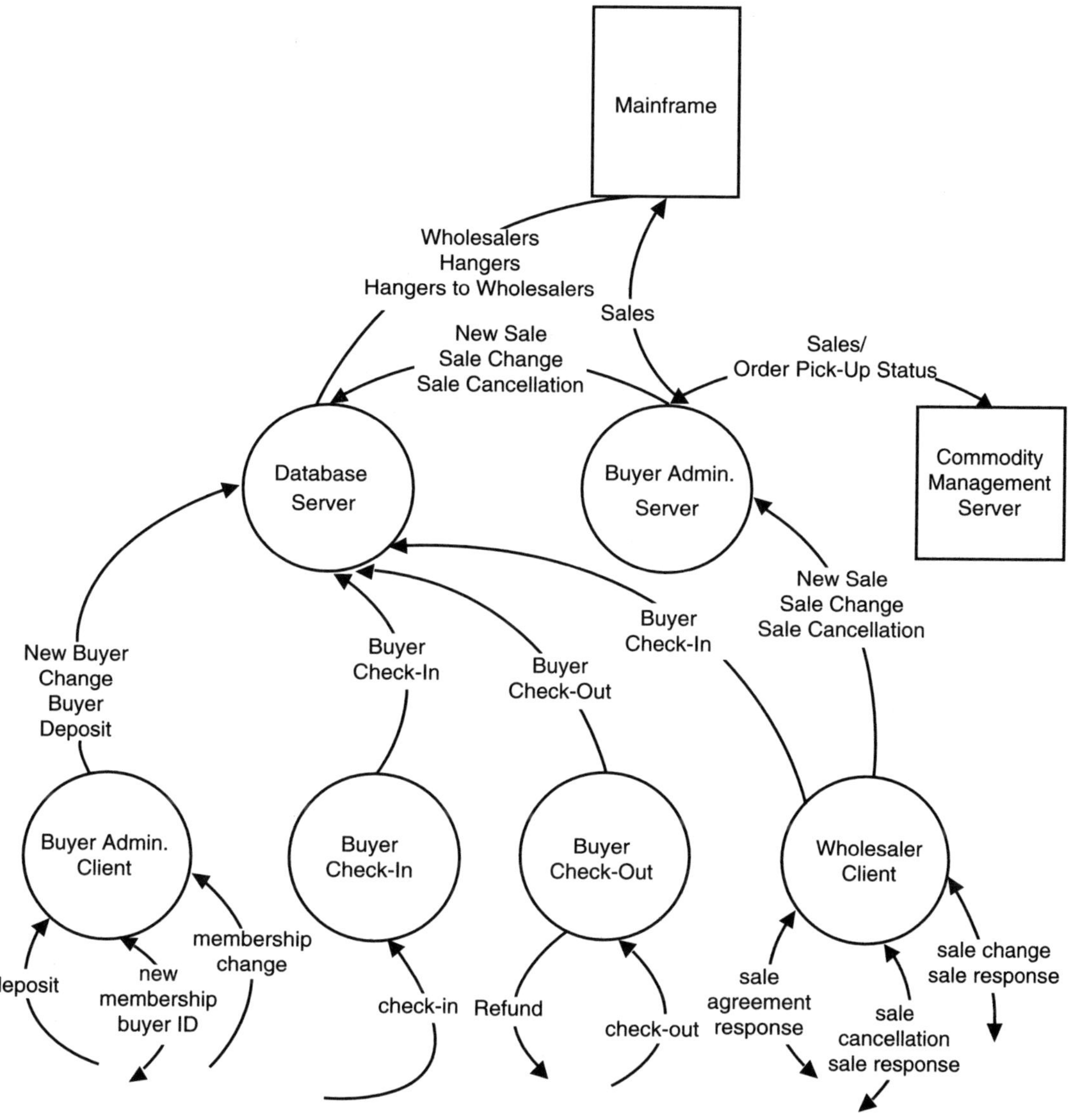

Figure 23–9 Alternative Processor Data Flow Diagram

Charts and other tools for creating detailed specifications, please refer to Chapter 15, section 15.5.

23.4.7 Presentation Design of Fleury Wholesaler Client

Once the logical clients were defined in the Multi-Tier Partitioning Aspect, part of the design team started prototyping the presentation screens with the business users. Figure

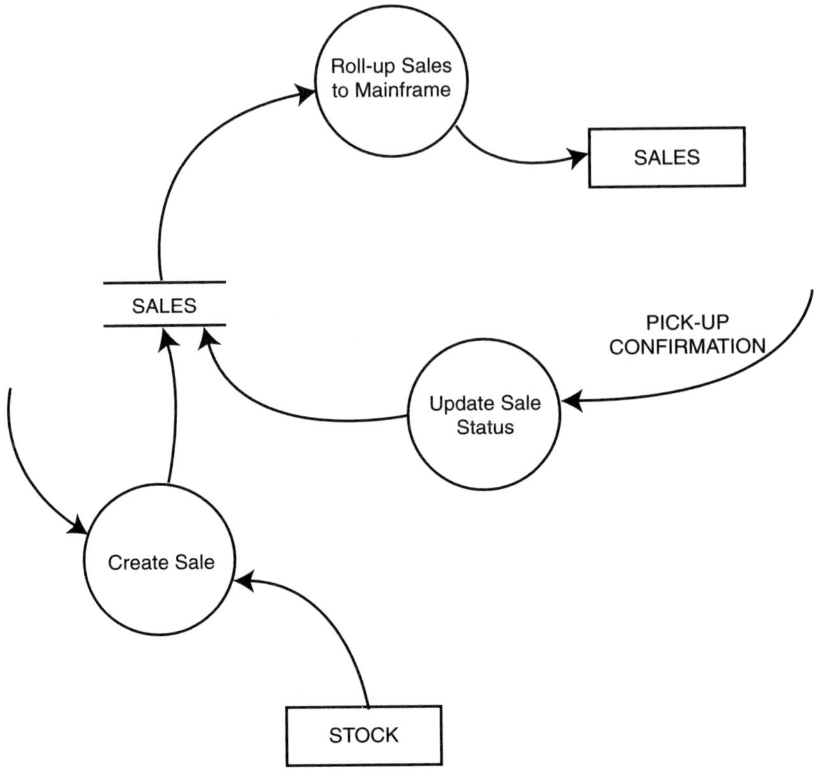

Figure 23–10 Detailed DFD for Creating a Sale

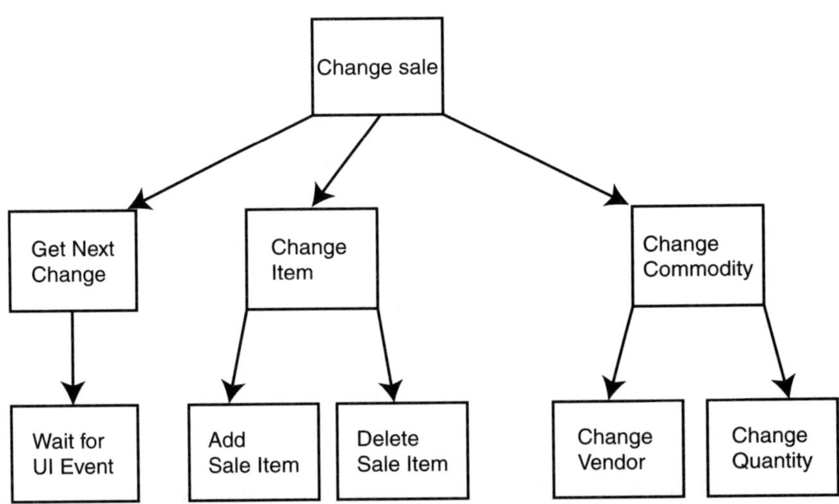

Figure 23–11 Structure Chart for Change Sale

Sale Form	Wholesaler	**Marcel Boucher et Cie**	Note if you have a Carte Fleury Insert it now!	Date 1 Nov	Wholesaler ID 0098 Buyer ID 0234 Hanger ID RQ1180

Line Items

#	Commodity	Description	Vendor	Qty	$	Total
01	CH023	Brie	Best Class	12	1.23	14.76
02	CH077	Camembert	Budget	10	1.57	15.70

Total	30.46

Agree	**Change**	**Cancel**

Figure 23–12 Presentation Design for Wholesaler Client

23–12 was their initial design for the Wholesaler Client. The Team identified all events which would be managed by each client machine, and began prototyping the user interface. The process for prototyping was done in very short and highly iterative design cycles. They had weekly reviews with the business users to define how they would perform the business processing.

23.4.8 State Transition Diagram (STD) for Agree to Sale Presentation Logic

Along with the prototypes, the team developed STDs for each event, to define the processing which occurred behind the GUI screen, once the button was pushed or option entered. These STDs became very useful for documenting design decisions, because object oriented 4GL programming techniques often place code behind objects, sometimes making it difficult to change the program later on.

STDs are extremely effective in portraying the detailed processing that happens once the "Agree" button (or any other button) is pushed. The Team created an STD for each process that required any complex logic (i.e., a programmer would not know what to program just by looking at the screen). For this screen, they created three STDs, one for Agree, one for Change, and one for Cancel. As an example, below is the STD depicting the logic for Agree to a Sale. For more information on creating STDs, please refer to Chapter 15, section 15.6.

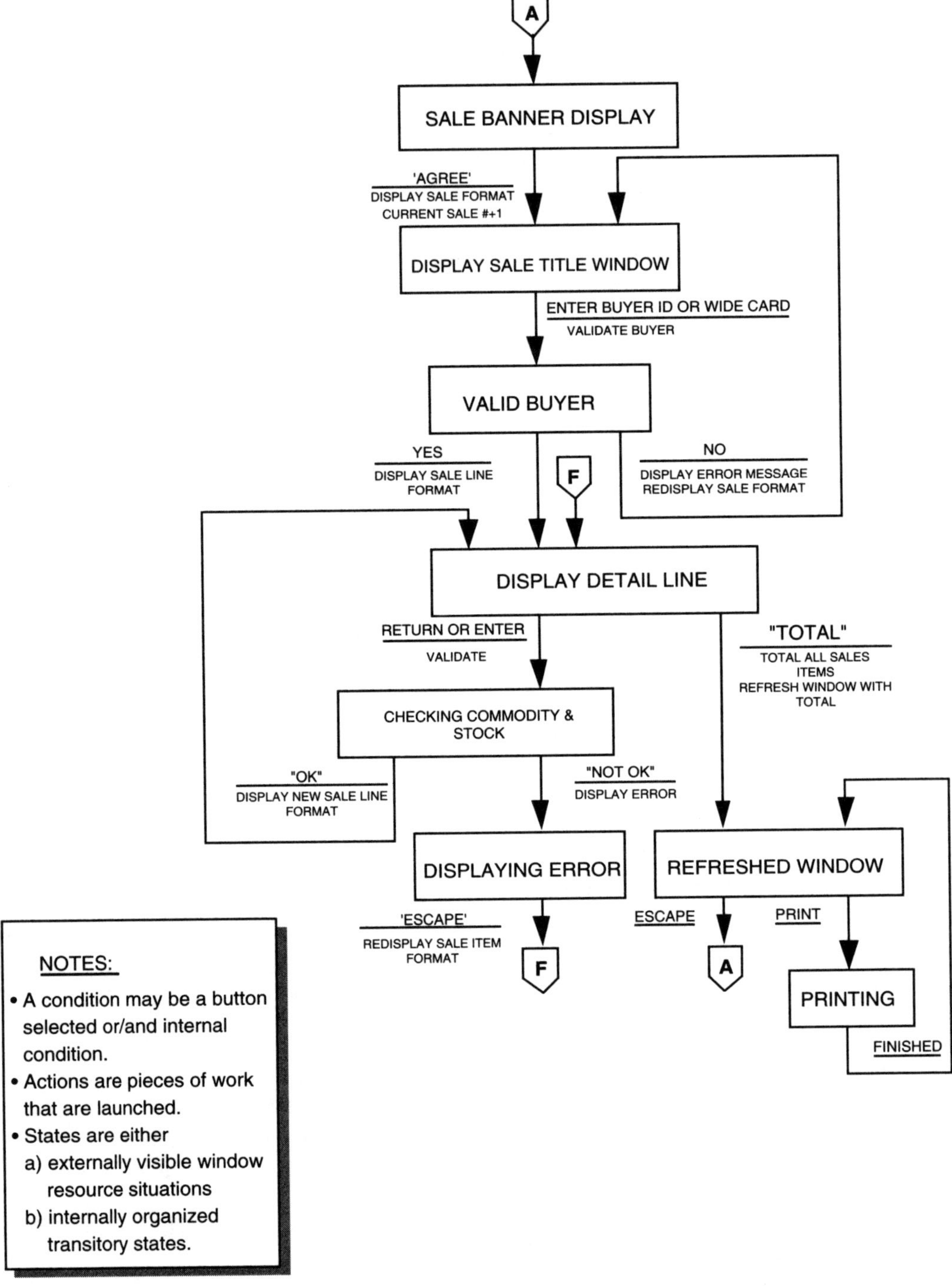

Figure 23–13 State Transition Diagram for Agree to Sale Presentation Logic

23.4.9 Entity Processor Table

Because we defined information requirements for events and responses, once the processes were distributed across processors, the design team could derive the information requirements for each processor. Creating the Entity-Processor Table (Figure 23–14) is an intermediate step before defining how the data will be partitioned across processors. It helps in deciding which processors will be the Authoritative Source of each entity. For more information on creating the Entity-Processor Table, please refer to Chapter 15, section 15.11.

23.4.10 Data Distribution Table for Fleury Market

By deriving the data requirements for each processor, the Design Team had enough information to determine where data should be stored, copied from, and replicated to. The team began by identifying Authoritative Sources, which are those locations responsible for the creation and deletion of an Entity. Figure 23–15 depicts how data will be distributed across processors. "Copy" indicates that a copy of the entity will be replicated from the Authoritative Source and stored on that processor. "Partial Copy" means that only part

Processor / Entity or Relationship	Buyer Admin. Client	Buyer Check In	Buyer Check Out	Whole-saler Client	Buyer Admin. Server	Data-base Server	Com-modity Mgmnt. Server	Main-frame Service Whole-salers
Buyer	c,u,m,r	r,u	r,u	r,u	m,r,u	c,u,d		
Wholesaler				m,r	r	r		c,u,d
Sale <Wholesaler> sells to <Buyer>				c,r,u,d	u	c,u,d		r
Sale Item <Commodity> is item of <Sale>			r,u	c,r,u,d	r	c,u,d	r	
Commodity			r	m,r		r	c,u,d	
Stock <Wholesaler> stocks <Commodity>				r		r	c,u,d	
Hanger				m,r		r		c,u,d
<Hanger> is located at <Wholesaler>				m		r		r
<Hanger > assigned to <Sale>				c,d		c		r

Figure 23–14 Entity Processor Table for Fleury Market

Processor / Entity or Relationship	Buyer Admin. Client	Buyer Check In	Buyer Check Out	Whole-saler Client	Buyer Admin. Server	Data-base Server	Com-modity Mgmnt. Server	Main-frame Service Whole-salers
Buyer	Copy	access	access	Copy	access	AS		
Wholesaler				Partial Copy	access	Copy		AS
Sale <Wholesaler> sells to <Buyer>				Copy (original source)	access	AS		Copy
Sale Item <Commodity> is item of <Sale>			access	Copy (original source)	access	AS	Copy	
Commodity			access	Partial Copy		Copy	AS	
Stock <Wholesaler> stocks <Commodity>				Partial Copy		Copy	AS	
Hanger						Copy		AS
<Hanger> is located at <Wholesaler>				Partial Copy		Copy		AS
<Hanger > assigned to <Sale>				Copy		AS		Copy

Figure 23–15 Data Distribution Table for Fleury Market

of the full table will be replicated. "Access" means that the data will not have a persistent store on that process, but may be called or accessed at run time.

The replication tools from the database vendor can automatically handle the replication processing. The Data Distribution Table, combined with the Entity Processor Table, defines all the requirements for programming the replication tool and access rights for each data store. After this step, both database and replication programming may begin, even as further design activities are going forward. For more information on creating the Data Distribution Table, please refer to chapter 15, section 15.12.

23.4.11 Data Distribution Options

There are always different options for distributing data and processing. The team decided to document these decisions (Figure 23–16). They did this so future design teams would understand why certain decisions were made and could make more informed decisions when designing future releases and upgrades to the system. This is an optional step, but useful for thinking through and documenting decisions.

Entity	Possible Redistribution Type	Pros	Minus Factors
Buyer	Replicate to Buyer Admin. and Wholesaler clients.	Availability of buyer info for all transactions	Increased storage necessary on clients, but data volumes are manageable.
Commodity	Option 1: Copy of all the Commodities to each client machine. OR Option 2: Copy only the commodities that each Wholesaler deals in.	Easy Speedy Specific and Efficient	Requires more storage capacity on clients. Requires more processing—simplified with subscribe and publish replication.
Stock	Replicated copies to local database server. Replicate partial copy specific to each Wholesaler. Issue is when to replicate changes in stock.	Specific and Efficient	More complex processing. Preferably would like to use event triggers to update wholesaler copies.
Sale/Sale Item	Each originating sale begins on Wholesaler client then is rolled up to server.	Wholesalers need to "own" their sales	Possible "traffic jams" for uploads at check-out time.
Hanger	Each Wholesaler is issued a set of Hangers at Market opening.	Efficiency in Storage	Upload when buyer checks out.
Wholesaler	Authoritative system is commodities system—replicated copies to other systems.	Simple design	Increased storage requirements.

Figure 23–16 Data Distribution Options

23.4.12 Message Specification Table

The processor DFD shows the messages between processors. To fully define all message traffic, the Message Specification Table was created (Figure 23–17). This table provides the programmer(s) with the necessary information for coding RPCs, messages, and extracts, and SQL calls. For more information on creating the Message Specification Table, please refer to Chapter 15, section 15.14.

23.5 GEOGRAPHIC DISTRIBUTION ASPECT

Creating Design Specifications for Each Location

After completing the distributed design for Fleury, the team turned their attention to the other locations and created a set of artifacts for each location. A large percentage of the artifacts they had already completed were reuseable for describing the other geographic locations. However, the team learned that there were slight differences at each location. They merely adjusted to models to account for these differences.

From Processor Name	To Processor Name	Message Name	Message Content	Message Type
Service Wholesalers Mainframe	Database Server	Wholesalers Info	Wholesaler Record	ASCII Extract
		Hanger Assign-ment	Wholesaler ID, Hanger#	ASCII Extract
Buyer Admin. Server	Service Wholesalers Mainframe	Sales	Wholesaler ID, Buyer ID, sale total	Async. Message
Buyer Admin. Server	Commodity Mgnt. Server	Sales	Wholesaler ID, Hanger#, Sale Items	Async. Message
Commodity Mgnt. Server	Buyer Admin. Server	Pick-up Status	Hanger#	Async. Message
Buyer Admin. Server	Database Server	Add Buyer	Buyer ID, Name, Restaurant, Address, Tele#, Bank Info	RPC or Async. Message
		Change/Delete Buyer	Buyer ID, Change Info	RPC or Async. Message
		Deposit	Buyer ID, Amount	RPC or Async. Message
		Add Sale	Buyer ID, Wholesaler ID, Sale Item(s), Item Price, Hanger#	RPC or Async. Message
		Change/Delete Sale	Buyer ID, Wholesaler ID, Hanger#, Item Changes	RPC or Async. Message
		Buyer Check-In	Buyer ID, Status	RPC or Async. Message
Buyer Admin. Client	Buyer Admin. Server	Add Buyer	Buyer ID, Name, Restaurant, Address, Tele#, Bank Info	RPC or Async. Message
		Change/Delete Buyer	Buyer ID, Change Info	RPC or Async. Message
		Deposit	Buyer ID, Amount	RPC or Async. Message
Buyer Admin.	Buyer Admin. Client	Add Buyer Response	Message Status	Async. Message
		Change/Delete Buyer Response	Message Status	Async. Message
		Deposit Response	Message Status	Async. Message

Figure 23–17 Message Specification Table

Processor / Response	Wholesaler Booth Client	Buyer Membership Admin. Client	Check In / Check Out Client	Service Buyers Admin. Server	Commodity Mngmnt Server	*Service Wholesalers Mainframe*
1. Add buyer		Add buyer presentation		Execute add buyer rules		
2. Check in buyer			Checkin buyer presentation	Update buyer status		
3. Create sale	Create sale presentation			Update sale status Add sale Add line item Update buyer balance Assign hanger to sale Notify service buyers of account debit	Update hanger status Check stock level Reduce stock level	*Update wholesaler sales*
4. Check out buyer	Buyer check-out presentation		Check out buyer presentation	Update sales status Update buyer status	Release hanger from sale Update hanger status	
5. Record pick-up				Update sales status		
6. Market closes/cancel uncollected sales				Cancel uncollected sales Update buyer status Update sales status	Release hanger from sale Update hanger status	*Update wholesaler sales*
7. Note membership change		Membership change presentation		Change membership info		
8. Change sale	Change sale presentation			Update buyer balance Send message to commodity mgnmt.	Check stock Reduce stock Increase stock	
9. Cancel sale	Cancel sale presentation			Update buyer balance Update sales statu Send message to commodity mgnmt.	Release hanger from sale Update hanger status	
10. Add deposit		Add deposit presentation		Add deposit to balance		

Figure 23–18 Processor Distribution Table for Lyon

23.5.1 Processor Distribution Table for Lyon

The only difference between processor distribution for Lyon and Fluery is that there is no mainframe at Lyon. On Figure 23–18 this is depicted by italics in the mainframe column.

23.5.2 Processor Distribution Table for Bordeaux

Bordeaux differs from Fleury and Lyon in a number of ways. Bordeaux has no Wholesaler Clients, no Buyer Membership Admin. Clients, and no mainframe. The client processors do not appear on Figure 23–19 because they are not needed at Bordeaux. The mainframe does appear because although there is no mainframe at Bordeaux, there is still mainframe integration and communications.

23.5.3 Processor Data Flow Diagram for Lyon

The Processor DFD for Lyon differs from Fleury because there is no separate database server for Lyon. The market is small enough that both the Buyer Admin. Server and the DBMS will be on one processor, as depicted in Figure 23–20. The design will be the same, but at Lyon, all the DBMS functions and the application server functions will reside on one box.

Processor / Response	Check In / Check Out Client	Service Buyers Admn. Server	Commodity Mngmnt. Server	*Service Wholesalers Mainframe*
2. Check In Buyer	Check in buyer presentation	Update buyer status		
4. Check Out Buyer	Check out buyer presentation	Update sales status Update buyer status	Release hanger from sale Update hanger status	
5. Record Pick-up		Update sales status		
6. Market Closes/ Cancel Un-collected Sales		Cancel uncollected sales Update buyer status Update sales status	Release hanger from sale Update hanger status	*Update wholesaler sales*
9. Cancel Sale		Update buyer balance Update sales status Send message to commodity mgnmt.	Release hanger from sale Update hanger status	

Figure 23–19 Processor Distribution Table for Bordeaux

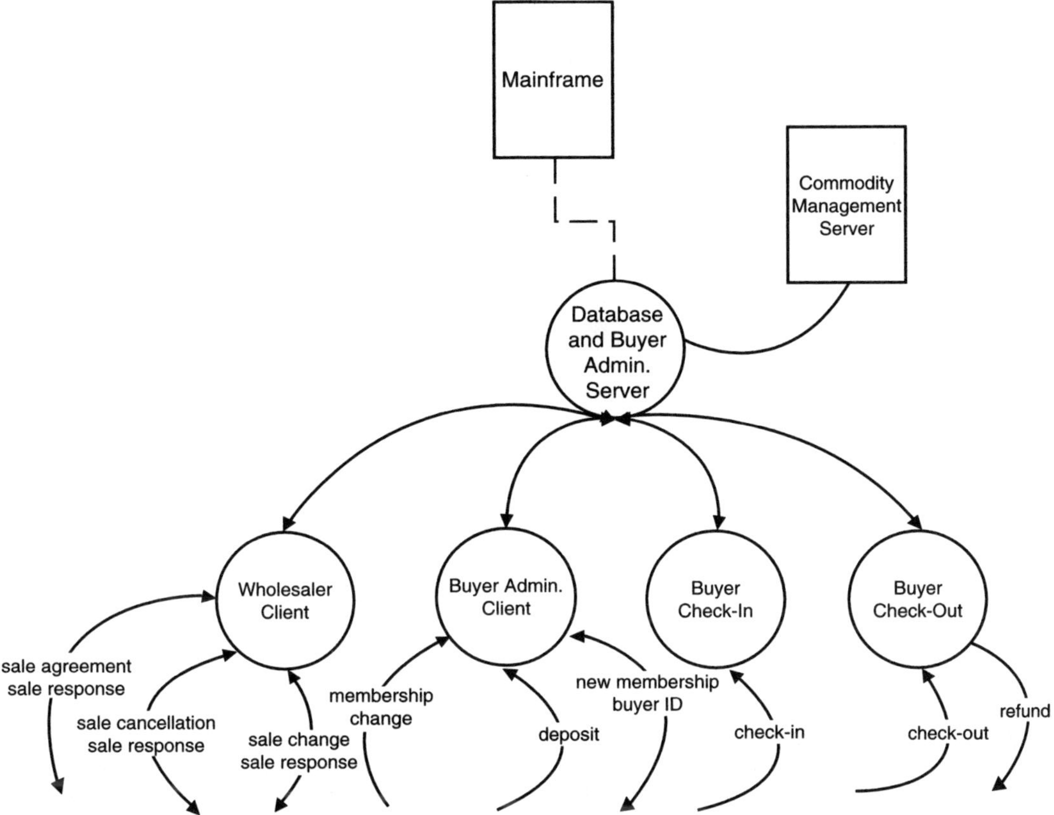

Figure 23–20 Processor Data Flow Daigram for Lyon

23.5.4 Processor Data Flow Diagram for Bordeaux

The Processor DFD for Bordeaux (Figure 23–21) looks very different than the Fleury and Lyon DFDs. There is only a Buyer Check-In/Check-Out client. There is only one server for both the DBMS and Buyer Admin. functions. Only the software components that manage Buyer status and process order pick-ups need to be distributed to the Bordeaux server. The entire database would probably be replicated to Bordeaux, because as the Entity Event Table showed, a sale involves every entity in the database.

23.5.5 Processor Data Flow Diagram Across Locations

The enterprise Processor DFD (Figure 23–22) highlights the communications between geographic locations. Note that site to site communications occurs between servers. At each individual location is a client/server architecture. Across locations there is a distrib-

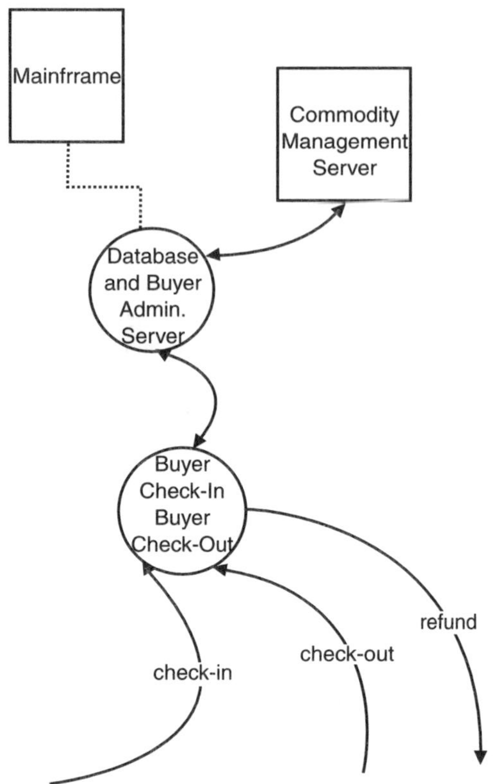

Figure 23–21 Processor Data Flow Diagram for Bordeaux

uted peer-to-peer architecture. The server at each site can act as either a server or a client to other sites.

23.5.6 Enterprise Data Distribution Table

The design team created an Enterprise Data Distribution Table (Figure 23–23), defining Authoritative Sources for all enterprise level data. This table supplied information for enterprise-wide data administration and for programming replication services.

23.5.7 Data Distribution Table for Lyon

After creating the Enterprise Data Distribution Table, it was fairly straightforward to create one for each geographic location. We know from the enterprise table that Lyon is the Authoritative Source (AS) for Lyon Sales, Sale Items, and Hangers. In other words, it is the AS for its own data. What needs to be decided at this point, is where to store data, and

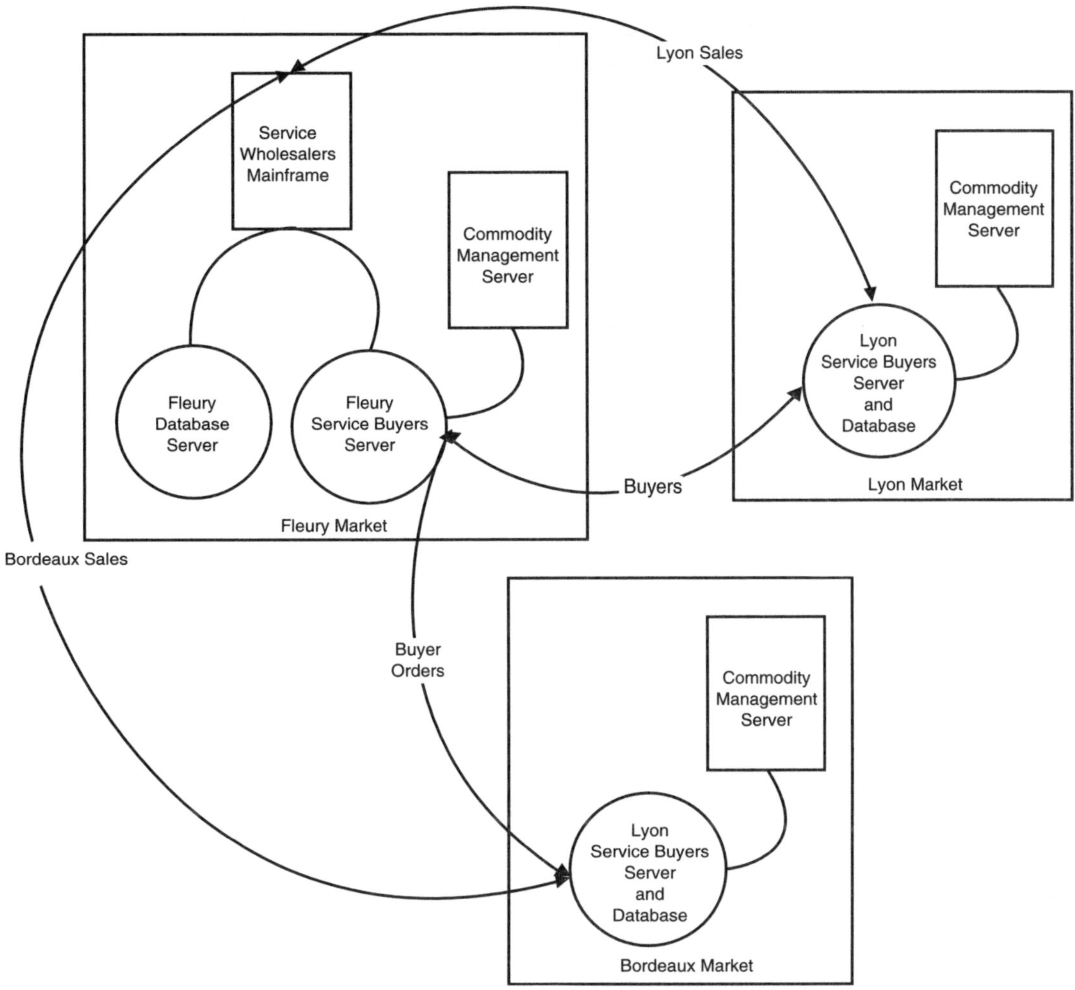

Figure 23–22 Processor Data Flow Diagram Across Locations (Enterprise View)

whether data will be replicated. Figure 23–24 represents the data distribution decisions for Lyon.

23.5.8 Data Distribution Table for Bordeaux

From the Enterprise Data Distribution Table we know that Bordeaux is not the AS for any data. The decision that must be made here is whether data should replicated or whether Bordeaux should access the data it needs. As Figure 23–25 depicts, it was decided to replicate data to Bordeaux to enable faster access.

Processor / Entity or Relationship	Fleury Database Server	Lyon Buyer Admin./ Database Server	Bordeaux Buyer Admin./ Database Server	*Commodity Mgmnt. Server*	*Mainframe Service Wholesalers*
Buyer	AS	Copy	Copy		
Wholesaler	Copy	Copy	Copy		AS
Sale <Wholesaler> sells to <Buyer>	AS (for Fleury & Bordeaux)	AS (for Lyon only)	Copy		Copy
Sale Item <Commodity> is item of <Sale>	AS (for Fleury & Bordeaux)	AS (for Lyon only)	Copy	Copy	
Commodity	Copy	Copy	Copy	AS	
Stock <Wholesaler> stocks <Commodity>	Copy	Copy	Copy	AS	
Hanger	Copy	Copy			AS
<Hanger> is located at <Wholesaler>	Copy	Copy			AS
<Hanger > assigned to <Sale>	AS (for Fleury only)	AS (for Lyon only)			Copy

Figure 23–23 Enterprise Data Distribution Table

Processor / Entity or Relationship	Buyer Admin. Client	Buyer Check In	Buyer Check Out	Wholesaler Client	Buyer Admin./ Database Server	Commodity Mgmnt. Server	Mainframe Service Whole-salers
Buyer	Copy	access	access	Copy	AS		
Wholesaler				Partial Copy	Copy		AS
Sale <Wholesaler> sells to <Buyer>				Copy (original source)	AS		Copy
Sale Item <Commodity> is item of <Sale>			access	Copy (original source)	AS	Copy	
Commodity			access	Partial Copy	Copy	AS	
Stock <Whole-saler> stocks <Commodity>				Partial Copy	Copy	AS	
Hanger					Copy		AS
<Hanger> is located at <Wholesaler>				Partial Copy	Copy		AS
<Hanger > assigned to <Sale>				Copy	AS		Copy

Figure 23–24 Data Distribution Table for Lyon

Processor / Entity or Relationship	Buyer Check-In/ Check-Out Client	Bordeaux Buyer Admin. Server	Commodity Mgmnt. Server	Mainframe Service Whole-salers
Buyer	access	Copy		
Wholesaler		Copy		AS
Sale				
<Wholesaler> sells to <Buyer>		Copy		Copy
Sale Item <Commodity> is item of <Sale>	access	Copy	Copy	
Commodity	access	Copy	AS	
Stock <Wholesaler> stocks <Commodity>		Copy	AS	
Hanger				AS
<Hanger> is located at <Wholesaler>				AS
<Hanger > assigned to <Sale>				Copy

Figure 23–25 Data Distribution Table for Bordeaux

23.6 TRAFFIC ANALYSIS

Determining Feasibility and Optimizing the Design for the Network

The team did a traffic analysis study for each of the proposed designs (strict multi-tier, mixed multi-tier/two-tier). This was reviewed by the Network Architect, who was able to determine if there were any areas of concern, risk, or unfeasibility due to contention with existing network traffic, existing network infrastructure, or the design itself. The information was also used in the network capacity planning process (outside the scope of this project).

23.6.1 Partial Traffic Analysis Table for Fleury

The Processor DFDs show all processor-to-processor dialogs. The names of the dialogs appear on the lines between the processors. We have specified the contents of the messages. From the Measurement Aspect we can determine the frequency of the messages. At this point, we just need to do the arithmetic to determine the network traffic the proposed design will generate. Figure 23–26 is a partial analysis of Fleury Market. The notes in-

From Processor Name	To Processor Name	Message Name	Avg. Freq.	Peak Freq.	Peak When	Message Size	Avg. Traffic	Peak Traffic
Service Wholesalers Mainframe	Database Server	Whole-salers Info	Nightly batch	None	None	250	6250	None
		Hanger Assignment	Nightly batch	None	None	5	12500	
For Wholesaler Info multiply message size of 250, taken from Entity Relationship Measurement Table (Figure 10–7) by number of Wholesalers (25) (Figure 10–3). *For Hanger Assignment multiply number of wholesalers (25) by average number of hangers per wholesaler (100), by size of message (5).*								
Buyer Admin. Server	Service Wholesalers Mainframe	Sales	480	1248	Thur.	100	48000	124800
Multiply number of peak buyers (156 on Thursday as per Figure 10–3) by number of average sales per buyer (8).								
Buyer Admin. Server	Commodity Mgnt. Server	Sales	1416	2784	Thur	50	70800	139200
Commodity Mgnt. Server	Buyer Admin. Server	Pick-up Status	177	313	Thur	5	885	1565

Figure 23–26 Partial Traffic Analysis Table for Fleury Market

cluded with the Traffic Analysis Table are important for documenting assumptions and algorithms used to derive traffic estimates. As these change over time, this documentation will make it easier to recalculate the estimates, because the original algorithms are explicitly defined.

23.6.2 Partial Enterprise Traffic Analysis Table

Traffic analysis is an important, and time-consuming step. The design team now has sufficient information for determining estimated traffic between locations. The information is derivable from the message specifications in the Process Distribution Aspect (and the estimate of how often these dialogs occur from the Measurement Aspect of the Essential Model). The first focus of the design team is to determine any obvious bottlenecks and address them as soon as possible. They were most concerned with the traffic between Fleury

From Processor Name	To Processor Name	Message Name	Avg. Freq.	Peak Freq.	Peak When	Message Size	Avg. Traffic	Peak Traffic
Fleury Buyer Admin.	Bordeaux	Sales	200	500	Thur.	100	20000	50000
		Buyers	30	60	Thur	200	600	1200

Figure 23–27 Partial Enterprise Traffic Analysis Table

and Bordeaux (Figure 23–7). The next step is to determine overall traffic estimates for the entire system, in order to provide capacity planning information to the network architects.

23.6.3 Traffic Flow Diagram

Data flow diagrams are the most descriptive and easily understood artifacts for depicting the movement of data across networks. This is an invaluable tool for speaking with the network architects regarding expected network traffic. When evaluating different designs from the viewpoint of network traffic, alternative traffic flow diagrams can be created.

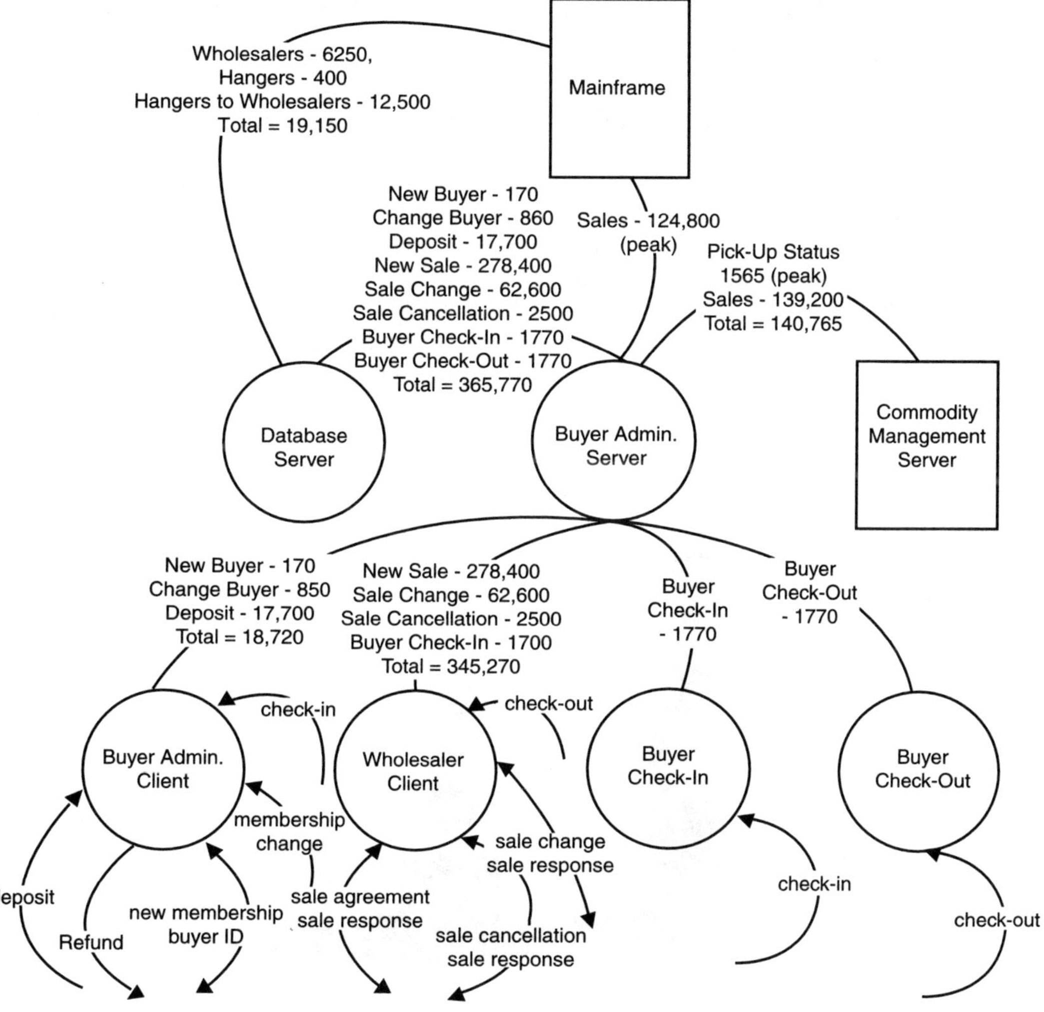

Figure 23–28 Traffic Flow Diagram

Figure 23–28 includes the estimated number of bytes for each type of message for a single day. The numbers, for the most part, represent peak estimates. For more information on creating the Network Flow Diagram, please refer to Chapter 17, section 17.3.

23.6.4 Frequency Distribution Graph

In cases where defining average and peak processing is not sufficient because of the complexity of the process, the distribution graph is helpful. It provides a graphical view of a series of peaks during the day. Figure 23–29 depicts the average frequency of buyer check-in between the open and close of a market day.

23.6.5 Processing Load Analysis Table for the Service Buyers Admin. Server

The Processing Load Analysis Table was created to address potential areas of concern or risk. Creating this table is useful if one server is going to be used for multiple applications. A processor design with granular servers dedicated to particular applications makes processor contention less of a risk or concern. If the application outgrows the processor, it is then relatively easy to upgrade for the application, and it will not impact other applications. That is why the design team decided to have separate servers for Service Buyers and Commodity Management systems.

The team also used the processing Load Analysis Table to size the server, because it estimates the processing load on the server. To determine the processing load on the Service Buyers Admin. Server, the team determined the message volume for each mes-

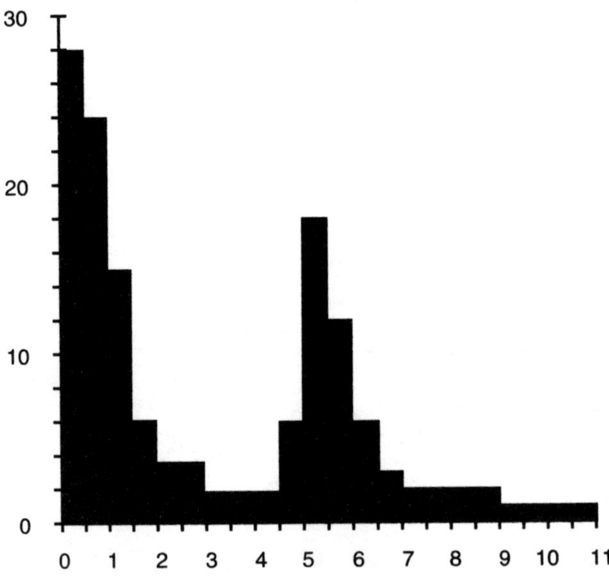

Figure 23–29 Frequency Distribution Graph for Sales Peaks

Server	Critical Peak Loads when	Critical Peak Loads	Solution
Buyer Admin. Server	Market Closes	# Messages = 5,500 #Transactions =50,000	Stagger processing—Update database and commodity management servers real time, batch sales to mainframe.

Figure 23–30 Processing Load Analysis Table for the Service Buyers Admin. Server

sage type (Figure 23–30). That server simultaneously handles *six* dialogs: Buyer Check-In, Buyer Check-Out, Wholesaler Booth, Buyer Membership, Service Wholesaler, and Buyer/Commodity. The transactions generated from the event/response processing defined in the Processor Distribution Table were also added.

This analysis is recommended for critical areas of potential risk. It may be necessary at times to redesign processing and data distribution to solve some load balancing issues. It is also possible with today's technology to implement the system with clustered processors and software, including some transaction monitors, which provide automatic load balancing.

Appendix A

Data Flow Diagram Language

The symbology used for creating data flow diagrams is listed here. The language uses boxes to represent things, circles to represent processes, and arrows to represent data or data accesses.

Terminator—An animate or inanimate thing in the environment which generates events and/or receives responses.

Process—A system activity which either receives events and generates responses or recieves and generates data.

Data Flow—The information generated during an event, generated during response, or produced during a system activity.

Data Store—A repository of information that persists over time.

Data Access—The access of a data store by a system activity.

Appendix B

Entity Relationship Diagram Language

The symbology used for creating entity relationship diagrams is listed here. The language uses boxes to denote information entities and lines and arrows to represent relationships among those entities.

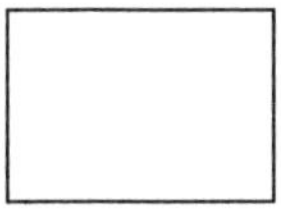

Entity—An animate or inanimate thing in the environment or the system which can be identified, which persists over time, and which has identifiable properties.

Relationship—A collection of entity occurrences.

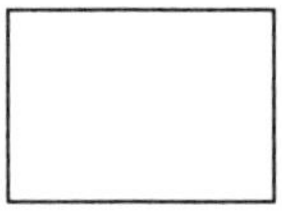

Associative Entity—A relationship that also acts as an entity.

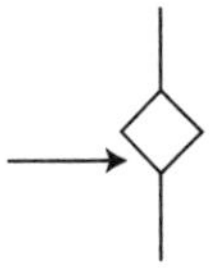

Associative Relationship—The participation of an associative entity in a relationship with other entities.

Typing Relationship—The indication that an entity has properties that are deemed to be generic in nature. Other entities inherit those properties as a result of participating in the relationship.

Appendix C

State Transition Diagram Language

The symbology used for creating state transition diagrams is listed here. The language uses boxes to represent the states of entities and arrows to represent transitions between states.

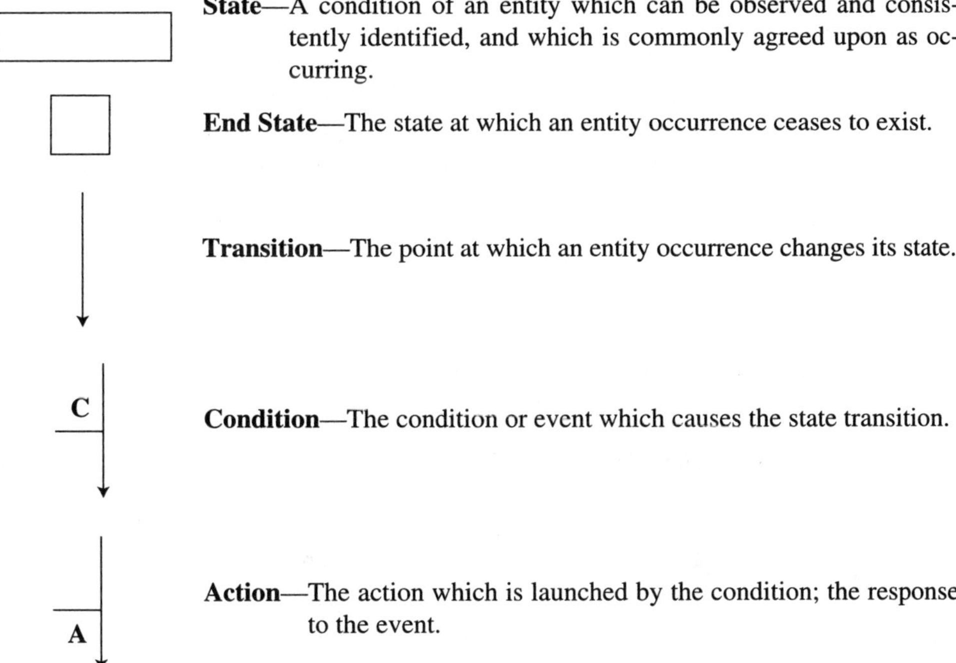

State—A condition of an entity which can be observed and consistently identified, and which is commonly agreed upon as occurring.

End State—The state at which an entity occurrence ceases to exist.

Transition—The point at which an entity occurrence changes its state.

Condition—The condition or event which causes the state transition.

Action—The action which is launched by the condition; the response to the event.

Appendix D

Processor Diagram Language

The symbology used for creating Processor Diagrams is listed here. The language uses circles to represent processors and arrows to represent either events or processor-to-processor dialogs. The Processor Diagram is the end result of the steady evolution of the Essential Model and Technical Architecture. The same notation is used for processes in the Data Flow Diagrams of the Essential Model and processors in the Implementation Model. This helps establish the connection between the business event and the technical implementation of the system.

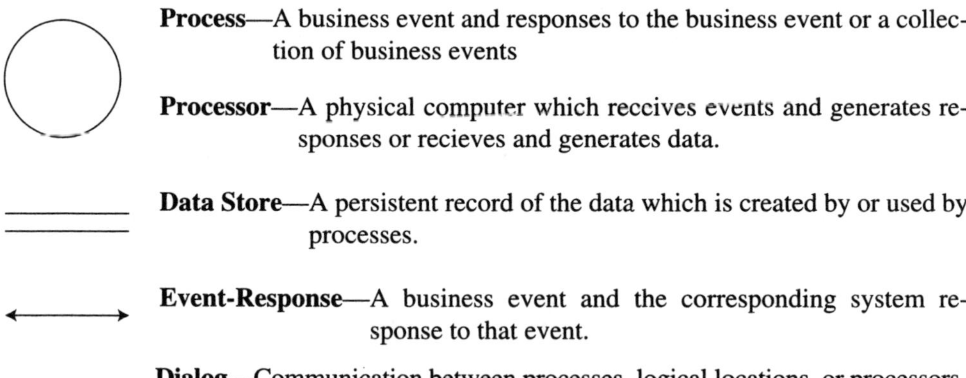

Process—A business event and responses to the business event or a collection of business events

Processor—A physical computer which reccives events and generates responses or recieves and generates data.

Data Store—A persistent record of the data which is created by or used by processes.

Event-Response—A business event and the corresponding system response to that event.

Dialog—Communication between processes, logical locations, or processors.

Appendix E

Structure Chart Language

The symbology used for creating Structure Chart Diagrams is listed here. In the language, a box is a software module, a line is an invocation (for example, a subroutine call), a triangle is a decision (for example, if-then-else), a looped arrow stands for iteration (for example, a do-loop or for-loop), and an arrow represents data passed between modules.

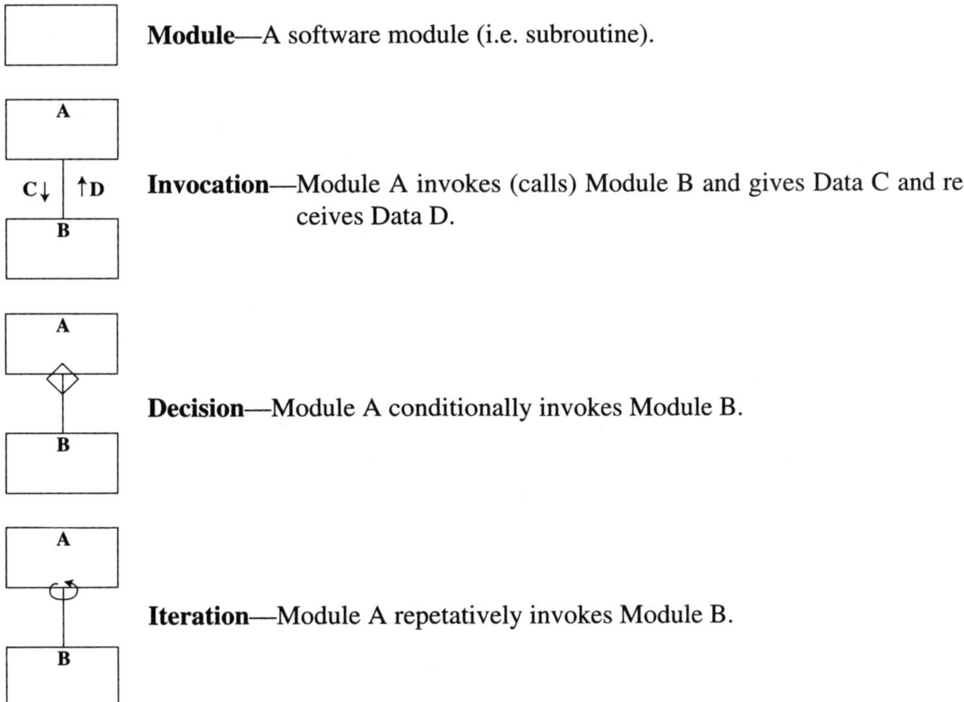

Module—A software module (i.e. subroutine).

Invocation—Module A invokes (calls) Module B and gives Data C and receives Data D.

Decision—Module A conditionally invokes Module B.

Iteration—Module A repetatively invokes Module B.

Appendix F

Model Artifacts

ESSENTIAL MODEL

Aspect	Activity	Artifact/View	Mandatory/ Optional/ Recommended
Statement of Purpose	Define business purpose, metric	Statement of Purpose Diagram	Mandatory
Environmental Aspect	Identify system boundaries	Context Diagram	Mandatory
		Data Flow Specification	Mandatory
		Data Store Specification	Optional
		Terminator Specification	Optional
	Identify business events	Event Table	Mandatory
Information Aspect	Define business entities, relationships, attributes	Entity Relationship Diagram	Mandatory
		Entity Specification	Mandatory
		Attribute Specification	Optional
		Relationship Specification	Optional
Bridge Aspect	Define data used by events	Entity/Event Table	Mandatory
	Define data over time	Entity State Transition Diagram	Recommended
Behavioral Aspect	Define System Responses	Event Response Table	Mandatory
		Event Response DFD	Mandatory
		Detailed DFD	Optional
	Define data for responses	Entity Response Table	Recommended
	Detail requirements	Minispecs	Optional
Event Distribution Aspect	Determine how events are grouped by function	Event Distribution Table	Mandatory
		Event Distribution by Logical Location	Recommended
	Determine where events occur	Logical Location/ Response Distribution Table	Mandatory for Multi-sites
		Geographic Distribution Table	Mandatory for Multi-sites
		Logical Location Distribution Diagram	Optional
Component Measurement Aspect	Determine frequency of business events; number of human terminators; and size of data stores	Terminator Measurement Table	Mandatory
		Event Measurement Table	Mandatory
		Entity Relationship Measurement Table	Mandatory

IMPLEMENTATION MODEL

Aspect	Activity	Artifact/View	M/O/R
Design Metrics	Define metrics to evaluate design	Statement of Design Goals	Mandatory
Multi-Tier Partitioning Aspect	Map Business Components to multi-tier architecture	Multi-Tier Model	Optional
	Define Application Architecture (centralized, 2-tier, or multi-tier)	Application Architecture	Mandatory
Technical Architecture Design	Define the business drivers	Business Drivers section of Architecture Data Form	Mandatory
	Create a comprehensive inventory	Current Technical Architecture Inventory	Mandatory
		Application Inventory	Recommend
		Skills Inventory	Recommend
	Define the technical components	Tool Selection Form	Optional
		Technical Processor Model	Mandatory
		Technical Architecture Specification	Mandatory
		Support Table	Recommend
		Logical Network Diagram	Optional
	Do Gap Analysis	All sections of Architecture Data Form	Mandatory
	Create Migration Plan	Architecture Data Form for each project to fund	Optional
Processor Distribution Aspect	Distribute events and responses across processors	Processor Diagram	Mandatory
		Processor Distribution Table	Mandatory
		Processor Data Flow Diagram	Mandatory
		Lower Level DFDs	Optional
	Model the presentation tier	Prototype	Mandatory
		State Transition Diagram	Recommend
	Distribute data across processors	Entity Processor Table	Mandatory
		Data Distribution Table	Mandatory
	Define communications between processors	Message Specification Table	Mandatory
Geographic Distribution Aspect	Distribute processing across geographic locations	Processor Distribution Table for Each Location	Mandatory
		Processor DFDs for Each Location	Mandatory
		Enterprise DFD	Mandatory
	Distribute data across geographic locations	Enterprise Data Distribution Table	Mandatory
		Data Distribution Table for Each Location	Mandatory
Traffic Analysis	Estimate network traffic	Traffic Analysis Table	Mandatory
		Traffic Flow Diagram	Mandatory
		Enterprise Traffic Table	Mandatory
		Frequency Distribution Graph	Optional
		Load Balancing Analysis	Optional

Appendix G

Issues List

Use this Issues List to track questions that arise during the design process.

Issue Description	Owner/ Resources	Start Date/ Promise Date	Resolution
1.			
2.			
3.			
4.			
5.			
6.			
7.			
8.			
9.			
10.			

Bibliography

Allen, C., *Effective Structured Techniques.* Prentice-Hall, Incorporated, 1991.

Boar, B., *Implementing Client/Server Computing.* McGraw-Hill Publishing Company, 1993.

Jayachandra, Y., *Re-Engineering the Networked Enterprise.* McGraw-Hill Publishing Company, 1994.

Kimball, Ralph, *The Data Warehouse Toolkit: Practical Techniques for Building Dimensional Data Warehouses.* John Wiley & Sons, 1996.

Koelmel, R., *Implementing Application Solutions in a Client/Server Environment.* John Wiley & Sons, Incorporated, 1995.

Krantz, S., *Real World Client/Server.* Maximum Press, 1995.

Marca, D., "Requirements Elicitation and Specification of Computer-Supported Cooperative Work," in *The HandPublishing of Software Engineering Productivity.* McGraw-Hill Publishing Company, 1992.

Marca, D, and C. McGowan, *IDEF0: Business Process and Enterprise Modeling.* Eclectic Solutions, Incorporated, 1993.

Marca, D., S. Schwartz, and G. Casaday, "A Specification Method for Coordinated Work," in proceedings of the 4th International Workshop On Software Specification, April 1987.

Marion, W., *Client/Server Strategies.* McGraw-Hill Publishing Company, 1994.

Ofali, R., and D. Harkey, *Client/Server Survival Guide.* Van Nostrand Reinhold, 1993.

Smythe, C., *Internetworking: Designing the Right Architectures.* Addison-Wesley Publishing Company, 1995.

Yourdon, E., *Modern Structured Analysis.* Prentice-Hall, Incorporated, 1989.

Yourdon, Inc., *Yourdon™ Systems Method.* Prentice-Hall, Incorporated, 1993.

Yourdon, E., *Object-Oriented Systems Design.* Prentice-Hall, Incorporated, 1994.

Index

About the Authors

Beth Gold-Bernstein is President of IllumiSys™ Corporation. She specializes in enterprise multi-tier client/server systems, data warehousing, technical architectures, client/server design methods, and developing client/server curriculum. She has worked with financial institutions, retail chains, manufacturers and state and local governments on assignments involving the planning, design, and implementation of nationwide distributed systems based on client/server architecture. Beth founded the Client/Server Group of the Boston Computer Society (BCS), and was the director for five years until the BCS closed its doors in September 1996. She was the director of the Architecture Planning and Implementation Advisory Service for DeBoevor Architectures, Inc. Over the past seven years she has educated hundreds of people on all things client/server. She has written numerous articles and is a frequent speaker at national conferences including *Database and Client/Server World, Software Development*, and others. Beth holds a Master of Science with High Distinction in Computer Information Systems from Bentley College.

In her spare time, Beth volunteers on the Lexington Technology Committee. She has been working for the past ten years to bring technology into the public schools. She has practiced yoga for twenty-one years, teaches weekly classes, and is grateful to Kali Ray for the knowledge of this path. Most of all, Beth enjoys spending time with her wonderful family: husband Ira, daughter Leah, and son Jacob. Beth can be reached at E-mail: bgb@illumisys.com, phone 617-863-8589, or fax 617-861-0261.

David A. Marca is founder of OpenProcess, Inc. He specializes in Internet technologies, workflow, process modeling, metrics definition, JAD, facilitation, business process reengineering, and groupware. For twenty years, David has designed and implemented high performance work environments for government agencies, large and small commercial firms, and the Department of Defense. He has also modeled and redesigned processes for numerous organizations and industries, and has developed workflow systems for computer manufacturing and software product development. David has spoken at several groupware and workflow conferences. He helped start the groupware field in 1984 and holds one of the first groupware patents: a system for coordinating autonomous agents. He has published eighteen papers and six books in the areas of systems analysis, groupware, workflow, client/server, TQM, and software engineering. He chaired the International Workshop on Software Specification and Design.

David volunteers personal time to public service. He has helped the Boston public schools effectively use the Internet and is a Massachusetts Literacy Volunteer. He also maintains a high altitude hiking trail in New Hampshire. David can be reached at: E-mail: dmarca@openprocess.com, phone: 617-646-0065, fax: 617-646-0065, or Internet: www.openprocess.com.